# NATIONAL SECURITY STRATEGY

## SECURING INDIA INTERNALLY AND EXTERNALLY

### (With Solutions of Previous Year Questions)

## By Umesh Kumar

### (IIM Kozhikode, Faculty Alchemy IAS)

#### With Team ARSu

# REFERENCES

- Constitution of India
- Ministry of Home Affairs and its publications
- Ministry of Defence and its publications
- Ministry of External Affairs and its publications
- Indian Armed Forces
- Central Armed Police Forces
- Survey of India
- Journals and other publications from Defence establishments
- Defence PSUs
- ISRO and DRDO
- Stockholm International Peace Research Institute (SIPRI)
- Center for Strategic & International Studies (CSIS)
- National Security Strategy from the USA
- Speeches from NSA Ajit Doyal
- https://www.totallytimelines.com
- Centre for Land Warfare Studies (https://www.claws.in/)
- Newspaper articles from TOI, The Hindu etc.

## GS-3 Syllabus Topics Covered

- Linkages between development and spread of extremism;
- Role of external state and non-state actors in creating challenges to internal security;
- Challenges to internal security through communication networks, role of media and social networking sites in internal security challenges, basics of cyber security; money-laundering and its prevention;
- Security challenges and their management in border areas - linkages of organized crime with terrorism; and
- Various Security forces and agencies and their mandate

# DISCLAIMER

This book is based on the limited available literature on the topic and the official information, reports or any other material available in the public domain. Publicly available opinions of experts and of institutions are incorporated with the flow of the book to make it more meaningful for the readers or students preparing for various examinations. While every effort is made to make this book useful on the topic, in no way it is connected to the official views, strategies, policy-measures or plans from the executive or its institutions like defence forces, police, intelligence etc. in the past, present or future.

# PREFACE

If we believe in Indian ethos and values of "Vasudhaiva Kutumbakam" (i.e. the world is one family) and wishes to have an ordered family based on Dharma (Righteousness) and compassion for each other, it is important that we should work on building a strong, prosperous and confident India. Only a strong, prosperous and confident India can work towards the establishment of righteousness at local, regional and international level; promoting Indian ethos and values of respecting each life form and a lifestyle which is socially and environmentally sustainable.

*'National Security Strategy: Securing India Internally and Externally'*, touches the first aspect of this, i.e. how we can build a strong, prosperous and confident India, by exposing our readers to finer details on internal and external security threats/challenges. It discusses basic ideas on National Security Strategy like the need for vision, leadership etc. and how India can develop its own National Security Strategy to build a safe and secure India.

Along with the development of vision on National Security Strategy and need of leadership from institutions, it is vital that the people should feel the need of such a strategy and become a partner in its implementation. This is achieved through the promotion of strategic thinking among the people. Therefore, to connect the citizens with the ideas of India and help in the promotion of strategic thinking, efforts are made to give a brief introduction to the rich Indian Cultural Heritage and events from the past which are significant to understand Indian conscience and value system.

Though the book is nowhere connected with the official views or strategies from the executive, we hope that it will be helpful in creating awareness towards the strategic objectives which India should pursue and the likely threats/risks it may face. We wish that the readers will take it positively and work on finding ways to aid India in its pursuit of creating a responsible world.

Umesh Kumar

# CONTENTS

# PROLOGUE

*"Your neighbor is your natural enemy and the neighbor's neighbor is your friend"*

-   *Kautilya, (Rajamandala Theory)*

Kautilya, also known by the name Chanakya or Vishnugupta, was one of the earliest philosophers and advisor to the king who made national security as the first responsibility of a king. The vision of Kautilya on national security can be traced to his Magnum Opus "**Arthashastra**" (a treatise on statecraft, economic prosperity and military strategy), where he discussed about the protection of sovereign identity of a nation and suggested a national security framework by integrating the four different fields of state i.e. diplomacy, information, economy and military (today identified by *acronym* DIME) towards it.

**Home Nation**

**Natural Enemy**

**Enemy of Natural Enemy**

**Friend of Natural Enemy**

*Circle of Friends and Enemies based on Rajamandala Theory*

Figure 1 Rajamandala by Chanakaya

According to Kautilya, it is important for a nation to identify its enemies and allies; which usually lies as per the Rajamandala theory or the circle of kings. In simple words, it means that the friends and enemies of a nation exist in circles (Mandala) with their own nation being at the centre.

Apart from the identification of enemies and allies, Kautilya advised the king of a nation that a strong vigil should be kept on all possible threats to its sovereignty such as:

a)   Internal threats,
b)   External threats,
c)   Externally-aided Internal threats, and
d)   Internally-aided External threats.

Therefore, in order to secure a nation, we need to look at not just the external threats but the internal also. According to Kautilya, this is done through a number of steps as:

1)   King acted as a parent for its citizens and worked towards the welfare of its people or helping them in fulfilling their works.

Activities like Setu-bandha for farmers, safety for traders are such activities.

2) Building of a strong military and economy with taxes to upkeep the military strength. Strong army helps in gaining allies with an effective expression of the needs/interests of the nation and its allies.

3) Use of spies to keep a vigil within the nation and in enemy nations,

4) Classify other nations into different categories based on the attitude of other nations as- i) Friends (Mitra), ii) Enemies (Ari), iii) Mediators (Madhyama), and iv) Neutral (Udasina) and try to create mutual interests with mediators and neutral nations, as "There is some self-interest behind every friendship". According to Kautilya, it can start with simple engagements with efforts to develop a complex relationship, a precursor to a strong partnership.

5) Use the policy of Sama (alliance building), Dama (Price or the gifts), Bheda (Logic or values) and Danda (use of force or war) to protect the nation and its interests.

This pragmatic approach and planning from Kautilya not only helped Chandragupta Maurya in becoming a king; it also laid the foundations of a strong pan-Indian empire by spreading the boundaries of the previous Nanda kingdom till modern-day Afghanistan. Inner chapters of the book discuss the potential National Security Strategy for India with the usage of modern-day terminologies, ideas and examples, without compromising on the values and the character of our great nation. As Kautilya said,

**"The fragrance of flowers spreads only in the direction of the wind. But the goodness of a person spreads in all directions."**

# CHAPTER 1 - UNDERSTANDING NATIONAL SECURITY

*Fearlessness, purity of heart, perseverance, yoga-meditation, charity, self-restraint, study of the Vedas, uprightness, ahimsa, truth, freedom from anger, freedom from fault-finding in others, renunciation, tranquility, compassion, absence of covetousness, gentleness, modesty, vigor, forgiveness, firmness, cleanliness, absence of quarrelsomeness, freedom from vanity, O Bharata, all these belong to him who is God-like.*

*— Krishna, Bhagavad Gita*

Nations are made and governed by the people living in a particular geography. As an entity, a nation lacks any virtue or character of its own. The individuals who live in it, especially the ones who run/administer the nation do have their values, aspirations and biases. When these values and aspirations are accepted by the nation, either through force or through shared socio-cultural heritage, they become national values, aspirations and biases which are protected and promoted by the nation.

Today's humankind is identified more with the vices rather than virtues. E.g. The 18th and 19th centuries were wasted by many because of the greed and arrogance of European nations (Colonialism). The colonial greed and arrogance of European nations ended by the end of the first half of the 20th century but it took two world wars of greed among themselves to end it.

Post World Wars, the greed of colonialism was replaced by ideologies and a struggle between ideologies of nations. The biggest example of it was the ideological clash between the Capitalism of the USA and the Socialism of the USSR. Similar battles existed between North and South Korea, North and South Vietnam etc. By the end of the 20th century and disintegration of USSR, the battle of ideologies was replaced by the unrestrained terrorism with States/nations using terrorism as a tool against other nations.

The continued struggle for energy resources along with the developmental and technological hazards like Global Warming, Climate Change, Cyber Surveillance etc. have become new security risks for various nations including existential risk for many small island nations.

## National Security and National Security Strategy

Under today's circumstances, National Security is defined as "*the security of a nation-state from all internal and external threats, including the threats to its citizens, economy, culture, institutions, environment, infrastructure etc. from state and non-state actors.*" The important point to be observed in the definition is that the risks can emanate from not just outside the nation but also from inside. Another important point is that the security risk can be posed by the state as well as non-state actors.

It highlights the increasing security risks, the security risks which have forced many nations to move away from the traditional position of treating military strategy as the only national security measure. The new challenges are addressed effectively by a nation through *National Security Strategy*, which is defined as "*the art and science of developing and using the diplomatic, economic and informational powers of a nation, together with its armed forces, during peace and war to secure national objectives.*"

The foundations of National Security Strategy, also known as the grand strategy or simply as national strategy, was first laid in USA when Goldwater-Nichols Legislation of 1986 tried for synchronizing the defence chain of command and strengthen civilian authority over the defence because of the failure of USA in dealing with Vietnam War, Iranian revolution and the hostage crisis. In 1987, the USA came with the first National Security Strategy.

National Security Strategy is prepared by the highest level executive body of the nation, serving as guidance on the national security concerns and the ways and means to tackle them. The concerns can be of international, regional or local (internal) level; focusing on the interests of the nation and resource generation to implement it. Along with risk management, it also helps a nation in prioritizing its resources and development of strategies to gain various resources.

## Principles of National Security Strategy

Before going into the principles of the National Security Strategy, it is important for a nation to first identify whether it can afford to have a written National Security Strategy. In our competitive world, a written National Security Strategy removes the secrecy from the motives/interests of the nation and exposes it to the countermeasures from enemy nations or nations who feel that it can be harmful towards their interest.

Being the most powerful and influential nation with large public support, the USA can afford to have a written National Security Strategy towards global order. For others, it can be risky, including China (which restricts its strategy to the identification of security threats with no specifics on the solution), because the removal of secrecy makes them vulnerable to clash with the written or unwritten interests of other nations; attracting counter strategies or unwillingness to engage with it at strategic level.

E.g. The reactions received by the '*String of Pearls*' strategy of China were far more lukewarm or retaliatory in comparison to its recent '*One Belt One Road*' initiative for being explicit in approach (direct engagement of its armed forces). As a matter of fact, because of being projected as a purely economic measure, one belt one road has received greater interests from smaller nations; as they are ambiguous on real motives and they can avoid confrontation from other nations by citing economic benefits.

Being discreet or secret in approach is also preferable for nations like Pakistan who use terrorism or other non-state actors in its policy. Secrecy helps them in avoiding direct linkage with terrorism and denounce if required. It also helps them in partnering with other nations in different fields while avoiding scrutiny on unwritten interests. Therefore, an unwritten National Security Strategy helps a nation by:

- Avoiding countermeasures from other nations in the form of imposition of Physical or Monetary Constraints because of interest clashes,
- Remaining discreet on the leadership role in order to avoid the development of leader cult,
- Remaining discreet on the enemy nations. It helps in avoiding the development of public opinion or popular sanction against it in those nations. Present day, it is vital to avoid information warfare or any other direct threat from it, and
- Avoiding penalties from international community/organizations for violation of International Laws by non-state actors operating from its land and actively used by it to target other nations.

So, a nation should understand it carefully whether it really wants and can fulfil its goals through a written National Security Strategy. Once it has zeroed on having a written National Security Strategy; it should make all efforts to have an effective National Security Strategy, by focusing on three key requirements from it, as:

1. **Vision for the Nation:** National Security Strategy of a nation acts as the first-hand document/guidance for a nation and its institutions at the Global, Regional and Local level while dealing with other nations, international organizations, making domestic laws on economical, environmental, technological or public order-related matters. Therefore, the National Security Strategy should be able to give a vision/direction to the nation on each dimension of national security.

2. **<u>Development of Positive Leadership:</u>** One of the basic requirements for the implementation of National Security Strategy is to have a Leadership which can ensure primacy to national needs and national security by all executive bodies, decision-makers, institutions etc., through the incorporation of strategic thinking in their areas of expertise.

3. **<u>People Participation:</u>** Participation from people/citizens become critical from two major perspectives. First, it helps in bringing continuity to the strategy by having allegiance to the National Security from all political parties because of being supported by the people. Two, it helps in creating an awakened citizenry who can avoid propaganda from other nations and reciprocate to the national needs when called to do so.

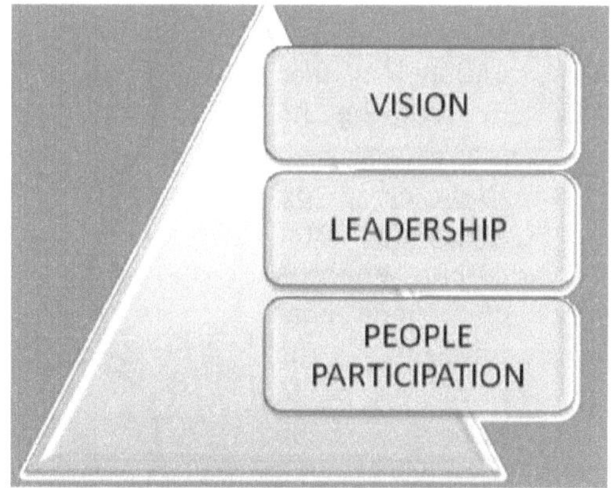


Figure 2 Requirements for an effective National Security Strategy

## Formation of National Security Strategy

Formation of National Security Strategy is a critical process for every nation as once formulated (either as written or unwritten) it can bring significant changes in the outlook and responses from a nation at the internal and external level. Being considered as the official government statements of strategy, it may lead to significant changes/shifts in the tools of strategy implementation i.e. diplomacy, information system, military responses and economic system of the nation.

At the same time, every nation is unique in terms of its security needs, threats/risks, ethos and values, resources at the disposal, the structure of institutions, availability of leadership etc. Therefore, we lack a standard process on the formation of the National Security Strategy. Every nation is required to develop a process which can serve its requirements best. As a customary practice, a nation can start with the identification of the need for having a National Security Strategy. Once identified, it can follow the steps, as:

1. **<u>Appraisal of the national security:</u>** The first step towards the formulation of National Security Strategy is to have an honest

assessment of the internal and external situation of the nation from a national security perspective.

2. **Identifying national interests along with future challenges, opportunities and risks:** After proper appraisal of the national situation, the next step is to identify the national interests from short to long-term perspective along with the future challenges in achieving those interests. What are the likely risks or threats, and the opportunities which the nation may face in securing its interests?

3. **Dialogue on Priorities:** After careful analysis of national interests, the next step is to prioritize the national interests through dialogue between senior leaders and organizations

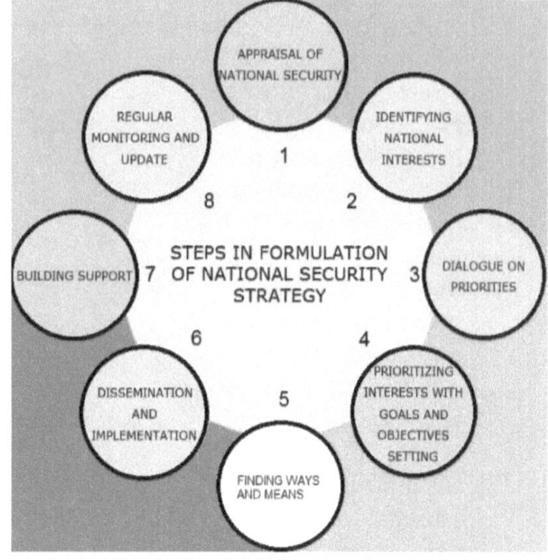


Figure 3 Steps in Formulation of National Security Strategy

responsible for achieving those interests. E.g. The current US National Security Strategy formulation involves a large number of participants like- The White House, Department of Defence, Department of State, Department of Homeland Security, Department of Energy, the Intelligence Community, Department of the Treasury, Department of Commerce, Department of Health and Human Services, and Congress. Wider participation helps in broadening the scope of thinking and helps in building larger consensus and commitment towards its implementation.

4. **Prioritizing Interests with the setting of Goals and Objectives:** The next step is to rate and prioritize those interests in order of importance from present to future scenarios. Ordering of interests helps in the identification of core interests, easing the process of setting implementation goals and objectives for various organizations.

5. **<u>Finding ways and means:</u>** After setting goals and objectives, the next step is to identify the ways and means to achieve the desired goals and objectives. This step is important because all nations suffer from the limitations of resources. It can be in terms of availability in the nation or in terms of quantity. It helps in identifying the resource situation of the nation and allocating them on the basis of priorities. It can also help in working towards resource security through strategic partnerships or innovations.

6. **<u>Dissemination and Implementation:</u>** The next step is to disseminate those ideas to all the subordinate actors/institutions by moulding those objectives in their language. It is vital to bring clarity among them and match the expectations of the leadership.

7. **<u>Building Support:</u>** For a vibrant and participative democracy like India, implementation of national security strategy requires support from the non-executive institutions, people, private industries and allies. Therefore, efforts should be made to build internal support and external support towards the national security strategy.

8. **<u>Regular Monitoring and Update:</u>** A nation should be agile towards the changes in the dynamic and competitive world, where self-interest is the biggest driver for individuals and nations. Also, some security threats like Climate Change, Energy Security etc. require technological changes. Therefore, arrangements should be made for regular monitoring and make changes in the strategy, as and when the situation demands.

## Tools to Implement National Security Strategy

Traditionally, threats to national security emanated from **Land** and **Water** (mainly through the sea). Being the traditional dimensions of warfare, the responses towards national security was also traditional, i.e. fighting fire with fire. Therefore, the building of strong armies and naval supremacy remained the main focus for National Security.

The Second World War added **Air** as the third dimension of national security. Start of the Cold War added **Space** and **Information** (Psychological warfare of ideologies) as new dimensions of National Security; the responses were more or less of the same magnitude and direction. Race for space and war of ideologies between USA and USSR with respective allies remained the strategy for national security.

As we discussed earlier, because of the problems which emerged during the Vietnam War and subsequent development in West Asia like Iranian Revolution and the hostage crisis; the USA was forced to move away from fighting fire with fire and explore the use of alternatives, often called using water against fire.

Development of National Security Strategy to synchronize the efforts of all institutions under the executive command was a result of it with recognition of Diplomacy, Information, Military and Economy (*termed as DIME*) as the tools for Implementing National Security Strategy.

As a matter of fact, it was the combined effort of diplomacy, military, economic, and information actions which helped the USA in Containment

Figure 4 Tools of National Security Strategy

or isolation of Soviet Union, eventually leading to the defeat of Soviet Union. We will discuss in detail about the components of each tool and their role with examples, like the use of institutions, conferences and diplomats in Diplomacy or use of intelligence agencies, people, universities, satellites and psychology as parts of information, while implementing a National Security Strategy.

## Features of National Security Strategy

    a.  It is living document and continuously evolves to meet the traditional and evolving international and national risks;

    b.  It is made by the executive, as its implementation starts with the most powerful leader of the nation;

    c.  It can be a written (either detailed or skeleton only) or unwritten document (based on the interests and risks of a nation);

    d.  It can be inward-facing, outward-facing or mix of both (based on the origins of threats);

    e.  It acts as the starting document on future dialogue and strategies of a nation;

## Benefits of having a National Security Strategy

As we discussed earlier, having a National Security Strategy increases the number of risks for the nation. At the same time, the National Security Strategy brings a number of benefits to the nation, as:

1. As soon as a nation starts the exercise of its preparation, it also works on the risks involved in furthering its National Interests or the likely reaction from other nations; leading to the preparation of better strategies and selecting the form of National Security Strategy which can help in preserving the national Interests.
2. National Security Strategy helps in building support for National Interests and promotes Strategic Thinking among various political parties, experts and the people; leading to better resource utilization toward its implementation.
3. It helps in developing a common understanding and synchronizes the working of all institutions of the nation like executive and the parliament, defence and foreign, defence and information etc.
4. It helps a nation in communicating its national interests to other nations in an effective manner; helping in bringing stability in the region and to move towards rules-based international order.
5. It helps in the promotion of the ethos and values of the nation.
6. It helps in prioritizing the national interests, thereby removing the errors caused by a lack of clarity on priorities. Through the National Security Strategy, every actor with participation in decision-making knows about the national interests to be preserved and promoted. This clarity of interests help in removing the problems like- i) Promoting lowest-common-denominator interests or the priorities set through old consensus based approach with interests of organization kept above the national interests; ii) Lacking forthrightness or directness in decision-making for fear of alienating an interest group or groups; iii) Inefficient resource utilization because of weak connection between the goals/objectives of the nation and resource usage; and iv) Internal conflicts causing slowness of response to the changing national security environment.
7. It helps a nation in structuring the flow of information in the system, whether it is for the elevation of issues to the senior levels or to communicate a decision to lower levels or the public, National Security Strategy helps in synchronizing all.

## Position of India on National Security Strategy

In India, National Security is talked for long by politicians and military establishments in an isolated manner. In 2007, an effort was made by the Integrated Defence Staff to have a National Security Strategy. But it failed to get the approval from the Cabinet Committee on Security. Subsequently, we faced some of the worst threats to our National Security from various state and non-state actors like 26/11 attack on Mumbai, 2010 Dantewada Maoist attack, worldwide surveillance from National

Security Agency (NSA) of USA, increasing cyber-attacks, climate challenge etc.

Sadly, we failed to build a consensus and the approach of India to security risks remained fragmented. E.g. Post 26/11, National Investigation Agency (NIA) was created as a central agency to combat terrorism but the set up of National Counter Terrorism Centre (NCTC) to synchronize the efforts of centre and state was objected by various States. In 2010, 76 CRPF personnel were killed by Maoists. It created national outrage and our Prime minister declared it as the biggest threat to National Security. But it was very short-lived, because of our divided information system and lack of coordination among forces responsible for the maintenance of public order and internal security.

Similar reactionary steps were taken against other pressing challenges to National Interests like the National Action Plan on Climate Change (NAPCC) in 2008 after the 2007 report from the Intergovernmental Panel on Climate Change. National Cyber Security Policy in 2013 after the release of large scale surveillance activity from NSA. Similarly, Strategic Oil Reserves are developed by India along with various partnering nations from the Middle-East and so on.

The fragmented institutions and impulsive reactions from India show that we are yet to have a critical appraisal/assessment of our national interests and security risks. Lack of strategic thinking or purpose is against the interests of our great nation; lowering the morale of our forces and institutions. In a rapidly changing and challenging environment, it restricts our capabilities to utilize them for our interests and promote a better global order.

With more than one-sixth of the humanity living in India, it is in the best interest of mankind to have Indian voice in its decision-making. A nation which has the longest continuous history of the world and rich in the God-like virtues mentioned by **Krishna**, it is important that we work towards having a National Security Strategy. It will help in not just securing our nation and its interests but it will also expand our vision and responses to the global problems; helping in building a global value system which promotes peace, non-violence, compassion and modesty with lack of anger, vanity and fault-finding approach.

The establishment of a Defence Planning Committee by the executive (in 2018) with official mandate to work on the preparation of National Security Strategy can be taken as a silver-lining; giving us hope that in near future we will have the necessary vision along with the leadership and vital public support to create a safe and prosperous India.

# CHAPTER 2 - CONFLICT, NEGOTIATIONS AND WAR

*If the resources of the earth are properly developed, she is then like an all-yielding cow, from which the threefold objects of Dharma, Artha and Kama might be milked. With the desire of enjoying the earth, men have become like dogs that snatch meat from one another.*

*— Sanjaya, Bhishma Parva*

*Survival of the fittest* is a universal law of nature. Whether it is the plant kingdom or animal kingdom, all jostle for survival. This struggle for survival is won by individuals with a high level of fitness and ability to adapt to nature. On marginalization or decreased chances of survival, threatened individual's try to develop a symbiotic relationship, with the members of same species or of different species, in hope that it will help in their survival.

Based on the challenges and available opportunities, humans also organized themselves into various symbiotic relationships with members of their own species or from different species; leading to the formation of societies and activities to harness those relationships. Domestication of plants and trees for food grains, fruits etc., or animals like cow and buffalo for needs of milk, fuel (from cow dung), fertilizers etc., all are part of that struggle for survival.

The improved survival opportunities through collective efforts helped humans to go through a series of physical and cultural evolutions, leading to increased desires and aspirations of the human mind. Whether it was the battle of Ramayana, Mahabharata, the expedition of Alexandra etc. from ancient past or the events of invasions, colonialism and World Wars from recent past; human desires and aspirations were the guiding forces.

These negative influences of desires and aspirations on human character, whether for Artha (material gains), Kama (love/desire) or both were recognized long ago, leading to the introduction of Dharma by Saptrishis (through Vedas). Dharma, **i.e. the cosmic laws of right behavior and social order**, a tool to understand the nature of everything and help in balancing the human passion with self-regulation through the introduction of reason and sympathy.

In words of Adam Smith, this duality i.e. presence of passion along with reason and sympathy in human character, serves both to pit individuals against one another and provide them with the rational and moral faculties to create institutions by which the internecine struggle can be mitigated and even turned to the common good.

With nations being made of individuals, this duality can prevail within a nation or between nations and higher level, i.e.

I. When individuals pit against each other within a nation, it leads to internal conflicts;

II. When individuals pit against the people of other nation, it leads to external conflicts;

III. When individuals of a nation are driven through common goal, it leads to the formation of the strong federation like the USA; and

IV. When individuals of various nations are driven through common goals, it leads to the formation of a Union like the European Union.

## Understanding Conflict in Context of People and Nation

We live in a society, where each individual has some responsibilities or is supposed to behave in a certain way. E.g. As a child you expect that your parents should fulfil your wants. At the same time, your parents feel that being the parent it is their obligation to fulfil your certain needs. Similarly, in the husband-wife relationship, both are expected to behave in a certain manner to meet the individual and joint needs or obligations of each other and towards society to keep the relationship going.

Based on the relationship, these wants, obligations or necessities from an individual change. E.g. If we talk about it in context of Vedic India, we will observe a range of Dharma's (*Raja Dharma, Putra Dharma, Shishya Dharma etc.*) defining the obligations of each individual based on his/her relationship with another individual or role in society. When an individual or group of people fail to meet those expectations or wish to carry out mutually inconsistent acts concerning their wants, obligations and necessities, we have a high probability of having a conflict. E.g. The conflict of Mahabharata i.e. war between Kauravas and Pandavas was caused because of the violation of obligations from Kauravas.

So, conflict is defined as *the clash of interests or incompatibilities/disagreements among living beings.* Such disagreements or clash of interests happen mainly because of the passion of individuals and common among family members, friends, neighbours, tribes or societies. Such interests exist at the national level also and it is normal to have differences of interest among nations. Situations, where we have such variance of interests among nations, who want to protect their interests passionately; a conflict between the nations is likely to occur.

If we look at the present world, we can observe such conflicts between two nations or at regional and international level. E.g. The conflict between two Koreas (South Korea and North Korea) or between India and Pakistan is an example of a conflict between two nations. Similarly, the conflict in the South China Sea region is an example of a regional dispute where a number of nations sharing the South China Sea have a clash of interests. And, the conflicts like terrorism, narcotics, trafficking etc. can be considered as international or global conflict with a large number of nations having a conflict of interests with some state and non-state actors.

## Understanding Negotiations and its Importance

*Success that is obtained by negotiations and other means is the best. Success which is secured by creating disunion amongst the enemy is temporary.*

*Success secured by battle is the worst.*

*— Vyasa, Bhishma Parva*

Conflicts are common to occur. We hardly have any relationship or affiliations where conflicts don't occur. Siblings have conflicts among them; some children have conflicts with parents, neighbors have conflict among them or at a higher level, we have conflicts among nations and a group of nations. So, the issue is not of conflict but it is how we handle and resolve those conflicts.

If we try to understand it from the perspectives on the conflict of Mahabharata i.e. war between Kauravas and Pandavas, we will observe the importance of attempts made by Krishna and Vyasa to avoid war and resolve the matter through negotiations. Krishna asking for only five villages or Vyasa describing the evils of war represents the attempts made to resolve the matter through negotiations. It was only when Dhritarashtra remained adamant on his decision of having his son as king with no village to the Pandavas, the battle of Mahabharata happened and the worst of it is evident from the war history where all just war laws were broken and the damages caused were beyond imagination.

Similar observations can be made at the end of World War I. E.g. after the end of World War I; the only attempts of allies were to create disunion in Germany. A large sum of economic reparations, territorial concessions to self and the limitations on the German armed forces; all made the life of Germans miserable and created a sense of anger among them. As Ferdinand Foch, the Commander-in-chief of the allies said-

**"This is not peace. It is an armistice for twenty years."**

And in nearly twenty years we had the Second World War. Similarly, the end of the Cold War between the USA and USSR was because of USSR disunion rather than negotiations. The signs of limited success are visible through the struggle for defence supremacy and almost opposite views/engagements from the USA and Russia in Ukraine, Syria etc. Therefore, it is vital to understand the importance of negotiations.

Negotiations are defined as the dialogues or discussions carried out by people or nations to make another side(s) aware of the interests of self and identify a common agenda, securing maximum interests of each other. Negotiations are more beneficial and successful in resolving issues as compared to war or disunion by:

- Removing the distrust on each other and work towards the building of a collective mindset;
- Helping the people or nations in overcoming the feelings of entitlement;
- Overcoming the emotions of injustice or helplessness among weaker people/nations by providing a common platform;
- Enhancing commitment to the negotiated agenda with reduced uncertainty of action among the actors; and
- Negotiations also help in removing the confirmatory bias.

When it comes to negotiations between conflicting interest groups or nations, it is essential that each actor comes with a flexible approach. The flexible approach helps in the success of negotiations and helps in creating common interest among them. Also, it requires confidence-building measures from each actor; displaying the will of each towards negotiated outcomes. Without a flexible approach and implementation of confidence-building measures, the conflict can further escalate by creating doubts and uncertainties among them.

E.g. In 1948, India lodged its complaint in the United Nations (UN) on the Pakistani invasion in parts of Jammu and Kashmir (J&K). On 13 August 1948, the UN Security Council passed a negotiated resolution on J&K with following steps:

1) First Pakistan will remove its troops, Pakistani Nationals and tribesmen who are not normally resident therein from Jammu and Kashmir;

2) The vacated territory will be administered by local authorities and the commission will verify and notify such vacation of Pakistani troops and others to the Government of India;

3) Once notified, the Indian Government will remove the bulk of Indian forces from J&K in stages to be agreed upon with the commission. Pending such acceptance of the conditions, Indian Government will maintain within the lines existing at the moment of the cease-fire the minimum strength of its forces which in agreement with the commission are considered necessary to assist local authorities in the observance of law and order;

4) Indian Government will ensure that the State Government takes all measures within its powers to make it publicly known that peace, law and order will be safeguarded and that all human and political rights will be guaranteed; and

5) The future status of the State of Jammu and Kashmir shall be determined by the will of the people and to that end, upon acceptance of the truce agreement.

As the implementation of the negotiated resolution required Pakistan to take the first step, the resolution was never implemented because of the lack of confidence-building measures being taken from Pakistan. The removal of forces from Pakistan occupied Kashmir (PoK) remained a dream, leading to wars fought by the two nations to decide the fate of the state rather than the people deciding the fate. Signing of the Shimla Agreement in 1972 ended the UN resolution mandate from Indian point of view as both nations agreed to settle their differences by peaceful means through bilateral negotiations.

Today, both nations seem to have accepted the current situation with no progress on confidence-building measures or negotiations happening between the two nations.

## Understanding War and Its Evils

*There are many evils in battle: the first and the foremost is slaughter. Victory is always uncertain. It depends on chance. Even those that obtain victory have to suffer losses.*

*— Vyasa, Bhishma Parva*

War is the evilest face of conflict and it can occur between the nations or people when their interests are against each other with no hope of negotiations or failure of negotiations. Traditionally, war is defined as the state of armed conflict between nations, societies, informal groups or non-state actors like insurgents, militias or mercenaries and people. It is also known as Conventional War, as it involves physical confrontation with the use of weapons, military technologies/equipment and operational strategies.

Conventional wars are evil because of the nature of aggression, destruction and violence resulted by it. Though conventional wars are not linked with the use of nuclear, biological and chemical warheads, they are becoming part of conventional wars since the First World War. E.g. if in First World War chemical weapons or toxin gases were used; in Second World War Nuclear Bombs were used. Though Geneva Protocol of 1925 outlawed the use of Chemical Weapons in war, as recently as in April 2017 (Syrian Civil War) chemical weapons with toxic gas (Sarin Gas or a similar substance) were used by the Government Forces.

So, it is not just that the wars between nations but even in the civil war[1] a nation can see the use of armed forces along with their technologies/equipment and weapons of mass destruction.

### Weapons of Mass Destruction (WMD)

Weapons of Mass Destruction are the nuclear, biological, chemical or any other weapons which are able to cause widespread devastation and loss of life. The devastation can be in the form of damage to human-made infrastructure, environment or usable natural resources. The major weapon categories included in weapons of mass destruction include:

1) **Nuclear Weapon:** Nuclear Weapon, also known as Atom Bomb, is an explosive device which uses nuclear reactions (either fission or fusion) to create mass destruction. Though possessed and tested by a number of nations, as of date only two fission-based nuclear bombs are used in War (both by the USA on Japan) as- i) On 06 August 1945, a Uranium based fission bomb nicknamed as *Little Boy* was used on Hiroshima city, and ii) On 09 August 1945, a Plutonium based fission bomb nicknamed as *Fat Man* was used on Nagasaki city;

2) **Chemical Weapons:** Chemical Weapons are the weapons which use harmful chemicals rather than explosives in the munitions to create mass destruction. Typically, the harmful chemicals used in chemical weapons are the toxic chemical substances (either in gaseous, liquid or solid form) which are capable of killing humans or cause temporary incapacitation/sensory irritation. The common examples include mustard gas, phosphine gas, sarin gas etc.

3) **Biological Weapons:** Biological Weapons are the weapons which use biological agents or bio-agents to create mass destruction. The most common biological agents include bacterium, virus, fungus protozoan or parasite. These biological weapons have the ability to kill or to adversely affect human health. Usually, these are genetically-modified to increase potency as most of them have become part of the human environment. E.g. Before European Colonialism, the original inhabitants of America were not exposed to plague and other viruses. When European arrived in these nations, more people died because of plague and other viruses as compared to the deaths during the war. Even in India which had hardly

---

[1] *Civil War is considered as the war between the forces or political entities of same nation.*

seen large scale viral attacks or diseases; a large number of diseases came with the British causing large scale deaths and reduced life expectancy.

4) **Radiological Weapons:** Radiological weapons are the weapons which use radiological substances or radiation poisoning to create mass destruction. As of date, radiological weapons are used for targeted killings through the exposure of a person to radioactive substances like Polonium-210. E.g. Russian secret agency FSB, earlier known as KGB, killed Alexander Litvinenko through radiation poisoning.

Apart from Conventional Warfare, we can have other forms of Warfare as:

a) **Unconventional Warfare:** Unconventional Warfare is a form of warfare, where attempts are made to win control over the state and military through control over the mind of the civil population. Unlike direct military fights in conventional warfare, unconventional warfare involves the use of acquiescence, capitulation, or clandestine means to gain control over the state. Unconventional warfare means are usually employed by the communists or guerrilla forces, where the minds of civilians are targeted to garner support for their activities.

b) **Total Warfare:** Total Warfare is a form of warfare, where all possible means are used against the enemy in disregard of any laws of war, morals or ideologies. These are the no limit wars where civilians are as much targeted as legitimate military installations. Weapons are used along with the ideologies and other tactical means to win the war and submission of civilians.

c) **Cyber Warfare:** Cyber Warfare is defined as the use of computer technology by nation-states or organizations to disrupt the activities of another state or organization, especially the deliberate attacking of information systems for strategic or military purposes.

d) **Terrorism:** Terrorism is broadly defined as the unlawful use of violence and intimidation, especially against state or civilians, in the pursuit of political or social aims.

e) **Insurgency:** Insurgency is a rebellion against authority, where unlawful combatants or a group of people attempts to take control of their country by force.

f) **Information Warfare:** Information Warfare, also termed as information operations, is a form of warfare to achieve information superiority by effective protection and use of own information assets and systems with the destruction of adversaries' information assets and systems. The information assets and systems largely include the computers and networks that support the four critical infrastructures, as- power grid, communications, financial, and transportation.

## Evils of War:

Modern-day Polemologists (those who study about war), have recognized a number of evils caused by the conventional, unconventional and total war between nations, like:

- **Human Casualties:** The number of casualties in a war can be too high. E.g. estimates on World War-II suggest that from 60.7 to 84.6 million deaths happened in the six-year period of war, i.e. from 1939 to 1945. The damages were on both sides, with USSR despite being the winner suffering maximum losses.

- **Damage to bodily integrity and psychological balance:** Physical and mental injuries like amputations, diseases, mental fatigue, anxiety, depression, confusion, obsession and character disorders are common among military personnel who serve in war. A study done by Swank and Marchand's on WWII found that after serving for sixty days of continuous combat, 98% of all surviving military personnel will become psychiatric casualties.

- **Civilians and critical infrastructure:** Exposing civilians to diseases, famine, genocide or death through direct attack or through destruction of infrastructure are major threats for civilians. We learn from history and the rising incidents of terrorism, civilians and critical infrastructures are always under danger as it makes the life of people miserable and reduces the morale and capabilities of the army and the people. E.g. nearly 2/3rd of people who died during World War II were civilians. Like soldiers, civilians are also vulnerable to psychological imbalances because of war.

- **Economy:** Development of a strong army and weapons for war or fighting a real war, a large amount of economic wealth and resources are required to do so. At the same time, the economy of a nation is first to be affected during the war because of the renewed priorities of a nation/society, inflation and the destruction caused by the war. Sometimes, it may add the burden of reparations or ceding of territory (like Alsace-Lorraine by Germany to France through the Treaty of Versailles) on a defeated nation(s).

- **Art and Culture:** The recent damages from ISIS to the ancient cities of Palmyra and Aleppo in Syria, destruction of Buddha's statue of Bamyan by Taliban and the long history of looting, invasions and conversations tell us that the art and culture are the important targets in wars based on ideology. Apart from the tangible damage to the art and culture, it can be intangible damage through the propagation of false ideas or adding motivated explanations to the interpretations of ancient texts.

## Minimizing Evils of War: Just War Theory

*Everything rises from the earth and when destroyed everything goes into her. The earth is the stay and the refuge of all creatures. The earth is eternal.*

*— Sanjaya, Bhishma Parva*

Reason and sympathy are the controllers of human passion and often these controllers fail to check human passions. When such passion is of the King, a group or state, it leads to war and its evils. Bhishma Parva, the sixth Parva among the 18 Mahabharata Parva, is the first and most influential text on rules/principles of warfare to minimize the evils of war. The first chapter of JAMBUKHANDAVINIRMANAPARVA (part-I of Bhishma Parva) talks about the special rules made before the battle of Mahabharata to keep it moral and ethical, as:

1. No enmity should be observed after the sunset;
2. The existence of mutual love, battle of speech should be done only with those who are indulged in it, killing a person, who is out of the army is condemned;
3. A foot-soldier, a horse-soldier and an elephant-soldier should fight with their equals only;
4. One should make an enemy alert and fight with him alone, who is equal to him in ability, zeal and strength;
5. One should not fight with the person who is not unprepared or with a scared person;
6. The war is condemned with a person, who is fighting with others, a refugee, a person who is out of war and a person with tainted weapons; and
7. A charioteer, the player of the kettle drum, a conch-blower and the supplier of weapons should not be attacked.

With thousands of wars since Mahabharata, these principles of a moral and ethical war have transformed into a written code as **Just War Theory**. The modern-day principles of Just War have their origins in the ideas of classical Greek and Roman philosophers like Plato and Cicero with additions from Christian theologians like St. Augustine and St. Thomas Aquinas. St. Thomas Aquinas in '***Summa Theological***' described the situations of justification of war and the kinds of activity permissible (for a Christian) in a war. Today, Just War Theory is made up of three elements as:

a) ***Jus ad Bellum (right to war):*** It is the first element of Just War Theory, describing the unfriendly acts and circumstances created by others under which a nation is justified to declare war as Just War or use its military forces against another nation, as:

I. *Just Cause:* A Just War requires a just or righteous cause, i.e. a nation should be able to show sufficient gravity to merit large-scale violence or war as a solution to it;

II. *Just Authority:* A Just War must be declared by the lawful or competent authority, like the elected political authority of the nation;

III. *Just Intentions:* The just belligerent (aggressive) nation must have rightful intentions, i.e. to advance good (self-defence) and curtail evil (balance of power through preemptive strikes against hegemonic power);

IV. *Reasonable Chance of Success:* The just belligerent nation must have a reasonable chance of success;

V. *Last Resort:* The war must be the last resort to fulfil the just cause; and

VI. *Ends proportional to Means:* The ends being sought through a war must be proportional to means being used in war.

b) ***Jus in Bello (right in war):*** It is the second element of Just War Theory, describing the set of ethical rules or principles which should govern the conduct of a nation during the war to fight a war in an ethical manner. Originally, it was to describe the just conduct during the war through two main principles of proportionality and discrimination. A third principle, as a principle of responsibility, is added to the traditional principles to identify where the responsibility for war lies. These principles of Jus in Bello helps in separating the causes of war from the actual conduct during the war and guide the behavior during the war through these principles, as:

I. **Principle of Proportionality:** It overlaps with the last principle of Jus ad Bellum, i.e. *ends proportional to means*, by restricting the indiscriminate use of force. Principle of proportionality describes the amount of force which is morally appropriate to achieve the ends sought or respond to the injustice suffered. This principle becomes important in war because of the presence of WMDs.

II. **Principle of Discrimination:** Principle of Discrimination is the second principle to be followed during the war. This principle helps in determining the legitimate targets in a war, by extending immunity to non-combatants from war violence through the separation of combatants from non-combatants. This separation helps in the avoidance of war crimes and helps in keeping the legitimacy of Just war from a nation.

III. **<u>Principle of Responsibility:</u>** The principle of responsibility helps in conducting military activities in a responsible manner and avoid the blames of unexpected side effects as long as it adheres to the following three conditions of a responsible behavior, as- I) The action must carry the intention to produce good consequences; ii) The bad effects were not intended; and Iii) The good of the war must outweigh the damage done by it.

c) ***Jus post-Bellum (right after War):*** It is the third element of Just War Theory, describing the ethical rules to be followed after the war. From a nation and its military perspective, a war can end with three possible outcomes as- I) It is on the winning side, ii) It is on the defeated side or iii) the war ends with a ceasefire. Jus post-Bellum helps in dealing with these situations and helps in having Just peace agreements or termination of war through:

I. *Principle of Discrimination* should continue and even after war nations should avoid imposing punishments on innocents or non-combatants;

II. *Principle of Proportionality* should be applied in the peace agreements and the claims sought after the war must be proportional (i.e. reasonable and fair) to the war's character and it should not be a burden on civilians;

III. *Rehabilitation* of aggressors or re-education must be done of the aggressor without damaging the basic human rights and traditions of such aggressor; and

IV. The Punishments of aggressive leaders, who caused the war, shall be delivered through a transparent and free trial.

A Just War is justified as long as it is started, carried and ends in just manner. Every war, even if it is for noble causes, becomes unjust if it goes away from such principles. History of India and of the world (from Mahabharata to the world wars of the twentieth century) tells us that it takes little to turn a Just War into unjust because of the emotions, aggressions and need of victory felt during the war. E.g. Despite the best of warriors, Mahabharata witnessed many diversions from the agreed war rules. The USA used nuclear bombs against Japan despite being in a favourable position with the allies of World War II.

At the same time, such events also act as an eye-opener for us and help in identifying the limitations of existing principles; thus helping in revitalization of existing principles and framing of International Law on legitimate war. The philosophical works of **Michael Laban Walzer** (Just and Unjust Wars in 1977), **Barrie Paskins** and **Michael Dockrill** (The Ethics of War in 1979) or from **Brian Orend** (War and International Justice: A Kantian Perspective in 2000), are such works which have expanded our understanding on Just War with increased ethical understanding on human life.

Presence of international organizations like the United Nations has helped in the development and propagation of these principles. With large scale religious/cultural differences of our world and rising power asymmetries/disagreements among nations; it has become a necessity for people to realize that unlike imaginary heaven, the earth is the base and abode of all creatures.

Therefore, it is important that individuals/nations overcome their desires or narrow-mindedness and become a Karma Yogi, performing selfless deeds which are good for the earth and the rest of movable and immovable living beings on it. This can be done by understanding and promoting the strong ethical values enshrined in our Dharma, helping people in overcoming the selfishness or arrogance; and helping all in performance of their duties toward the family, society and earth. As Rig Veda says:

आत्मनोमोक्षार्थम्जगत्हितायच

*" Atmano Mokshartham Jagat Hitaya cha "*

(I.e. for the salvation of our individual self and for the well-being of all on earth)

# About India

*"The ultimate source of the prosperity of the kingdom is its security and prosperity of its people"*

*-Kautilya, Arthashastra*

India is home to 1/6th of humanity with probably the largest diversity of the world as part of one nation. This large population and diversity is an asset as well as an obligation on India. On one hand, India can present a model to the world by building a secure and prosperous nation without compromising on its large diversity. On the other hand, a large population of India with an equally diverse profile of people makes it difficult for the policymakers to properly allocate and use the limited resources for the benefit of all. The big rural-urban divide or inter-state dividers are an example of it.

These developmental imbalances and a mix of physical and socio-cultural differences among people create uncertainty in the minds of people. These uncertainties are further influenced by the rapidly changing external environment. Failures in addressing those uncertainties lead to divisions and situations which exposes our nation to a large number of internal and external threats. Therefore, it is important that people should feel connected with India and its future even if their aspirations and expectations are failed by the policymakers.

The importance of this connection can be realized from the history of our nation, as whenever India i.e. Bharat acted as one nation; it moved towards the peak and a divided nation was easily conquered and exploited even by island nations. It can be easily identified from some examples of our past.

1.  The regime gained by Nanda Dynasty from Shishunaga Dynasty (344BCE) was massive. It shattered the confidence of Greek Army and forced the King Alexandra to end his campaign and retreat from River Beas (in 326 BCE). Maurya Dynasty (321-184 BCE), under the guidance of Kautilya, further strengthened it. Under King Ashoka (last Major Maurya Ruler), the use of soft-power diplomacy started and he exported not just Buddhism to different parts of world but developed strong relationships with almost all major powers of the time like Greece, Rome, China etc.

2.  The weak successors of Maurya Dynasty and the increased internal divisions of India made it so weak in no time that soon a series of external aggressions started from the North-West part of India and the newly rich kingdoms of Central Asia like Indo-

Bactrian, Kushans, Indo-Parthians etc. started to migrate towards India through power.

3. Rise of the Gupta Dynasty (300-550 AD) once again strengthened the native rulers and once again India started to flourish with defeats of the aggressive Central Asian Kings. This increased prosperity in India. During Gupta Dynasty India witnessed a series of scientific, economic and socio-cultural developments. Temple construction, improvements in cave architecture with building of Ajanta Caves, set up of Nalanda University, composition of large number of literary texts from Kalidasa and other Navratanas of Gupta Dynasty, astronomical discoveries and works from Aryabhatta and Varahamhira are some example of same. Indian trade with the world increased and the internal economy also became strong with Indian coin-making reaching its peak.

4. The Pushyabhuti Dynasty (550-750AD) kept that supremacy for some time under King Harsha. But the fight of the Pushyabhuti Kingdom with the Gaud Kingdom and the start of tripartite war between the three major native Kingdoms (Pratiharas of Gujarat, Palas of Odisha and Rashtrakutas of Deccan region) from 750-1000 AD for control over Kanauj after Death of Harsha, weakened the native rulers and increased internal divisions. As a result of this, the invasions which started with raids from Mahmud of Ghazni ended with a series of bloody invasions from Huns, Mongols, Turks and Afghans with some being able to rule the major part of India.

5. These internal divisions among Indian rulers remained for almost 900 years leading to exploitation of the same situation by European Colonial Powers like Portugal, Britain and France. It was the French who started to exploit these internal divisions among native rulers for personal benefits through the extension of support to one native ruler over others and use of Indian's as soldiers to serve in French Army. In comparison, initially the British relied on European soldiers with use of internal dissents within the natives or use of money to bribe and gain people from the opposing side. The *Battle of Plassey* and the succession war for Nizam of the Carnatic were fought by the British through this approach. With the expansion, British realized merit in French approach and under Warren Hastings they shifted to the "***Policy***

*of Ring Fence[2]*". Soon, they recruited Indians as Sepoy to build a large army with avoidance of the loss of Englishmen and started to exploit the divisions among Indian rulers. With the rise of British power, Lord Wellesley added the "***Policy of Subsidiary Alliance***", a scheme to make Indian Kings weak through subsidiary alliances and increase in own military strength through the use of resources from Indian Kings to upkeep the forces. Under the policy of the subsidiary alliance, native rulers remained as symbolic King, even through adoption in case of no legal heir, with British interference in decision-making and alliances entered by the King (a form of dual government).

In 1813, the Policy of Ring Fence was replaced by "***Policy of Subordinate Isolation[3]***" but it remained a non-starter because of certain apprehensions about people's reaction. In 1834, the Board of Directors issued guidelines to the East India Company (which itself was transformed into a complete political authority through the Charter Act of 1833) to annex Indian states wherever and whenever possible. To supplement those efforts of the Company, Governor-General's Council was established under the Charter Act of 1833 to advise the Governor-General of India.

T. B. Macaulay, the first law member of the Governor-General's Council, brought a shift in British strategy. The use of internal divisions among native rulers was replaced by the idea of marginalization of traditional Indian Culture and learning's; the only common and shared heritage of people from different parts of India. Our heritage restricted the claims of British supremacy, a newly civilized nation facing the grand old civilization. This policy is also known as '**Macaulayism**'. As Macaulay said in his minute on Education (02-Feb-1835):

*"I have no knowledge of either Sanskrit or Arabic. But I have done what I could to form a correct estimate of their value. I have read translations of the most celebrated Arabic and Sanskrit works. I have conversed both here and at home with men distinguished by their proficiency in the Eastern tongues. I*

---

[2] *Policy of Ring Fence was the policy practiced by the East India Company in India from 1765-1813 for protection of British Frontiers by creating Buffer Zones between the East India Company Frontiers and the native rulers through use of treaties on non-annexation of each other territory and mutual help in case of aggression from other native rulers.*

[3] *Policy of Subordinate Isolation was the policy practiced by the East India Company in India from 1813-1858 for its relations with native rulers with features like-acknowledgement of British Supremacy and restrict themselves to internal administration with external sovereignty being surrendered to British administration.*

*am quite ready to take the Oriental learning at the valuation of the Orientalists themselves. I have never found one among them who could deny that a single shelf of a good European library was worth the whole native literature of India and Arabia. The intrinsic superiority of the Western literature is indeed fully admitted by those members of the committee who support the oriental plan of education."*

Macaulay's strategy initially succeeded in dividing Indians through active use of newly educated Indians as interpreters between the British and the millions governed by them. As Macaulay described their use in changing the Indian culture and tradition:

*"We must at present do our best to form a class who may be interpreters between us and the millions whom we govern; a class of persons, Indian in blood and colour, but English in taste, in opinions, in morals, and in intellect. To that class we may leave it to refine the vernacular dialects of the country, to enrich those dialects with terms of science borrowed from the Western nomenclature, and to render them by degrees fit vehicles for conveying knowledge to the great mass of the population."*

> To learn more about the Macaulay's minute use the link below:
> (https://drive.google.com/open?id=1adiaiUtg6sY_A9w7aIPuA4OmTMQ5D
> JLq)

The implementation of the *Policy of Subordinate Isolation* and the 1834 guidelines seemed feasible and soon the annexation of various territories was started by the British to expand and protect the British territories in India. E.g. Annexation of Sindh, First Anglo-Afghan War, 1st and 2nd Anglo-Sikh war, Annexation of Lower Burma etc. With the introduction of '***Doctrine of Lapse***', annexation of other major Indian states like Satara, Jaipur, Sambalpur, Nagpur, Jhansi, Berar and Awadh was completed under Dalhousie.

The subsequent Revolution of 1857 by certain native rulers and a large section of people helped the British in realizing the problems in their policy of subordinate isolation, rapid social changes through law and the importance of loyal native rulers as "***Breakwaters in the Storm***[4]". It was only because of indifference from a section of native rulers and active help

---

[4] *Breakwaters in the Storm was the term used by the Governor-General Canning for the native rulers and chiefs who helped the British in countering the 1857 revolution through instant support, which otherwise would have removed the British rule in India because of its swiftness.*

from a large number of kings, Nawabs, Chiefs and other big Zamindars; the British were able to restrict the revolution.

This incident helped the British in realizing a few important lessons like:

- Native Rulers and Chiefs are largely selfish and can be trusted more than the people, who largely follow them;
- For upkeep of British rule they need to keep loyal native rulers as chiefs, as they can offer instant help with zones of calm under any revolution with time and other considerations being a barrier from getting help through Britain and other colonies;
- Indian people use these opportunities to settle own scores (e.g. many villagers first targeted the money-lenders who held their land), so we need to create more divisions among Indians to scatter their instant anger within;
- Indian Merchant class was largely profit-minded, as most of them refused to help the rebels and hid their wealth and goods. In fact, because of the profit-considerations merchants from port-regions like Madras, Bengal and Bombay helped them.
- Sections of people who are established and nurtured by the British are largely loyal to them. E.g. the Zamindars and the western educated people remained alien to the revolution.

On the basis of these inputs, the British came with the unofficial policy of '**Divide and Rule**[5] **Policy**', for the people and the ***Policy of Subordinate Union***[6] for the native rulers. In order to strengthen their ties with the native rulers and bind Indian people with Britain, three Delhi Durbars (also known as Imperial Durbars) was organized by the British in 1877, 1903 and 1911, as:

a) During the first Imperial Durbar (1877) Queen Victoria was proclaimed as the empress of India in 1877, As Queen Victoria described the importance of it:

*We trust that the present occasion may tend to unite in bonds of close affection ourselves and our subjects; that from the highest to the humblest,*

---

[5] *Divide and Rule Policy was first explained by Traiano Boccalini in La Bilancia Politica, as a technique used by the King to strengthen his rule over the subjects by dividing them, who collectively might be able to oppose the sovereign.*

[6] *Policy of the Subordinate Union was used by British towards native rulers after the 1857 revolution, with treatment of Indian Princely States as subordinate to the British Crown with British Government having power to interfere in the internal matters. It ended the policy of annexation and replaced it with British power to govern the succession of Princely States under all conditions.*

*all may feel that under our rule the great principles of liberty, equity, and justice are secured to them; and to promote their happiness, to add to their prosperity, and advance their welfare, are the ever present aims and objects of our Empire.*

b) The second Imperial Durbar was held to celebrate the succession of Edward VII and Alexandra of Denmark as Emperor and Empress of India under Viceroy Curzon.

c) The Third Imperial Durbar was held in 1911 with King George and Mary of Teck attending it as Emperor and Empress of India. Though the loyal native rulers attended these functions with a full display of loyalty, the newly rising educated political elites who attended these durbars started to feel it as a waste of Indian time and money. Because of this and other reasons, the fourth planned Durbar of 1937 was officially boycotted by Indian National Congress.

The roots of this decision in 1937 Durbar from Indian National Congress can be traced to the rise of Mahatma Gandhi in the Indian National Congress. As we learnt from the events of the 1857 revolution, the British were able to continue their rule over India because of active help from Indian. E.g. in 1919, the state of Punjab was going through a phase of protests making British fearful of a possible Ghadarite uprising.

Under those tense situations, on 13 April 1919 Jallianwala Bagh Massacre happened in Amritsar. In this massacre, more than 300 Indians were killed with nearly 1500 being injured. The saddest part of the massacre is that though it happened on order from Brig-Gen Reginald Dyer, the soldiers who fired on the people were Indians as part of the British Indian Army.

This incident had a far-reaching impact on the Indian National Movement. Many moderate Indians who till now acted as loyal to the British started to become nationalist. Mahatma Gandhi also realized the evils of Divide and Rule Policy from British where Indian people feel higher loyalty to British over fellow citizens. Therefore, he promoted the idea of Indian unification with people from all religions, regions and Caste coming together for Indian independence.

Whether it was the Non-Cooperation Movement, Civil Disobedience Movement or Quit India Movement; all had separation of Indian from British Raj as an important consideration to make people realize that British rule is alien to the Indians. Though the movements from Mahatma Gandhi largely focused on the civilians, the impact of it on Indians serving in British Indian Army was visible when a platoon from Royal Garhwal Rifles refused to fire on Satyagrahis in Peshawar.

Later, Subhash Chandra Bose through the Indian National Army (INA) initiated the Indianization of armed forces by bringing the nationalist aspirations among the Indians serving in the Armed Forces. A large section of soldiers from the British Indian Army, Royal Indian Navy and Royal Indian Air Force started to identify with the idea of India as a nation, leading to service discontent and changed behavior towards India because of

a)  The stories of bravery from INA's fight against the British in Imphal and Burma; and

b)  The Red Fort Trial of General Shah Nawaz Khan, Colonel Prem Sehgal and Colonel Gurbaksh Singh Dhillon from Indian National Army (INA, also known as Azad Hind Fauz).

This discontent was displayed by the soldiers through the acts of open defiance of orders and rules. Finally, the Royal Indian Navy Mutiny of 18 February 1946 (considered as the last nail in the coffin of British colonial aspirations in India) made British realize the rising Nationalist mood of Indians, leading to the freedom of India.

But the tools developed by the British to Divide and Rule the Indians are still present in our society, acting as a barrier to the built-up of internal peace and calm. The interpretation of Indian History and Culture in a way which disconnects its people from our own heritage is one such way. The acceptance of such poor interpretations on Indian history and culture by the people in India is just a tip of the **melting Indian cultural iceberg** among the minds and hearts of Indian people.

Today, those interpretations are often used by ideologues of anti-India establishments and allure people against the state. In their zeal towards accepting the views of an educated person what we miss is that the person is neither learned on Indian culture nor a neutral personality. Understanding Indian Culture is impossible through the west standards. One can't identify the reason behind a cultural practice without understanding the thinking behind it.

What people fail to understand is that in the guise of explanations or understanding of Indian heritage and culture, attempts are made to spread hatred against it. This hatred helps them in dividing our society or nation and restricts the coming together of Indian people for making a strong nation among its diversity. It is true that we lack equal participation and representation in National Growth and Development. But it is a universal truth and impossible for any society of such wide diversity like ours.

# CHAPTER 3 - Our Leadership Structure & Mandate of Executive Agencies

The success of the National Security Strategy depends on three key factors:

a) *Vision of the Strategy,*

b) *Leadership from the executive, and*

c) *Support from the citizens.*

For a nation, its vision on National Security Strategy is guided by the diversity of threats it faces. Based on threats, we have different executive agencies or specialized agencies with specific role in national security and prosperity. This role plays a vital role in the National Security Strategy.

Among them, some executive agencies work on identifying the threats to National Security and prepare holistic solutions and strategies to avoid or minimize the risk possessed by those threats. The expertise of the executive agencies helps in early identification of imminent threats and the future risks involved in our changing environment. Based on this, they can identify ways to make our nation more resilient and secure against threats with alignment of agency objectives and national security.

Being a democracy, the governance of India as a nation is headed by the political heads with different executive agencies working under them. Therefore, leadership from the political heads or the topmost executives is important for alignment of the objectives and co-ordination among all. It starts from the effective leadership of the topmost executive or the Prime Minister, enjoying greatest support from the citizens. Support from citizens helps in the promotion of informed decisions on national security and gives continuity to it.

Therefore, before learning about the National Security of India, it is essential that we learn about the Indian Governance Structure and the executive bodies which have an important role in our National Security.

## Structure of Indian Leadership

India runs on the basis of fundamental principles and established precedents of the Constitution of India. Whether it is the state or the organizations/agencies established by it, all are supposed to work without compromising on the principles laid in the Constitution. These organizations are required to serve different functions on National Security, requiring effective leadership to harmonize the efforts of all. Based on the mandate and capabilities of various executive agencies this leadership starts from the Union.

The Constitution of India provides for a parliamentary form of democracy. We have a democratically elected government at the centre and state level. Both of them work on the basis of separation of powers between Centre and State, as given in the Seventh Schedule of the Constitution.

With Foreign Affairs (Diplomacy), Defence of India and major economic matters being part of the Union List (Seventh Schedule) and duty of the Union to protect States against external aggression and internal disturbance (Article 355), it is imperative to have National Security in the domain of the Union or Central Government. Governments in State and in Union Territories, if any, are to aid the efforts of the centre by fulfilling their functions under the Constitution or any other responsibility given by the Parliament in a cooperative and efficient manner.

Based on our Constitutional scheme, we have a President (to act as the nominal executive of India/de jure executive) and a Prime Minister (to act as the real executive/de facto executive) of India. E.g. under Article 53(2), the President of India holds the supreme command of the defence forces of the Union. He appoints the service chiefs of various armed forces. As the Supreme Commander of armed forces; he declares war and concludes peace subject to parliament approval.

But all these functions are carried by the President in accordance with the aid and advice of the Council of Ministers headed by the Prime Minister. So, the **first leadership** to the nation and its executive branches comes from the **Prime Minister (PM) of India** for being the head of the government.

Under Article 75, all other Ministers are appointed by the President on his advice. He is free to keep any ministry with himself or give charge to someone else. The appointed Ministers can be removed on his advice or he can reshuffle their portfolio. Based on his advice, the duties and responsibilities of various ministries can be changed. He can

Figure 5 Relation of Prime Minister with other Executive Agencies

create new ministries or end the old ones.

The Prime Minister decides the foreign policy of the nation and represents India at major international, multilateral and bilateral forums and talks. He is the Chairman of Niti Aayog, National Development Council, National Integration Council, National Water resource Council, Inter-State Council etc. He is the political head of all forces and of disaster management.

The Prime Minister, through secretarial assistance from the Cabinet Secretariat, heads the Cabinet. He defines the vision of the government. He presides over the Cabinet meetings and plays an important role in cabinet decision-making. He influences the working of different ministries and holds the responsibility to coordinate their functioning.

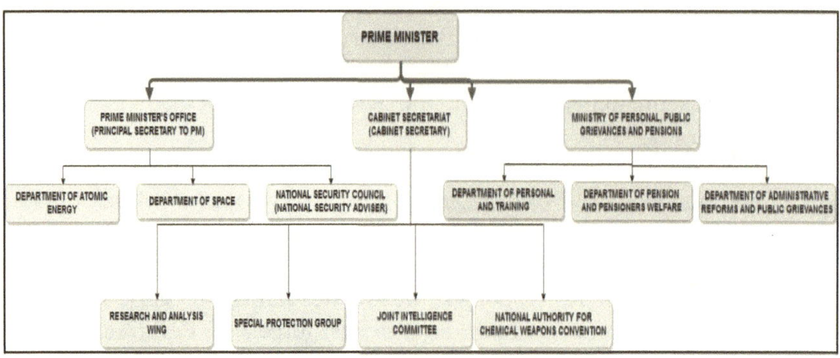


Figure 6 Executive Agencies working directly under Prime Minister

Prime Minister's Office (PMO), under Principal Secretary to PM, provides the secretarial assistance to the PM for looking after the functioning of ministries or departments kept by PM with himself. E.g. Traditionally the Ministry of Personnel, Public Grievances & Pensions, Department of Space and Department of Atomic Energy are kept with the PM. With Space and Atomic Energy being critical to National Security, PM through PMO controls the policy measures and functioning of important organizations engaged in Atomic Energy and Space Research and development like BARC, ISRO etc.

After the Prime Minister, the **second leadership** is provided by the Minister In-charge of Ministries with an important role in National Security. E.g. We have the Ministry of Home Affairs (MHA) headed by the Home Minister, to look after internal security through help from state government and organizations working under it. We have the Ministry of Defence (MoD) headed by the Defence Minister, to look after the external security through armed forces and other defence organizations. So, it is important to know about the structure and function of Ministries with control over agencies responsible for National Security.

### 1. *The Ministry of Finance*

Today, money is the most universal and powerful medium of exchange. Just like an individual or household requires money to purchase different goods and services in order to fulfil the basic needs and comfort in life; a nation also requires money for administration and help people in their pursuits of life securely.

In India, the responsibility of this lies with the Ministry of Finance. It looks after the overall **economy of India** and plays an important role in the mobilization of national resources for the welfare of people and the security needs of our nation. Strong economy helps in gaining allies through stronger economic relations and extends the influence of India. Strong economy helps in strengthening our forces through advanced weapons and facilities leading to better protection of borders or sovereignty. Being of such high importance, finance of a nation is also on the list of state and non-state adversaries.

Therefore, it is important that the Ministry of finance not just mobilize the resources for National Security but protect them from the rising threats. The structure of the Ministry of Finance is as follows:

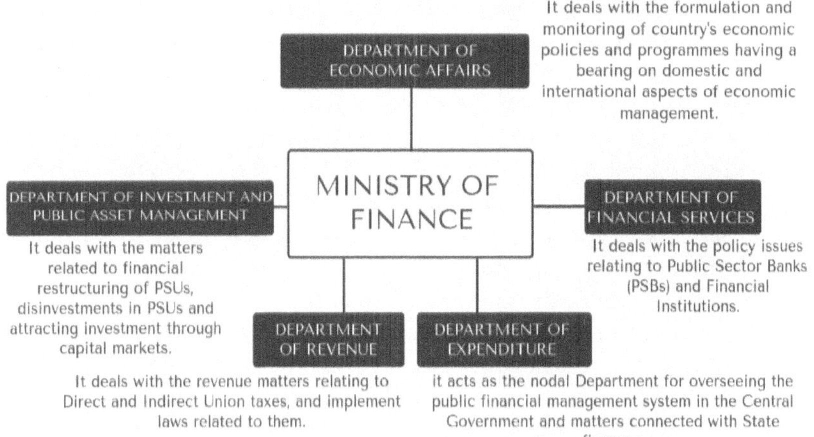


Figure 7 Various Departments under the Ministry of Finance

The five departments under the Ministry of Finance are further divided into a number of executive agencies like Central Board of Direct Taxes (CBDT), Central Board of indirect Taxes and Customs (CBIC), Reserve Bank of India (RBI) etc. The functions of these departments include:

1. **<u>Department of Economic Affairs:</u>** Department of Economic Affairs is responsible for the formulation and monitoring of economic policies for India. Most important among them are the Union Budget and Economic Survey. With the Union Budget dealing with the demand of grants from various central ministries and departments, its role is very important in national Security.

2. **<u>Department of Expenditure:</u>** Department of Expenditure oversees the public financial management system of the Central Government and matters connected with State finances. It keeps an eye over the expenditures from Central Ministries/Departments through Financial Advisors, carries pre-sanction appraisal of all major schemes/projects at the centre level, transfers central resources to various states and implements the recommendations of Finance Commission and Central Pay Commission.

3. **<u>Department of Revenue:</u>** Department of Revenue deals with the revenue matters of the Central Government. Through CBDT and CBIC, it looks after the revenue matters relating to Direct and Indirect Union taxes. In addition to that, it is entrusted with the administration and enforcement of regulatory measures provided in the enactments concerning Central Sales tax, Stamp duties and other relevant fiscal statutes.

4. **<u>Department of Investment and Public Asset Management:</u>** With significant contributions in Indian Economy being made by the Public Sector Undertakings (PSUs), Department of Investment and Public Asset Management is entrusted with the responsibility of financial restructuring, disinvestments and attracting investments in PSUs.

5. **<u>Department of Financial Services:</u>** Department of Financial Services deals with the policy matters of Public Sector Banks (PSBs) and other Public Financial Institutions in sectors like agriculture credit, insurance, pension etc. It administers the Financial Inclusion programmes, Social Security Schemes and other targeted schemes aimed at facilitating the flow of credit to the people.

So, the Finance Minister is an important part of second leadership. Through efficient mobilization of national resources, he works toward the meeting of financial needs from the people and various executive agencies including the ones with a very high role in National Security.

*2. The Ministry of Home Affairs (MHA)*

According to Kautilya, threats to the sovereignty of a nation are of four types:

a)  *Internal threats;*
b)  *External threats;*
c)  *Externally-aided Internal threats; and*
d)  *Internally-aided External threats.*

Under the constitutional scheme of India and the set precedents, it is the Ministry of Home Affairs (MHA) which is entrusted with the maintenance of *internal security, i.e. to deal with internal threats.* Apart from this, MHA deals with a number of other issues like border management, Centre-State relations, administration of Union Territories, management of Central Armed Police Forces, disaster management or protection of every State from external aggression and internal disturbance (Article 355).

To fulfil these obligations, the work of the Ministry of Home Affairs is divided into six departments viz. Department of Home, Department of States, Department of Border Management, Department of Official Languages, Department of Internal Security and Department of Jammu and Kashmir (J&K) Affairs, with a large number of divisions and executive agencies working under the political leadership of Home Minister and the administrative leadership of Home Secretary. The role of these six departments and some of the major national security matters dealt by various divisions under them are as follows:

Figure 8 Various Departments under the Ministry of Home Affairs

Major National Security matters dealt by various Divisions of MHA:

1. ***Intelligence:*** Through the Intelligence Bureau (IB) and National (NATGRID) Internal Security-I Division helps the MHA in keeping a vigil over the activities of potential internal security threats and aid provided by the external agencies to them. E.g. A few years back, IB helped in identifying the role of foreign NGOs in instigating protests against the developmental projects in India.

2. ***International Border Management:*** Management of international borders is necessary not just from the security perspective; it also involves a range of economic, administrative, diplomatic and developmental issues. Through Border Management Division-II, MHA plays its part in the management of international borders of India and participates in the border areas development programmes.

3. ***Radicalization:*** One of the major global challenges of 21st-century Internet-enabled Terrorism is the radicalization[7] of vulnerable people/communities by terrorist organizations. To keep a check on such radicalization and counter the misuse of people emotions/sentiments against the state, MHA has established a Counter-Terrorism and Counter Radicalization Division which deals with a matter relating to terrorism, counter-terrorism, radicalization and counter-radicalization along with other responsibilities like UAPA, NIA Act, FICN, FATF.

4. ***Cyber Security:*** We live in the age of Cyber Era. The process of digitization which started under the Third Industrial Revolution[8] is now merging with the life of people. If this increased integration of technology in our system and processes make them more accessible and efficient, it also makes them more vulnerable to attacks because of being critical. MHA has established a Cyber and Information Security (C&IS) Division to address matters

---

[7] *Radicalization: Radicalization is defined as the action or process through which individuals or groups adopt radical/extreme positions on political ideals, religious beliefs or social issues.*

[8] *Industrial Revolution: As of now we have seen three complete industrial revolutions and the fourth one is in progress. The First Industrial Revolution was dominated by the Steam-powered factories and engines; Second Industrial Revolution led us to the era of mass-production and manufacturing; and the third industrial revolution started the process of digitization through increased use of electronics and information technology. Fourth Industrial Revolution is the era of technology where technologies like artificial intelligence, genome editing, augmented reality, 3-D printing etc. are getting fused with the processes and systems, blurring the lines between the physical, digital, and biological spheres of our life.*

related to Cyber Security, Cyber Crime, National Information Security Policy & Guidelines (NISPG) and implementation of NISPG, NATGRID etc.

5. ***Jammu & Kashmir:*** The UT of Jammu & Kashmir and the UT of Ladakh comes among the states with a high risk of Terrorism[9]/militancy[10]. Therefore, to keep these UTs safe and deal with the constitutional or policy matters, Jammu and Kashmir and Ladakh Affairs is established by the MHA.

6. ***Left-Wing Extremism:*** Left Wing Extremism (LWE) is among the biggest challenges to the internal security of India. In terms of its ideological and operational spread, it covers nearly 11 states with 90 districts of India (once it was nearly 200). Therefore, to coordinate the efforts of various state and central agencies and implement holistic policy measures, the Left Wing Extremism Division was created on October 19, 2006. Today, it carries out a number of functions like review of security situation, issuing advisories to the concerned State Governments, capacity building of states to combat LWE, deployment of Central Armed Police Forces (CAPFs), providing funds to CAPFs for infrastructure/Helicopters/civic action etc. and coordinate for the implementation of LWE related Schemes of other Central Ministries for LWE affected districts.

7. ***North East:*** North-East region of India holds an important strategic and socio-cultural place in India. Different states of this region share borders with nations like China, Bhutan, Myanmar and Bangladesh. Because of its geography, socio-economic issues and historical factors like language/ethnicity, tribal rivalry, migration, control over local resources, feeling of exploitation and alienation, the North-East region has posed many challenges to our internal security and maintenance of law & order situation. A significant number of extremist or Indian Insurgent Groups (IIGs) exist in the region. To deal with the insurgents and have peaceful resolutions through talks with various extremist groups, MHA has established a North-East Division. It also coordinates with the friendly neighbouring nations like Myanmar and Bangladesh to strengthen the security situation.

8. ***Women Safety:*** The decreasing values in our society and the rising crimes against women (including girl child) has made

---

[9] *Terrorism: Terrorism means the use of or threat to use violence to strike terror amongst the people.*

[10] *Militancy: It is the use of confrontational or violent methods in support of a political or social cause.*

women safety a major challenge for all. In order to strengthen the measures toward the safety of women and to instil a greater sense of security in them, MHA has set up a Women Safety Division on 28 May 2018. The primary motive of the division is to achieve a speedy and effective administration of justice. This division works toward the creation of a safer environment for women by carrying out the work of policy formulation and assistance to the States/Union Territories in planning; formulation, coordination and implementation of projects/schemes undertaken by MHA towards the women safety like Emergency Response Support System, Safe City projects etc; improve the efficiency of criminal justice delivery through use of IT interventions like Crime and Criminal Tracking Network and Systems-CCTNS, Inter-operable Criminal Justice System-ICJS, Investigations Tracking System for Sexual Offences-ITSSO, National Database on Sexual Offenders-NDSO etc.; look after the matters relating to Trafficking in Persons and Smuggling of Migrants and the two protocols of United Nations Convention against Transnational Organized Crime (UNCTOC) namely, the 'Protocol to Prevent, Suppress and Punish Trafficking in Persons, especially Women and Children' and the 'Protocol against the Smuggling of Migrants by Land, Sea and Air' etc.

We can sum up the importance of MHA and of leadership from the Home Minister in our National Security through its role of continuous monitoring of the internal security situation, issuing appropriate advisories, sharing intelligence inputs, extension of manpower support through deployment of CAPFs, capacity building through financial and technological support and its responsibility towards the maintenance of security, peace and harmony inside India without encroaching upon the constitutional rights of the States.

### 3.    *Ministry of Defence (MOD)*

International Law [Article 2(4) of the UN Charter] prohibits the use of force from one state against the territorial integrity or political independence of another state. Still, because of personal enmity between nations, the dominance of revisionist powers in neighboring nations along with the greed and lack of trust on others, modern-day nations are required to raise and maintain significant armed forces. Though they are primarily raised to protect the nation from external threats, their services are often used by many nations in internal matters also.

Because of our troubled neighborhood with unsettled issues and certain internal concerns, India maintains one of the biggest and strongest Armed Forces of India. Indian Armed Forces consist of Indian Army, Indian Air Force and Indian Navy with active support from Indian Coast Guard to maintain Maritime Security and a number of Paramilitary Forces like Border Security (BSF), Indo Tibetan Border Police (ITBP) etc. helping in External Border Security.

According to the Constitution of India, the Supreme Command of the Armed Forces is vested in the President of India. In actual, it is the Government of India, working through the Council of Ministers (with National Defence as a responsibility of Cabinet), who is responsible for ensuring the defence of India and every part thereof. Therefore, the Prime Minister either himself or appoints someone from the Cabinet as Defence Minister (Raksha Mantri) of India.

The Defence Minister heads the Ministry of Defence and provides leadership to it. The major responsibilities of the Ministry include- to obtain policy directions of the Government on all defence and security related matters, communication of national defence policy framework among all the services along with the provisioning of necessary wherewithal (means/resources) to Armed Forces for policy implementation and in discharge of their other responsibilities in context of national defence and welfare of its personnel.

In order to carry out these functions effectively and efficiently, the work of the Ministry of Defence is divided into four departments viz. Department of Defence, Department of Defence Production, Department of Defence Research & Development and Department of Ex-Servicemen Welfare. The functions of these departments are:

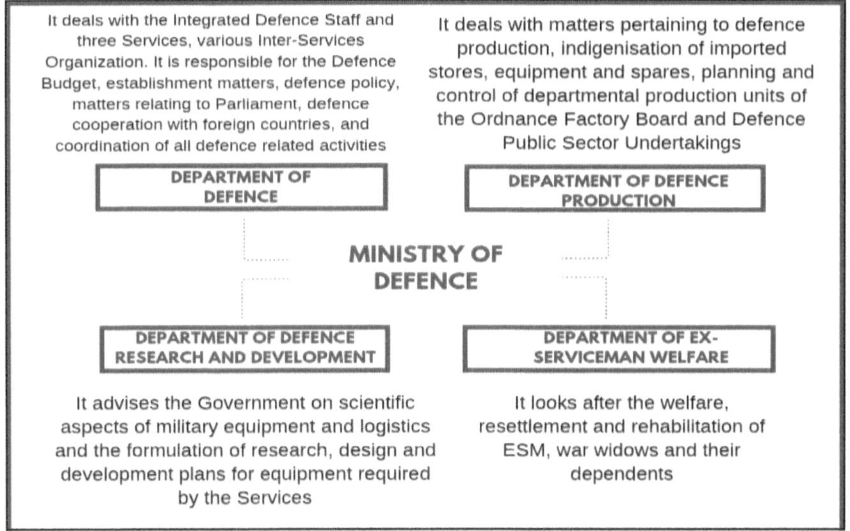


Figure 9 Various Departments* under Ministry of Defence

*Note: In 2020, a new department is added to the Ministry of Defence as the Department of Military Affairs with the Chief of Defence Staff as its head. While the complete details are yet to come out but the available information is discussed while explaining about the Chief of Defence Staff.*

The timeline of major structural changes in the Ministry of Defence from the times of the Interim Government of 1946 is as follows:

- On 02 September 1946, Ministry of Defence was created under the Interim Government with Baldev Singh as the first Defence Minister (earlier these functions were carried by the British Commander in Chief of the Indian Army);
- Post-Independence, Minister of Defence was made part of the Cabinet and each service was placed under its own Commander-in-Chief;
- In November 1962, a Department of Defence Production was set up to deal with research, development and production of defence equipment.
- In November 1965, the Department of Defence Supplies was created for planning and execution of schemes for import substitution of defence requirements.
- These two Departments were later merged to form the Department of Defence Production and Supplies and in 2004, the name of the Department of Defence Production and Supplies was changed to Department of Defence Production.
- In 1980, the Department of Defence Research and Development was created.
- In 2004, the Department of Ex-Servicemen Welfare was created.
- In 2020, the Department of Military Affairs was created.

### 4. *Ministry of External Affairs (MEA)*

As we discussed earlier, the National Security Strategy of a nation requires synchronization in the four key areas viz. Economy, Information, Military and Diplomacy. This last area, i.e. Diplomacy of India is looked after by the Ministry of External Affairs, also known as Foreign Ministry. MEA is the principal organization with the responsibility of overall supervision and coordination on international relations of India. It works under the External Affairs Minister with its work divided under five secretaries on the basis of territorial and functional responsibilities of secretaries. The work under the secretaries is further divided into various divisions.

Overall Coordination and supervision of work; EA (only China & Japan), AMS (only US), North, BM, IOR , PAI Division; EW Division (only UK, France, Germany); ERS Division (only Russia); RIC; D&ISA Division; Administration, Establishment, Projects, CNV, BOS, PP&R, Finance, and EG&IT Division; ICCR,CCCS

EA (except China & Japan), AMS( Canada), Southern Division; Indo-Pacific Division, ASEM, EAS, MGC, Nalanda, BIMSTEC & SAARC; LAC Division, MERCOSUR, CARICOM; A&RM, RTI Division; CT, XPD; Parliament & Coordination, Rajbhasha & Bharatiya Bhashayein

EU, Europe West (except UK, France and Germany), Central Europe Divisions; ERS Division (except Russia); Multilateral Diplomacy – UN, NAM, CHOGM, UNCTAD; SCO, G-20; L&T, Protocol and Conference Division, Coordination of events related to commemoration of Gandhi@150

**SECRETARY OF FOREIGN AFFAIRS**

**SECRETARY OF EAST**

**SECRETARY OF WEST**

# MINISTRY OF EXTERNAL AFFAIRS

**SECRETARY OF ECONOMIC RELATIONS**

**SECRETARY OF CONSUL, PASSPORT, VISA AND OVERSEAS INDIAN AFFAIRS**

Development Partnership Administration, MER, Investment & Trade Promotion; WTO Policy; WIPO, GCI, ED & States; Gulf, Special Kuwait Cell, WANA, GCC, India-Arab League, Maghreb Union; East & Southern Africa, Central and West Africa Division; AU, African Regional Economic Communities (SADC, IGAD, TEAM-9 and COMESA), India-Africa Forum; IBSA, BRICS

OIA-I, OIA-II,OE & PEG, CPV & PSP, PBK

## ORGANIZATION STRUCTURE

Figure 10 Various Departments under the Ministry of External Affairs

The major terms and abbreviations in the functions of various secretaries are as follows:

**AMS:** *Americas*

**ASEM:** *Asia-Europe Meeting*

**AU:** *African Union*

**BIMSTEC:** *Bay of Bengal Initiative for Multi-Sectoral Technical and Economic Cooperation*

**BM:** *Bangladesh Myanmar*

**BOS:** *Bureau of Security*

**BRICS:** *Brazil, Russia, India, China and South Africa*

**CARICOM:** *Caribbean Community*

**CCCS:** *Center for Contemporary Chinese Studies*

**CHOGM:** *Commonwealth Heads of Government Meeting*

**CNV:** *Cypher, NGO & Vigilance*

**COMESA:** *Common Market for Eastern and Southern Africa*

**CPV:** *Consular, Passport and Visa*

**CT:** *Counter-Terrorism*

**D&ISA:** *Disarmament & International Security Affairs*

**EA:** *East Asia*

**EAS:** *East Asia Summit*

**ED:** *Economic Diplomacy*

**EG&IT:** *E-Governance & Information Technology*

**ERS:** *Eurasia*

**EU:** *European Union*

**EW:** *Europe West*

*G-20:* Group of Twenty

*GCC:* Gulf Cooperation Council

*IBSA:* India, Brazil and South Africa

*ICCR:* Indian Council for Cultural Relations

*IGAD:* Intergovernmental Authority on Development

*IOR:* Indian Ocean Region

*LAC:* Latin America & Caribbean

*L&T:* Legal & Treaties

*MER:* Multilateral Economic Relations

*MERCOSUR:* Southern Common Market (South American Trade Bloc)

*MGC:* Mekong–Ganga Cooperation

*NAM:* Non Aligned Movement

*OIA:* Overseas Indian Affairs

*PBK:* Parvasi Bhartiya Kendra (now renamed as Sushma Swaraj Bhawan)

*PP&R:* Policy Planning & Research

*PSP:* Passport Seva Programme

*RIC:* Russia-India-China

*RTI:* Right to Information

*SAARC:* South Asian Association for Regional Cooperation

*SADC:* Southern African Development Community

*SCO:* Shanghai Cooperation Organisation

*TEAM-9:* Techno-Economic Approach for Africa-India Movement

*UN:* United Nations

*UNCTAD:* United Nations Conference on Trade and Development

*WANA:* West Asia & North Africa

*WIPO:* World Intellectual Property Organization

*WTO:* World Trade Organization

*XPD:* External Publicity Division

**This list of terms and abbreviations is provided in order to help the readers to know about the major divisions under which the Ministry of External Affairs divides its work and to benefit them in their preparation on International Relations by knowing about the way the Ministry of External Affairs looks at our International Relations.**

The high dependence of India on fuel imports for its energy security with rising geopolitical tensions in West Asia, North Africa and South America region and increasing global problems like Climate Change, loss of flora and fauna etc. has increased the scope of National Security Strategy beyond the DIME, i.e. Diplomacy, Information, Military and Economy. E.g. the recent set up of Jal Shakti (Water Power) Ministry by merging the Ministry of Water Resources, River Development and Ganga Rejuvenation and Ministry of Drinking Water and Sanitation is based on the increased realization of *water scarcity*[11] in India and the need to take immediate steps for water security.

Similarly, some other ministries like the Ministry of Petroleum and Natural Gas, Ministry of Coal etc. have an important role to play in our energy security and so on. You can read more about such fields and their role in National Security from Sustainable Development perspectives given in **"Sustainable Development Goals: Directive Principles for Sustainable India by 2030"**. Here, our discussion is restricted to Ministries and Executive Agencies as per DIME approach.

## Important Executive Agencies and Their Mandate in National Security

### Indian Armed Forces

Establishment of universal peace and Dharma (order) is an integral part of National Security. As 'Yajur Veda' says:

*"May the sky be peaceful; may the atmosphere be peaceful; may the earth be peaceful; may eternal peace cometh upon us"*

In order to build that peace for India, under the administrative structure of the Ministry of Defence, we have Indian Armed Forces, divided into three arms as:

    I.    Indian Army;
   II.   Indian Air Force; and
  III.   Indian Navy.

The prime responsibilities of our armed forces include:

a) Affirmation and protection of the Indian territorial integrity;
b) Engage in warfighting in order to secure our nation from any external aggression and internal subversion, if required;
c) Provide Military assistance to friendly nations along with participation in United Nations peacekeeping operations in order to fulfil our commitments to other nations and to the UN Charter; and
d) Aid the efforts of our Civil Authorities at times of disasters like flood, cyclones, earthquakes, insurgency, proxy wars etc.

### Indian Army

Indian Army is the biggest (around 1.2 million active army personnel) and most decorated Indian Armed Force; dedicated towards its

---

[11] *As per Niti Aayog study on Indian water crisis, by 2020 nearly 21 cities of India like Delhi, Chennai, Hyderabad, Bengaluru etc. will run out of groundwater, affecting around 100million citizens, with 6% of GDP loss by 2050 if no steps are taken to mitigate the crisis.*

responsibility of preserving the national interests by safeguarding the sovereignty and territorial integrity of India. It is headquartered in New Delhi and acts as ground defence from Indian Armed Forces.

It traces its roots to the British Indian Army and post-independence it was brought under the Ministry of Defence. Till 1955 all armed forces functioned under the Commander-in-Chief when all of them were renamed as Chief of the Army Staff (COAS), Chief of the Naval Staff (CNS) and Chief of the Air Staff (CAS). The motto of the Indian Army is **"Service Before Self"**, and every time it lives to its motto because of the edifice around which its fundamental framework is built. Indian Army is guided by the Just War principles and each rank and file of the Indian Army is driven by the values of:

1) **Esprit-de-Corps: It represents** the spirit of comradeship and brave brotherhood among all members of the force, regardless of caste, creed or religion.

2) **Spirit of Selfless Sacrifice:** It represents the do or die approach for the three "Ns"- i) Naam, i.e. name-honour- of the unit/Army/Nation, ii) 'Namak'(salt) i.e. loyalty to the Nation, and iii) 'Nishan', i.e. the insignia or flag of his unit/regiment/Army/Nation which the soldiers hold afloat willingly and without any question on all.

3) **Valour:** Show fearlessness in combat and in the face of the enemy even when fighting against great odds or even when facing sure death.

4) **Fairness and Honesty:** Live by the spirit of honesty and fair play. He fights for a just cause that extends even to the enemy (prisoner or wounded).

5) **Non-discrimination:** The Indian Army does not discriminate on account of caste, creed or religion. A soldier is a soldier first and anything else later. He prays under a common roof. It is this unique character, which makes him bind in a team despite such diversity.

6) **Discipline and Integrity:** Discipline and integrity impart the feeling of patriotism, honesty and courage under all circumstances, however strong be the provocation otherwise.

7) **Fidelity, Honour and Courage:** He is a man on whose shoulders lies the honour and integrity of his nation. He knows that he is the last line of defence and he cannot fail the Nation.

8) **Forthrightness:** A soldier has to be forthright, for on his word the men he leads are going to lay down their lives without questioning why.

9) **Death to Dishonour:** A close bond amongst soldiers forces them to choose death to dishonour. The concept of 'IZZAT' (HONOUR)

in the clan/unit enables them to shun the fear of death; to be called a coward in the peer group is worse than death.

## The journey of the Army from the British Indian Army to Indian Army

Having the Army for territorial integrity is not new and from the time of our grand epics i.e. 'Ramayana' and 'Mahabharata', the presence of proper armies is recognized. These documents are also among the first documents to lay stress on not just having an army but to use it for Just War only. Mahabharata is among the first documents to have troops divided into various units, as "Akshaunis" with different compositions and capabilities in terms of chariots, horses, elephants and foot soldiers. With time the compositions and capabilities of armies changed and many kingdoms came and went.

The present-day Indian Army traces its origin and evolution in the early sixteenth century efforts from the trading companies of European nations. The most important among them is the East India Company (EIC). It started with the recruitment of local soldiers to oversee the safety of trading posts and to protect the European units sailing into India. Indian Kings allowed them to do so because of various reasons, like immediate financial benefits, other local kings considered as a bigger threat than European companies and little or no vision towards the future.

As we discussed earlier, the use of trained Indians as regular soldiers by French against local kings inspired the East India Company to recruit and train local people for wars. A first authentic record of a regular battalion on Indian soil dates back to the year 1741, raised to carry out the garrison duties in Bombay Castle. In 1748, Major Stringer Lawrence, also known as 'the father of the Indian Army', was appointed as the Commander-in-Chief of East India Company's field forces in India (HQ @ Fort St. David, 12 miles from Pondicherry).

The ever increasing colonial hold from the British across the world and tensions in Europe like war with France forced the EIC to enroll more local troops for military services. While the local kings were occupied by bitter internal fighting and lack of scientific outlook, the EIC forces gained strength and technology. This helped in increasing the gap between the two. The victory in the Battle of Plassey (in 1757 under Robert Clive) helped EIC to go for further territorial expansion with an increased base for recruiting troops. Soon, Robert Clive created fully equipped regular Indian infantry battalions under the command of the British captain.

Post Battle of Buxar, EIC further enlarged/diversified its operations and became an administrator from a mere trading company. But the increasing corruption in the activities of company officials (because of which they became famous as Nabobs in Britain) forced the British Government to appoint the Board of Directors in 1784-85. Under this, full military powers including the power to appoint the Commander-in-Chief were given to the Board of Directors. By1790 the total strength of the combined British-Indian Army was 80,000.

With some hiccups, internal mutinies (e.g. Vellore Mutiny of 1806) and staggering casualties suffered in some battles like Bharatpur, British had overcome most of the local resistances by 1850 and gained the significant territory which can be defined as India. This led to a massive expansion of the Army and by 1857, the total strength of the combined British Indian Army increased to 2,33,000 Indian serving the three Presidency Armies of Bengal, Bombay and Madras along with 36,000 British troops under command of British officers.

In 1857, major Sepoy Mutiny happened (largely among soldiers of the Bengal Presidency Army) and the mutinous sepoys joined the local Kings as part of the 1857 revolution. With local help and superior tactical knowledge, the EIC was able to suppress the revolution. But it led to significant compositional and recruitment changes. After suppressing the mutiny and local kings, on **1st November 1858** British Crown under Queen Victoria took the complete governance charge of India, ending the role of East India Company. Strength of British troops was increased to one-third in each garrison of the Army.

With command of the Army coming under the British Crown, the use of Indian troops increased to not just secure and expand local interests but to strengthen foreign expeditions of British like Egypt (1882), Sudan (1884-85), China (1900) and Tibet (1904). On 1 April 1895, the Army was further restructured. The existing Presidency Armies were abolished and all were merged into one army as British Indian Army. It was then divided into four commands as- Punjab, Bengal, Madras and Bombay command. By 1903, the number of commands was reduced from four to two as- Northern Army and Southern Army and the battalions were also reorganized in order to suit the regional recruitment patterns. The raising of battalions like Marathas, Rajputs, Jats, Sikhs etc. happened during this time under Commander In-chief Kitchener. Later they served in World War-I and II from the British side.

By end of Second World War the mood of Independence prevalent across the nation set in the Armed Forces as well; leading to revolts/mutinies within the rank and file of all Armed Forces. With these revolts, the British also realized that it will be impossible for them to keep the same discipline and loyalty in forces as they enjoyed earlier because of the changed mood. Soon India was declared Independent and on 15 January 1949, last serving British Commander-in-Chief of Indian Army Francis Butcher handed over the command of Indian Army to Field

Marshal K.M. Cariappa. This day is also celebrated as the **Army Day** in India.

With the partition of India on religious lines, the unsettled neighbourhood became a gift for India from Britain. Because of it, we had our first brief war with Pakistan in the year of partition itself. Indian Army aided the efforts of our leaders towards Indian integration. E.g. It carried out 'operation polo' in order to end the atrocities of Razakars on people and integrate Hyderabad with India. In 1962 we had the Indo-China war because of Chinese aggression. Though the Indian Army lost in that war because of various reasons, the stories of bravery from its soldiers are still fresh in the minds of people.

In 1965, Pakistan again forced a war on India and Indian Army dealt with it victoriously. In 1971, the atrocities from West Pakistan on East Pakistan became so high that a lot of human rights violations and migration to India happened. It forced the Indian Government to take the decision of supporting the efforts of the Bangladeshi Liberation Army (*Mukti Bahini*). Pakistan took it as offensive and dragged India into another War to be fought on two fronts i.e. on the Eastern and Western side of India.

India responded with a calibrated approach with being offensive on the eastern border and defensive on the western border. The war ended on 16 December 1971 (now celebrated as **Vijay Diwas**) with unconditional surrender from Pakistan Army and the secession of East Pakistan (as Bangladesh) from West Pakistan. In order to stop future wars between the two nations, the Prime Ministers of both nations signed the "**Simla Agreement**" on 2 July 1972.

But because of rogue behavior from Pakistan, the border tensions between the two nations are yet to die down. Frequent ceasefire violations and use of terrorists or guerilla warriors have become part of the new approach from Pakistani military establishments. Indian Army has responded well to all such adventures from Pakistan and turned them into misadventures. Whether it was the Kargil War or the proactive surgical strikes in Pakistan Occupied Kashmir (POK) to avenge the Uri attack, Indian Army has shown that in order to fulfil its duty to defend India it can go offensive and beyond Indian territories.

Today, Indian Army is headquartered at New Delhi with the President of India as the Supreme Commander. The organisation of the Indian Army is divided into seven commands with six as operational commands and one as the Training Command on the basis of geography and operations. These seven commands are:
1) Northern Command (HQ: Udhampur),
2) Western Command (HQ: Chandimandir),
3) Eastern Command (HQ: Kolkata),

4) Southern Command (HQ: Pune)
5) Central Command (HQ: Lucknow)
6) South-Western Command (HQ: Jaipur), and
7) Army Training Command (HQ: Shimla).

## Indian Air Force

Indian Air Force (IAF) was raised under the British rule on **8 October 1932 (celebrated as Air Force Day)**. It started with an initial fleet of four Westland Wapiti army co-operative by-planes, six RAF trained officers and 19 Hawai Sepoys. Today, Indian Air Force stands as the 4th largest Air Force of the world and second among the Indian Armed Forces with a strength of around 1.4 lakh Air Force personnel.

Like the Indian Army, Indian Air Force also remained under the command of British even after independence. It was only on 1 April 1954 that the command of Indian Air Force was taken by an Indian when Air Marshal Subroto Mukherjee became the first Indian Commander-in-chief of Indian Air Force. In 1955, the Commander-in-chief was renamed as Chief of the Air Staff (CAS) with the rank of Air Chief Marshal.

The prime responsibility of the Indian Air Force is to safeguard the Indian Skies (Indian Airspace) from enemy invasion and work in conjunction with other armed forces to defend Indian territorial integrity. To fulfil its responsibilities, Indian Air Force is divided into seven different commands, out of which 5 are categorized as operational commands and two are recognized as functional commands as:
1) Central Air Command (HQ: Prayagraj, erstwhile Allahabad),
2) Eastern Air Command (HQ: Shillong),
3) Southern Air Command (HQ: Thiruvananthapuram),
4) South Western Air Command (HQ: Gandhinagar), and
5) Western Air Command (HQ: Delhi).

The two functional commands are:
1) Training Command (HQ: Bengaluru) and
2) Maintenance Command (HQ: Nagpur).

These commands are further divided into different Air Force Stations, Air Force Stations into different wings and wings into different squadrons and units, safeguarding Indian skies.

The motto of Indian Air Force is taken from Srimad Bhagavadgita as:

नभःस्पृशं दीप्तमनेकवर्णं व्यात्ताननं दीप्तविशालनेत्रम् ।
दृष्ट्वा हि त्वां प्रव्यथितान्तरात्मा धृतिं न विन्दामि शमं च विष्णो ॥

Lord, seeing your form Touching the Sky with Glory, effulgent, multi-coloured, having its mouth wide open and possessing large flaming eyes, I, with my innermost self frightened, have lost self-control and find no peace.

**-Srimad Bhagavadgita, Chapter XI, Verse 24**

This touching the Sky with Glory was started by Indian Air Force from its first war assignment itself, i.e. from World War-II with its officer KK Majumdar being rated among the 12 best airmen from the allied forces. Post-independence, because of financial constraints and technological limitations, the IAF role was limited in the 1962 war with China. It was the Chinese war when the need for active participation from the Indian Air Force was realized and since then it has played aggressive and defensive roles in order to protect Indian sovereignty and territorial integrity.

E.g. in the 1965 war, the Indian Air Force was given the task of neutralizing the air attacks from Pakistan. In the 1971 war, Flying Officer *Nirmal Jit Singh Sekhon* became the first IAF person to be awarded Param Vir Chakra (posthumously) for his role as the lone air defence warrior of Srinagar air base. Apart from that, it helped in Kargil War through one of the most unique and difficult operations, called as 'Operation Safed Sagar', carrying attacks at unprecedented heights with snow-covered terrain and hostile climatic conditions.

The other major functions of IAF include the extension of logistical support to Indian Army defence posts at difficult terrain (e.g. Siachen Glacier post), helping in relief & rescue operations post-natural disasters and to serve in UN peacekeeping missions as and when Indian Government commands it to do so. The Balakot airstrike of 2019 was a major event in the history of IAF when it went deep into Pakistani territory and attacked the installations of a terrorist organization; showing IAF capability to play the role of aggressor.

It shows that IAF has developed strong technical and strategic capabilities. Today, it is ranked among the strongest Air Forces of the world using some of the most advanced technologies of the world. IAF is made part of Integrated Space Cell along with other armed forces, Department of Space and Indian Space Research Organisation (ISRO). This Integrated Space Cell carries the responsibility of protection and effective utilization of the country's space-based assets towards military purposes.

## Indian Navy

The Indian Navy completes the triad of Indian Armed Forces by providing safety and security to India from any attack through above, on and below the Indian Ocean surface. The present Indian Navy was established under British India but the presence of maritime traditions is part of

Indian history for a long. Therefore, before we go through the development of Indian Navy, let's look at the brief naval history of India and the Indian Ocean.

## Naval History of India and the Indian Ocean

Use of small boats or arrangements for fishing, navigation and other activities through water bodies is known for long. E.g. Kevat, the community identified as boatmen, is recorded since the time of Lord Ram when a Kevat ferried Lord Ram and others across Ganga at the start of his exile in the forest.

Figure 11 Indus Valley Civilization

In terms of material evidence, the first signs of navigation in India are traced to the sea links built around 3000 BC by Indus Valley Civilization for trade and other purposes. Indus Valley Civilization (IVC) established maritime trade links with Mesopotamia and other parts of prehistoric civilizations. At Lothal (in modern-day Gujarat), one of the major cities of IVC, a dry-dock is found with the presence of berth and servicing facilities for ships, dating back to around 2400 BC.

In our recent history, the literary records of Greeks and Romans (from the time of Nanda and Maurya dynasty, i.e. from 340 to 300 BC) talks about maritime trade relations with India. This was also the time when the importance of naval security was realized in India. Megasthenes (a Greek ethnographer and Macedonian ambassador to Chandragupta Maurya) and Chanakya talked about the presence of naval security. E.g. in Arthashastra, Chanakya talks about the waterways department under Navadhyaksha (Superintendent of the ships) to look after the maritime trade accounts and maintain security over the waterways.

During the Gupta Period, Chinese scholars Fa-Hien, who visited India to learn Buddhism, sailed back to China via sea-route. He started from Bengal and after visiting places like Ceylon (modern-day Sri Lanka), Nicobar, Java etc. he reached China. The work from astronomers like Aryabhata and Varahamihira towards the movement of large celestial bodies and identification of stars position further helped in navigation; making maritime trade routes more predictable and safer.

The peninsular kingdoms or the southern dynasties of India had more developed maritime and versatile trade links. Satavahanas (200 BC–220 AD), with Amravati and Pratishtana as Capital City, ruling over the Deccan region, were the first native rulers to inscribe ships on their coins. Other Southern Dynasties like Cholas, Cheras and Pandyas with their knowledge on monsoonal winds, established trade and cultural links with other kingdoms.

E.g. the Pandyas were distinguished sailors and had control over the pearl trade. They established trade links over vast geography spread from Rome and Egypt in the West to China in the East. Similarly, the Cheras had a flourishing trade relationship with the Greeks, Arabs and the Romans. They carried forward their trade by navigating through various rivers opening

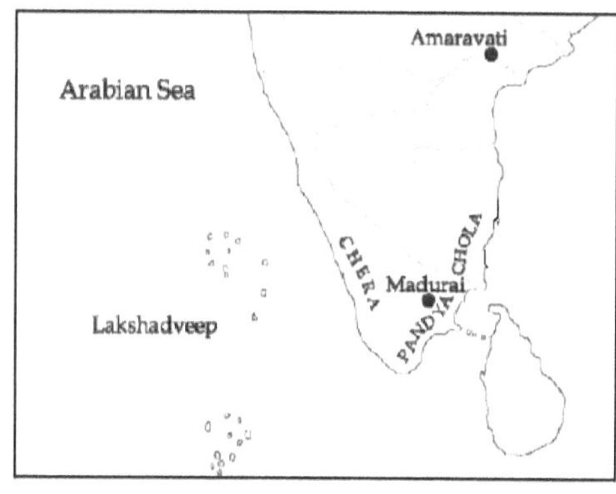


Figure 12 Southern Dynasties

into the Arabian Sea and used the monsoon winds to sail through the Indian ports like Muziris port (at Pattanam near Kochi).

But the most significant among them was the Cholas. They were located on the eastern coastal side of India and had strong trade links with Southeast Asian nations. They raised a strong naval force and launched a number of naval expeditions. E.g. **Rajaraja I** (985-1014 AD) used naval expeditions to gain control over the Maldives and Northern Sri Lanka, as they were the vital sea links for trade with Arabs, Southeast Asia and China.

His son, **Rajendra I** carried forward the policy of strong naval force and extended the influence of the Chola Dynasty from the coastal cities of River Ganga in North India to deep in Southeast Asia. In 1017 AD, he completed the Chola control over Sri Lanka by gaining control over Southern Sri Lanka also. Next year he gained control over the Cheras and Pandyas. In 1019 AD he defeated King **Indraratha** of Kalinga and King **Mahipala**, Pala king with Patliputra as the capital city. He commemorated the victory on Patliputra, a city on the coast of River Ganga, by the establishment of Gangaikonda Cholapuram as Capital of Chola in Tamil Nadu.

He furthered the commercial and cultural interests of Chola. In 1025 AD, he extended support to Suryavarman *I*, King of Khmer (now Cambodia) over his fight against the Tambralinga *Kingdom* of Malay Peninsula. With the Srivijaya Kingdom of Shailendra Dynasty (spread across the Indonesian Islands) being on the side of Tambralinga

Kingdom, Rajendra I attacked the *Srivijaya Kingdom* and established supremacy over the region.

All this was made possible by the naval superiority of the Chola Dynasty. They built different types of vessels which were classified as:

- **Dharani:** Warship for high sea combats (an equivalent of a modern-day *destroyer* in terms of purpose).
- **Loola:** Light combat Warship to escort the trading ships (an equivalent of modern-day *corvettes*).
- **Vajra:** A defence ship with the ability to attack quickly (an equivalent of modern-day *frigates*).
- **Thirisadai:** The biggest warship with the ability to engage a number of enemies at one time and for days.

Because of this massive influence of Chola Dynasty under Rajendra 1, the Indian Navy commemorated the completion of 1000 years of coronation of great Chola King *Rajendra 1* in 2014. The influence of Cholas is also recorded by Chinese Song Dynasty when a mission was sent by Cholas to China for trading purposes and helped Chinese through the transfer of Chola ship designs, weapons like flamethrowers and all-important Mariner Compass for navigation.

Though the influence of Indian culture and language on Southeast Asian nations is older, these trade links helped in revival and protection of those cultural and linguistic links. Even today we have nations in Southeast Asia which celebrate Indian festivals like Ramayana and Mahabharata or use Sanskrit words. It is also famous for some of the most scientific temple complexes like Angkor Wat.

With the onset of outside rule over Delhi, popularly known as Delhi Sultanate, the security veil enjoyed by Southern Dynasties from land attack came to an end and their attention shifted to internal events. The rising Arab Merchant class, which entered the maritime trade in the 8th Century, soon replaced the Southern Dynasties in the sea. They gained control over the trade routes and developed West Asian ports as the nodal point for trade between Europe, Southeast Asia and India.

In 14th century, i.e. during the phase of instability in Delhi, also known as the down phase of Delhi Sultanate because of weak rulers and Mongol invasions, Vijaynagar Kingdom (1336–1646 AD) tried to regain that lost control over maritime trade routes by developing strong links with European (e.g. Portuguese travellers like Niccolo De Conti, Domingo Paes visited their court) and Southeast Asian nations. During the regime of Krishna Deva Raya (1509-1529 AD), Vijaynagar Kingdom became the strongest and most prosperous kingdom of India. It had control over complete South India.

But soon after the death of Krishna Deva Raya, the empire started to disintegrate. The Deccan Sultanates, also known as Bahmani Kingdoms, who were defeated by Krishna Deva Raya came together. In 1565 the decisive Battle of Talikota was fought between the Vijaynagar kingdom and the Deccan Sultanates. Despite being stronger and in winning position, the forces of the Vijaynagar Empire under Aliya Rama Raya lost because of betrayal from two army generals.

Though Vijaynagar Kingdom continued to exist until 1646 AD, it never regained its military strength because of weak leadership. During this fall of Indian Naval power, we had probably the strongest Delhi Sultanates of Medieval India with stability under Mughal Rulers. But all of them focused only on revenues through excessive taxation on land and agriculture. Even whatever trade activities happened under their regime they were largely land-based. The Indian Ocean remained an open political affair.

With no Indian kingdom being in the position to extend patronage for peaceful sea-borne commerce, Indian coastline, port infrastructure and trade between the east and west was up for grabs. This lack of patronage from strong political power served the interests of rising European nations and their trading companies found it appropriate to have direct sea route trade with India. It also helped in the expansion of European trade companies and soon they started to gain upper hand over the Indian Ocean trade and commerce.

The first Europeans to arrive at Indian shores directly were the **Portuguese**; with Vasco da Gama reaching the shores of Calicut (Kozhikode) on 20 May 1498. He travelled from Portugal to India via Cape of Good Hope (in Africa), i.e. oceanic route of entering the Indian Ocean through the Atlantic Ocean. Though Vasco da Gama failed to have a commercial treaty with the Calicut King it opened the direct route for trade with Calicut, famously known as the City of spices. It also opened the routes of imperialism and colonialism.

E.g. in his second voyage, as 4th India Armada, Vasco da Gama came with an armed fleet of ships and trained soldiers to achieve political gains. He looted Arab vessels and killed people including the passenger ships like *Miri*. Though he failed to gain any significant victory against the Calicut king it was enough to disturb the peaceful trade of the Indian Ocean.

Soon, Portuguese established their factories at Calicut (1500 AD), Cochin (1500 AD), Cannanore (Kannur) (1502 AD), Kollam (1503 AD), Goa (1510 AD; as the biggest and seat of the Portuguese Viceroy), Daman and Diu (1529 AD) Surat (1534 AD), Mumbai (1534 AD), Hooghly-Chuchura (1579 AD) etc. In order to take full control over oceanic trade, they captured all major connecting trade ports like Hormuz, Socotra, Aden and Malacca from Arabs. The wealth accumulated by Portuguese through the trade of spices and control gained over the important trade routes inspired other European nations to establish their own trading companies and have direct trade through the Indian Ocean with subsequent political and religious gains.

The **Dutch** started their voyages in 1595 under various companies, in 1602 they were merged and one Dutch East India Company was established as Verenigde Oost-Indische Compagnie or VOC, meaning United East India Company. The VOC was granted with trade monopoly from east of the Cape of Good Hope to the Straits of Magellan (linking the Pacific Ocean with the Atlantic Ocean). From British end, Ralph Fitch was the first English merchant to arrive at the court of Akbar in 1585. But he travelled through the old route. The sea voyages via Cape of Good Hope were initiated only after the establishment of East India Company.

On 31 December 1600, **British** Queen Elizabeth-I gave English Royal Charter for the establishment of East India Company (EIC) with the grant of trade monopoly with countries east of the Cape of Good Hope. In 1601, East India Company started its first voyage under James Lancaster on 'Red Dragon' Ship. In 1603, they established their first factories in Indonesia at Java and Spice Islands (now as the Maluku Islands). In 1607, Captain William Hawkins (on ship Hector) started his sail towards India and arrived at Surat. Captain Hawkins visited the court of Jahangir at Agra in 1609 and the Mughal ruler allowed their trade with Mughal dominions.

Being the dominant sea power of trade over the Indian Ocean, the Portuguese felt infuriated by the Jahangir order and under Portuguese pressure the permission was soon revoked. The EIC established its first factory in India at Masulipatnam in 1611 (Andhra Pradesh) and in the same year, under Captain Middleton, they were able to convince the local Mughal Governor for grant of trading rights. Once again the Portuguese opposed but it was crushed by Middleton through a crushing blow in the Battle. In 1612, they established Surat as a trade point and in 1615, their representative **Thomas Roe** was able to get exclusive rights for building factories at Surat from Mughal King Jahangir.

By 1623, the VOC, i.e. Dutch East India Company was able to throw British East India Company out of Indonesia. So, the British East India Company started to strengthen their Indian interests. In 1639, they established Fort Saint Gorge at Madras and with the establishment of Town it became their first major territorial possession in India. Soon they expanded to Bengal and from Bengal, their colonial aspirations started.

Meanwhile, the VOC established by Dutch had the colonial aspirations since its inception as it was established not just to conclude treaties with native rulers alone or to build factories but to have powers for building forts, keeping armed forces for the security of its interest and engaging in administrative activities. Because of Portuguese dominance over Indian water, they started from Indonesia and established their first trading post at Batavia (Jakarta in Indonesia). Though they tried to expand and established their trading facilities in India also, like Masulipatnam (1605), Pulicat (1608), Surat (1616), Bengal (1627) etc. but these were established after permission from Portuguese.

They established Ambon (in Indonesia) as their headquarters. With the decline of Portuguese power, the Dutch EIC expanded its interests and by 1640 it started to overtake Ceylon (Sri Lanka). In 1652, they established an outpost at the Cape of Good Hope and by 1659 it established full control over the Ceylon coasts. In 1661, they fought successfully against Portuguese to establish control over the forts on Malabar Coast and protect their possession over Ceylon (Sri Lanka). They primarily traded in textiles, precious stones, indigo, silk, opium, cinnamon, pepper etc. and by 1669 it became the richest company of the world.

But VOC failed to bring any significant challenge to the British possession in India. In 1664, Jean Baptiste Colbert (serving as Minister of Finances under King Louis XIV) established French East India Company to trade with the Eastern Hemisphere or the Orient Nations. Though they were late to enter the waters of the Indian Ocean in a short period they developed themselves as the biggest threat against British interest in the Indian Ocean.

In 1668 they established their first factory of India at Surat and in 1669 they established another factory at Masulipatnam. In 1673 they were able to convince local Mughal Governor of Bengal to establish a trading post with town Chandernagore and in 1674 they convinced the Sultan of Bijapur to establish a similar town at Pondicherry. In 1710, they occupied Mauritius and developed it as the port of call and strong naval base for future operations. Though the French were forced to leave some old factories like Surat and Masulipatnam, they added new gains like Mahe, Yanam and Karaikal.

By 1740, French became a force to reckon in the Indian Ocean Region and a threat to British colonial interests in India under declining local rulers. This battle for supremacy in the Indian Ocean continued between the two from 1744 and 1760, through repeated attacks on each other's coastal forts and towns. Under Dupleix, the French achieved some initial political or diplomatic successes inside India and against British.

With the arrival of Robert Clive in 1744, the situation changed and by 1754 they were able to force the French's for recall Dupleix to home. Though the French were still able to get some initial successes, their defeat in the Battle of Wandiwash (Vandavasi in Tamil Nadu) in 1760 gave a serious blow to their Indian aspirations. All their Indian possessions were taken by the British. The Treaty of Paris (1763) allowed them to keep possession over Pondicherry, Mahe and Karaikal but these possessions were to be maintained under the British Protection.

Among Indians, the Maratha Navy raised under Shivaji and his successors were the only prominent local navy which offered strong resistance to British. He built a number of coastal forts along the Konkan coast regions like Sindhudurg, Vijaydurg, Ratnagiri and Kolaba. For some time the Maratha navy was weakened after the death of Shivaji but soon it started to gain strength under the command of Kanhoji Angre. In fact, it was the Marathas under Kanhoji Angre who destroyed the naval power of the Portuguese over the Indian Ocean and forced them to sign a peace treaty with Marathas. He challenged the British Navy on many occasions and both navies had many wars against each other. But the defeat of the Maratha Navy in 1756 at Vijaydurg ended the challenge from the Marathas.

After the end of all these struggles over the Indian Ocean, the British were left as the only naval power with the ability to extend patronage towards Indian Ocean trade. The British were also aware of it and soon they strengthened their naval bases in India and increased the strength of the Navy. This dominance from British continued till 18 February 1946, when Indian origin sailors and officers of the Royal Indian Navy rose against discrimination, popularly known as *Royal Indian Navy Mutiny*. The support from other Armed forces, i.e. The Army and Air Force, along with the local police and masses of Bombay made the British realize that their days in India are limited.

With the adoption of Indian Constitution and India becoming a republic, the name of Royal Indian Navy was changed to Indian Navy on 26 January 1950 and Admiral Ram Dass Katari became the first Indian Chief of the Naval Staff in 1958.

Today, Indian Navy has developed itself into one of the most advanced navies of the world and holds multidimensional abilities to respond against the enemy from below, on and above the ocean surface in order to protect the Indian maritime territorial integrity. It is based on the invocation to Lord Varuna (The Sea God of Vedas) and carries it as their emblem with "**Sham no Varunah**"- meaning: "**Be auspicious unto us Oh Varuna**" as its Motto.

Post-independence, it played an important role in the liberation of Goa (through operation *Vijay*) and again in the 1971 war against Pakistan (through Operation *Trident*). From 1972, the day of successful naval operations under the operation *Trident* (04 December) is celebrated as the Navy Day, replacing the English navy Day of 21st October since 1944. The Headquarters of the Indian Navy is located in New Delhi along with other armed forces and it has three Naval Commands under the control of a Flag Officer Commanding-in-Chief as:

1) The Western Naval Command (an operational command with Headquarters at Mumbai);
2) The Eastern Naval Command (an operational command with Headquarters at Visakhapatnam); and
3) The Southern Naval Command (a Training Command with Headquarters at Kochi).

The naval bases of Indian Navy are spread across the Eastern and Western coasts of India including the Indian Island groups; with the defence of the Andaman & Nicobar Islands under a Tri-Services Command, i.e. a joint responsibility of all the three armed forces, with Headquarter at Port Blair. This was set up in 2001, headed by a Commander-in-Chief, appointed in rotation from the three Services.

The prime reason for this unique structure is the presence of Indian strategic interests in Southeast Asia and the increasing militarization around the Strait of Malacca. In comparison, the defence of the second Indian island group, i.e. The Lakshadweep group of islands is kept under the Navy. The fleet of Indian Navy, i.e. ships, submarines and aircraft are divided among the Eastern and Western Command.

The comparative hierarchical positions of the three armed forces at officer level are as follows:

| INDIAN ARMY | INDIAN AIR FORCE | INDIAN NAVY |
| --- | --- | --- |
| General | Air Chief Marshal | Admiral |
| Lieutenant General | Air Marshal | Vice Admiral |
| Major General | Air Vice-Marshal | Rear Admiral |
| Brigadier | Air Commodore | Commodore |
| Colonel | Group Captain | Captain |
| Lieutenant Colonel | Wing Commander | Commander |
| Major | Squadron Leader | Lieutenant Commander |
| Captain | Flight Lieutenant | Lieutenant |
| Lieutenant | Flying Officer | Sub-Lieutenant |

## Intelligence Agencies

According to Chanakya, the threat to peace and prosperity of a nation can come from outside or from inside of the nation. Under the evolved domestic and global environment of the 21st century, though the spheres of the threat to national peace and prosperity are the same yet the nature of threats faced by nations have diversified. These diversities are added by the increased connectivity of the world at the physical, economic and intellectual level, influencing not just the state actors but also the non-state actors.

At the time of our independence we had limited threats to our national security from some state actors like Pakistan, China or from few ethnic identities wanting to separate from India. But today we have an additional set of new threats working against our National Interests. E.g. We have intellectuals who spread false notions about India and instigate Indian people to revolt against the state. Through internet-enabled terrorism, non-state religious actors try to sow the seeds of disharmony among Indians and recruit Indian people for global radicalism. The list is long and we need agencies that can recognize these threats in advance and help our leaders and security agencies to secure the interests of India through credible intelligence.

Credible intelligence includes objective and insightful information on security risks, allowing our leaders to identify the national priorities and make informed decisions. Most importantly, it keeps us aware of the strategies from our adversaries, helping in timely up-gradation of our national security strategy and to make our nation more secure. For India, this function of Intelligence is performed by the two premier agencies- Intelligence Bureau (IB) and Research and Analysis Wing (RAW) for a long. Many new agencies have also joined into the efforts of IB and RAW with the prime goal of securing India and its interests through credible intelligence collection for better decision making. The mandate of these executive agencies is as follows:

### 1) Intelligence Bureau (IB)

The Intelligence Bureau (IB) is the first intelligence agency of India tasked with the responsibility of keeping a close eye on the internal affairs of India and to inform the central and state government about the upcoming dangers. It works under the Ministry of Home Affairs (MHA) as maintenance of internal security is one of the responsibilities of MHA.

It traces its origin to the Central Special Branch established by British in 1887 to keep a watch on the social, political and economic conditions of India along with a careful watch on the expanding Russian troops' deployment on the Northwest Border (near Afghanistan region). After a number of changes in name and functions; finally, it was named as Intelligence Bureau (IB) in 1920 and since then continues with that name.

Though still a classified document, the increasing Chinese activities on the Tibetan side and fear of Chinese takeover of Tibet led to the formation of 'North and North East Border Defence Committee', popularly known as Himmat Singh Ji Committee. Among its recommendations on the improvement of Indian Border Defence along

66

the Tibetan Border, it recommended the use of IB to keep a watch on the Chinese troop movement on the Border.

Though IB carried this responsibility of internal and external intelligence till 1968 but the lapses on getting timely information on Chinese strategy before the 1962 war and on Pakistan attack in 1965, the Indian government was forced to look for alternatives. Finally, in 1968 the Research and Analysis Wing (RAW) was established to keep a watch on external threats. Today, IB is involved in the internal intelligence activities related to counter-terrorism (foiling terrorist acts), counter-intelligence (foiling enemy intelligence agencies network in India), Border Intelligence, VIP security and giving clearance on the names recommended for key posts like Indian Diplomats or Judges of High Court and Supreme Court.

## 2) Research and Analysis Wing (RAW)

The Research and Analysis Wing (RAW) is the premier external intelligence agency of India. It was founded in 1968 with the primary target of foiling the Chinese influence. It justified its set up under guidance of very first RAW Director, Rameshwar Nath Kao by helping in the formation of Bangladesh, keeping India's first Nuclear Test 'Smiling Buddha' under security cover before the test and convincing the rulers of Sikkim to merge with India. Based on its initial successes, it has expanded a lot and today its network is spread across the globe with the primary objective of securing Indian interests through advanced information and countermeasures.

RAW is headquartered at New Delhi and works under the direct command of the Prime Minister through the Cabinet Secretariat. The primary duty of RAW is to protect and promote India's strategic interests on foreign soil by gathering actionable intelligence on foreign soil for our policymakers and security agencies. Like IB, it helps in countering terrorism operations and has the major responsibility towards securing Indian Nuclear programme from proliferation. Though shrouded in secrecy, RAW assets include a number of Aviation Research Centres involved in aerial surveillance, Signal intelligence, border monitoring, Imagery intelligence etc. Some experts believe that after the set up of NTRO, some of those functions and assets are transferred to Directorate of Air Force intelligence and NTRO.

## 3) Joint Intelligence Committee (JIC)

The Joint Intelligence Committee is part of National Security Council and it was established to analyze the intelligence data from different intelligence agencies like Intelligence Bureau, RAW, Directorate of Military Intelligence, Directorate of Naval Intelligence, Directorate of Air Intelligence etc. It has its own secretariat under the Cabinet Secretariat.

## 4) Defence Intelligence Agency

The nature of our defence establishments is such that even after having the support from premier Intelligence agencies like IB and RAW, they need to have their own intelligence network in order to keep a close watch on the movement of terrorist organizations and enemy nations army movement in their areas of operation. It helps in securing own assets and responding early to the potential or actual security risks like border intrusions, terror attacks etc. To do this, all three armed forces of India have their own intelligence directorates as Directorate of Military Intelligence, Directorate of Naval Intelligence and Directorate of Air Intelligence.

Though all of them reported to respective Armed Forces Headquarters functioning from South Block in New Delhi, under the Ministry of Defence but for long they failed to share information and coordinate with each other even in joint areas of operation. One such failure of coordination was 1999 when intelligence agencies of our Armed Forces failed to get early evidence on Pakistani infiltration.

To overcome this, in March 2002 Defence Intelligence Agency (DIA) was created under the Ministry of Defence to share each other resources for intelligence gathering and better coordination of operations; by combining the Directorates of Military Intelligence, Directorates of Air Force Intelligence and Directorates of Naval Intelligence with prime responsibility of gathering first-hand actionable intelligence for Indian Armed Forces. They track the troop movements in our neighbouring nations and the terrorist groups operating within India and outside.

### 5) National Technical Research Organisation (NTRO)

National Technical Research Organisation (NTRO) was established in 2004 as National Technical Facilities Organisation (NTFO) for specialized technical intelligence gathering activities and to improve our signal intelligence through active monitoring of National Critical Information Infrastructure like Satellites monitoring, terrestrial monitoring or internet monitoring. The increasing space of Critical Information Infrastructure makes the role of NTRO all more important under the changing circumstances.

In order to perform its role par excellence, NTRO has established the National Critical Information Infrastructure Protection Centre (NCIIPC). NCIIPC carries the responsibility to conduct periodic security reviews and sensitization of all stakeholders (e.g. Ministries, Regulators, Enterprises etc.) through regular workshops and periodic guidelines for identification of Critical Information Infrastructure.

It works under the National Security Adviser (NSA). NTRO also helps other intelligence agencies in gaining technological advancement and help in providing actionable intelligence. E.g. in recent Balakot strikes on Terrorist Camps of Pakistan, NTRO helped the Indian Air Force in ascertaining the presence of terrorists. With increasing cyber threats to Government IT infrastructure especially the critical infrastructure with changing technical landscape like the introduction of Internet of Things (IoT), 5G etc. the role of NTRO in general and its unit NCIIPC, in particular, becomes crucial.

### <u>Networks and Software for Security</u>

In 2001, i.e. before the attacks of 9/11 on World Trade Towers (New York), USA lacked the presence of an integrated surveillance mechanism for its security agencies. Because of this, despite having the name of many 9/11 perpetrators in the terrorist watch list, the state agencies failed to give an early response. In this backdrop, (i.e. post 9/11) the State launched a massive mass surveillance mechanism in order to avoid the repeat of incidents like 9/11. This led to the rise of Panopticon State, an idea first developed by Jeremy Bentham for an institutional building and a system of control where one security guard can observe all the prisoners without the prisoners being aware of being watched.

Post 9/11, India also realized the need for better surveillance and coordination among its agencies, leading to preparatory work on the development of mass surveillance networks with the joining of a global movement towards peace with security. But under our federal set up responsibilities of state and union government are well defined. With public order being a state responsibility, the union government moved slowly on it. Also, many such projects are against some fundamental rights of individuals like Right to Privacy and personal liberty.

Therefore, it picked pace only after the 26/11 attacks on Mumbai in 2008. The Mumbai attack exposed poor intelligence gathering, lack of coordination and operational failures from union and state governments to address such large scale attacks inside India. Since then, India has developed important mass surveillance networks and software for early information and better coordination among different agencies. This includes-

**1. National Intelligence Grid (NATGRID): NATGRID** is an integrated intelligence grid which connects the databases of core security agencies under the Government of India along with personal databases like data on financial transactions (tax, bank account, card details etc.), travel (rail and air travel), immigration details etc. of citizens in order to collect comprehensive patterns of intelligence with easy access to 10 central intelligence agencies as- RAW, CBI, IB, DRI, CBDT, CBEC, ED, NCB DGCEI and

FIU. It was first proposed in the aftermath of the 2008 Mumbai attacks, along with the National Intelligence Agency (NIA) and the National Counter Terrorism Centre (NCTC). After the initial hype, the project started to crumble as it is yet to become operational as it is seen in violation of Right to Privacy by collecting confidential and personal information of citizens by many. It consists of complex technologies and programs as it requires synchronization of at least 21 databases from different agencies into one form. Also, it lacks a mechanism to share intelligence inputs with state agencies. While the initial proposal included the setting up of **National Counter Terrorism Centre (NCTC)**, as a federal anti-terror agency of India (i.e. agency with participation from state and central agencies) based on the model of National Counterterrorism Center (USA) but no alternative is explored after the protests from Chief Ministers of various states against NCTC for being against the Indian federalism. With the increased pace of NATGRID in the last few years, it is hoped that by the start of 2020 it will become operational.

**2. NEtwork TRaffic Analysis (NETRA):** NETRA is an indigenously built software network from Centre for Artificial Intelligence and Robotics (CAIR), a laboratory under the Defence Research and Development Organisation (DRDO), used by three agencies of India as- Cabinet Secretariat, Intelligence Bureau and Research and Analysis Wing (RAW) for intercepting and analyzing the internet traffic on real-time basis through use of predefined filters. It can intercept and analyze the text as well as voice messages flowing through the internet networks in India. Similar systems are developed by other nations also. E.g. the five eyes of the world i.e. USA, UK, Canada, Australia and New Zealand use the 'Echelon' software network. Similarly, we have a Prism network used by NSA of the USA along with GCHQ (UK intelligence agency). Under present circumstances, NETRA is vital for tackling the growing menace of internet-enabled terrorism where internet use by terrorist organizations for recruitment, fundraising and instigation purposes has increased a lot.

**3. Central Monitoring System (CMS):** If NETRA helps in tacking voice and text messages on the internet, the **Central Monitoring System (CMS)** acts as a centralized telephone interception provisioning system used for automatic monitoring of communications on mobile phones, landlines and the internet in the country for national security and lawful interception purposes. It was installed by the Centre for Development of Telematics (C-DOT), an Indian Government-owned telecommunications technology development centre, and operated by Telecom Enforcement Resource and Monitoring (TERM) Cells. Under this, a Central Monitoring Centre (CMC) is already set up in Delhi with Regional Monitoring Centre's (RMC) becoming operational across states of India.

## Other Security Forces and Agencies

The mandate of the Indian Armed Forces is primarily to secure Indian territorial integrity from external threats or aggression. Though armed forces aid Civil Authorities at times of disasters like flood/cyclones/earthquakes/insurgency/proxy wars etc. yet, for routine activities or peacetime purposes we have a number of security forces to protect Indian borders.

Also, at the state level, the maintenance of law and order is State Government responsibility (under Schedule 7) which is shouldered through State Police. But at times to maintain law and order, carry out disaster relief operations, to deal with national threats within India or to improve the capabilities of forces working within India, a number of Central Armed Police Forces and other agencies (established for specific tasks) operate in the country. A number of them are described in following articles:

### 1.   *Indian Coast Guard*

Under present conditions, maritime areas are as important for the security and economic prosperity of a nation as the mainland. If we look at India, we have a coastline of 7516.6 km (5422.6 km of the mainland and 2094 km of Island Territories) with territorial waters[12] area (up to 12 nautical miles) of 1,93,834 km$^2$ and an Exclusive Economic Zone[13] of 2,305,143 km$^2$. Add to that, we have a large diversity of marine environment (presence of coral reefs, mangroves, marine algae, sea grasses and marine life) and economic activities like fishing, oil exploration and production, large and small ports with LNG terminals etc. being located in and around our maritime area.

Therefore, in 1978 the Indian Coast Guard was formally established (on 18 August 1978 by the *Coast Guard Act, 1978*) to look after the Coastal Security of India including the safety and security of its

---

[12] *Territorial Waters area refers to the area which comes within the 12 nautical miles or 22. Km from the baseline of the coastal state. The baseline is usually the low-water line of the coast as recognized by the state.*

[13] *Exclusive Economic Zone is a sea zone prescribed by the 1982 United Nations Convention on the Law of the Sea (UNCLOS) over which the state holds special rights of exploration and use of marine resources. Presently it extends to 200 nautical miles with India submitting its claim to extend it up to 350 nautical miles as our Continental Shelf extends up to 350 nautical miles.*

EEZ area, Offshore activities, Marine Safety and protection of Marine Environment with help in Scientific Assistance programs and aid to the efforts of Navy towards National Defence in War situations.

Indian Coast Guard started its journey with its ensign (flag) being hoisted for the first time on Indian Coast Guard Ship Kuthar on 19th August 1978. It is headed by the Director General Indian Coast Guard (DGICG) with its headquarters located at New Delhi. The duties of the Indian Coast Guard include:

a) Ensuring the safety and protection of artificial islands, offshore terminals, installations and other structures and devices in any maritime zone,

b) Providing protection and assistance to fishermen in distress while at sea,

c) Preservation and protection of our maritime environment including prevention and control of marine pollution,

d) Assisting the Customs and other authorities in anti-smuggling operations,

e) Enforcement of Maritime Zones of India Act, and

f) Precautionary measures for the safety of life and property at sea and the collection of scientific data.

In order to carry out its duties effectively and efficiently the Indian Coast Guard has divided the Indian Maritime surface into five Coast Guard Regions, namely, North-West (covering maritime area of Gujarat), West (complete western sea of India except Gujarat, i.e. Maharashtra, Goa, Karnataka, Kerala and Lakshadweep), East (covering the entire coastline from Poovar in Kerala to Ichchapuram in Andhra Pradesh), North-East (covering the entire coastline from Sunderbans of West Bengal to Gopalpur in Odisha) and Andaman & Nicobar, with the respective Regional Headquarters located at Gandhinagar, Mumbai, Chennai, Kolkata and Port Blair. In order to fulfil its duties, the Indian Coast Guard has developed capabilities to perform sea surface and air operations.

Among all, the western coastal area is far more important as it is the sea link of Pakistan as well as the presence of the Sea Lanes of Communication (SLOCs) passing through Indian maritime area with a large number of oil and gas tankers passing through it. Because of this high commercial activities and ships, the threat of pirates and the risk of oil pollution are very high in the western coastal area.

### 2. Territorial Army

The Territorial Army (TA) is an army of volunteers first raised by the British in 1920 through Indian Territorial Act of 1920 with two wings, namely – 'The Auxiliary Force' for Europeans & Anglo-Indians, and 'The

Indian Territorial Force' for Indian Volunteers. Post-Independence, the Territorial Army Act was passed in 1948 to make it a part of Regular Army with role to relieve the Regular Army from static duties and assist civil administration in dealing with natural calamities and maintenance of essential services in situations where life of the communities is affected or the security of the country is threatened and to provide units for Regular Army as and when required.

As of date, the TA units have played an active role in-

- War efforts of 1962, 1965 and 1971;
- Operations like OP PAWAN in Srilanka, OP RAKSHAK in Punjab and J&K, OP RHINO and OP BAJRANG in the North East; and
- Numerous activities to aid the efforts of civil authorities during Industrial unrest and natural calamities like the earthquakes in Latur (Maharashtra) and Uttarkashi in Garhwal Himalaya; the Super Cyclone in Odisha etc. With the establishment of the National Disaster Relief Force (NDRF), some of the functions of TA are taken by them.

### 3. *National Cadet Corps (NCC)*

On 29 September 1946, under the chairmanship of H.N. Kunzru, a Cadet Corps Committee was formed to carry out an exhaustive study on the problems of youth in India. After studying the youth in all the main provinces of erstwhile India and the functioning of the youth and cadet organizations of Britain and France, the committee submitted its report to the Government of India in Mar 1947. It recommended the setting up of a National Cadet Corps in India.

Independence brought a lot of unprecedented troubles like partition/large scale migrations/ communal violence/the struggle to integrate princely states in India including the Kashmir War of 1948. These troubles made the need for the National Cadet Corps more pronounced than ever. So, the recommendations of Kunzuru committee were placed before the Constituent Assembly (Legislature) on 13 Mar 1948 after receiving answers from various provincial governments. The draft Bill on NCC was sent to the Constituent Assembly (Legislative) on 19 Mar 1948. Finally, the bill was passed by the Assembly on 08 Apr 1948.

On 16 April 1948, the bill received assent from the Governor-General of India and the National Cadet Corps came into being by an Act of the Parliament Act No. XXXI of 1948 designated 'The National Cadet Corps Act 1948'. The prime purpose for the creation of NCC was to have sufficient strength of reserves in India, who could take up arms when required by giving military training of young men and women from schools and colleges throughout the country.

The activities of the NCC are managed by the Director General NCC with its Headquarters in Delhi and Colonel Gopal Gurunath Bewoor (who served as 9th COAS, after the retirement of Sam Manekshaw) as the first Director of the NCC on 31 March 1948. It started to enroll the students from the schools and colleges of independent India from 15 Jul 1948 and today it has become the largest uniformed youth organisation in the world with more than 13 lakh cadets on its rolls. These cadets are divided into a variety of units like Armoured Corps, Artillery units, Engineers units, Signals units, Medical units and 83 companies of Infantry.

### 4.  *Central Bureau Of Investigation (CBI)*

The Central Bureau of Investigation, popularly known as CBI, traces its origin to the Special Police Establishment (SPE), started by British in 1941 to investigate cases of bribery and corruption in transactions with the War & Supply Department of India during World War II. With bribery and corruption being part of the system, the need for such an establishment to investigate the central government employees was felt.

In 1946, through the Delhi Special Police Establishment Act, the superintendence of the SPE was transferred to the Home Department with enlargement in its scope of the investigation to all departments of the Government of India, Union territories and to the States (if consented by the concerned State Government).

On 1st April 1963, the name of DSPE was changed to its present name as *Central Bureau of Investigation (CBI)*, through a Home Ministry resolution. Today, it covers a number of other organizations like public sector undertakings, Public Sector Banks etc. with some key investigations which are essential for national security like Economic offences and crimes by terrorists on a selective basis.

### 5.  *Bureau of Police Research & Development (BPR&D)*

It was established on 28 August 1970 by the Government of India, under the Ministry of Home Affairs to replace the Police Research and Advisory Council (1966) and to work on modernization of police forces. BPR&D performs its duties by a speedy and systematic study of the problems faced by the police and promotes the use of science and technology in the methods and techniques used by police.

### 6.  *National Crime Records Bureau (NCRB)*

In order to improve the confidence of people in police and to promote greater efficiency and effectiveness in the police, it is important that the crimes are recorded and analyzed properly. It helps in the prevention and detection of crime. Based on the recommendations of the National Police

Commission-1977, the Ministry of Home Affairs constituted a Task Force in 1985 to work out the modalities for setting up of the National Crime Records Bureau (NCRB).

It was important as police is a State subject under the Indian constitution with Central Government activities being largely restricted to offering assistance and to aid the States in the modernization of the State Police Forces through the Ministry of Home Affairs. Based on the recommendations of the Task Force, National Crime Records Bureau (NCRB) was established in January 1986 with its headquarters at New Delhi. Today, NCRB performs a number of functions as:

- To create a comprehensive and integrated nationwide networking infrastructure, like **Crime and Criminal Tracking Network & Systems** (CCTNS), a Mission Mode Project under the National e-Governance Plan (NeGP), to enhance the efficiency and effectiveness of policing throughout India by providing an IT-enabled-state-of-the-art tracking system for Investigation of crimes and detection of criminals.
- To look after the administration of the **Central Finger Print Bureau** (CFPB), Kolkata. The charge of CPFB was given to NCRB in July 1986, before which it was first under IB from its start in 1955 to 1973. From 1973 to 1986 it remained under the CBI.
- To carry out the statistical works through its **Statistical Branch**, transferred to NCRB from the Statistical Section of the Bureau of Police Research and Development (BPR&D).
- To build up, update and maintain a secure National Database on crimes, criminals and property through its **Data Centre & Technical (DCT) Branch**, helping in accurate and timely availability of information online to all State forces and Central agencies for the purpose of improving day-to-day functioning in terms of crime detection, crime prevention and maintenance of public order.
- To impart training in Information Technology (IT) and FingerPrint Science to police forces through its Training Branch, for capacity building of Police Forces to control Cyber Crimes, use of Digital Forensics, CCTNS, etc. in Law Enforcement and crime investigations.

### 7. *National Investigation Agency (NIA)*

National Investigation Agency (NIA) is a central investigation agency established by the Indian Government in the aftermath of the 2008 Mumbai attacks to combat terror in India and act as the Central Counter-Terrorism Law Enforcement Agency. It came into existence on 31 December 2008, with the enactment of the National Investigation Agency Act 2008 by the Parliament of India.

The establishment of NIA was essential to tackle the increasing problems of terrorism, insurgency, militancy, Left Wing Extremism and organized crimes like drugs and arms smuggling, circulation of counterfeit currency, infiltration etc., which are often linked to each other and have complex inter-state and international linkages. NIA fits in to investigate such crimes as in the performance of its duties it doesn't require special permissions from the states concerned.

In the recent past, the role of NIA as Central Counter Terrorism Law Enforcement Agency has gained significance with the rise of Internet-enabled terrorism. Today, NIA has developed itself as a professional investigative agency with high standards of excellence in counter-terrorism and other national security-related investigations with an enviable conviction percentage of 91.3%.

E.g. in the recent past, NIA cracked the terror funding network in Jammu and Kashmir, Khalistani terror plot with attempts to revive terror activities in Punjab etc., helping in creating deterrence for existing and potential terrorist groups/individuals.

### 8. *Lok Nayak Jayaprakash Narayan National Institute of Criminology & Forensic Science (NICFS):*

It was established in 1972, based on the recommendations of the UGC for setting up of a central institute for teaching criminology and Forensic Science. Initially, it was established within the Bureau of Police Research and Development. In 1976 it became an independent department under MHA and in 1991 it was upgraded to a national institute, as National Institute of Criminology and Forensic Science (NICFS). In 2003, it was renamed as Lok Nayak Jayaprakash Narayan NICFS in 2003. NICFS carries out training activities for criminal justice functionaries and others through its Master of Arts and Master of Science courses in Criminology and Forensic Science.

### 9. *National Disaster Response Force (NDRF):*

National Disaster Response Force (NDRF) is a statutory force established under the Disaster Management Act, 2005 for the purpose of specialized response to natural and man-made disasters, including chemical, biological, radiological and nuclear (CBRN) emergencies. The need for such a force was long felt by India especially during the events which led to the passing of Disaster management Act, i.e. the Super Cyclone of Odisha (1999), Gujarat Earthquake (2001) and Indian Ocean Tsunami (2004).

As international focus also increased on Disaster preparedness and response through Yokohama Strategy (after World Conference on Natural Disaster Reduction in Yokohama, 1994) and Hyogo Framework for Action, 2005, the need for a comprehensive disaster management plan from India also became important. This led to the enactment of the Disaster Management Act on 26 December 2005 with the setting up of a National Disaster Management Authority (NDMA) to lay down the policies, plans and guidelines for disaster management.

Accordingly, NDRF was constituted in 2006 with 8 Battalions contributed by the Central Armed Police Forces. Since February 2008, NDRF has made a dedicated force for disaster response related duties, under the unified command of Director General, NDRF. At present, NDRF has 12 Battalions with a total strength of 1149 personnel. Each Battalion has 18 self-contained specialist search and rescue teams with engineers, technicians, electricians, dog squads and medical/paramedics to support the operations. The composition of 12 Battalions, based on the parent force is as follows- three each from the BSF and CRPF and two each from CISF, ITBP and SSB.

In addition to the security forces and agencies we discussed above, a number of **Central Armed Police Forces**, also known as **Paramilitary Forces** because of their similarities with armed forces in terms of organizational structure, tactics, training, subculture, and some functions but not being formal part of our armed forces, functions under the **Ministry of Home Affairs** to enable the MHA perform its functions of Border Management and Internal Security. It includes seven forces as:

### 1.  *Assam Rifles (AR)*

Assam Rifles is the oldest paramilitary force, established in 1835 as a militia called the 'Cachar Levy' for protection of British Tea estates and settlements from tribals. With an increase in its scope of work or area of action like the conduct of punitive expeditions even outside Assam it was renamed as the 'Frontier Force'. Soon it became Assam Military Police and helped the British in the expansion of their trade in the region.

During the First World War, they served as part of the Rifle Regiments of the British Army in Europe and the Middle East Successfully. As recognition of their services, the name of the force was changed to its present name of Assam Rifles in 1917. Today, Assam Rifles serves as the 'Sentinels of the North East', also the motto of Assam Rifles, and serves in the remote and underdeveloped regions of India.

Today, it serves as the peace-keeping force in North-Eastern areas suffering from problems of tribal unrest or insurgency by maintaining law & order and countering insurgency. At times, it also strengthens the efforts of Armed Forces by helping in combat operations (during Sino-Indian War of 1962) or in peacekeeping efforts (as part of Indian Peace Keeping Force to Sri Lanka, 1987). To fulfil its duties it has raised 46 battalions, providing a sense of security to the local people and gaining the confidence of locals, ensuring their smooth integration with the mainstream of India.

## 2. *Border Security Force (BSF)*

Before the existence of Border Security Force i.e. before 01 December 1965, the borders shared by India with Pakistan were manned by CRPF and State Armed Police Battalion. The Pakistani Army attack on a number of posts in the Kutch region during 1965 war (operation Desert Hawk) was an eye-opener for the Government of India, as it exposed the inadequacy of the Armed Police to respond to aggression from the trained army. Therefore, the need of having a specialized (well-armed and trained) and centrally controlled Border Security Force was realized to man the Indian Border shared with Pakistan.

Based on recommendations of the Committee of Secretaries, the Border Security Force (BSF) came into existence on 01 Dec 1965, with K F Rustamji as its first chief and founding father, guarding Indian borders shared with West Pakistan and East Pakistan (now Bangladesh). The motto of BSF is "Jeevan Paryant Kartavya" and it has lived up to its motto with the commendable role since its inception including its role during the 1971 War and 1999 Kargil War.

The task of BSF is divided into two categories as follows:

I.    *Peace Time Task:*  To promote a sense of security among the people living in the border areas through prevention of trans-border crimes, smuggling and other illegal activities, unauthorized entry into or exit from the territory of India, prevention of smuggling and any other illegal activity.

II.   War Time Task: To hold its ground across sectors manned by it in case of attack or even hold it during the war, helping Indian Army to work on offensive defence and reinforce or relieve BSF as suits the need of war. Under the Army's operational command, BSF also helps the Armed Forces in the protection of vital installations/air-fields from enemy raids. Take aggressive action against similar or irregular forces from the enemy and gain intelligence along the line of duty or as called by the Armed Forces to do so.

In the recent past, BSF has also been deployed for counter-insurgency and internal security duties. Under special circumstances, it can be used to maintain law and order in enemy territory administered under the control of the Army. It can also be used to guard the prisoners of war cages, aid efforts of civil police in control of refugees etc.

## 3. *Central Industrial Security Force (CISF)*

The Central Industrial Security Force (CISF) was established through "Central Industrial Security Force Act, 1968", an act of parliament for having dedicated armed police to provide security to the premises staff along with the security of infrastructure or establishments which are critical for the nation. Today, with strength of over 1.4lakh CISF provides security to the strategic establishment, including the Department of Space, the Department of Atomic Energy, Sea Ports and the Airports, the Delhi Metro, vital PSUs, the historical monuments and the basic areas of Indian economy such as petroleum and natural gas, electricity, coal, steel and mining.

People covered under the Z Plus, Z, X or Y security cover are protected by the CISF and its services are also used by some private sector units (e.g. Infosys campus in Mangaluru), private citizens etc. by paying for it.

### 4. *Central Reserve Police Force (CRPF)*

The Central Reserve Police Force (CRPF) is the second oldest and largest paramilitary force of India, established as the Crown Representative Police by British in 1939. It was raised by the British to maintain the law and order in the princely states of India because of increasing political unrest/agitations in their territories with Indian National Congress merging their political agitations with national independence movement through its Madras Resolution of 1936.

Post-Independence, the Crown Representative Police was renamed the Central Reserve Police Force (CRPF) on December 28, 1949, through CRPF Act 1949. The objective of this Act is to provide for the constitution and regulation of an Armed Central Reserve Police Force of the Union. Today, it is considered as the premier central police force of the Union of India playing an all-important role in the maintenance of internal security through its multidimensional role, as envisaged by Sardar Vallabhbhai Patel, the first Home Minister of India.

During initial years of independence, it helped in checking infiltration and trans-border crimes along the Kutch, Rajasthan and Sindh Border with an all-important role in the smooth amalgamation of the princely states with Indian Union by controlling a number of rebellious princely States like Junagarh and Kathiawar in Gujarat. They guarded the Indian border shared with Pakistan in Jammu and Kashmir and with China in Ladakh region.

The National Police Commemoration Day observed every year on 21 October to remember the brave policemen who sacrificed their lives while discharging their duties is celebrated in honor of CRPF personnel who bore the brunt of the first Chinese attack on India at Hot Springs (Ladakh) on October 21, 1959. On this day, a small CRPF patrol was attacked by the Chinese Army leading to the martyrdom of ten policemen.

CRPF helped the Indian Army during 1962, 1965 and 1971 war. In fact, before the raising of BSF in 1965, it was CRPF who guarded the India-Pakistan Border. It was also part of Indian Peacekeeping Force to Sri Lanka and of the UN Peacekeeping Force in Haiti, Namibia, Somalia and Maldives. But the most important role of CRPF is in the maintenance of internal peace by playing the role of counter-insurgency forces of India in Left-Wing Extremist areas, Tripura and Manipur. In 2008, Commando Battalion for Resolute Action (COBRA) was added to CRPF for controlling the Naxalite movement.

CRPF also holds a number of Rapid Action Force (RAF) battalions, raised 10 battalions internally in October 1992 with the addition of 5 more in 2018. RAF is a specialized force set up to deal with riots and riot-like situations, to instil an immediate sense of security and confidence amongst all sections of the society and also handle internal security duty. It is called the Rapid Action Force as it is a zero response force which gets to the crisis situation within a minimal time.

### 5.   *Indo Tibetan Border Police (ITBP)*

Indo-Tibetan Border Police was initially raised with 4 battalions under the CRPF Act of 1949 on October 24, 1962, i.e. during Sino-Indian War for reorganizing the frontier intelligence and security set up along the Indo-Tibetan border. Post-war, it was entrusted with other functions like border guarding, engaging in counter-insurgency operations and internal security through acts and rules like Indo-Tibetan Border Police Force Act of 1992 and its rules of 1994. With increased functions, the manpower (56 Battalions) and technological capabilities of ITBP also increased.

In 2004, in pursuance of Group of Ministers (GoM) recommendations on "One Border One Force", ITBP was assigned with the responsibility to guard the entire stretch of India-China Border of 3488 Kms, replacing Assam Rifles from border areas in Sikkim and Arunachal Pradesh. Along with guarding of borders, ITBP carries out other functions like detection and prevention of border violations; promotion of the sense of security and confidence among the local people; Check illegal immigration, trans-border smuggling and crimes; give security to sensitive installations, banks and protected persons; and restore & preserve order in any area in the event of disturbance.

### 6.   *National Security Guard (NSG)*

On lines of SAS of the UK and GSG-9 of Germany, National Security Guard (NSG) was created by the Union Cabinet in 1984 as a Federal Contingency Force. It is headed by a Director General and comprises highly motivated, well trained and equipped personnel. Through the passage of the National Security Guard Act, 1986 NSG got formal recognition as armed forces of the Union to combat terrorist activities and protect states against internal disturbances.

NSG is headquartered at New Delhi with an operation and training centre at Manesar, Gurugram (Haryana). NSG is designed for a swift and speedy strike with immediate withdrawal from the theatre of action (which can be inside or outside India). For its operations, NSG is divided into two elements- *Special Action Group (SAG)* as the main offensive or core operations group (containing Army Personnel), and *Special Ranger Group (SRG)* to support SAG, look after high-risk VIP/VVIP security and other functions including specific counter-terror operations (containing personnel from Central Armed Police Forces and State Police Forces as well).

Being a specially equipped and trained force, the use of NSG is usually done in exceptional circumstances to thwart acts of terrorism. It includes operations like Black Thunder I and II, protection of hostages in hijacking incidents and numerous terrorist attacks including the 2008 Mumbai Attacks and 2016 Pathankot Attack. The National Bomb Data Centre of India (established in 1988) is located at NSG Manesar facility and engaged in collecting data on all bombing related incidents in India and outside (which are deemed significant) to analyze them and identify patterns and gather other actionable inputs from them.

### 7.  *Sashastra Seema Bal (SSB)*

In the aftermath of Chinese conflict in 1962 many changes were introduced to make India secure. One such change was the establishment of a Special Service Bureau (SSB) in 1963, now recognized as Sashastra Seema Bal. SSB was established to gather foreign intelligence, to protect Indian borders and develop a good rapport with the locals thereby, helping in the development of nationalistic feelings among them and gain unwavering support from a committed border population.

Increased contact with locals is important as they have in-depth understanding or familiarity with the terrain and it helps in understanding the culture and ethos of our border population. So, SSB was the first CAPF which was established as a specialized force for border guarding with its unique or unconventional relation with locals, considered as important because of its far-flung/remote location with presence of climatic and strategic vulnerabilities.

It started its duty under its founder Director of Special Service Bureau B N Mullik from North Assam, North Bengal, North-East Frontier Agency (NEFA, now recognized as Arunachal Pradesh), hill districts of Uttar Pradesh (now Uttarakhand), Himachal Pradesh and Ladakh region. SSB is guided by its motto of "Service, Security and Brotherhood", and works towards 'Total Security Preparedness' in its area of operation, including the 'stay-behind' role of Guerrilla force with locals in the event of a war.

The jurisdiction of SSB was extended to Manipur, Tripura and Jammu in 1965, Meghalaya in 1975; Sikkim in 1976; Rajasthan in 1985; and South Bengal, Nagaland and Mizoram in 1989. Through its National Integration Programmes of the 1970s, SSB has helped in the development of a trained volunteer force among locals acting as the eyes and ears of SSB. Post-Kargil war, the K. Subramanyam Committee's recommended for assigning one border for the operation to each paramilitary force.

So, in 2001 SSB was declared a Border Guarding Force under the Ministry of Home Affairs with its mandate of being the Lead Intelligence Agency and guarding of the 1751 km long **Indo-Nepal border**. Its name was changed to "Sashastra Seema Bal" on *15th December 2003*. On 12 March 2004, it was given the added responsibility of acting as Lead intelligence and guarding the Indo-Bhutan Border.

In 2004 it was awarded President's Colour and in 2007 Sashastra Seema Bal Act, 2007 was passed to define its role, duties, functions, service conditions etc. SSB is headquartered at New Delhi with its three frontier headquarters at Lucknow, Patna and Guwahati to look after its work along the International open border across Uttarakhand, UP, Bihar, West Bengal, Sikkim, Assam and Arunachal Pradesh. The present charter of duties of SSB includes:

- Safeguard the security of assigned borders of India and promote a sense of security among the people living in border areas;
- Prevent trans-border crimes, smuggling and any other illegal activities;
- Prevent unauthorized entry into or exit from the territory of India;
- Carry out civic action programme in the area of responsibility; and
- Perform any other duty assigned by the Central Government. (SSB is being deployed for Law & Order, Counter Insurgency Operations and Election duty.

**List of Important Training Establishments of our Armed Forces**

| S. No. | Training Establishment | Commissioning and Location | For |
|---|---|---|---|
| 1. | National Defence Academy (NDA) | In 1954 at Khadakwasla (Pune) | Tri-services academy of Army, Air Force and Navy |
| 2. | National Defence College (NDC) | In 1960 at New Delhi | Officers from the Armed Forces and Civil services |
| 3. | Defence Services Staff College (DSSC) | In 1905 at Deolali (near Nashik). Now at Wellington in Nilgiris (TN) | Officers from tri-services for Defence and Strategic Studies |

| | | | |
|---|---|---|---|
| 4. | Rashtriya Indian Military College (RIMC) | In 1922 at Dehradun | School Education from 8th to 12th as a feeder to NDA, NAVAC etc. |
| 5. | Indian Military Academy (IMA) | In 1932 at Dehradun | Training Army cadets for Lieutenant |
| 6. | College of Defence Management (CDM) | In 1970 at Sainikpuri (Secunderabad) | Officers from Tri-Services for Management Training |
| 7. | Military Institute of Technology (MILIT) | In 1952 as Institute of Armament Studies at Pune | Tri-Services officers and staff for Technical Training |
| 8. | Indian National Defence University (INDU) | In 2010 at Binola (Gurugram) | Mix from Indian Armed forces (66%) and rest from CAPF, State Police and Civilians for courses on war and peace |
| 9. | Armed Forces Medical College | In 1948 at Pune | For under-graduate and postgraduate medical and nursing education for future medical personnel in defence services |

**Important Training Establishments of Indian Air Force and Indian Navy**

| INDIAN AIR FORCE | | | |
|---|---|---|---|
| S. No. | Training Establishment | Commissioning and Location | For |
| 1. | Air Force Academy | In 1969 at Dundigal (Hyderabad) | For flying, technical and ground duty training for Air Force and others like Indian Army, Indian Navy and Indian Coast Guard |
| 2. | Air Force Technical College | In 1949 at Bangaluru | For technical training on aircraft, weapon and support system to IAF officers and |

| S. No. | Training Establishment | Commissioning and Location | For |
|---|---|---|---|
| | | | technicians |
| 3. | Air Force Administrative College | In 1943 at Pune. Now at Coimbatore since 1946 | Officers from Tri-services for professional knowledge courses |

INDIAN NAVY

| S. No. | Training Establishment | Commissioning and Location | For |
|---|---|---|---|
| 1. | Indian Naval Academy | In 1969 at Kochi. Now at Ezhimala (Kannur) | Induction Training for Officers of the Indian Navy and Indian Coast Guard |
| 2. | INS Garuda | In 1953 at Willingdon Island in Kochi | For aviation-related training like maritime reconnaissance, patrol, evacuation and search and rescue, aircraft maintenance, naval aviation etc. |
| 3. | INS Satavahana | In 1974 at Visakhapatnam | Integrated training facility for submarine, escape and undersea warfare training of Indian Navy personnel |
| 4. | INS Agrani | In 1965 at Puliakulam (Coimbatore) | Leadership Training Institute for Indian Navy |
| 5. | INS Shivaji | In 1945 at Lonavala | For Marine Engineering, Naval Engineering and NBCD training for Indian Navy and Coast Guard |

**Conclusion on Forces**

| S.No. | Force | Formation Day | Motto |
|---|---|---|---|
| 1. | INDIAN ARMY | 15 JANUARY | Service before Self |
| 2. | INDIAN NAVY | 04 DECEMBER | "Sha-no Varuna" (May the Lord of the oceans be |

| | | | auspicious unto us) |
|---|---|---|---|
| 3. | INDIAN AIR FORCE | 08 OCTOBER 1932 | Touch the Sky with Glory |
| 4. | INDIAN COAST GUARD | 01 FEBRUARY 1977 | Vayam Raksham (We Protect) |
| 5. | CENTRAL RESERVE POLICE FORCE | 27 JULY 1939 | PeaceKeeper to the Nation |
| 6. | BORDER SECURITY FORCE | 01 DECEMBER 1965 | Kartavya Jeevan Paryant (Duty unto death) |
| 7. | SASHASTRA SEEMA BAL | 20 DECEMBER 1963 | Service, Security and Brotherhood |
| 8. | INDO-TIBETAN BORDER POLICE | 24 OCTOBER 1962 | *Shaurya Dridhata Karamnishtha (Valour, Steadfastness and Commitment)* |
| 9. | CENTRAL INDUSTRIAL SECURITY FORCE | 10 MARCH 1969 | Protection and Security |
| 10. | ASSAM RIFFLES | 24 MARCH 1835 | Sentinels of the North East |
| 11. | NATIONAL SECURITY GUARDS | 16 OCTOBER 1984 | SARVATRA, SARVOTTAM, SURAKSHA (Omnipresent omnipotent security) |
| 12. | NATIONAL CADET CORPS | 15 JULY 1948 | Unity and Discipline |

## Other Organizations with an important role in National Security

### INDIAN SPACE RESEARCH ORGANISATION (ISRO)

With the end of Second World War two new powers i.e. The USA and USSR emerged as the global powers. This led to a bitter rivalry between the two, also known as the cold war, for having greater influence over other nations through their principles of the economic system and technological advancement over others. One such field was space in the 1950s, which lead to significant developments in the field of space, especially outer space[14].

Through these developments, the world realized that use of space isn't just limited to the exploration of space or physical laws but it can be the battle of dominance over space and the next theatre of operations for war. E.g. in the early 1960's we had USA and USSR having programmes like Manned Orbiting Laboratory (MOL) and Almaz respectively towards surveillance of satellites in space and destruction of enemy satellites through the deployment of weapons. Though **Outer Space Treaty** was enacted in 1967 to allay the fears of different nations by making the use and exploration of space (including celestial bodies like the moon and other) free for all nations by formulation of international laws on use of outer space along with prohibition on placing nuclear weapons in space, the fears still remain.

Indian Government also recognized the importance of space exploration. Accordingly, the Department of Atomic Energy (under Homi J. Bhabha) was given the responsibility to carry out space research in 1961. In 1962, the Department of Atomic Energy (DAE) formed the Indian National Committee for Space Research (INCOSPAR), with Dr. Vikram Sarabhai as its chairman. In November 1963, Dr. Sarabhai established the Thumba Equatorial Rocket Launching Station (TERLS) in Thiruvananthapuram for upper atmospheric research and in 1969; INCOSPAR was reconstituted as an advisory body under the India National Science Academy (INSA) with setting up of Indian Space Research Organisation under Dr Vikram Sarabhai to carry out space research.

Today, ISRO is among the six largest space agencies of the world. As a responsible nation, India promotes the peaceful use of outer space but it recognizes the threat to its national security which can emanate from space (including outer space). Also, it has identified the direct and spin-off uses of the highly sophisticated space technology to ensure national security.

.Since its inception, ISRO has developed a large network of satellite-based services and technologies helping our armed forces and intelligence agencies. E.g. As part of Integrated Space Cell, ISRO works along with the armed forces, Department of Space etc. to execute the responsibility of protection and effective utilization of the country's space-based assets towards military purposes.

---

[14] *Outer Space, also called as space, refers to the relatively empty regions of the universe outside the atmospheres of celestial bodies. Though a standard or definite altitude from Earth's surface isn't defined, outer space is mainly considered to be above the Karman Line or the edge of earth's atmosphere. It lies 100 km above Earth's mean sea level.*

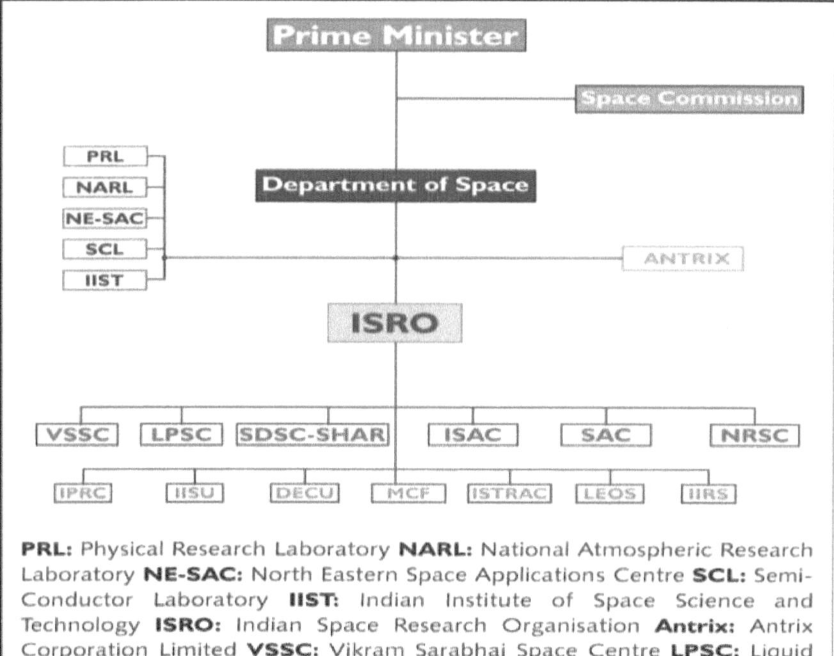


**PRL:** Physical Research Laboratory **NARL:** National Atmospheric Research Laboratory **NE-SAC:** North Eastern Space Applications Centre **SCL:** Semi-Conductor Laboratory **IIST:** Indian Institute of Space Science and Technology **ISRO:** Indian Space Research Organisation **Antrix:** Antrix Corporation Limited **VSSC:** Vikram Sarabhai Space Centre **LPSC:** Liquid Propulsion Systems Centre **SDSC:** Satish Dhawan Space Centre **ISAC:** ISRO Satellite Centre **SAC:** Space Applications Centre **NRSC:** National Remote Sensing Centre **IPRC:** ISRO Propulsion Complex **IISU:** ISRO Inertial Systems Unit **DECU:** Development and Educational Communication Unit **MCF:** Master Control Facility **ISTRAC:** ISRO Telemetry, Tracking and Command Network **LEOS:** Laboratory for Electro-optic Systems **IIRS:** Indian Institute of Remote Sensing

Figure 13 ISRO Administrative Structure and Facilities (Image Courtesy: ISRO)

Some of the major technologies with high usefulness for our defence forces include:

a) **<u>Communication Satellites:</u>** The communication needs of India including our armed forces are fulfilled by the Indian National Satellite (INSAT) system, with the first satellite of INSAT series INSAT-1B being launched in 1983. With the launch of GSAT-17, the total number of operational satellites under INSAT has gone to 16 (INSAT-3A, 3C, 4A, 4B, 4CR and GSAT-6, 7, 8, 9, 10, 12, 14, 15, 16, 17 and 18) orbiting in Geosynchronous orbit. These communication satellites use C-band, Extended C-band and Ku-band for transponders. Some important uses of these communication satellites in defence forces include communication services, weather forecasting, disaster warning and Search and Rescue operations.

b) **<u>Earth Observation:</u>** The earth observation functions are performed by Indian Remote Sensing satellites with IRS-1A as a starting point in 1988. Today, 13 Sun-synchronous orbit satellites (RESOURCESAT-1, 2, 2A CARTOSAT-1, 2, 2A, 2B, RISAT-1, 2, 2B and the recent RISAT-2BR1 (by PSLV-C48 in December 2019), OCEANSAT-2, Megha-Tropiques, SARAL and SCATSAT-1) and 4 Geostationary orbit satellites (INSAT-3D, Kalpana & INSAT 3A, INSAT -3DR) helps in different fields of remote sensing like agriculture, water resources, urban planning, rural development, mineral prospecting, environment, forestry, ocean resources, disaster management etc. For the Surgical Strike of 2016, India used earth observation satellites of the Cartosat series. With the plan of sealing the International border shared with Pakistan 24x7x365 through Five-layer lock[15] Being approved, also known as the Comprehensive Integrated Border Management System (CIBMS), these low earth orbit surveillance satellites have an important role to play in terrain mapping and prevent infiltration through round-the-clock surveillance. E.g. RISAT (Radar Imaging Reconnaissance Satellites) series satellites, launched after the 2008 Mumbai Attacks, are the only satellites having Synthetic Aperture Radar system (SAR) making it capable of all-weather and time (day and night) surveillance. Presently, 3 of them are functional and plan to have two more soon.

c) **Satellite Navigation:** Satellite-based Navigation (popularly known as GPS on the basis of US satellite navigation system) is an emerging commercial and strategic satellite use with Civil Aviation, Defence Forces and independent citizens as the main users. Satellite Navigation is used for the needs of positioning, navigation and timing. E.g. **GPS Aided Geo Augmented Navigation (GAGAN)** system is developed by ISRO with Airport Authority of India (AAI) for Civil Aviation purposes. Similarly, **Indian Regional Navigation Satellite System (IRNSS) or Navigation with Indian Constellation (NavIC)** is a satellite navigation system to provide navigational services in India and neighbouring countries (up to 1500 km). IRNSS provides two types of services: i) Standard Positioning Service (SPS), and ii) Restricted Service (RS). The SPS is available to all while RS is

---

[15] *Five-layer locks for Border security/surveillance include CCTV cameras; Thermal imaging and night-vision devices; battlefield surveillance radar; underground monitoring sensors; and laser barriers. In 2017, MHA formed Madhukar Gupta committee on Security and Border Protection with specific task of recommending technological solutions for securing international borders with identification of gaps and vulnerabilities under present conditions.*

made available to specified security agencies.

d) **Other Technologies with Spin-offs:** The propulsion system and fuels used in Satellite Launch Vehicles can also be used for carrying the explosives by missiles. E.g. Russia backed out from the transfer of technology for GSLV stage 3 engine, i.e. technology of cryogenic engine to India, because of being in violation of Missile Technology Control Regime (MTCR). Similarly, the validation of technologies like hypersonic flight, reusable technology with reusable thermal protection system, autonomous navigation, guidance and control etc. are some technologies which can help Indian Missile programme as well. Recently, with the success of **Scramjet-TD**, India became the fourth country to demonstrate the flight testing of a Scramjet[16] Engine.

e) **<u>Disaster Management Support:</u>** India is among the most vulnerable nations to a natural disaster because of the big variations in the geo-climatic conditions across India. Floods, droughts, cyclones, earthquakes and landslides are the major natural disasters with nearly 60% of the landmass being prone to earthquakes, over 40 million hectares is flood-prone area, around 5,700 km of the 7,516 km long coastline of India is prone to cyclones, and nearly 68% of the cultivable area is susceptible to drought. In 2004 we faced a Tsunami on the Andaman & Nicobar Islands and the East coast. In Himalayan states, the cloudbursts and landslides are very common. The rising temperature and changing livelihood patterns has increased the incidents of forest fires in the deciduous/ dry-deciduous forests. Satellites from ISRO help us in every stage of disaster management support from the identification of the hazard to the dissemination of information with track on the progress of the disaster as well as the rescue operations.

---

### INDIA AND FOUR MULTILATERAL EXPORT CONTROL REGIMES

In the last few years, India has emerged as a major global power. Be it the economic sphere of influence or the political sphere of influence, Indian recognition at the global level has only risen because of our increasing economic clout and advances in defence capabilities. E.g. At the start of 1990's we introduced the economic liberalization and today with the US $2.9 trillion economies (as per IMF World Economic Outlook Database

---

[16] *Scramjet, along with Ramjet and Dual Mode Ramjet (DMRJ, is among the three concepts of air-breathing engines developed by various space agencies with scramjet as a technology based on Air Breathing Propulsion System, i.e. instead of taking the oxidisers with itself from mission start, the engine takes it from environment.*

2020) we are the 5th biggest economy of the world.

First on 18 May 1974 (*Operation Smiling Buddha for fission based nuclear weapon*) and again on 11 and 13 May 1998 (*Operation Shakti with five tests including the nuclear fission and thermonuclear[17] based nuclear weapon*), India displayed its capability as a full-fledged Nuclear State, the biggest deterrent of modern times. But in between these two tests, a number of Multilateral Export Control Regimes were formed to impose restrictions on access to such technologies for nations like India.

Multilateral Export Control Regimes are the voluntary and non-binding export regimes or arrangements which aim to prohibit the proliferation goods and technologies which are considered as weapons of mass destruction[18] and their delivery means or the equipment and technologies which are related to them. Though we have a legally binding United Nations Security Council Resolution 1540 (dated 28 April 2004) which requires state to take and enforce effective measure to establish domestic controls for the non-proliferation of weapons of mass-destruction but these export control regimes were formed much before that and therefore, act as an independent body (i.e. outside United Nations Control).

Presently, we have four major Multilateral Export Control Regimes, which tries to organize the export control system of member nations in accordance with national laws and practices. With India's track record as a responsible nuclear power with non-proliferation as a major part of its Nuclear Programme, the Multilateral Export Control Regimes which were once created to impose restrictions on nations like India are getting engaged with India. India has joined three of them and is making efforts to join the remaining one.

These four major Multilateral Export Control Regimes are:

1) Nuclear Suppliers Group (NSG), for non-proliferation of nuclear weapons,
2) Australia Group (AG), to minimize the risk of assisting proliferation of biological and chemical weapons,

---

[17] *Thermonuclear or fusion-based nuclear weapon is the second generation of nuclear weapons with greater destructive power and more compact size.*

[18] ***Weapons of Mass Destruction (WMD)*** *are the weapons carrying nuclear, radiological, chemical, biological, or any other form of explosive/weapon that can kill and cause significant harm to large number of people or cause high order of destruction to human-made structures (e.g., buildings), natural structures (e.g., mountains), or the biosphere itself.*

3) Missile Technology Control Regime (MTCR), for non-proliferation of unmanned delivery systems capable of delivering WMD, and

4) Wassenaar Arrangement (WA), to promote transparency and responsibility in the transfer of both conventional weapons and sensitive dual-use goods and technology.

All these Multilateral Export Control Regimes have specified the controlled items in its list and include goods (like equipment, materials etc.), software and technologies. Their origin, mission, functioning and Indian membership status is as follows:

## NUCLEAR SUPPLIERS GROUP (NSG)

NSG was established in 1974, in response to our first Nuclear Weapon Test i.e. Smiling Buddha or Pokhran-I of 1974, to prevent the proliferation of nuclear equipment, materials and technologies which are used or can be used to manufacture nuclear weapons. The responsibility of **NSG** is somewhat similar to the work of Zangger Committee[19] and Non-Proliferation Treaty (NPT) towards non-proliferation by framing and implementing guidelines on export of nuclear equipments and related exports for nuclear supplier countries.

Presently, it has forty eight (48) participating supplier countries to follow its export guidelines; guidelines which cover the nuclear equipment, material and technologies which may be considered dual-use, ensuring the nuclear trade for peaceful purposes and avoiding the proliferation of nuclear weapons or other nuclear explosive devices. Since 2010, i.e. after the Indo-US Nuclear Deal of 2008, the United States has shown interest towards Indian aspiration of being the member of all four Multilateral Export Control Regimes.

In 2010, The United States President Barack Obama endorsed the Indian entry to all of them in a phased manner. India applied for the membership of NSG in 2016 but it is yet to become a member because of Chinese objection to India becoming part of NSG. (*Please note that all the decisions of NSG are taken on the basis of consensus and objection from any*

---

[19] *Zangger Committee, also known as the Nuclear Exporters Committee, was first established under Prof. Claude Zangger to interpret the article III, paragraph 2 of Nuclear Non-Proliferation Treaty (NPT) of 1970 regarding the equipment or the material for the processing, use or production of special fissionable material. Based on it, the Zangger Committee maintains a Trigger List (triggering safeguards as a condition of supply) of nuclear-related strategic goods to assist NPT Parties in identifying equipment and materials subject to export controls. Presently, it has 39 members.*

*one nation is considered as no*).

Before we look at the importance of NSG membership for India we must know about the criteria or factors which are taken into consideration before a nation becomes a member of NSG. These factors include:

- the ability of a nation to supply items (including items in transit) covered by the Annexes to Parts 1 and 2 of the NSG Guidelines;
- adherence to the Guidelines and action in accordance with them;
- enforcement of a legally based domestic export control system which gives effect to the commitment to act in accordance with the Guidelines;
- full compliance to the obligations of one or more of the following: the Treaty on the Non-Proliferation of Nuclear Weapons (NPT), the Treaties of Pelindaba, Rarotonga, Tlatelolco, Bangkok, or an equivalent international nuclear nonproliferation agreement; and
- Support from international efforts towards non-proliferation of weapons of mass destruction and of their delivery vehicles.

Based on the criteria, we can identify that NSG membership will not just give recognition to Indian Nuclear Capabilities and its behavior as a responsible state but it will also help us in making India energy secure by getting necessary help in terms of nuclear power plant equipments and parts through entry to comprehensive group of nuclear supplier nations. Though India already enjoys the NSG waiver under the Indo-US nuclear deal of 2008 it requires India to have negotiations with each supplier nation and a favorable agreement.

E.g. The Nuclear plant set up from US companies required India to have a favorable response from Japan also as many parts or components to them were supplied by Japanese companies or they have a stake in them. Such conditions not only delays the set up of nuclear reactors in India but also limits the expansion of our civilian nuclear power generation plan of 63,000 MW of nuclear power capacity by 2031-32 set after the 2008 deal.

So, NSG membership can be of great help in our civilian nuclear programme and entice nuclear companies to invest and set plants in India, helping in expansion of the use of nuclear energy. Because of non-membership of NSG and other reasons like Nuclear Liability Legislation, India has already reduced the ambitious target of 63,000 MW to 22,480 MW by 2031.

NSG membership will enable India's entry in the export market of nuclear suppliers and enjoy commercial and strategic benefits through addition of some of its nuclear expertise like Pressurized Heavy Ware Reactors (PHWRs) of 220 and 540 MW or other related items including goods and services. It will also help India in becoming part of the rule-making body and push for rules which are more favorable to its interests. If agreed, membership of NSG can help in increasing the international profile and role of India and bring it closer to reforms in the United Nations Security Council (UNSC) with increased probability of membership.

Some points which are raised against the membership of India to NSG include the facts that India is non-signatory of Non-proliferation Treaty (NPT) which remained a precondition till 2001 but the 2001 guidelines at Aspen made it the guiding principle for consideration on membership. China links the Indo-US Nuclear Deal, also known as the 123 Agreement or US-India Civil nuclear Agreement, with its Nuclear Deal with Pakistan and demands similar waivers and membership to Pakistan as well.

The other points raised by China include the need of having a norm-based entry for nations who are not part of NPT and the risk of disturbing the nuclear-arms balance in favour of India in the South Asian region with increased nuclear weapons and war risks. Though the questions raised by China on Indian membership are largely driven by its insecurities due to rise of India in Asia, yet India has already done much to allay those concerns.

E.g. The membership of NPT isn't mandatory to be a member of NSG since 2001. In 2016, Rafael Mariano Grossi, the present Director General of the International Atomic Energy Agency (IAEA) and former President of NSG formulated a draft formula for membership of non-NPT nation's membership to NSG. This is also known as Grossi Process and it proposed "nine general commitments" that non-NPT countries "would need to make" in order to receive the "fullest" atomic trading privileges.

As a responsible nation, India already fulfils all the nine general commitments for non-NPT nations with an impeccable record on non-proliferation, also endorsed by NSG through its waiver of 2008. Pakistan, whose membership is linked with Indian membership by China, had a dubious record on non-proliferation with its Scientists like Abdul Qadeer Khan or others being involved in the selling of nuclear technology and materials to other nations like Iran, Libya and North Korea.

Voluntarily, India has adopted its Nuclear Policy Doctrine[20] in 2003

---

[20] *Nuclear Policy Doctrine or Nuclear Doctrine is a policy statement from a nation describing how a nuclear weapon state would use its nuclear weapons during peace*

with some important basic principles of- i) To build and maintain a **Minimum Credible Deterrence;** ii) **No First Use** of nuclear weapons, i.e. only to be used in retaliation against a nuclear attack on Indian Territory or on Indian forces anywhere; iii) nuclear weapons **not to be used against non-nuclear states**; iv) to continue its support towards **nuclear free world**; v) may use **Nuclear Weapons in case of Chemical or Biological Weapon attack** based on the decision by decision-makers (as they are already outlawed by international laws so nuclear weapons won't be used against any international law compliant nation); vi) the **command and control** on use of nuclear weapon remain with **political leadership**[21]; vii) **No Proliferation** through strict controls on export of nuclear and missile-related materials and technologies etc.

Therefore, India has a strong track record and policy framework to live up to its responsibilities as a responsible state and member of NSG. With separation of Civilian nuclear programme from the Military nuclear programme, following IAEA guidelines on Civilian nuclear programme, being open to IAEA inspections; no genuine reason is left to deny Indian entry to NSG.

## AUSTRALIA GROUP

The Australia Group (AG) was established in 1985 at Brussels, after the use of Chemical Weapons by Iraq in 1984 against Iran, as an informal forum of countries which, through the *harmonization of export controls*, seeks to ensure that exports do not contribute to the development of chemical or biological weapons.

So, the AG works against the would-be proliferators through the development of ways and means to minimize export and transshipping risks, such that the would-be proliferators are not able to obtain necessary inputs for chemical and biological weapons. This is done through better coordination of national export control measures among its participant nations to fulfil their obligations under the Chemical Weapons Convention[22]

---

*and war. The first draft of Indian Nuclear Doctrine was prepared by K. Subrahmanyam in 2001. In 2003, India adopted its official Nuclear Doctrine.*

[21] *The command and control function is performed by 3-tier Nuclear Command Authority with- political council, executive council and strategic forces command as 3-tiers of it.*

[22] *Chemical weapons Convention (CWC) is an arms control treaty, which entered into force on 29 April 1997, prohibiting States Parties from assisting, encouraging or*

and the Biological and Toxin Weapons Convention[23] to the fullest extent possible.

One way developed to reduce this risk includes the setting up of the **Licensing Authority** over a wide range of chemical weapons. All member nations of AG require licenses for the export of dual-use chemical manufacturing facilities, equipment, and related technology, plant pathogens, animal pathogens, biological agents, and dual-use biological equipment.

The participating country in the Australia Group has grown from 15 in 1982 to 43 member nations including the European Union. Because of our strong commitment to bring our export control system into alignment with the Australia Group and to contribute to the global effort to prevent the proliferation of CBW in the security interests of all members of the international community, India got the membership of Australia Group on 19 January 2018 as 43rd member.

The absence of China from the forum also helped us as it acts as the traditional opposition to Indian membership on such forums including the UNSC. Apart from China factor, a number of other factors like- the membership of India to related Conventions of CWC and BWC; our strong track record and commitment to prevent Chemical and Biological Weapons proliferation and large chemical and biotech industry which manufacture, export or transship the AG controlled items.

## <u>MISSILE TECHNOLOGY CONTROL REGIME (MTCR)</u>

Missile Technology Control Regime (MTCR) was formed in 1987 as an informal group to restrict the proliferation of missiles, complete rocket systems, unmanned air vehicles, and related technology for those systems capable of carrying a 500 kilogram payload at least 300 kilometres, as well as systems intended for the delivery of weapons of mass destruction (WMD).

The founding members of MTCR were the Group of Seven (G7)

---

industrialized nations (Canada, France, Germany, Italy, Japan, the UK, and the United States) to address the increasing proliferation of nuclear weapons by addressing the most destabilizing delivery system for such weapons. Since then its membership and scope of control have grown a lot. Today it covers the delivery systems for all the Weapons of Mass Destruction (WMD), i.e. nuclear, chemical and biological weapons with 35 member nations, including India as its last member (joining it on 27 June 2016).

MTCR helps in the maintenance of world order by minimizing the proliferation risks of the Weapons of Mass Destruction (WMD) delivery systems through common **export control** policy guidelines applied to an integral list of controlled items under different heads as Category I and Category II. Category I include items with an unconditional strong presumption of denial as:

- **Complete rocket systems** (to include ballistic missiles, space launch vehicles (SLVs), and sounding rockets),
- **Unmanned air vehicle** (UAV) systems (to include cruise missiles, drones, UAVs, and remotely piloted vehicles (RPVs)), and
- **Software and Technologies including production facilities** which are related to the first two.

**Category II** includes items whose export is subject to licensing requirements taking into consideration the non-proliferation factors specified in the MTCR Guidelines. These items are less-sensitive and dual-use missile-related components, as well as other complete missile systems capable of a range of at least 300 km, regardless of payload.

Apart from export control, other mechanisms to restrict the proliferation include **meetings** among MTCR partners regularly to exchange information about relevant missile non-proliferation issues and the **dialogue and outreach** activities by the MTCR Chair and MTCR Partners with non-Partners in order to keep them informed about the group's activities and to provide practical assistance regarding efforts to prevent the proliferation of WMD delivery systems.

**<u>No Undercut:</u>** It is an important part of its export control policy, introduced in October 1994, in order to make the enforcement of MTCR Guidelines more uniform. No undercut means that if one member denies the sale of some technology to another country, then all members must adhere.

Among the four Multilateral Export Control Regimes, MTCR is

considered very significant as it attempts to stop the proliferation of weapons and technologies which are considered the major threat to international peace and security. But at times it has failed to control such exports from members and non-members. E.g. China, who is yet to become a member of MTCR, has a record of the shady transfer of missile technology to Pakistan and North Korea.

One mechanism developed by MTCR to counter this threat is the Hague Code of Conduct (HCOC) or the International Code of Conduct against Ballistic Missile Proliferation (ICOC). ICOC was launched in 2002 at The Hague with the objective of prevention of ballistic missile proliferation by calling for restraint on their production, testing and export. It was opened for voluntary subscription and as of today, 130 nations have subscribed to this code. The other measure to stop proliferation includes constant vigilance over the transfer of missile equipment, material, and related technologies usable for systems capable of delivering WMD.

Indian entry to the MTCR is significant as the MTCR members have allowed India to retain its ballistic missiles with the ability to deliver a 500 kg payload at least 300 km. This will help in keeping India secure and improve over it by easy buy opportunities for high-end missile technology and enhance our global partnership with nations like Russia (our Joint Venture of Brahmos). It will also help in getting a favorable response on the export of Category 1 UAVs (Reaper and Global Hawk) from the USA to India, very useful in counter-terrorism operations.

The retention of our ballistic missiles and enhanced global partnership will help in export of missiles like Brahmos, helping India to emerge as an arms exporter for high-end technology. It will boost our research and production programmes through better economic viability and better international relations through strategic offers. It helps in the improved global position of India by making India as part of international policy making forum working against the proliferation of WMD missile technology.

<u>**WASSENAAR AGREEMENT**</u>

Wassenaar Agreement was established in 1996 at Wassenaar (a suburb of Hague in the Netherlands) as a voluntary export control regime to contribute to regional and international security and stability, by promoting transparency and greater responsibility in transfers of conventional arms and dual-use goods and technologies, thus preventing destabilizing accumulations. It is considered as the successor of the Cold War-era Coordinating Committee for Multilateral Export Controls (COCOM), which was created to restrict exports to the former Soviet Union and Eastern bloc.

Unlike COCOM, Wassenaar Agreement doesn't target any specific group or bloc and it calls on states to make a series of voluntary information exchanges and notifications on their export activities related to weapons and items appearing on its control lists (first on *Conventional Weapons* and second on *Dual-Use Goods and Technologies*). Through the Wassenaar Agreement the participating States seek, through their national policies, to ensure that transfers of these items do not contribute to the development or enhancement of military capabilities which undermine these goals, and are not diverted to support such capabilities. The aim is also to prevent the acquisition of these items by terrorists.

Export controls on specific arms and technologies help in the preservation and maintenance of regional and international security by promoting transparency and responsibility in transfers of conventional arms and sensitive dual-use (civilian/military) goods and technologies. It helps in prevention of destabilizing accumulations of weapons and technologies in volatile regions around the world.

It has 42 members with India as the 42nd member, joining the agreement in 2017. Like other two Multilateral Export Control Regime, India got the membership of this agreement because of its strong record on non-proliferation on WMD with the implementation of UNSC Resolution 1540 through The Weapons of Mass Destruction and their Delivery Systems (Prohibition of Unlawful Activities) Act, 2005. Membership of the Wassenaar Agreement will help India in becoming part of the policymaking group and gain access to dual-use technologies[24]. Other benefits include the rise in Indian stature at a global level and a boost to not just the NSG membership of India but also of UNSC.

## Conclusion:

With India already becoming part of three Multilateral Export Control Regimes, the Indian efforts toward the integration of its non-proliferation of WMD with the global non-proliferation efforts are becoming true. It helps in our efforts toward order based export of arms and related technologies, securing them from going into the hands of irresponsible nations or groups. It will also increase the Indian defence trade and technology transfer,

---

[24] *Dual-use technologies are the technologies which can be used for both civil and military purposes. The common technologies of such nature include the goods and technologies in aerospace, telecommunication, computing, navigation, electronics, sensors and lasers.*

making our nation more secure and promote our efforts on Make in India in the Defence sector.



## *Defence Research and Development Organisation (DRDO):*

Defence Research and Development Organisation (DRDO) is a Research and Development organisation working under the administrative control of the Department of Defence Research and Development of the Ministry of Defence. DRDO is headquartered (HQ) at Delhi and works on the fields related to Military's Research and Development, helping Indian Armed Forces and other security agencies through empowering cutting-edge defence technologies.

DRDO was established in 1958 through the amalgamation of the Technical Development Establishments (TDEs) of the Indian Army and the Directorate of Technical Development & Production (DTDP) with the Defence Science Organisation (DSO). Since then the number of establishments or laboratories of DRDO and its area of work has expanded a lot. From 10 laboratories in 1958, the number of its research and development labs has gone to 52 laboratories with each lab working on a variety of subject disciplines.

E.g. through the Integrated Guided Missile Development Programme of 1980's **Defence Research and Development Laboratory (DRDL)** lab of DRDO developed a range of missiles with different capabilities for India as- i) **Prithvi** (a Short-range surface-to-surface missile; ii) **Trishul** (a Short-range low-level surface-to-air missile; iii) **Akash** (a Medium range surface-to-air missile; iv) **Nag** (a Third-generation anti-tank missile; and v) **Agni** (an intermediate-range ballistic missile). The IGMDP ended with Agni-3 as the last missile to be tested in 2007 (with official closure in 2008).

From outside the programme, it has developed other variants of Agni also. The whole IGMDP was executed under guidance of our ex-President Dr. Abdul Kalam (also known as Missile Man of India), who was the project director of ISRO SLV-3 programme, an example of dual-use of technology i.e. SLV and Missiles. Since its establishment, DRDO has helped our nation in achieving self-reliance in major/critical defence technologies and systems.

This helps in fulfilling the requirements laid down by our three Armed Services in order to secure our nation by equipping them with state-of-the-art weapon systems and equipment. Some of the other major developments from the DRDO's pursuit of achieving self-reliance and successful indigenous development and production of strategic systems and platforms include- **Tejas** (a light combat aircraft); **Pinaka** (a multi-barrel rocket launcher; **NETRA** (a software network); and a wide range of radars and electronic warfare systems with basic necessities of defence personnel's on field requirements like combat vehicles, state-of-the-art sensors, weapon launch platforms, nutritious and ready to eat food, mosquito repellent, armaments, explosive detection kit, agriculture, information systems, UAVs, advanced computing and simulation, instrumentation, special materials etc., in line to its motto of "Balasya Mulam Vigyanam", i.e. the source of strength is science.

Overall DRDO has 52 laboratories across India with most of them engaged in the technological Research and Development activities. The work across these technological laboratories is divided into seven different technology clusters through which DRDO perform its important functions as:

| S. No. | Cluster | Functions and Labs |
| --- | --- | --- |
| 1. | Aeronautical Systems (AS) Cluster | It is engaged in the design and development of state-of-the-art Unmanned Aerial Vehicles (UAVs), Aero Gas Turbine Engine Technology, Airborne Surveillance Systems, Parachutes, Decelerators and Lighter-than-Air Systems. The cluster comprises of four labs Aeronautical Development Establishment (ADE), Aerial Delivery Research and Development Establishment (ADRDE), Centre for Airborne Systems (CABS), Gas Turbine Research Establishment (GTRE) and a Centre for Military Airworthiness & Certification (CEMILAC) which provides concurrent airworthiness certification, support to indigenous development to certify upgrades and integration of imported and indigenous systems |
| 2. | The Naval Systems & Materials (NS&M) Cluster | It is responsible for the cutting edge naval technology and material solutions for the Armed Forces like state-of-the-art underwater sensors and surveillance systems; underwater weapons and associated systems; Air Independent Propulsion systems; protection technologies for marine platforms; stealth and camouflage technologies for land, air and naval platforms; advanced metallic, ceramic, polymeric and composite materials for structural and functional application; and |

| | | nuclear radiation management technologies. It is headquartered at Visakhapatnam with six labs as- Naval Physical & Oceanographic Laboratory (NPOL) at Kochi, Naval Science & Technological Laboratory (NSTL) at Visakhapatnam, Naval Materials Research Laboratory (NMRL) at Ambernath, Defence Metallurgical Research Laboratory (DMRL) at Hyderabad, Defence Materials Stores Research & Development Establishment (DMSRDE) at Kanpur, and Defence Laboratory (DLJ) at Jodhpur. |
|---|---|---|
| 3. | Armament & Combat Engineering Systems (ACE) Cluster | This cluster primarily focuses upon research & development of armaments, explosives, land-based combat vehicles & engineering equipment. While many armament production activities of these labs are done through Transfer of Technology a high degree of self-reliance is also achieved in areas, viz., armaments, ammunition, missiles, gun propellants, high explosives for warheads, pyrotechnics for various applications, synthesis and characterization of new energetic materials, electro explosive devices, high energy materials and pilot plant facilities. Under the Combat Engineering Systems, the production of various platforms for use of Armament is carried out like Main Battle Tank (MBT), bridging systems, launchers for missiles & wheeled as well as tracked vehicles with components like transmission & suspension for tracked vehicles, hydro-pneumatic systems for launchers, accurate forecast & control of avalanches, etc. Under this cluster we have eight labs as– Advanced Centre for Energetic Materials (ACEM), Armament Research & Development Establishment (ARDE), Combat Vehicles Research & Development Establishment (CVRDE), Defence Terrain Research Laboratory (DTRL), High Energy Materials Research Laboratory (HEMRL), Proof and Experimental Establishment (PXE), Research & Development Establishment |

| | | |
|---|---|---|
| | | (Engineers) R&DE (E), Snow and Avalanche Study Establishment (SASE), Vehicles Research and Development Establishment (VRDE). |
| 4. | Missiles and Strategic Systems (MSS) Cluster | In order to defend our nation and create deterrence among enemies, it is important that a nation possesses state-of-the-art Missiles and Strategic Systems. In India, this development is largely (with few exceptions like Brahmos under JV with Russia or imported missiles) done through five MSS Cluster labs as- Defence Research and Development Laboratory (DRDL), Research Centre Imarat (RCI), Advanced Systems Laboratory (ASL), Terminal Ballistics Research Laboratory (TBRL), Integrated Test Range (ITR) and centres used for testing, integration and analysis of the systems being designed. The major defence technologies on which MSS cluster works include Aerodynamics and Airframe Design; Solid, Liquid, Ramjet and Scramjet Propulsion; Navigation, Control, Guidance and Homing Systems; On-board Power Supply, Warhead Systems, Launch Systems as well as the Command and Control Systems for missile systems. |
| 5. | Micro Electronic Devices, Computational Systems & Cyber Systems (MED & CoS) Cluster | In recent times, this cluster is the most expanding cluster in terms of functions and importance as it covers the modern warfare space of Micro Electronic Devices and Cyber World. Under this, the Micro Electronic Devices (MED) sub-cluster focuses on technologies and emerging areas related to Microwave Tubes, Solid State Electronics including Micro Electronic Device design and manufacturing through its three labs namely, Advanced Numerical Research and Analysis Group (ANURAG), Hyderabad, Microwave Tube Research & Development Centre (MTRDC), Bengaluru, and Solid State Physics Laboratory (SSPL), Delhi. The second sub- |

| | | |
|---|---|---|
| | | cluster, i.e. Computational Systems (CoS) focuses on systems and technologies related to Artificial Intelligence, Robotics, Command and Control, Networking, Information and Communication Security, Secure/Trusted Computing Platforms, HPC, Cryptology, Information Security, and Cyber Security. The labs under this sub-cluster include Centre for Artificial Intelligence & Robotics (CAIR), Bengaluru and Scientific Analysis Group (SAG), Delhi. The products developed by this sub-cluster are Critical products for battlefield communication and security of the modern-day critical infrastructure. |
| 6. | Life Sciences (LS) Cluster | Along with the best, cutting-edge weapon systems and platforms, our services also need to match the integral human component of the war machine in order to achieve their intended purpose. Our service personnel face lots of challenges because of difficult terrain and environmental pressures of work along with human elements. It is necessary for us to optimize the integral human component of the war machine in terms of psychological, physiological and nutritional well-being, with life support systems and protection from all conceivable operational hazards. <br><br> Therefore, DRDO has established a group of laboratories under the Life Sciences (LS) cluster which focuses on the R&D efforts starting from the selection of officers and men for various types of jobs in the Armed Forces, promulgating optimized ration scales with provisioning of fresh and processed foods tailored to the Indian dietary habits and operational needs, developing acclimatization schedules for harsh terrain, specialized protective clothing, biomedical devices and protective gear, life support systems in hostile and challenging environments, countering strategies to overcome Chemical, Biological, Radiological and Nuclear (CBRN) threats in terms of its |

| | | |
|---|---|---|
| | | early detection, protection, decontamination and medical management of CBRN eventualities. Further, it focuses upon the development of psycho-socio-behavioral methodologies to cope with stresses, alternative systems/ strategies to enhance performance etc. The laboratories under this cluster include Defence Bioengineering and Electro-medical Laboratory (DEBEL), Defence Food Research Laboratory (DFRL), Defence Institute of Bio-Energy Research (DIBER), Defence Institute of High Altitude Research (DIHAR), Defence Institute of Physiology & Allied Sciences (DIPAS), Defence Institute of Psychological Research (DIPR), Defence Research & Development Establishment (DRDE), Defence Research Laboratory (DRL), Institute of Nuclear Medicine and Allied Sciences (INMAS). |
| 7. | Electronics and Communication Systems (ECS) Cluster | The seventh cluster of DRDO is the ECS Cluster with the mandate to design and develop electronic, electro-optical and laser-based sensors and systems. The products from ECS cluster laboratories play a pivotal role in Indian security as the state of art technologies developed by it in the fields of Electronic Weapon Systems, Radars, Electro-optic Equipment, Laser Sources & sensors, Directed Energy Weapon Systems and Communication Systems is used in various Flagship Programmes and platforms of other DRDO clusters or labs viz., Missile programmes, Unmanned Air Vehicles, Airborne Early Warning & Control System (AEWCS), Aerostats, Main Battle Tank (MBT), Integrated Coastal Surveillance System and Light Combat Aircraft (LCA) etc. The laboratories under ECS cluster include Defence Avionics Research Establishment (DARE), Defence Electronics Applications Laboratory (DEAL), Defence Electronics Research Laboratory (DLRL), Electronics and |

| | | Radar Development Establishment (LRDE) Instruments Research and Development Establishment (IRDE), Laser Science and Technology Centre (LASTEC) and the Cognitive Technology Lab. |
|---|---|---|

The vision of *empowering the nation with state-of-the-art indigenous Defence technologies and systems* which started with the setting up of DRDO in 1958 has achieved a lot in the last 60+ years. Whether it is the explosives or missile, their launching platform or enabling radar mechanisms, DRDO has made a great contribution towards making our armed forces strong and India as a self-reliant nation.

## Equipments used by our defence forces (Platform, Weapons, Ammunition and Enabling System) and beyond

At the time of Independence, India inherited a significant number of ordnance factories, shipbuilders, and aircraft repair and maintenance facilities. But as a sector, the defence sector requires technology which is step ahead of the present. With limited money and technical knowhow, Indian armed forces suffered a lot with the problems of inadequate and outdated weapons. This was visible in the 1962 war with China and even in the 1965 war with Pakistan. Though the battle was dominated by the fight between the infantry and armored units of both sides of the army with India having superiority in numbers in terms of equipment it was largely a neck and neck battle.

This was all because of the USA help to Pakistan in terms of the supply of aircraft, submarine (PNS Ghazi), tanks and other artillery while India has a mix of them like aircraft from the Soviet Union and the United Kingdom, tanks from a mix of USA, France, UK and Soviet Union etc. with most of them outdated. At the outbreak of the 1965 war, 10 out of the 20 vessels of Indian Navy, including the aircraft carrier, were under refit. Like 1962, 1965 war also helped India to learn a lot of lessons:

1)  The first important lesson was the need for advanced information on such adventurism from neighbouring nations. Because of the absence of credible intelligence, Indian armed forces failed to anticipate Pakistan attack and strategy with most of them being caught off guard.

2)  The second important lesson was the open support from China to Pakistan with threats to India including the use of Nuclear Weapons. It necessitated for India to fast develop its own nuclear weapons.

3) The third lesson was the active help from the USA to Pakistan in terms of advanced weapons and military tactics.

4) Another important lesson was the need to rethink on Indian strategy of Non-Alignment under the Non-Aligned Movement (NAM). Indonesia under its President Sukarno, an important leader of NAM, helped Pakistan in the 1965 war and despite India being the defender, the UK Prime Minister Harold Wilson condemned India for aggression.

All of these events forced India to move beyond non-alignment and actively engage with the Soviet Union. The active collaboration with the Soviet Union paid a lot and by the start of 1980's India (via Defence Research and Development Laboratory), India developed enough of expertise in propulsion, navigation and aerospace material technologies that it launched its own missile development programme as "Integrated Guided Missile Development Programme (IGMDP)" on 26 July 1983, under the leadership of Dr A. P. J. Abdul Kalam.

Before we look at the missiles developed under this programme and other technologies or equipment used by our armed forces and other security agencies it is important to know that in the last 55 years, i.e. since 1965 war, India has moved a lot. Today, it is recognized as the fourth strongest military power[25] of the world; behind USA (1), Russia (2) and China (3) and fourth among all nations in terms of military expenditure[26] with a defence budget of nearly US$ 66.5 billion.

This is made possible by the joint efforts of the organizations working within India (i.e. the network of 52 DRDO laboratories, 40 Ordnance Factories, Eight (08) Defence Public Sector Undertakings and number of Private Sector Companies) and other nations along with their organizations in meeting the defence needs of Indian Armed Forces. The DRDO laboratories and their work are already discussed. Here, we will discuss other agencies and defence equipment used by Indian security agencies on the basis four areas of defence needs identified by defence experts, as- Weapons Platform, Weapons, Ammunition and Enabling Systems.

1. **Weapons Platform:** It includes the system or structure on which a weapon can be mounted. The major weapon platforms include

---

[25] *The Military Strength ranking of India is based on the Global Firepower's 2019 Military Strength Ranking, based on its PowerIndex score.*

[26] *The military expenditure ranking is based on the Stockholm International Peace Research Institute (SIPRI) annual report of 2019. The first three nations in the list were- USA (spending US$694billion or 36% of the total global military expenditure of US$1.82trillion), China (US$250billion) and Saudi Arabia (US$67.6billion).*

the Ships, Submarines, Aircraft carriers, Aircraft, Launchers, Tanks, Unmanned Aerial vehicles (UAV) etc.

2.  **Weapons:** Weapons, also known as arm or armament, means the thing, implement or the device which is used for inflicting damage or harms in conflict. It includes the Rifles, Missiles, Howitzers, High Energy weapons like Laser and Microwave etc. used by the security agencies. Weapons are also used to avoid damage or harm from enemies if they are used against the enemy weapons like Anti-aircraft missiles, Anti-tank missiles etc.

3.  **Ammunition:** Ammunition represents the firepower or the object which is fired, dropped or detonated by the weapon. It includes the bullet fired from the gun, shells fired from artillery or the bombs/Thermobaric explosives carried by the weapons.

4.  **Enabling Systems:** Enabling System is the support system which helps all the above three in improving their capability, i.e. to create maximum impact or output, by providing guidance on its position, enemy position, targets etc. The major enabling systems of modern-warfare include a communication system, satellites, radars etc.

Weapon Platforms used by Indian Armed Forces (As of 2019 end):

## SHIPS:

| S. No. | Class (Ships in Service) | Built by | Specifications |
|---|---|---|---|
| _Frigates (Frigates are the warships with features varying between corvettes and destroyers. Today, they form the second line of Defence)_ | | | |
| 1. | Brahmaputra Class (INS Brahmaputra, INS Betwa & INS Beas) | Designed by Directorate of Naval Design and Garden Reach Shipbuilders (GRSE) and built by GRSE | 03 guided missile frigate as a follow-up of Godavari class with steam turbine based propulsion. |
| 2. | Talwar Class (INS Talwar, INS Trishul, INS Tabar, INS Teg, INS Tarkash & INS Trikand) | Follow-up of Krivak-III class frigates of Russia with design and built by Russia. The ships were made in two | 06 Semi-stealth guided missile frigates with gas-based propulsion. The work is on to have 4 more with 2 being built by |

| | | batches with first three ship given in 2003-04 while other 3 given in 2012-13 | Russia while the other 2 by Goa Shipyard |
| --- | --- | --- | --- |
| 3. | Shivalik Class (INS Shivalik, INS Satpura & INS Sahyadri) | Designed by Directorate of Naval Design and built by Mazagon Dock Limited (MDL) | 03 multi-role stealth-based guided-missile frigates with Combined diesel or gas propulsion system |
| 4. | Nilgiri Class[27] (INS Nilgiri, INS Himgiri, INS Udaygiri, INS Dunagiri, INS Taragiri, INS Vindhyagiri & INS Mahendragiri) | Under construction with 1st four to be built by Mazagon Dock Limited and other three by Garden Reach Shipbuilders | 07 multi-role stealth guided-missile frigates as a follow-up of Shivalik Class |
| 5. | INS Godavari Class | Follow-up of 1st Nilgiri Class frigates designed and built by Mazagon Dock Limited | 03 guided missile frigates with steam-based propulsion. Presently, only one i.e. INS Gomati is in service. |

***Destroyers (Destroyers are the warships which are faster, have high manoeuvrability and long. Because of these features, they form the first line of defence and second in the offence, i.e. next after submarines)***

| | | | |
| --- | --- | --- | --- |
| 1. | Rajput Class (INS Rajput, INS Rana, INS Ranvir & INS Ranvijay) | Based on Soviet Kashin class destroyers built at 61 Kommunara Shipbuilding | 05 Guided Missile Destroyers with Gas Turbines based propulsion. The 1st ship was |

---

[27] *Six NIlgiri Class ships were built from 1972-81 at Mazagon Dock Limited. Under P-17A, 07 follow-on ships are under construction with the first six carrying the old names of the 1st Nilgiri Class ships.*

| | | Plant, now known as Mykolaiv Shipyard in Ukraine. | commissioned in 1980. Four of them are active in service while one ship (INS Ranjit) was decommissioned in 2019. |
|---|---|---|---|
| 2. | Delhi Class (INS Delhi, INS Mysore & INS Mumbai) | Designed by Directorate of Naval Design and built by Mazagon Dock Limited | 03 Guided Missile Destroyers with Gas Turbines based propulsion. $1^{st}$ ship was commissioned in 1997 and presently all three ships are in service. |
| 3. | Kolkata Class (INS Kolkata, INS Kochi & INS Chennai) | Designed by Directorate of Naval Design and built by Mazagon Dock Limited | 03 Stealth[28]-Guided Missile Destroyers with Gas Turbines based propulsion. Presently, they are the largest destroyers of the Indian Navy |
| 4. | Visakhapatnam Class (INS Visakhapatnam, INS Mormugao, INS Imphal & INS Porbandar) | Designed by Directorate of Naval Design and built by Mazagon Dock Limited | 04 Stealth Guided Missile Destroyers with Gas Turbines based propulsion. They are follow-on of Kolkata Class and once completed, they will become the most advanced destroyers of Indian Navy |
| **Corvettes (small warships), Replenishment Ships (oil tankers), Patrol Vessels etc.** | | | |

---

[28] *Stealth Ships are the ships with stealth technology, i.e. technologies used in construction which makes it harder to detect through radar, sonar, infrared, visual or any other detection means used by others. The usual stealth technologies include the design of ship, use of materials which absorb or deflect the waves, technology which reduces the signature of the ship like controlling its acoustics, visual camouflage etc.*

| Corvettes | Veer Class, Abhay Class, Khukri Class, Kora Class & Kamorta Class | Mainly built by GRSE, MDL and Goa Shipyard with some imported from the Soviet Union. Today these ships are also made by Indian PSUs for Friendly foreign Navies like Brazil, Philippines, Mauritius etc. | Mainly built for specific purposes. E.g. Kamorta Class for Anti-submarine warfare while Kora Class for surface Combats using Guided-Missiles. The length of Indian corvettes usually varies from approximately 60metres to 109metres |
|---|---|---|---|
| Offshore Patrol Vessels | Sukanya Class & Saryu Class | Mainly built by Hindustan Shipyard Limited and Goa Shipyard with 1$^{st}$ three ships of Sukanya Class from Korea | Larger Patrol Vessels (around 100metres) to man the Exclusive Economic Zone of India with ability to function as temporary frigate through upgrade These vessels are also used in Anti-piracy operations, fleet support, offshore assets protection etc. |
| Offshore Patrol Vessels | Shachi Class | Five Ship project under-construction at Reliance Defence and Engineering | To be the 1$^{st}$ privately built Naval vessels. Once operational, it will add to our ocean surveillance and patrolling capabilities. Such vessels are also used by the Coast Guard |

| | | | |
|---|---|---|---|
| *Adding to the offshore patrol vessels, a number of smaller patrol vessels and boats are also used by Indian Navy for quicker response.* | | | |
| Amphibious Transport Dock | INS Jalashwa | Ex-US navy ship (USS Trenton) purchased by India. The indigenous ships built for this purpose includes the landing crafts built by GRSE or troopships | Mainly used for transportation of service personnel for expeditionary warfare missions. In India, it is used for evacuation purposes (e.g. from Libya) as the US restricts its use in war operations |
| Landing Ships | Kumbhir Class, Magar Class & Shardul Class | Mainly built by GRSE and Hindustan Shipyard Limited | These ships are used for carrying the tanks, vehicles, troops and other cargo used in military operations |
| Replenishment Ships | Jyoti Class, Aditya Class & Deepak Class | Barring INS Aditya (made by GRSE) others are purchased from other nations. E.g. INS Jyoti was from the Soviet Union and Deepak Class (INS Deepak & INS Shakti) are purchased from Italy | These are replenishment oilers or replenishment tankers used to supply fuel and dry cargo to other ships in the deep sea. In terms of length, with 170metres or more they are next to aircraft carriers of Indian Navy |
| *Along with these ships or vessels, many other vessels are also used for other purposes like Training, Sailing expeditions, Hydrographic surveys, Marine Acoustic Research, Dredging etc.* | | | |

## SUBMARINES:

| S. No. | Class (Submarines in Service) | Built by | Major Features |
|---|---|---|---|
| 1. | Chakra Class | Based on Akula | One Nuclear Powered Attack |

| | | | |
|---|---|---|---|
| | (INS Chakra) | Class submarines. Built by Amur Shipyard. | Submarine commissioned in 2012 on a 10-year lease from Russia. The second submarine of this class will join the Indian Navy by 2025. |
| 2. | Sindhughosh Class (INS Sindhughosh, INS Sindhudhvaj, INS Sindhuraj, INS Sindhuratna, INS Sindhukesari, INS Sindhukirti, INS Sindhuvijay & INS Sindhurashtra) | Based on Kilo-class submarines of the Soviet Union. Built by Sevmash of Russia (erstwhile Soviet Union). | 10 Diesel-Electric Attack Submarines with 8 still serving while 2 as decommissioned. The decommissioned submarines include INS Sindhurakshak because of explosion and INS Sindhuvir which is transferred to Myanmar. |
| 3. | Shishumar Class (INS Shishumar, INS Shankush, INS Shalki & INS Shankul) | Based on Type 209 submarines of Germany with 1$^{st}$ two built-in Germany while the other two are built by Mazagon Dock Limited under technology transfer from HDW, Germany. | 04 Diesel-Electric attack submarines with the 1st being commissioned in 1986. As of the end of 2019, all four are in active service. |
| 4. | Kalvari Class (INS Kalvari & INS Khanderi) | Based on the Scorpene-class Submarine of France with all six to be built by Mazagon Dock Limited under technology transfer from DCNS, France. | 06 Diesel-Electric Attack Submarines with the last two to be equipped with Air-independent propulsion developed by DRDO. 1$^{st}$ submarine (INS Kalvari) was commissioned in 2017 and 2$^{nd}$ (INS Khanderi) in 2019. 3$^{rd}$ and 4$^{th}$ submarine i.e. INS Karanj and INS Vela are launched and the other two are yet to be launched. |
| 5. | Arihant Class (INS Arihant) | Built by Navy Shipbuilding | 04 Nuclear Powered ballistic missile submarine built under |

| S. No. | | Centre, Visakhapatnam with an 83 MW pressurized water reactor built by BARC to power it. | Advanced Technology Vessel Project, designed as strategic strike nuclear submarines to complete the nuclear triad[29] of India. 1st submarine, INS Arihant was commissioned in 2016. The second submarine, INS Arighat, was launched in 2017. These submarines have the capacity to carry 12 K-15 (Sagarika) missiles of 750 km range or 04 K-4 missiles of 3500 km range. The other two submarines will be larger and capable of carrying 24 K-15 or 8 K-4 missiles. |
|---|---|---|---|
| 6. | P-75-I | Yet to be decided with MDL as PSU and L&T as Private players being the main contenders. | 06 submarines to be built with foreign collaboration and transfer of technology with an expression of interests from different nations. |
| 7. | S-5 Class | Yet to be decided | 03 Nuclear Powered Attack Submarines to be built as follow up of Arihant Class |

**AIRCRAFT CARRIERS: Warship which serves as an airbase in sea**

| S. No. | Aircraft Carrier | Built by | Major Features |
|---|---|---|---|
| 1. | INS Vikramaditya | Purchased from Russia in 2004. Earlier it was part of Soviet Navy from 1987 and later of Russian navy after Soviet disintegration as Admiral Gorshkov. | Kiev Class Aircraft Carrier commissioned on 16 November 2013 into Indian Navy. It is the biggest aircraft carrier ever operated by the Indian Navy with a displacement of 45,400 tonnes, steam turbines |

---

[29] *Nuclear Triad is the three-pronged capability of a military force to launch nuclear missiles from land, air and deep sea, i.e. through land based launchers, aircrafts with nuclear bombs or missiles and submarines with nuclear missiles.*

| | | | based propulsion and a length of 283.5metres. |
|---|---|---|---|
| 2. | INS Vikrant | Designed by Directorate of Naval Design and to be constructed by Cochin Shipyard, Kerala | 1st Indigenous Aircraft Carrier to be built by India and expected to join by 2022. It will have a displacement of 40,000 tonnes, gas turbines based propulsion and a length of 262metres |
| 3. | INS Vishal | Presently it is in the design stage. | It is likely to be of 65,000 tonnes with Integrated Electric Propulsion and 284metre length provided the UK agrees to share HMS Queen Elizabeth as the base for designing INS Vishal. |

- HMS means Her Majesty's Ship

Before INS Vikramaditya, Indian Navy operated two Aircraft Carriers purchased from the UK as INS Vikrant (started by British Royal Navy as HMS Hercules) purchased in 1957. It was commissioned in 1961 and served till 1997. During its tenure, it played an important role in the 1971 war by enforcing a naval blockade of East-Pakistan. The second was INS Viraat (part of the Royal Navy as HMS Hermes from 1959 to 1984). It was commissioned in 1987 and served till 2017.

The other known Aircraft carriers include USS Gerald R. Ford Class as the biggest and the most advanced aircraft carriers of the world with a length of 337metre and displacement about 1lakh tonnes, i.e. just 5metres long than the USS Nimitz class aircraft carriers (length 332.8metres and displacement of 97,000 tonnes). Both of these classes of aircraft carriers are nuclear powered. USS Nimitz Class has 10 aircraft carriers with 1st commissioned in 1975. USS Gerald R. Ford-class is a follow up of Nimitz and it will also have 10 aircraft carriers.

In comparison, China at the moment has only two aircraft carriers in service as Liaoning (304.5metre long and 62,000 tonnes displacement) and Shandong (315metre long and 66,000 plus tons full load). But it is fast catching up with the USA. Shandong was the first indigenously developed aircraft carrier and after its success, China has planned 06 other aircraft carriers with the introduction of Integrated

Electric propulsion system as compared to steam turbines on the first two.

## AIRCRAFTS:

| S. No. | Aircrafts | Built by | Specifications |
|---|---|---|---|
| | | FIGHTER/COMBAT AIRCRAFTS | |
| 1. | MIG-21 | Originally built by Mikoyan-Gurevich of Soviet Union and | It is the 2nd generation fighter and interceptor aircraft[30] operational in IAF since 1963. |

---

[30] *Fighter aircrafts are the aircrafts which are built for air-to-air combat with enemy aircrafts in order to establish air supremacy. Thus, these aircrafts require features of speed and maneuverability along with the firepower. Based on the evolutionary history of jet fighter aircrafts they are divided into different generations as:*
*1st **Generation:** It was the first type of jet fighters built during the Second World War with ME 262 of Germany as the first aircraft with a jet engine, replacing the piston engines.*
*2nd **Generation:** It includes the jet aircrafts built from 1950s to 190s and over passed the speed of sound and sustained the sonic speed because of better aerodynamics, propulsion system and aircraft material. They used semi-guided missiles in comparison to machine guns, cannons and unguided bombs used in the 1st generation.*
*3rd **Generation:** It includes jet aircrafts with better flight control, higher maneuverability and ground strike capabilities as compared to 2nd generation along with improvements in weaponry (laser guided bombs), radar system etc.*
*4th **Generation:** It includes jet with highly sophisticated avionics and weapon systems, giving not just speed and precision in multiple roles but the ability to quickly change the speed, altitude and direction in order to gain air supremacy Relaxed static stability and fly-by-wire became the standard of this generation aircrafts. Presently, most of the fighter aircrafts are of this generation. Stealth technology was also introduced in this generation aircrafts.*
*4.5 **Generation:** It is an intermediate range between the 4th and 5th generation where the aerodynamics of 4th generation aircrafts is boosted by communication technologies of 5th generation like AESA radar. It is mainly because of the high cost of 5th generation aircrafts making it economical to upgrade or advance the 4th generation aircrafts and the end of the weapon race because of the end of the cold-war era. Major features of this generation aircrafts include- stealth technology, advanced digital avionics with highly integrated weapons and communication systems to perform different roles in the air GPS-guided weapons, Beyond Visual Range Air-to-Air Missiles and helmet-mounted sights are part of this generation aircrafts.*
*5th **Generation:** These are the fighter aircrafts with capability of 'first look, first shot, first kill", i.e. first to identify the target, first to take the shot hit and first in hitting the target. This is made possible by its active phased array radar using AESA technology with very high speed integrated circuits and greater stealth capabilities, by keeping even the primary weapons in internal bays without compromising on the aerodynamics.*
*6th **Generation:** Presently it is in the concept stage and considered as the next generation tactical aircrafts which will dominate the sky from 2030 to 2050.*

|  |  | under licence by Hindustan Aeronautics Limited (HAL) | IAF pilot Abhinandan Varthaman, who drowned 4th generation F-16, was flying MIG-21 Bison aircraft |
|---|---|---|---|
| 2. | JAGUAR | Originally built by SEPECAT (a joint-venture of UK and France) with under-licence production from HAL | It is the 3rd Generation attack aircraft inducted by IAF in 1979. It is named as 'Shamsher' and has the capability to fly low with high speed and deliver heavy bombs at long range |
| 3. | MIG-27 | Originally built by Mikoyan-Gurevich[31] of Soviet Union and under licence by HAL | It is the 3rd Generation ground attack aircraft inducted by IAF in 1979. It was named as 'Bahadur' and retired from active service in December 2019 because of safety issues. During service, it was popular as Swing-wing fighter |
| 3. | MIG-29 | Originally built by Mikoyan-Gurevich of Soviet Union and under licence by HAL | It is the 4th Generation multirole fighter aircraft inducted by IAF in 1985 and used as a defence aircraft by India. It is named as "Baaz" & with upgrades, i.e. MIG-29K & MIG-29UPG variants; MIG-29 has joined 4.5 Generation aircraft. Presently, it is the only combat aircraft used by Indian Navy from INS Vikramaditya. |
| 4. | MIRAGE 2000 | Manufactured by Dassault Aviation, France | It is the 4th generation multirole single-seat single-engine fighter aircraft inducted by IAF in 1985. It is also known as 'Vajra' and extensively used during the Kargil War and the |

---

[31] *In 2006, Russia merged different aircraft manufacturers like Mikoyan, Sukhoi, Ilyushin, Tupolev etc. into one organisation as "United Aircraft Corporation"*

|  | | | |
| --- | --- | --- | --- |
| 5. | SUKHOI SU-30 | Manufactured by Sukhoi Corporation, Russia and under licence by HAL | recent Balakot strike because of being the fastest (Mach 2.5 speed) serving aircraft in IAF<br><br>It is the 4.5 Generation all-weather twin-seat twin-engine multirole fighter aircraft inducted by IAF in 2002. It uses avionics from different nations, i.e. Russia, India, France and Israel in its different variants with a top speed of Mach 2. It is among the most advanced fighter aircraft of IAF and recently it is equipped with BrahMos Missile to make it more lethal |
| 6. | TEJAS | First indigenously built aircraft from HAL with Aeronautical Development Agency (established in 1984) to design and develop Tejas with participation from many other agencies | It is the 4th Generation light combat fighter aircraft inducted by IAF in 2016 with **Flying Daggers** as 1st squadron. It is equipped with digital fly-by-wire technology with capabilities of interception and anti-ship operations. With increasing stealth and other capabilities, it will join 4.5 Generation aircraft with induction in the Indian Navy also. |
| 7. | RAFALE | Manufactured by Dassault Aviation, France | It is the 4.5 Generation multirole fighter aircraft with formal handing of the first aircraft done on 08 October 2019. The first Rafale squadron, i.e. Golden Arrows squadron will be based at Ambala Air Force Station and another squadron to be placed at Hasimara Air Force Station Rafale means 'gust of wind' |

| | | | and its claim air supremacy through its AESA radar and its unique technology of long-range optronique secteur frontal (OSF) to search and track targets through infra-red. It will be inducted as a Medium Multi-Role Combat Aircraft. The plan to introduce it in the Indian Navy is under consideration. |
| --- | --- | --- | --- |
| 2. | | | |
| **TRANSPORT AIRCRAFTS** | | | |
| 1. | AVRO HS-748 | Originally built by Hawker Siddeley with under-licence production by HAL (production in India started with IAF Aircraft Mfg. Unit, Kanpur. | It is a twin-engine turboprop, military transport and freighter with the capacity to transport 48 paratroopers or 6 tonnes freight with a max speed of 452 km/h. |
| 2. | 737-200 & 737-700 | Built by Boeing of USA | It is a twin-engine turbofan aircraft used for VVIPs/VIPs movements within India and abroad. It has a total seating capacity of up to 60 passengers with a max speed of 943 km/hr |
| 3. | IL-76 | Heavy lift aircraft built by Ilyushin of Soviet Union (now Russia). Before C-130J, IL-76 was the main transport aircraft of IAF | It is a four-engine heavy duty/long haul military transport aircraft known as 'Gajraj' in IAF. It has the capacity to carry 225 paratroopers or 40 tonnes of freight, wheeled or tracked armoured vehicles. |
| 4. | AN-32 | Built by Antonov of Soviet Union in the 1970s, now part of Ukraine | It is a twin-engine turboprop, medium tactical transport aircraft with capacity to carry 39 paratroopers or a max load of 6.7 tonnes at a max speed of |

| | | | 530 km/h. |
|---|---|---|---|
| 5. | C-17 Globemaster-III | Large military transport aircraft manufactured by Boeing of USA (started by McDonnell Douglas of USA). It was inducted by IAF in 2013-14 | It is a four-engine heavy-duty strategic transport aircraft capable of carrying a payload of 40-70 tons up to a distance of 4200-9000 km in a single hop. It is unique in terms of its ability to take-off from a short runway of 1.1km with as narrow as 27metre with the ability of rapid turnaround |
| 6. | C-130J SUPER HERCULES | Heaviest transport aircraft manufactured by Lockheed Martin of the USA. It was inducted by IAF in 2013 | It is a four-engine turboprop tactical transport aircraft capable of performing operations like paradrop, heavy drop, casualty evacuation etc. It has the ability to operate from short and semi-prepared surfaces and in 2013 IAF landed it at Daulat Beg Oldi airstrip of Ladakh, the highest landing of the aircraft. |
| 7. | ERJ-135 | Built by Embraer of Brazil | It is used for VVIPs/VIPs movements within India and abroad. |
| 8. | Do 228 | Originally built by Dornier of Germany with licensed production by HAL | It is a twin-engine aircraft used by IAF, IN and Indian Coast Guard for transport because of its feature of Short takeoff and Landing (STOL) |
| *Airborne Early Warning and Control (AEWCS) Aircrafts (these aircraft are used for surveillance for air defence and early warning and to aid in the tactical missions or offensive strikes by gathering intelligence)* | | | |
| 1. | A-50 | Manufactured by Beirev of Soviet Union with IL-76 airframe as base | It uses the EL/W-2090 AEW&CS radar system jointly developed by Israel Aerospace Industries and Elta Electronics Industries of Israel for surveillance. |
| 2. | EMB-145 | Built by Embraer | It uses the NETRA AEW&CS |

| | | S.A. of Brazil as R-99 | of DRDO with AESA primary radar or the long-range multimode radar built by LRDE Lab and other parts by other labs of DRDO with 240-degree coverage. |
|---|---|---|---|
| 3. | C-295 (Proposed) | Built by Airbus | DRDO has planned to build six new upgraded AEW&CS on C-295 with 360-degree coverage and range of 300 km |
| 4. | Ka-31 | Military helicopter built by Kamov of Soviet Union | It is the naval airborne early warning and control system used by Indian Navy |

Adding to the above list of combat aircraft, transport aircraft and AEW&CS, a number of trainer aircraft (BAE Hawk, HAL Kiran, HJT-36 an Intermediate Jet Trainer, Pilatus PC-7, Pipistrel Virus or Garud), Aerial Refueling tanker aircraft (Ilyushin Il-78), reconnaissance aircraft (Boeing 707, Global 5000, Gulfstream G100), Maritime Patrol and Anti-submarine warfare aircraft (Boeing P-8, Dornier Do 228, Britten-Norman BN-2 and Ilyushin IL-38, used by Indian Navy) and Electronic warfare aircraft (Gulfstream III) are also operated by Indian Air Force, Indian Navy and other Security Agencies.

## Search for most advanced aircraft from India

In 2007, India and Russia agreed for a joint programme for co-development and production of 5th generation aircraft. Initially, it was code-named T-50. Later, it was named as Sukhoi PAK FA or Sukhoi/HAL Fifth Generation Fighter Aircraft with Sukhoi from Russia and HAL from India as the participating agencies. It was supposed to be an upgrade of Sukhoi Su-57 but because of the delays in its development, the poor performance of the prototype (in terms of engine performance and stealth capabilities) and other related issues like cost, work from HAL etc. India withdrew from the programme in 2018.

As an alternative, India is working on two new plans. The first plan is to develop its own fifth-generation fighter aircraft as "Advanced Medium Combat Aircraft", a stealth all-weather multirole fighter for IAF and Indian Navy with Hindustan Aeronautics Limited and Aeronautical Development Agency (ADA) as lead agencies. It will also focus on increasing participation from the private sector by engaging them in its development and production. The second plan is to work on up-gradation of Sukhoi Su-35, a multi-role super-manoeuvrable fighter aircraft which possess greater stealth capabilities with lower cost and is the most advanced aircraft used by China at the moment.

## HELICOPTERS:

| S. No. | Aircraft Carrier | Built by | Specifications |
|---|---|---|---|
| 1. | CHEETAH & CHEETAL | Originally built by SNIAS of France, now known as Aerospatiale with under-licence manufacturing by HAL. Cheetal is the upgraded variant of Cheetah developed by HAL. With more power and ability to work at more harsh conditions. | It is a single-engine turboshaft helicopter built to work at hot and high altitude conditions of the Himalayas. In 1972, HAL started its production and subsequently it was inducted in IAF and Indian Army Aviation Corps (formed in 1986). It has 3 passengers or 100 kg load capacity with a max speed of 121 km/h. In 2006, HAL went for its upgrade, as Cheetal with a more powerful engine and ability to work continuously at Siachen Glacier |
| 2. | CHETAK | Originally built by SNIAS of France, now known as Aerospatiale with under-licence manufacturing by HAL | It is a single-engine turboshaft light utility helicopter used for Search and Rescue (SAR), Casualty Evacuation and Route Transport Role (RTR) operations by the IAF and Indian Army Aviation Corps. It has 6 passengers or 500 kg load capacity with a max speed of 220 km/h. |
| 3. | DHRUV & RUDRA | It was built by HAL and has been operational since 2002. RUDRA became operational in 2012 and either of one or both are used by all three armed services along with Indian | Dhruv is a twin-engine, multi-role, multi-mission advanced light helicopter (ALH) used by IAF and others for communication, SAR, Casualty Evacuation and other roles. Rudra is the armed version of Dhruv, equipped with an anti-tank guided missile, rocket |

| | | Coast Guard, National Disaster Management Authority etc. | pods, thermal imaging and infrared and air-to-air missiles. |
|---|---|---|---|
| 5. | CHINOOK CH-47 F (I) | Heavy-lift helicopter built by Boeing Rotorcraft Systems of USA. It was inducted by IAF in 2019. | It is a twin-engine tandem-rotor transport helicopter with vertical lift features and ability to work at high altitudes. It can operate in all-weather conditions with state-of-art night vision goggles to carry out SAR and other operations even at night, It has a carrying capacity of 9.6 tonnes of payload |
| 6. | MIL MI-17 V5 | Medium-lift Helicopter built by Kazan Helicopter Plant of Soviet Union, now Russia. | It is a twin-turbine transport helicopter with the ability to operate at hot and high conditions; and it is equipped with state-of-art navigational equipment, avionics, all-weather radar with NVG-compatibility. |
| 7. | MIL MI-26 | Heavy-lift Helicopter built by Moscow Helicopter Plant of Soviet Union, now Russia. | It is a twin-engine turboshaft transport helicopter with a carrying capacity of 70 combat-equipped troops or 20,000 kg payload at a max speed of 295 km/h. |
| 8. | MIL MI-25/ MI 35 (export versions of MIL MI-24) | Attack helicopter built by Moscow Helicopter Plant of Soviet Union, now Russia | It is a twin-engine turboshaft large gunship assault and anti-armour helicopter capable of carrying 8 men assault squad with four-barrel 12.7 mm rotary gun in nose barbette and up to 1500 Kg of external ordnance including Scorpion anti-tank missiles. It has a max speed of 310 km/hr and protects the crew from Nuclear, Biological and |

| | | | Chemical (NBC) attacks. |
|---|---|---|---|
| 9. | Apache AH-64 | Advanced attack helicopter built by Boeing Defence of USA. It was inducted by IAF in 2019. | It is a twin-engine turboshaft advanced attack helicopter with front and rear rotors, suitable for air combat. It is equipped with night vision and nose-mounted sensors for target acquisition in all weather and attack targets through the helmet-mounted display. |
| 10. | KV-28 | Anti-submarine warfare helicopter built by Kamov of Soviet Union, now Russia. | It is a coaxial rotor anti-submarine warfare helicopter used by Indian Navy for anti-submarine warfare and transport with a capacity of 4 tonnes of payload and a maximum speed of 270 km/h |
| 11. | Sea King MK-42B and SH-3 | Medium-lift Helicopter built by Westland helicopters of UK (now AgustaWestland after the merger with Augusta of Italy) with Sikorsky S-61 of the USA as base | These are two different helicopters with the first being built for transport purposes while the other for anti-submarine and anti-shipping operations. Both of them are used by the Indian Navy since the 1970s by operating them from the frigates. |

## TANKS:

Tanks are the armoured (i.e. having a protective covering) front-line combat vehicles used by nations in war. Tanks are among the most powerful battle equipment used by ground forces. England built the 1st tank of the world during World War I and since then it has played an important role in almost all battles fought on ground, especially World War II.

This wide use of tanks is preferred because of their ability to break the enemy fronts through their bigger firepower which can be fired from its tank gun at a higher speed with greater manoeuvers and speed of attack. The tanks can be classified on a different basis. such as technology, role and weight etc. The most used criteria is technology, with technical features of tanks as:

  a) **First Generation Tanks:** General-purpose medium tanks which were used during World War II as an upgrade over the initial technology demonstrations and working tanks prepared since the end phase of World War I like cruiser tanks, infantry tanks, heavy tanks etc. with limitations because of a specific purpose.

b) **Second Generation Tanks:** Tanks with the introduction of a number of new technologies to improve the original function of high firepower like stabilized main gun and Infrared night vision devices along with improvements in security like Nuclear, Biological and Chemical (NBC) protection.

c) **Third Generation Tanks:** Tanks with further improvements over the previous features like NBC protection through the introduction of new technologies like thermal imagers, digital fire control systems and composite armour etc.

d) **Third Generation Advanced or Fourth Generation Tanks:** It includes the next-generation tanks under development by different nations including India, called the *"Future Ready Battle Tank."* Some of the features or desires from these tanks include real-time awareness with multilayered protection system (i.e. ability to respond against anti-tank and anti-aircraft threats) and lethal firepower with agility to dominate all the battlefields of its use (ground, desert, high altitude areas like mountainous terrain etc.) in quick time.

In between these generations, we have intermediate generations with the inclusion of some advanced technologies over the previous generation but considered as not significant enough to be classified as a separate generation.

| S. No. | Tanks | Built by | Specifications |
|---|---|---|---|
| 1. | Arjun | Designed by CVRDE Lab of DRDO with production at Heavy Vehicles Factory, Avadi (in Chennai). The development project of the Arjun tank was started in 1974. But because of various reasons, it was inducted only in 2004. | Arjun is a third-generation Main Battle Tank which boasts a 120mm main gun with armour-piercing fin-stabilized discarding-sabot ammunition. Other weapons include a PKT 7.62 mm coaxial machine gun and another machine gun of 12.7mm. The top speed of the Arjun tank is 67kmph with a 1400 BHP engine. |

| 2. | T-90S & T-90M Bhishma | Co-produced with Russia by Heavy Vehicles Factory, Avadi (in Chennai). | The T-90 tank is among the legendary Main Battle Tanks built by Russia. India purchased 310 T-90S tanks from Russia in 2001 under a co-production model. It is an upgrade to the T-72 tanks, used and co-produced by India before the introduction of T-90. The T-90M Bhishma is the upgraded version of the original T-90S co-produced by India and Russia with inputs from France as well. Major features of T-90S Bhishma tanks include Catherine-FC thermal sights (built by French company Thales) with Russian Kontakt-5 (K-5) explosive reactive armor plates. It boasts a 125mm smoothbore main gun and 12.7mm heavy machine gun. The top speed of Bhishma is 60kmph with an 1130 BHP engine. In 2019, India placed an order for 464 T-90MS tanks, the latest version of T-90 tanks with features like inertial navigation systems, new explosive reactive armour, steering wheel, video cameras and a thermal imager with a range of 3.3.km. |
| 3. | T-72 & T-72M1 Ajeya | Originally produced in the Soviet Union by Heavy Vehicles Factory, Avadi (in Chennai) with Co-production with | T-72 tanks are second-generation tanks built by the Soviet Union. In 1978 India purchased 500 T-72 to supplement firepower of the |

| | | Poland and Russia. | previous Main Battle Tank Vijayanta (built under license of Vickers Mk 1 by Heavy Vehicles Factory) which played an important role in the 1971 war. The T-72 Ajeya is an upgrade over the Soviet-made T-72 tanks with additional safety measures like explosive reactive armour. The main gun of the T-72 tank was 125mm. |

## Unmanned Aerial Vehicles (UAV's):

Unmanned Aerial Vehicles, also known as a drone, are the flying aircraft without any human pilot on board. The humans may or may not pilot it from the ground, i.e. fully automatic or remotely operated vehicles. So, a UAV involves three key technologies:

1) A flying Drone or UAV;
2) Ground-based controller of UAV (it can be remotely controlled from the ground or programmed for autonomous work; and
3) The communication system between the two.

Today, drones are used for many scientific and civil purposes but initially, they were developed for security purposes. Security purposes include surveillance purposes or to use them as a weapon platform (as target aircraft). Therefore, below we have given both types of UAVs used by our defence forces.

| S. No. | UAV | Built by | Specifications |
|---|---|---|---|
| 1. | Nishant | Built by DRDO for Indian Army in 1996 | Nishant is an aerial surveillance UAV designed by DRDO with the primary task of gathering intelligence over enemy territory. It is also used for other purposes like reconnaissance (for battlefield intelligence), training, surveillance, target and decoy, artillery fire correction, damage assessment, electronic intelligence (ELINT) and signals intelligence (SIGINT). Nishant has a range/endurance to fly for four hours and thirty |

| | | | minutes. |
|---|---|---|---|
| 2. | P-4 or Harop | Developed by Israel Aerospace Industries with capabilities to operate fully automatic or have a man-in-the-lope | Harop is a suicide drone, also known as loitering munition UAV, which loiters around the target in order to search and locate it with stealth and anti-radiation properties to primarily hit air defence targets of the enemy by hitting them. Its operating range is 1000 km with 6 hours of flight. |
| 3. | Heron | Developed by Israel Aerospace Industries with internal GPS and pre-programmed flight profile and fully automatic launch and recovery functions & manual override. | It is a medium-altitude long-endurance UAV for air surveillance with the ability to fly for 52 continuous hours at a speed of 130 miles/hr and up to a height of 35,000 ft (10.5 km). It is used by IAF and IN. It is claimed to be used by the IAF along with other surveillance and reconnaissance systems before the Balakot strike. |
| 4. | Searcher | Developed by Israel Aerospace Industries | It is a patrolling UAV used by IAF and IN for their aerial reconnaissance missions with the ability to fly for 18 continuous hours at a speed of 125 miles/hr and up to a height of 20,000 ft. |
| 5. | Lakshya | Designed by DRDO and built by HAL with features of pre-programmed and controlled flights for Indian Air Force (IAF), Indian Navy (IN) and DRDO | It is a pilotless target aircraft with features of remote operation and high speed to carry out aerial reconnaissance missions in war or otherwise. Its launch is assisted by a rocket while the recovery is assisted by parachutes. |
| 6. | Rustom & Rustom-II | Developed by DRDO to meet the needs of Indian Air Force (IAF), Indian Navy (IN) and Indian Army (IA) | It is a medium-altitude long-endurance UAV to supplement Heron in air surveillance through tactical and larger variants and has other variants with combat features |

| # | | | |
|---|---|---|---|
| 7. | Netra | Developed by DRDO in joint collaboration with IdeaForge (a private firm) to meet the needs of CRPF, BSF and other police forces. | It is a lightweight mini-UAV for surveillance and reconnaissance missions with features of Vertical Take-off and Landing (VTOL), high resolution charged coupled device camera with a flight range of 2.5km at an altitude of 200m. Today, it is widely used by police in SAR operations, disaster management, aerial photography, riot-control and to check crowd movement in large gatherings. |
| 8. | Ghatak | An Autonomous Unmanned Research Aircraft (AURA) under-development by DRDO for IAF | Ghatak is an autonomous unmanned Combat Aerial Vehicle (UCAV) with features like high-speed reconnaissance, stealth features and combat abilities to defend it or to carry attacks inside enemy territory. As a combat UAV, it will have precision-guided munitions, kept inside the internal bay to add stealth and on-board sensors for targeting and weapon guidance. It will be a medium-altitude drone with the capability to fly at 9.14 km. |

**Weapons used by Indian Armed Forces**

## MISSILES:

Missiles are the intelligent unmanned rockets designed to carry a payload with the aim of destroying the targeted-object. Like a rocket, a missile involves identification of the target, trajectory to be followed, range, warhead, velocity and launch platform to be used. The basic design of the missile includes the following components:

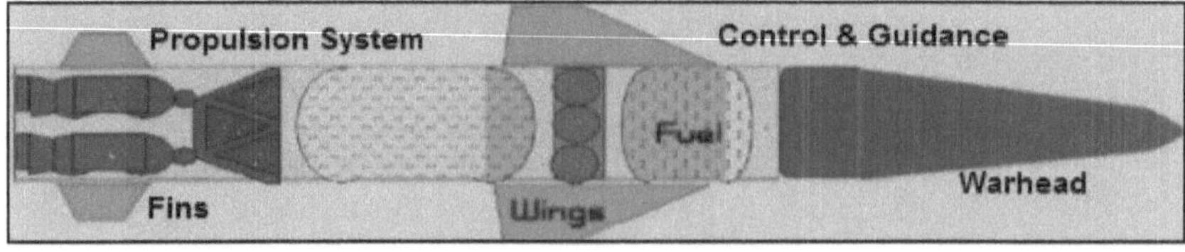


Figure 14 Components of a Missile (Image Courtesy: BrahMos Missiles)

The propulsion system includes the jet engine or the rockets used to propel the missile with either solid, liquid or both as fuel used in one stage or in multiple stages. The important terminal conditions of the missile operation like range, speed and warhead carrying capacity are determined by the propulsion system.

The next important component is the control and guidance system of the missile. The control includes the aerodynamic design of the missile with its fins, wings and tail used to steer the missile. The guidance system defines the path or trajectory to be followed by the missile and control its altitude along with control over flight features like pitch control, roll and yaw of the weapon etc. to dampen the fluctuations and to keep the missile on track to hit the target.

This guidance mechanism can be inbuilt in the missile computers or it can be achieved through external means. In addition to the above, we have precision missiles which use an active seeker to detect its target (using infra-red or laser devices) and to activate the warhead through trigger mechanism. Such missiles are known as 'fire and forget' missiles.

The last and most important component of a missile is the warhead or ammunition used in the missile. It determines the type of targets which can be destroyed effectively by the missile and the destruction which will be created by the missile.

## Major Classifications of the Missile

The missiles can be classified on the basis of a number of factors like the

| Category | Different Types of Missiles & their Features |
| --- | --- |
| Trajectory/ form of Missile | **Cruise Missile:** Cruise missiles are the jet engine based missiles which fly within the earth's atmosphere. These are self-propelled (till the time of impact) guided vehicle which travels through aerodynamic lift for most of its flight path with the primary purpose of placing the warhead or its payload on the target.<br>Within Cruise Missiles, we have different forms of missiles based on their speed, ability to penetrate, size, range or launching surface. The most commonly used categorization for cruise missiles is the speed with different forms as:<br>1) **Subsonic cruise missile**, missiles with travel speed less than that of sound. Usually, subsonic missiles are developed to travel at a speed of around 0.8 Mach[32]. |

---

[32] *Mach speed or Mach number is the ratio of speed of the object in consideration in comparison to the speed of sound. 1 Mach or the speed of sound is 332m/s or 1195km/hr, meaning a Mach number below 1 as speed less than that of sound and above 1 as speed greater than the speed of sound.*

Major subsonic missiles of the world include the Tomahawk and Harpoon of the USA and Exocet of France.

2) **Supersonic cruise missile**, missiles with a travel speed of 2-3 times greater than the speed of sound, i.e. around 2-3 Mach speed. The high speed of missile and good quantity with quality of warhead provides the supersonic missiles high kinetic energy to create a greater lethal effect on the target. Presently, **BRAHMOS** is the only known versatile supersonic cruise missile system which is in service.

3) **Hypersonic cruise missile**, missiles with a travel speed of more than 5 Mach. We are yet to have such a cruise missile but Russia and India are very close to achieving it through BrahMos-II. Many other nations are also working to develop hypersonic cruise missiles.

**Ballistic Missile:** Missiles which follow a ballistic trajectory over most of its flight path regardless of whether or not it is a weapon-delivery vehicle are called ballistic missiles. The range of ballistic missiles is primarily defined by its initial velocity or launch velocity and the launch angle and they may be of exo-atmospheric in nature, i.e. going out of the atmosphere before reentry to the atmosphere.

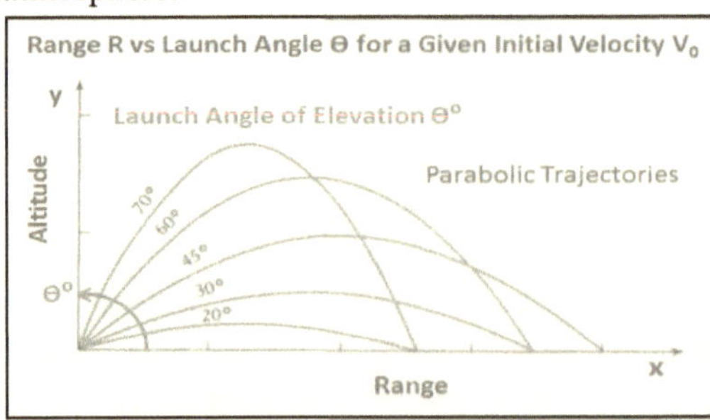


Figure 15 Ballistic Missile Trajectories

The Ballistic Missiles are primarily categorized on the basis of their range in terms of the maximum distance covered by it along the surface of earth's ellipsoid from the point of launch to the point of impact of the last element of their payload. Ballistic missiles carry a huge payload and are considered among the most deadly warheads because of their area of coverage.

| | |
|---|---|
| Range | Based on range, the missiles are primarily categorized in different categories as:<br>1) Short Range Missile,<br>2) Medium Range Missile,<br>3) Long Range Missile,<br>4) Intermediate Range Missile and<br>5) Intercontinental Ballistic Missile.<br><br>An important point to consider among these ranges is that the requirement of the travel distance varies for missiles based on their operational requirements and some categories may not be applicable to certain missiles. E.g. The distance requirements for surface-to-surface short-range missiles are different from Surface-to-air short-range missiles. |
| Mode of Launch | 1) **Surface-to-Surface Missile:** A guided projectile launched from the surface (ground) to attack targets on the surface.<br>2) **Surface-to-Air Missile:** Missiles which are launched from the ground to destroy aerial targets like aircraft, helicopters, UAVs or other ballistic missiles. Surface-to-air missiles are mainly built for air defence systems as they defend any aerial attacks by the enemy.<br>3) **Surface-to-Sea Missile:** Surface (coast)-to-sea missiles are the missiles launched from land to attack ship in the sea.<br>4) **Air-to-Air Missile:** Air-to-air missiles are launched from an aircraft/helicopter/UAV to destroy the enemy aircraft, UAVs or any other aerial target.<br>5) **Air-to-Surface Missile:** Missiles which are launched from armed forces aircraft/helicopters/UAV to hit the targets on land, at sea or both.<br>6) **Sea-to-surface Missile:** Missiles which are launched from the sea (via ship or submarine) to attack land-based targets.<br>7) **Sea-to-Sea Missile:** These are the missiles used by ships to attack another ship in the sea.<br>8) **Anti-tank Missile:** It is a guided missile designed to pierce and destroy the heavily-armoured tanks or other armoured vehicles. These missiles could be launched from aircraft, helicopters, tanks or from the shoulder-mounted launcher. |

| | |
|---|---|
| | 9) **Anti-submarine Missile:** It is a guided missile designed as an alternative to depth charges to target the submerged submarines while allowing standoff, i.e. to be launched from a distance sufficient enough to avoid defensive fire. |
| Propulsion System | 1) **Solid Propulsion:** The solid propulsion technology with missiles uses solid fuel for propulsion like aluminium powder. It is simple, easy to store & handle in fuelled condition with the ability to produce large thrusts or reach very high speeds quickly. Because of these properties, whether it is long-range heavy missiles or Satellite Launch Vehicles, the first stage uses solid fuel.<br><br>2) **Liquid Propulsion:** The liquid propulsion technology uses liquid as fuel, mainly hydrocarbons. Such missiles are difficult to store with fuel thus requiring fuel filling before launch, meaning high time to respond. But these missiles are far easier to control through restrictions on fuel flow and they have a high specific impulse in comparison to solid fuel.<br><br>3) **Hybrid Propulsion:** It is a mix of two fuel technologies with a propulsion system having two stages as- solid propulsion and liquid propulsion. This is done to compensate for the disadvantages of both propulsion systems and have the combined advantages of both.<br><br>4) **Ramjet:** Ramjet propulsion system is based on air-breathing engines which use the forward speed of the missile for intake and the compression of air rather than to use a turbine as used in turbojet engines.<br><br>5) **Scramjet:** Scramjet propulsion system is another form of an air-breathing engine with a difference that it works as a Supersonic Combustion Ramjet, I.e. The combustion takes place at supersonic air velocities in a scramjet engine.<br><br>6) **Cryogenic:** This propulsion system uses cryogenic propellants (liquefied gases stored at very low temperatures) as fuel. The most common combination used in cryogenic engines is liquid hydrogen as the fuel and liquid oxygen as the oxidizer. |
| Warhead | 1) **Conventional Warhead:** A conventional warhead missile contains high energy chemical explosives and |

| | | |
|---|---|---|
| | | relies on the detonation of the explosive and the resulting metal casing fragmentation as kill mechanisms.<br>2) **Strategic Warhead:** In a strategic warhead missile we have radioactive materials as warheads. When triggered, they release huge radioactivity capable of mass annihilation or strong enough to even wipe out complete cities, as did in Hiroshima and Nagasaki during World War II. |
| Guidance System | | Missiles are primarily based on two technologies, i.e. unguided missiles or guided missiles with a difference of the absence and presence of a guidance system. Among the guided missiles, we have different forms of guidance as:<br>1) **Wire Guidance:** Missiles which are guided by the signals sent through the wire which connects the missile with its guidance mechanism from the launch site after its launch. It offers the advantage of less susceptibility to electronic countermeasures but useful only for limited line-of-sight missiles like anti-tank missiles.<br>2) **Command Guidance:** Command guidance system involves the use of radar or optical instruments for tracking of the missile from the launch site or platform and use of radio, radar, or laser impulses or along thin wires or optical fibres to transmit commands.<br>3) **Terrain Comparison Guidance:** Terrain Comparison Guidance system, also known as TERCOM, is customarily used by cruise missiles to measure the profile of the ground directly below the missile and to check it with the stored information through the use of sensitive altimeters.<br>4) **Inertial Guidance:** Inertial Guidance system is integrated within the missile and used in the cruise missiles or the other surface-to-surface missiles. It uses three accelerometers, mounted on a platform space-stabilized by gyros, measure accelerations along three mutually perpendicular axes; these accelerations are then integrated twice, the first integration giving the velocity and the second giving position. The system then compares it with the programme feed prior to launch and directs the control system to preserve the pre-programmed trajectory. |

|  | 5) | **Terrestrial Guidance:** Like Inertial Guidance System, Terrestrial Guidance System involves pre-programmed angles before the launch of a missile. The guidance system constantly measures the star angles and compares them with the pre-programmed angles expected on the missile's intended trajectory; directing the control system to correct whenever an alteration to the trajectory is required. |
|  | 6) | **Beam Rider Guidance:** This system relies on external surface radar or ship-based radar to transmit a beam of radar energy towards the target. The surface radar tracks the target and transmits a guidance beam to the missile in order to adjust its angle as the target moves across the sky. |
|  | 7) | **RF and GPS Reference:** RF (Radio Frequency) and GPS (Global Positioning System) reference system uses the RF waves or the GPS signals to locate the target and adjust the trajectory of the missile-based on the commands from control surfaces. |
|  | 8) | **Laser Guidance:** Laser Guidance System uses a laser beam to focus on the target. The laser beam strikes the target and reflects off the target, thus getting scattered. The guidance system uses a laser seeker to detect the direction of the laser reflections and send the information to the guidance system, in order to enable the guidance system for steering the missile towards the source of laser reflections, i.e. the target. |

## Missiles of India

The Second World War was an important milestone in the warfare history of mankind. It started as a traditional war with main focus on having long-standing armies aided by technology. By the end of war, technology demonstrated that it can be relied more by armed forces because of its greater destructive capabilities in different forms. One such important form developed in this war was V-2 rockets used by Germany in 1944 to attack the allied nation cities.

With end of war, a race started among nations, especially between USA and USSR, to develop missiles which can carry one or more warheads (including thermonuclear warheads) to enemy nations to create maximum or targeted destruction of its assets like aircraft, tanks, defence installations, cities etc. while preserving its own assets.

Today, we have missiles developed by a number of nations varying from short-range ballistic missiles (operating within the Earth's atmosphere) to the intercontinental ballistic missiles following a sub-orbital trajectory; and cruise missiles with a powered flight. India also started its guided missile development research with the setup of a special weapons development team in 1958. In 1962, India started its programme for an intermediate-range surface-to-air missile with Switzerland. But it ended without any significant results.

In 1972, India started the development of an intercontinental ballistic missile (under Project Valiant) and a short-range surface-to-air missile (under Project Devil) with liquid-fuelled engines. But both the programmes were discontinued abruptly, Project Valiant in 1974 and Project Devil in 1980 without completion.

But Project Devil helped in gaining significant insights into the missile development with the development of different missile components. With the success of ISRO Satellite Launch Vehicle development (SLV-III which successfully deployed Rohini Satellite in near-earth orbit) in 1980, its project director Dr A. P. J. Abdul Kalam was again brought to DRDO to lead the Integrated Guided Missile Development Programme (IGMDP) of DRDO.

IGMDP was formally launched on 26 July 1983, as a research and development programme to develop a comprehensive range of missiles. This project achieved great success and on the basis of it, India has developed many more missiles on its own or through foreign collaboration. Add to that, we have purchased certain missiles from other nations also as:

| S. No. | Missile Name | Developed By | Features |
| --- | --- | --- | --- |
| 1. | PRITHVI | Five missiles developed by DRDL lab of DRDO under Integrated Guided Missile Development Programme (IGMDP). These missiles are mainly produced by Defence PSUs like Bharat | Short-range Surface-to-Surface Ballistic Missile with features as:<br>• First indigenously developed Ballistic Missile under IGMDP with a launch in 1988<br>• Only one stage as liquid<br>• 3 variants as- **Prithvi-I** (Range 150 km with a payload capacity of 1,000 kg); **Prithvi-II** (Range 350 km with a payload capacity of |

| | | Dynamics Limited (BDL), Bharat Electronics Limited (BEL) with some private players like Larsen & Tubro (Defence) and Tata Power Strategic Engineering Division. | 350-750 kg) and **Prithvi-III** (Range 350-600 km with a payload capacity of 500-1,000 kg) |
| 2. | AGNI | | Intermediate-range Surface-to-Surface Ballistic Missile<br><br>• Second Missile developed under IGMDP with a launch in 1989<br>• Also, the last missile to be launched under IGMDP as a technology demonstrator on Re-entry (Agni-III)<br>• But the development of Agni Missiles continued and today it comes in a number of forms as<br><br>**Agni-I**, a Medium-range Ballistic Missile with one stage and a range from 700-1200km;<br>**Agni-II**, an intermediate-range Ballistic Missile with two stages and a range from 2000-3500km;<br>**Agni-III**, an intermediate-range Ballistic Missile with two stages and a range from 3000-5000km;<br>**Agni-IV**, an intermediate-range Ballistic Missile with two stages and a range from 3500-4000km;<br>**Agni-V**, an Intercontinental Ballistic Missile with three stages and a range from 5000- |

| | | | | |
|---|---|---|---|---|
| | | | | 8000km;<br>**Agni-VI**, an intercontinental Ballistic Missile (under-development) with three stages and a range from 10000-12000km; |
| 3. | TRISHUL (Trident) | | | Short-range low-level Surface-to-Air Missile with features as:<br>● First launch in 1989<br>● Max Speed of Mach 2<br>● It has a range of 12 km with the capability to carry a 15 kg warhead.<br>● Though it was inducted in the Indian Army and Indian Air Force it failed to generate much confidence.<br>● Because of it, despite its use as an anti-ship and anti-sea skimmer missile, Indian navy went for Israeli Barak Missiles. |
| 4. | AKASH | | | Medium-range supersonic Surface-to-Air Missile with features as:<br>● First launch in 1990.<br>● Max Speed of Mach 2.5<br>● It has an intercept range of 30km.<br>● It uses Rajendra 3D Passive Electronically Scanned Array (PESA) Radar to identify the targets, and |

| | | | |
|---|---|---|---|
| | | | • It can neutralize aircraft as well as missiles. |
| 5. | NAG (Prospina) | | Third-generation Anti-tank Guided Missile based on the "Fire-and-Forget" technology (i.e. no guidance after its launch and need of the launcher being in line-of-sight of the target. It has a range of 500metre to 4 km. It is launched through NAMICA (Nag Missile Carrier) but a number of variants of it are also developed like HELINA. |
| 6. | BrahMos (Brah representing fury of Brahmaputra River and Mos representing the grace of Moskva River) | Developed by Joint Venture (JV) of DRDO from India and NPOM (Mashinostroyenia) from Russia since 12 February 1998. | Two-stage Supersonic Cruise Missile<br>• First Supersonic cruise missile of world<br>• The first stage as 'Solid Stage'<br>• The Second Stage is 'Ramjet Stage'<br>• Missile Range: 290 Km<br>• Missile Speed: near 3 Mach<br>• Operated on: 'Fire and Forget' Technology<br>• Stealth-based missile<br>• Warhead Capacity: 200-300 Kgs<br>• Launch: From land, Ships ($1^{st}$ from INS Rajput in 2005) and Air ($1^{st}$ from Sukhoi-30MKI)<br><br>It is a modular design missile |

| | | | with the capability of being launched at different orientations. Because of it, BrahMos can be integrated with a wide spectrum of platforms like warships, submarines, different types of aircraft, mobile autonomous launchers and silos. |
|---|---|---|---|
| 7. | BrahMos-II | Under-development by the above mentioned JV | To be the first Hypersonic cruise missile of the world, i.e. above 4 Mach Speed, by replacing the ramjet stage with a scramjet. MTCR membership will help India to build an upgrade with 450-600 km range |
| 8. | ASTRA | Developed by DRDO with production by BDL | It is a Beyond Visual Range Air to Air (BVRAAM) Missile to hit targets at varying ranges and altitudes. It has a speed of Mach 4.5 and a short-range of 20km in the tail chase while a long-range of 80-110km in head-on-chase. It is developed for IAF aircraft for high altitude warfare with a maximum range of 20 km height. Presently, it is installed on Su-30MKI, Mirage 2000, Tejas and MiG-29.<br>Further higher range Astra, as Mk 2 variant, is under-development giving it a range of 160km. |
| 9. | DHANUSH | Developed by DRDO | It is a modified version of Prithvi missile, a Short-range Ballistic Missile, which is developed for Indian Navy to launch from ship to attack other ship or land |

| Sl. | Name | Developed by | Description |
|---|---|---|---|
| 10. | BARAK 8 | Developed by Israel Aerospace industries with DRDO. For India, it is produced by BDL | targets with a range of 250-400 km Medium-Range Surface-to-air Missile with capabilities to hit aerial targets like aircraft, helicopters, UAVs etc. It comes in two variants as- Land and Ship version. It has a range of 70-100 km with a max speed of Mach 2 and 360-degree coverage. Also, an extended range Barak-8ER of the missile with a range of 150 km is under development. All modern warships and aircraft carriers since the Kolkata class have this missile. |
| 11. | ADVANCED AIR DEFENCE (AAD) & PRITHVI AIR DEFENCE (PAD). Also known as Ashwin Ballistic Missile Interceptor & Pradyumna Ballistic Missile Interceptor | Developed under Indian Ballistic Missile Defence Programme by DRDO in 2007 by making a number of missile technologies; radar and satellite technologies; and their command and control network as one integrated defence system operational through a Mission Control | Two-layer ballistic missile defence system with PAD for high altitude (exo-atmospheric, 50-80km) interception and AAD for low altitude (endo-atmospheric, up to 30 km) interception with a range of 5000km, i.e. to hit the medium and intermediate-range ballistic missiles in the terminal phase. India is the fourth nation of the world, after the USA, Russia and Israel to build such an anti-ballistic missile system. Once installed, Delhi and Mumbai will be the first cities to be protected by this system. The missiles used under the system are comparable to the Terminal High Altitude Defense (THAD) system of the USA with the |

| | | | ability of hit-to-kill interception of the missiles in their terminal phase. |
|---|---|---|---|
| 12. | NIRBHAY | Developed by DRDO | It is a long-range subsonic (0.6-0.7 Mach) two-stage Stealth Cruise Missile with all-weather capability and ability to carry conventional as well as a nuclear warhead. It has the loitering capability and can search target before hitting it. |
| 13. | HELINA | Developed by DRDO | HeLiNa (Helicopter Launched Nag) is the air-launched version of a NAG missile mounted on helicopters like Rudra. |
| 14. | S-125 | Built by the Soviet Union, now Russia | Short-range low-altitude surface-to-air missile to protect important installations from air attacks |
| 15. | S-200 (Vega) | Built by the Soviet Union, now Russia | Very long range medium-to-high altitude surface-to-air missile to protect important installations from air attacks |
| 16. | S-300 | An air defence system built by the Soviet Union, now Russia | Surface-to-air missile defence system to protect a long area from air attacks. |
| 17. | S-400 | An air defence system built by Russia. It was inducted by Russia in 2007 and in 2018, India signed the formal agreement for the purchase of S-400, despite | The most advanced mobile surface-to-air missiles or anti-ballistic missiles defence system with the capability to identify and neutralize the anti-stealth targets at high altitudes within range of 230 to 570 km (based on the attack method) or low altitude cruise missiles at 400km range. It can engage 80 targets at one time belonging to |

| | | | |
|---|---|---|---|
| | | threats from the USA to apply its CAATSA[33] Act for transactions with Russian defence sector. It is likely to be inducted in 2020 by the Indian Armed Forces. | different forms like aircraft, ballistic missiles, cruise missiles etc. within a response time of 9-10 seconds. to protect important installations from air attacks |
| 18. | QRSAM | Developed by DRDO and Produced by BEL and BDL | An all-weather all-terrain Quick Range Surface-to-Air Missile (QRSAM) with a 25-30 km range. It is developed to replace the ageing Soviet missiles for low-range air defence like Osa-Ak missile and medium-range air defence like 2k12 Kub Missile. Its development was completed recently in December 2019 and by early 2021 it will be inducted by the forces. |
| 19. | Mission SHAKTI | Anti Satellite Missile Test (ASAT) by DRDO | March 2019 test of Prithvi Defence Vehicle Mark-II to test anti-satellite weapons of India. With this, India became the fourth nation after the USA, Russia and China to develop an anti-satellite weapon and it is considered as part of the Indian Air Defence System by extending it to cover the intercontinental ballistic missiles and to protect |

---

[33] *CAATSA Act, also known as **Countering America's Adversaries Through Sanctions Act**,* is a US law passed in 2017 to impose sanctions on three nations i.e. Russia, Iran and North Korea.

| | | | the space assets of India. |
|---|---|---|---|
| 20. | PRAHAAR & PRAGATI | Developed by DRDO | It is a short-range Ballistic Missile with a range of 150 km with Mach 2 speed. It is developed to fill the range gap between the Pinaka Multi Barrel Rocket Launcher (with a range of 40-75 km) and Prithvi Ballistic Missile. Pragati is the export variant of Prahaar developed with a higher range of 170km |
| 21. | SAGARIKA (K-15) | Developed by DRDO under the Submarine-launched Ballistic Missile programme to give the second-strike capability to India | It is a Short-range Ballistic Missile with a range of 700-750 km and a number of guidance systems like inertial navigation system and GPS with terrain contour matching system in its terminal phase. It has the capability to carry a payload of 500-800kg |
| 22. | SHAURYA (K-4) | Developed by DRDO under the Submarine-launched Ballistic Missile programme to give the second-strike capability to India | It is an intermediate-range Ballistic Missile with a range of 3000-5000 km with a guidance system similar to Sagarika but the higher capability to carry a payload, i.e. it can carry a payload up to 2 ton. Presently work is speculated to be in progress for higher variants K-5 and K-6 with a range of 5000 km and 6000 km respectively |
| 23. | Spike MR | Developed by Rafael Advanced Defense Systems of Israel | It is a fourth-generation anti-tank guided missile based on fire-and-forget technology. It can be launched from a helicopter as well as from the ground. It comes with different |

| | | | ranges varying from 50m to 5 km i.e. from short to long (even an extended version with 8km range) with India ordering MR or Medium-range spike missiles with a maximum range of 2.5km |
| --- | --- | --- | --- |
| 24. | PRALAY | Under-development by DRDO | It is a surface-to-surface short-range ballistic missile. It is based on the Prithvi Defence Vehicle (PDV) exo-atmospheric interceptor missile with a 350-500km range. |

In addition to all the above explosive weapons or their platforms, our research laboratories have developed or are developing the non-explosive weapons which will rule the future non-contract wars. E.g. DRDO (from Public Sector) and Kalyani Group (from Private Sector) are working on LASER weapons, high energy or directed energy weapons (DEW) with capabilities to end the future war even before they begin. Similarly, BARC and DRDO are working together on KALI (Kilo Ampere Linear Injector), a linear electron accelerator to damage the on-board electronic system of enemy aircraft or missiles fired at India.

DEWs are devices which emit highly focused energy such as laser, microwave, electromagnetic radiation, radio waves, sound or particle beams in order to destroy or to make the enemy weaponry incapable. These DEWs direct high focused energy to destroy the enemy missiles, combat aircraft, UAVs and other weapons which are based on electronic circuitry. Some DEWs like electromagnetic weapons, using high power microwaves, are developed by few nations like the USA. Similarly, in 2014 the USA deployed operational Laser Weapon System (LaWS) on USS Ponce but its present capabilities involve tackling small UAVs or thin and soft boats.

Similarly, Russia has developed DEWs which can disable the guidance and navigation system of aircraft. Presently, nations like the USA, Russia, China, France, Israel and the UK are known to be working on DEWs apart from India. This large interest from already the most powerful nations of the world becomes clear from the features/advantages of DEWs like:

- Discrete use, because of no sound and invisible radiations if used above or below the visible spectrum;

- Precise aiming because of flat trajectory with infinite range and high speed (travels at speed of light) to target moving targets instantly;
- Reduced collateral human deaths and other damages.
- Capable to attack space assets, an important requirement of modern-day warfare; and
- Can be cheaper and easier to maintain with lesser manpower and infrastructural requirements.

## Defence Manufacturers of India

In early years post independence, Indian Government have established new units or nationalized the private industries engaged in weapon manufacturing to achieve following objectives:
- To let DRDO focus on its R&D activities,
- To enable India Armed Forces with sufficient firepower, and
- To achieve self-reliance in defence manufacturing through indigenization of technology purchased by India through Transfer of Technology or through in-house production.

Based on it, a significant number of Defence PSUs, ordnance factories and other agencies are manufacturing weapons across India. Post the licensing reforms, which limited the licensing requirement to four defence manufacturing fields, i.e.:
- Tanks and armoured fighting vehicle,
- Defence aircraft, spacecraft and parts,
- Warships of all kinds, and
- Arms and ammunition or allied hems of defence equipment parts and accessories;

a number of new private industries have also come up in defence manufacturing. Some of them have gained expertise and infrastructure well enough to enter the license-based defence manufacturing fields while a significant number of units acting as suppliers for existing public and private defence manufacturing organizations.

Part of the credit for present defence manufacturing establishments in India also goes to the East India Company and subsequent British authorities. For their economic interests and for greater control over the Indian subcontinent, they established a number of manufacturing facilities in India dedicated to military hardware. In 1775, the Board of Ordnance was established in Fort William, Kolkata and in 1787 the foundation of Gun Powder Factory was established at Ishapore.

In 1801, the first industrial establishment of ordnance factories came into the picture in the form of Gun Carriage Agency at Cossipore, Kolkata. When the British left India, we had 18 such ordnance factories and the government has further established many such factories (41, in total), working under the Ordnance Factory Board, established in 1979.

Before independence, we had a number of private shipbuilders and other factories also like the Hindustan Aircraft established by Walchand Hirachand Doshi. Post-independence, most of them were nationalized and brought under the Department of Defence Production. So, the present Indian defence manufacturing is dominated by Ordnance factories and a number of Central Public Sector Undertakings, also known as Defence Public Sector Undertakings (DPSUs) with some private industries. These Central Public Sector Undertakings or DPSUs include:

| S. No. | DPSU | Role |
|---|---|---|
| 1. | Hindustan Aeronautics Limited (HAL) | A Navratna company headquartered at Bengaluru. It was established in 1940 by Walchand Hirachand as Hindustan Aircraft. Today, it has 20 production divisions, 11 R&D centres and a Facility management Division spread across India with the prime responsibility of production, maintenance and overhaul of aircraft based on in-house technology or under license from other nation. |
| 2. | Bharat Electronics Limited (BEL) | A Navratna company headquartered at Bengaluru. It was established in 1954 and presently it has nine (09) units spread across India with core competencies in defence sectors like- Radars & Weapon Systems, Sonars, Communication, EWS, Electro-Optics and Tank Electronics. In the Non-Defence sector, BEL's product range includes EVMs, Tablet PCs, ICs, Hybrid Microcircuits, Semiconductor devices, solar cells etc. |
| 3. | Bharat Dynamics Limited (BDL) | A Mini Ratna (Category-I) company headquartered at Bengaluru. It was incorporated in 1970. The core competencies of BDL includes- Anti-Tank Guided Missiles (ATGM), Surface-to-air weapon systems, strategic weapons, launchers, underwater weapons, decoys and test equipment. |
| 4. | Bharat Earth Movers Limited (BEML) | A Mini-Ratna (Category-1) company headquartered at Bengaluru. It was established in 1964 and presently it has nine manufacturing units with core competencies in design, development and manufacturing of many defence and non-defence areas like defence vehicles, Rail & Metro products, Mining & Construction vehicles etc. |
| 5. | MISHRA DHATU | A Mini-Ratna (Category-1) company headquartered at |

| | | |
|---|---|---|
| | NIGAM LIMITED (MIDHANI) | Hyderabad. It was established in 1973 with the primary aim of achieving self-reliance in the production and supply of various superalloys, titanium alloys, special steels & stainless steels, soft magnetic alloys etc., required not just in defence sector but also for space, aeronautics, nuclear power, electronics, telecommunications and other strategic sectors. |
| 6. | MAZAGON DOCK SHIPBUILDERS LIMITED (MDL) | A Mini-Ratna (Category-1) company headquartered in Mumbai. Its first dock was created in 1774 and in 1934 it was established as a Private Limited Company. In 1960, it was nationalized and presently it is the leading Shipyard amongst all Defence PSU Shipyards of India engaged in the construction of Warships and Submarines. |
| 7. | GARDEN REACH SHIPBUILDERS AND ENGINEERS LIMITED (GRSE) | A Mini-Ratna (Category-I) Company headquartered at Kolkata. It was established in 1884 and in 1960 it was nationalized. The core competencies of GRSE include different type of Navy ships like Anti-Submarine Warfare Corvettes (ASWC), Landing Craft Utility (LCU) ships, Water Jet Fast Attack Crafts (WJFAC) with the introduction of Frigate manufacturing. |
| 8. | GOA SHIPYARD LIMITED (GSL) | A Mini-Ratna (Category-I) company headquartered at Vasco da Gama, Goa. It was established in 1957 by Portuguese and in 1961 it became part of Defence PSUs after Indian annexation of Goa. The core competencies of GSL include high technology ships like Offshore Patrol Vessel (OPV), Fast Interceptor Boats (FIB), Missile Corvettes, and Fast Patrol Vessel (FPV). Add to that, GSL is now engaged in Frigates and Mine Countermeasure Vessels. |
| 9. | HINDUSTAN SHIPYARD LIMITED (HSL) | A 100% State-owned Enterprise headquartered at Visakhapatnam. It was established in 1941 by Walchand Hirachand as Scindia Steam Navigation Co. In 1952 the Government of India purchased two-third of the company holding and named it Hindustan Shipyard Limited. With the purchase of the rest of the holding it was fully nationalized in 1961. In 2010, it was brought under the administrative control of the Ministry of Defence. Presently, it works as an important ship-repair and submarine refit facility because of its strategic location. The nuclear powered Arihant Class Submarine construction is also undertaken at HSL. |

In addition to the above organizations, Cochin Shipyard is working towards the production of 1st indigenously built aircraft carrier INS Vikrant. The major private companies engaged in defence manufacturing include L&T, Tata, Mahindra, and Reliance etc. In the last few years, special focus is given on bringing global defence manufacturers to India and further encourage the participation from our Private Sector in the Indian defence production and services sector because of various reasons like:

- Limited production capacities of our DPSUs with high defence imports.
- Poor track record of DPSUs in meeting the demands of defence forces (delays in delivery and quality issues),
- Urgent need of making Indian Defence Sector internationally competitive and efficient;
- To augment the efforts of existing organizations working towards Research, Design and Development with reduced government spending on one of its biggest expenditure item;
- High needs of our armed forces and other security agencies because of long unsettled land boundaries with a huge coastline and EEZ;
- It helps in minimizing the minimum inventory levels of many items;
- Presence of unfriendly nations in the neighbourhood;
- It acts as a tool for diplomacy and helps in building strong foreign relations through increased collaboration and help offered to other nations; and
- A large and dynamic defence production ecosystem in India can help in creating jobs; improve the level of technology in India with opportunities to earn large foreign exchange from a lucrative export market.

## Major Steps taken to promote Defence Manufacturing in India

For the past many years, Indian government has taken a number of initiatives in order to expand our defence production ecosystem through government policies and persuasions. As a sum of all those initiatives, the present shape of Indian defence manufacturing is as follows:

- Liberalization in the license requirements for defence manufacturing with nearly 70% of the items (parts, components, subsystems, raw materials etc.) being removed from the purview of industrial licensing with longer license duration (15 years);

- Introduction of defence offset[34] as part of the Defence Procurement and Procedure (DPP) Policy;
- Greater preference being given to Indian Designed Developed and Manufactured (IDDM), introduced in 2016 DPP Policy;
- Increased Foreign Direct Investment limits through automatic route (49%, 74% after Covid) with the option to allow even more through government approval, if it results in access to modern technology or for other reasons to be recorded.
- The earlier requirement of having a Single Indian Resident with 51% shareholding for any foreign-based company looking to establish a defence manufacturing unit in India is now removed.
- Promotion of greater synergies across sectors like security and aerospace.
- Push to Indian defence exports by Defence Production Department. One major step in this direction is the grant of *Open General Export Licence* (OGEL) for export of certain defence parts and equipment to nations like Belgium, France, Germany, Japan, South Africa, Spain, Sweden, UK, USA, Canada, Italy, Poland and Mexico. Presently, India is exporting to different parts of the world like USA, Israel, European Union, Africa, South Asia and Middle-East. In 2018-19, Indian defence exports stood at Rs 10,745 crore, up from Rs 4,682 crore in 2017-18. It is projected that the success of OGEL and Make in India through liberalized FDI will help India to achieve Rs 35,000 crore defence exports by 2024.

## Two Important Advisors to Shape Decisions of our Decision Makers

*Knowing a great deal is not the same as being smart; intelligence is not information alone but also judgment, the manner in which information is collected and used.*

- Carl Sagan

Whatever capacities our armed forces have and information gathered by our intelligence agencies, it is important that it is used wisely. Under our present set up, two people are most likely to identify that wise use and

---

[34] *Defence Offset is part of Indian Defence Procurement and Procedure (DPP) Policy, to counterbalance or compensate defence suppliers to place work of an agreed value with firms in the buying country i.e. India, over and above what it would have brought in the absence of the offset. The most recent policy on it is the DPP-2016 which increases the threshold for application of defence offset to Rs 2000crore from the current level of Rs 300crore under "buy" and 'buy and make" categories with an offset requirement of 30%.*

work towards National Security Strategy. The first one is National Security Advisor (NSA) and the second is Chief of Defence Staff (CDS).

NSA is a person with greater understanding on all aspects of national security (political, economic and security environment). And, the Chief of Defence Staff, being from the armed forces, is the one with greater understanding on the overall combat abilities of our armed forces and of our enemies. CDS can also help in identifying the future needs in order to enhance collaboration and synchronization of warfare efforts of all our armed forces in hybrid warfare strategies[35] of present time.

E.g. If we observe the present strategy adopted by Pakistan against India, we will realize that it largely uses the tools of hybrid warfare which it can afford because of the present economic crisis of Pakistan. Some of it includes:

- The internationalization of Indian affairs through sponsored journalism and protests at Indian Embassy,
- Starting an information warfare through use of fake news to incite religious hatred,
- Tacit support to non-state actors to conflict with Indian State, and
- Use of political activists/NGOs to promote Pakistan's own narratives.

Under such an atmosphere, these two persons are the most important advisors of the state to identify the intentions of other nations and calibrate its responses to make them more resilient and highly adaptable. But before we look at them, it is important that we should have proper awareness on the types of decisions required to be taken in national security interest and how these two people can help in the making these decisions.

Three types of Decision

1) **Operational Decisions:** Decisions which focus on day-to-day activities of an organization. These decisions are primarily taken at the individual organization level to ensure that daily activities proceed smoothly toward the strategic goal. E.g. the recruitment in armed forces, their training, regular military exercises represents some of the operational decisions.

---

[35] *Hybrid Warfare Strategies is the modern day military strategy which involves use of political warfare, i.e. to use political means in order to compel the opponent to do things as per its strategy through hostile intent; and use all the tools available at its disposal like conventional warfare, cyber warfare, irregular warfare (forcing non-state actors to have violent struggle against State) along with other tools like diplomacy, economy, fake news, political activism, NGOs, lawfare etc.*

2) **Strategic Decisions:** Decisions which influence or affect the long-term direction of the organization or nation are considered to be strategic decisions. These decisions are complex and often related to national security. Strategic decisions are primarily taken by the political leaders based on the advice from experts or advisors like NSA. E.g. The purchase of Rafale Combat Aircraft is a strategic decision taken to improve the capabilities of IAF for the coming decades and reverse the downtrend in its number of squadrons with a boost to the morale of IAF personnel.

3) **Tactical Decisions:** Decisions which focus on more intermediate-term issues and may involve one or more organizations, based on the nature of the decision. These decisions are largely taken in line with the strategic goal of the organization or organizations. E.g. it may be a decision taken by the Indian Army and BSF or any other force working in a close relationship.

## National Security Advisor (NSA)

On 19 November 1998, the Government of India established a three-tier security structure with 'National Security Council (NSC)' as apex body along with a Strategic Policy Group and National Security Advisor Board (NSAB)[36]. The prime of this was to bring synchronization of military interests with the scientific and political leadership of India. National Security Council works under the chairmanship of the Prime Minister of India along with the Home Minister, External Affairs Minister, Defence Minister, Finance Minister, National Security Advisor (NSA), Deputy National Security Advisor (DNSA) and Vice Chairman of Niti Aayog as members. The functions of NSC is

a) To constantly analyze security, political and economic threats and render continuous advice to the Government.

b) To carry out Strategic Defense Review in order to study and analyze the security environment and make appropriate recommendations to cover all aspects of defence requirements and organization.

One important official of the NSC is National Security Advisor (NSA) who also heads the Strategic Policy Group which involves experts from all important ministries, Chief of various armed forces and heads of different scientific bodies (DRDO, BARC etc.) along with intelligence agency chiefs and other officials. NSA also acts as the chief advisor to the Prime Minister on national security policy and international affairs.

---

[36] *NSAB is a group of eminent national security experts consisting of members from different fields like bureaucracy, armed forces, academics, economics, science and technology etc. with the function of providing a long-term analysis of the security situation and suggesting policy measures to remove issues.*

This helps NSA in becoming the major link between the political leadership and various executive agencies working towards any matter which can be important towards national security.

## Chief of Defence Staff (CDS)

Whether it was the 1965 war or the 1999 Kargil war, operational and tactical coordination between the armed forces of India has remained a cause of concern. E.g. when ceasefire was declared in 1965 war between India and Pakistan, India had an upper hand and when our Prime Minister Lal Bahadur Shastri consulted the service chiefs about the possibilities of India getting a decisive win over Pakistan if he delays the ceasefire by few days- Chief of the Army Staff suggested to avoid such delay while Chief of the Air Staff suggested delaying ceasefire.

Also, the armed forces have the feeling of being sidelined by the bureaucracy while dealing with service matters or their requirements, especially after the 3rd Finance Commission. The Kargil Review Committee, under K. Subrahmanyam (a retd. IAS and first head of NSAB), also stressed on the importance of having single-point professional military advice to the political representatives with the need of having better coordination between three services under the Chief of Defence Staff.

Though a tri-services theatre command was established immediately in 2001 (as Andaman and Nicobar Command) but not much happened after that to increase synchronization among armed forces. This synchronization is important for putting specific units of personnel from the three armed services of India under a common theatre command, helping in increased cohesion among the armed forces and to achieve greater rationalization of manpower and resources.

Subsequent committees and task forces like the Naresh Chandra task force in 2012 (by recommending for a Permanent Chairman Chief of Staff Committee, CoSC) and D.B. Shekatkar Committee in 2016 (Chief of Defence Staff, CDS) also stressed on the need of one command structure in order to bring synergy among the armed services and optimize the resource utilization. Naresh Chandra task force also identified that like Andaman and Nicobar Command we need tri-services theatre command in other areas also like cyber, space and special operations. Finally, in 2018, creation of the Defence Cyber Agency, Armed Forces Special Operations Division and Defence Space Agency was approved. In November 2019, Defence Cyber Agency started to function as part of integrated defence staff.

On 24 December 2019, Cabinet Committee on Security (CCS) chaired by the Prime Minister also gave nod to the creation of Chief of Defence Staff post with General Bipin Rawat as the first incumbent four-star general officer for a 3-year term. He will head the newly created Department of Military Affairs (DMA) under the Ministry of Defence and function as its secretary and also as the Permanent Chairman of the Chiefs of Staff Committee (COSC), the position which till now rotated based on the senior-most Chief among the three services.

Under present situations, the Chief of Defence Staff will help the armed forces a lot in overcoming the security challenges ahead of India under the hybrid warfare atmosphere of present time with structural and functional benefits like:

- Introducing long-term restructuring measures through completion of the theaterisation process. The current CDS said that he will complete the same in the next three years with Air Defence Command being the first step in this direction.
- To bring jointness among the armed forces in several areas like joint logistics command, joint medical arm or training activities like study and analysis of the UAVs feed etc.
- CDS, as secretary of DMA, will look after the affairs of Indian Army, Indian Air Force, Indian Navy and Territorial Army, including the revenue procurements and works of the three services.
- He will help in the promotion of indigenous equipment use by the services with a focus on trimming the weapon procurement procedure.
- He will be a member of the Defence Acquisition Council (under the Ministry of Defence) and the Defence Planning Committee (under the NSA).
- He will play the role of Military Advisor in the Nuclear Command Authority.
- In order to promote transparency in his functioning, the office of CDS is brought under the Right to Information (RTI) Act.

# CHAPTER 4 - Challenges to Internal Security of India & Solutions

*uttaraṃ yatsamudrasya himādreścaiva dakṣiṇam*
*varṣaṃ tadbhārataṃ nāma bhāratī yatra santatiḥ*

i.e. The country that lies north of the ocean and south of the snowy mountains is called *Bhāratam (Bharata Varsha)*; there dwell the descendants of Bharata."

—Vishnu Purana

The identity of India, i.e. Bharat, is probably the oldest one in this world, with its territory going from the snowy mountain ranges in North to the Ocean in South. In Sanskrit, *'Bha'* means Light or Knowledge while *'rata'* means "Devoted", meaning land which is devoted to light/knowledge. So, the identity of India, i.e. Bharat goes hand-in-hand with the devotion towards knowledge and it continued for many coming years because of the widespread belief in good karmas, in consequence of which men go to heaven, or obtain emancipation.

But it requires a lot of effort from each individual and ruler (government in the present context) to keep people devoted towards knowledge, in order to keep a nation secure from within. If the mind and perception of people get polluted or the ideas of a nation gets weakened in the society, the individual or society moves toward subversion/rebellion and other people/institutions of governance become the prime target of people.

Modern-day India also faces a large number of challenges to its internal security since its independence. Despite the best efforts from our security agencies and leadership towards proper identification and finding of solutions to them, many challenges still exist for decades. They are becoming more complex and varied because of many new challenges joining the existing challenges. Conservative estimates put more than 50% of India is affected by one or more of these challenges because of internal reasons as well as fueled by external reasons/actors.

These issues are not just law and order issues but also a greater concern to the future of the nation. Therefore, India needs to address these challenges by going into detail of each security challenge and work towards the establishment of a long-term true democracy. A democracy which not just protects the socio-cultural identity of each individual but also brings the sense of security, economic prosperity and feeling of political participation among all individuals in order to protect the mind and perception of each individual from getting polluted while changing the mind and perception of people towards India who work against the national interests.

## What is Internal Security?

Centre-State Relations Committee defined internal security as "Security against threats faced by a country within its national borders, either caused by inner political turmoil or provided, prompted or proxied by an enemy country, perpetrated even by such groups that use a failed, failing or weak state, causing insurgency, terrorism or any other subversive acts that target innocent citizens, cause animosity between and amongst groups of citizens and communities intended to cause or causing violence, destroy or attempt to destroy public and private establishment."

Kautilya also identified two kinds of threats to the internal security of a nation, as- internal threats caused by reasons within the nation and internal threats caused by Externally-aided reasons. In simple words, Internal Security means the security within the borders, i.e. maintenance of law and order, peace with upholding of sovereignty and unity of the nation.

Internal security challenges are very broad-based and multi-faceted for a nation. India also faces multiple challenges to its internal security caused by the domestic and global environment, which changes with time, requiring constant evaluation of challenges and opportunities from the nation. The major responsibility for this lies with the Ministry of Home Affairs.

## Challenges to Internal Security of India

The main challenges/threats to national security are classified into two categories as:

1) Traditional threats to the security of India, and
2) Modern/emerging threats to the security of India.

The traditional threats to internal security of India include Instability/Militancy in Jammu and Kashmir, terrorism/militancy through radicalization, Insurgency in North-East region, Language issues, Left-Wing Extremism/Naxalism, Communal Violence, Socio-political and economic isolation, Political sub-state movements, espionage, and security of the national infrastructure/assets related to the weapons of mass destruction.

The modern threats to the internal security of India include cyber threats, Organized Crimes like human trafficking, money-laundering and Narco-terrorism, Demographic Changes, Stress in financial institutions, Problems of Criminal Justice System, Revival of Khalistan movement, social media & the self-radicalization, water scarcity, Climate Change, unemployment etc.

## Traditional Threats to the Security of India and their Solutions

### <u>Instability/Militancy in Jammu and Kashmir</u>

Since the formation of India-Pakistan, Jammu and Kashmir have remained a bone of contention between two nations and a cause of concern for India despite being a part of India. In view of the demography of the region and other concerns, the Constitution of India provided for a unique position to it under Article 370. But it failed to meet the aspirations of not just India but of local people as well.

Before the 1980s, the violence in Jammu and Kashmir was largely because of direct action from Pakistan or the acts of waging war against India. But from the mid 1980s, Pakistan changed its strategy. Inspired by the events around the globe like the 1st Intifada of Palestine in 1987 and successful use of Mujahideen by the USA in Afghanistan against the Soviet Union (with active participation from Pakistan's ISI, which helped it in learning new tactics), Pakistan moved towards militancy in order win local support for its ambitions.

Since then, the focus of Pakistan has remained to create an internal security challenge for India, probably the biggest of Indian history in the recent past. In the last three decades, more than 42,000 innocent lives are lost because of the ongoing violence in the region through terrorism[37] and local Militancy[38]. The poor governance and the absence of true democracy on the ground further aided to the aspirations of Pakistan and built anger against India among the local people in Kashmir Valley.

This is visible through the increasing disengagement of the public from state and poor political participation because of boycott calls from the separatist elements. The prevalence of electoral malpractices and the changing demography of the Kashmir region because of the armed rebellion since 1989 have turned the equations in the region. If we look at the voting percentage in different regions of Jammu and Kashmir and compare it with the national average, it is quite clear that the social vibrancy of the region is damaged by the over-ground workers (OGW). OGW assist the terrorists in-

- Providing logistical support,
- Provoking local people against Indian Democracy,

---

[37] *Terrorism is defined as 'the unlawful use of violence and intimidation, especially against civilians, in the pursuit of political aims.'*

[38] *Militancy is defined as' the use of confrontational or violent methods in support of a political or social cause.'*

- Attracting youth towards militancy,
- Use of local people for illegal activities like espionage, drugs and fake currency circulation and intimidate local people working in Police, Army etc. through boycott with cover support in case of being attacked.

The results of provoking local people against Indian Democracy are visible through the voting percentages in the region. In Lok Sabha elections-2019, some constituencies of Kashmir valley like Shopian and Pulwama had voting percentages as little as below 3%. Other districts of Kashmir like Kulgam, Anantnag etc. had a voting percentage just above 10%. In comparison, the regions of Ladakh (now separated after The Jammu and Kashmir Reorganisation Act, 2019) or Udhampur (in Jammu region) recorded around 63% and 66.7% respectively.

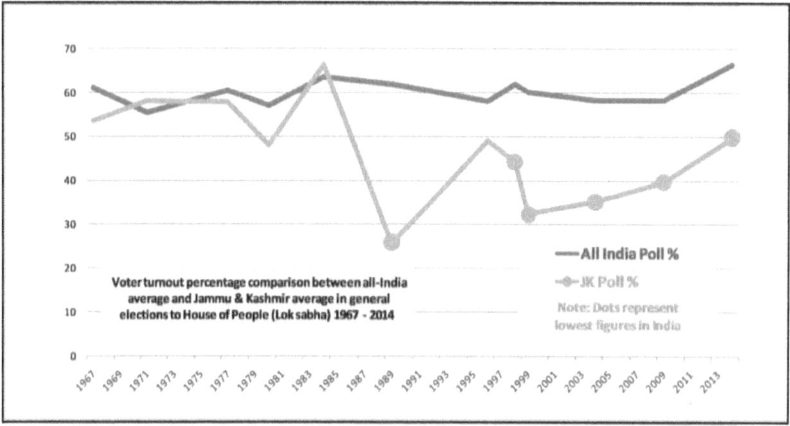


Figure 16 Comparison between All India Poll vs J&K Poll over the years (Source: Wikipedia)

High corruption with lack of economic and social development in the region further alienates the people from the idea of India. It attracts people towards militancy by presenting it as an indigenous movement against the State with lack of focus on development of physical and social infrastructure in the region. It also deprecates the democracy of India and shows the urgent need to restore the social vibrancy of the region in order to stop the alienation against India.

## Solutions:

As we know that the challenges to the internal security of India in Jammu and Kashmir region are not just because of the security reasons but also because of the social, economic and political reasons, we need to address all of them. Some of the much-needed steps, either implemented, under implementation or needs to be implemented, in this direction can be:

- ***Strengthen the Security Forces***: Powerful and prepared security forces acts as a deterrent not just to the activities of the militancy and terrorism but the external help as well. The aggressive stand taken by Indian Armed Forces, either in the form of 2016 surgical strikes across the Line of Control (LoC) or the 2019 Balakot strike in Pakistan territory has forced the enemies to think twice before the attack. It shows the political will from the MHA and MoD to work in cohesion and determination of Indian forces to expand the scale of operations beyond its territories.

- ***Restore Socio-cultural vibrancy***: As we learn from our great civilization, the presence of large interest groups and diversity is an important requirement to build an ever-lasting society. In order to build a sense of long-term peace and solidarity, control over the physical violence is important. Non-violent atmosphere gives an opportunity to restore the socio-cultural vibrancy which was once lost because of physical violence.

- ***Bring Economic Development***: An analysis done by '*The Hindu*' newspaper of Central and State Finance shows that 10% of all Central grants given to states over the 2000-2016 period were given to Jammu & Kashmir with just 1% of Indian Population. Even the biggest state of India (in terms of population), i.e. Uttar Pradesh has received lesser help at 8.2% or **mere Rs 4,300 per person** in comparison to **Rs 91,300 per person** received by Jammu and Kashmir. The worst is that despite the most magnificent help, the state has only fallen in Human Development Index ranking from **9** (in 1990) to **11** (in 2017) among states. This is largely because of the rampant corruption and presence of vested interests in the administration itself. Other factors like limitations on other Indians to purchase land in order to live or establish a business, uncertain tourism because of high terrorism or militancy and slow pace of infrastructure projects further deprived the region of economic development.

- ***Restore Political Democracy with a basis in Good Governance***: The elections for Panchayat elections in Jammu and Kashmir region were governed by the Jammu and Kashmir Panchayati Raj Act, 1989. But the first election was held only in 2001 and after a period of 10 years, we had second elections in 2011. It was only in 2014 that the J&K Cabinet approved the extension of the 73rd amendment of the Indian Constitution to the State and in 2018 first elections were held to have the same three-tier structure in J&K as well. But in most of the seats of Kashmir region, either there was no contestant or the person was elected unopposed. Therefore, there is an urgent need to improve the confidence of people in democracy at ground level and show that the ballot is stronger than a bullet. The 2018 Panchayat elections and the 2019 Block Development Council election served as an important input to the Union Government and it is hoped that appropriate action will be taken in order to establish democracy at the grass-root level and make all the political institutions more strong, transparent and functional in the region.

- ***Protection of regions which believe in Indian Democracy***: While carrying out the other steps to solve the problem of militancy, it is important that regions which participate in our democracy and want to grow with the idea of India should be protected and kept away from the expanded theatre of Jammu and Kashmir instability. This includes the region of Ladakh and Jammu where we see greater voting percentages.

The removal of all the clauses of Article 370 except 370 (1) and the reorganization of the State of Jammu and Kashmir into two Union Territories as the Union Territory of Jammu and Kashmir and the Union Territory of Ladakh is a major step in this direction. It will help in finding more realistic and implementable solutions to address the issues prevalent in the region.

Our security forces brought the region into peace a number of times but the lack of political will always turned the wheel back. For the first time, we are seeing a much-needed window of opportunity which will not only establish peace in the region but also bring long term gains for India. This will be achieved through greater efforts toward greater social, economic and political development in the region while protecting the cultural identity of the Union Territory of Jammu and Kashmir. It will also help in limiting the future plans of Pakistan i.e. to link it with the revival of Khalistan movement, in order to achieve its ulterior goals.

## Terrorism/militancy through Religious Extremism

In his speech at the United Nations Security Council in 1965, Zulfikar Ali Bhutto from Pakistan declared that Pakistan will have a thousand-year war against India. The military leadership of Pakistan turned it into a military doctrine of 'bleeding India through a thousand cuts'. After the humiliating defeat of Pakistan in 1971 war, the independent state of Bangladesh came into the picture, destroying the dreams of Pakistan to use East Pakistan to cut North-East of India.

Under General Zia-ul-Haq, Pakistani security establishments turned this doctrine to 'inflicting thousand cuts' through covert and low-intensity warfare against India. The basic strategy behind it is to create significant mayhem in India with large casualties to our security forces.

The insurgency in Jammu and Kashmir, support to Khalistan movement are all part of that strategy.

The basis of religious extremism, also known as Jihadi terrorism, is to spread religious extremism in order to radicalize people across India, using non-state actors. Major non-state actors helping Pakistan include Lashkar-e-Taiba (LeT) under Hafiz Saeed and its allies like Jaish-e-Muhammad (JeM), Hizbul Mujahideen and the Soviet-era Islamic Fundamentalist organizations like Harkat-ul-Jihad al-Islami (HuJI) with a network across South Asia and beyond. E.g. in 1992, it established its cell in Bangladesh as Harkat-ul-Jihad-ul-Islami Bangladesh (HUJBI).

HuJI was highly active in the first decade of 21$^{st}$ century and carried a series of bomb blasts like Varanasi bombing of Sanket Mochan Temple in 2006, a series of bombings in 2008 and the 2010 German Bakery blast. Many Indian militant groups like Students Islamic Movement of India (SIMI), Indian Mujahideen (IM) or their offshoots also helped them. Many such groups are also active in Bangladesh like Jamaat-ul-Mujahideen Bangladesh (JMB), Jamaat-e-Islami Bangladesh (JIB) and its student front Islami Chhatra Shibir.

Though the Government of India and Bangladesh have banned most of the organizations, some organizations are believed to be operating clandestinely even today. The prime reason for the continued existence of these organizations is their nexus with Pak-based jihadi organizations and the ISI. Some of them have extended to other nations like Myanmar and use the Rakhine issue to attract Rohingya Muslims.

The recent developments of Afghanistan, Syria and Iraq has increased the fear of entry from international radical elements belonging to terrorist groups like DAESH (also referred to as ISIL, ISIS or the Islamic State) and Al Qaeda (AQ)-linked groups. E.g. origins of religious extremist groups like Al-Shabaab in Africa can be traced to a small group of Somali citizens who fought in the Afghan war. On their return to the homeland, they created a militia of their own by recruiting vulnerable individuals and the Ethiopian invasion of Somalia in 2006 provided them with a perfect platform to rally the masses to their side.

According to the 2011 Census, India had around 172 million Muslims but only 180-200 Indian have been traced to join ISIS with nearly 45 from Kerala. While the numbers are insignificant, the death of Abu-Bakr Al Baghdadi has created the fear of some coming back to India and carrying out operations. Similarly, Al Qaeda is working for many years to enter India and likely to develop assets in some states. These terrorist organizations have the ability and resources to direct, enable and inspire high impact attacks across India with mass casualties.

**Solutions:**

Religious Extremism is an emerging challenge to the internal security of India and across the world. We need to take a number of steps in order to counter the violence caused by religious extremism at the local, national and international level. Some of the solutions to address this problem include:

- **Profiling of individuals** by taking the help of experts from different fields like psychology, religion, anthropology etc. in order to create a micro profile of vulnerable individuals. Social identity theory[39] and social movement theory[40] are both helpful for understanding the individual's radicalization, and the socialization context of that radicalization. It will help in not just early tracking of the potential radicalization targets but also help the law enforcement agencies in training their personnel.
- Enhancing **participatory decision making** with rights-based approach and involvement from all in civic space at the national and local level.
- Promote **Good Governance** by making administration more responsive and corruption-free in order to establish the rule of law and remove the governance gaps.
- Strengthen the local government capacity towards service delivery and security in order to extend social services to all and solve the complex problems of people.
- **Engaging faith-based organizations** and **religious leaders** towards disengagement of youth from radicalization. Deradicalisation can be done by countering the religious abuse used for radicalization. Further re-integration may happen through ideological, theological and organizational methods.
- Removal of socio-economic disparities in order to allay the fears of alienation and marginalization,
- Using media for public awareness programmes with a focus on the promotion of human rights and tolerance.
- Changes in the educational system with a focus on the promotion of human rights, diversity and philosophies like ***Vasudhaiva Kutumbakam*** with focus on **building community** resilience.

*Along with the above steps, we need to work with other nations in order to take necessary international action toward-*

---

[39] *Social Identity Theory studies the interplay between personal and social identities in order to specify and predict the circumstances under which individuals think of themselves as individuals or as group members.*

[40] *Social Movement Theory tries to explain the process of social mobilization in terms of why it occurs, forms of its manifestation and the potential social, cultural, and political consequences.*

- Internet-enabled Terrorism. It is the biggest cause of concern for security agencies in the 21st century as the internet has become the most vital part of modern society. It has created opportunities not just for the enemy nations to attack the cyber infrastructure of a nation but also gives easy access to the terrorist organizations in sharing their propaganda and operations-related content with lone-wolfs or creating self-radicalized individuals to carry lone wolf attacks. Therefore, we need to join the international Information Sharing mechanisms developed as a preventive measure by responsible intelligence agencies.

- Restricting the access of radical organizations to financing sources and building pressure on nations who actively help these agencies. Because of Pakistan support to LeT and JeM, India has worked hard for years to put Pakistan in the 'Black List' of Financial Action Task Force (FATF), (A Paris based intergovernmental body set up in 1989 to combat money-laundering and terror financing). Presently, Pakistan is in the Grey List. With an already fragile economy, Pakistan is in a situation where it can't risk too much and it will have to stop funding terrorist activities in order to avoid being put in Black List. Studies done in recent years suggest that these terrorist organizations get fund not just through the funding/charity or organized crimes like drugs or human trafficking but they themselves have developed different revenue sources through active engagement in various business activities like Real Estate, wildlife trade, Share market etc. So, we need to engage the international bodies like the UN to monitor these groups and take countermeasures.

Today, India is among the most dangerous nations of the world with 11 recognized terrorist organizations operating in it. According to Global Terrorism Index-2019, prepared by the Institute for Economic and Peace, India ranked 7th in the world. At the same time, the world has seen some of the most sophisticated and well-coordinated attacks in Paris and Brussels in November 2015 and March 2016 respectively.

Before the religious extremism in India takes the shape of the war of Islam, we need to purge such ideology from our society and stop people from believing in the legitimacy of joining a terrorist network or carrying out a terrorist attack. But in order to do that we need one Global definition of Terrorism. Though India is pushing for a Comprehensive Convention on International terrorism in the UN since 1986, yet it has not become a reality and some more efforts are required to make it happen.

# Insurgency in North-East region

India is a land of diversity. North-East region of India, also called as the land of the seven sisters, is home to more than 200 tribes and non-tribes spread across the mountains and plains of North-East with large scale socio-cultural, politico-economic, ethnic and linguistic differences among them. With mountains as a guard on all sides, the narrow stretch of Siliguri corridor is the only link for mainland India.

Because of this, they have largely remained isolated from external contact and their ethnic identities with diversity are as prominent as they were centuries ago. Also, the bad experiences of the outsider contact under the British Regime have caused many fears in their mind. Because of this, India's North-East region is called as the land of thousand mutinies with the presence of different forms of conflict like

- Tribal vs non-tribal,
- Resident vs non-resident, and
- Secession (separation from India) to sub-regional (greater power within the State to region), is going on in the region from pre-independence time with different means and strategies to achieve it.

To understand the problem properly and the steps taken by the government we have adopted the state-wise approach, detailing about the pattern of conflicts, their origins along with the bodies involved and their latest status. But before we look at each state lets understand a few things about ethnicity and ethno-nationalism.

### ETHNICITY AND ETHNO-NATIONALISM

**Ethnicity** is defined as the identification by a group as one based on socially perceived differences in national origin, biological inheritance, language and/or religion. It serves people as a basis for social categorization and at the national level we can have one, two or more ethnicities existing within one nation. E.g. If we talk about India, it is a multi-ethnic nation with presence of multi-religious, multi-biological and multi-linguistic people.

This large diversity of India leads to the creation of many sub-interest groups within India, with regionalism as the first common manifestation. Regionalism is considered as *the lack of commonality of ideals and shared emotional bonds and values among the people of a nation which leads to favouring a specific region over a greater area or nation.*

**Ethno-nationalism,** defined as the demand for a nation on the basis of biological, cultural, religious, linguistic or any other common identity, is a manifestation of regionalism where preference is given to a region or ethnicity over the nation. For a multi-ethnic nation like India, it has remained a major problem and threat to our democracy as some of them were violent and demanded separation from India.

These ethnicity-based movements can also be caused because of large unfulfilled aspirations of a group with a lesser voice in decision making in comparison to others who enjoy greater power and resources. The Constituent Assembly of India identified both forms of movement and tried to allay their concerns through constitutional mechanisms. The continuation of the previous measures from British India like Inner-Line Permits (ILP) or the insertion of constitutional safeguards under the 5th and 6th Schedule of the Constitution of India are some of the measures to preserve the multi-ethnic tribal regions of India.

Still the problems of regionalism and ethno-nationalism exist in India. The inadequate implementation of constitutional safeguards with fears of cultural hegemony, Land alienation etc. has fueled those movements. The North-East India is one such region where we have seen such movements from the marginalized ethnic identities as well as from the dominant ethnic identities of the region.

Some of these movements are considered to be supported by our neighboring nations in different capacities varying from providing a safe haven to direct help in terms of supply of weapons and other capacity-building measures.

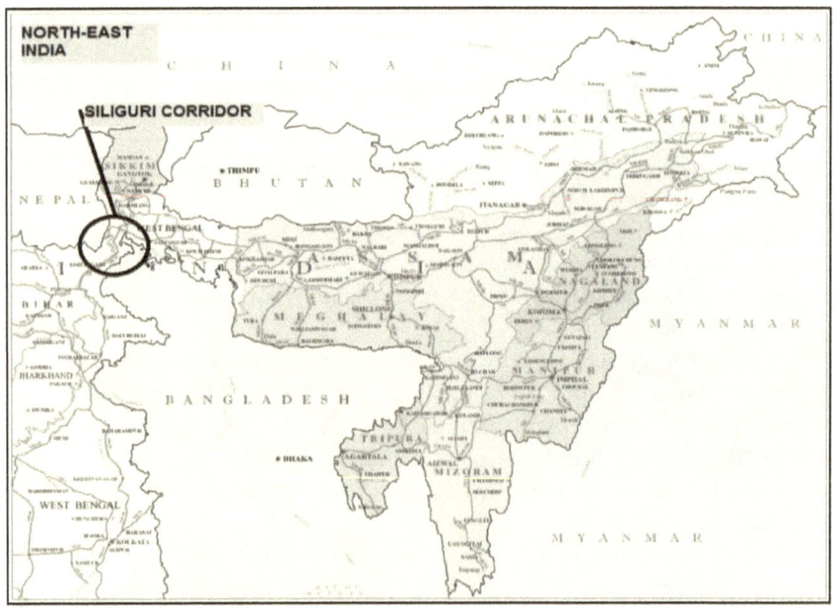


Figure 17 Map of North-East India (Image Courtesy: MDONER)

## ASSAM

Assam is the most-populated state of the North-East region. It is also the most connected to the mainstream in terms of infrastructure, culture etc. The first known civilizational contact with Assam goes to the time of Maharishi Vasistha, who had an ashram in Assam and brought Shaivism to Assam. In modern history, it was Srimanta Sankardev who revived the historical connect in form of Ekasarana Dharma, a Neo-Vaishnavite form of Hindu religion with numerous contributions to its art and culture like Sattriya (major dance form in Assam), Ankia naat and Bhaona (theatrical art form) or Borgeet (a form of music).

Though the works of Sankardev helped in building a commonly shared socio-cultural heritage yet the state suffers from problems of regionalism. This is also caused by the large influx of people from outside. First such influx happened during the British Regime, when Tea Plantation was introduced in the region. The second wave of such influx happened in the 1970s because of the large-scale atrocities on the people of East Pakistan (now Bangladesh) by West Pakistan.

These two waves of influx brought significant demographic changes to the region and local extremist outfits like the **United Liberation Front of Assam (ULFA)** emerged in the region. They gained larger public support because of the insecurities among the local population and the continued migration from our neighboring nation because of the religious persecution or better economic opportunities in India.

ULFA was created in April 1979 with the objective of establishing an independent state of Assam through armed struggle. Initially, it operated from Bhutan and enjoyed local support. By 1990, it started its operations against the security agencies. These indulgences in violence lead to large scale criminalization of ULFA cadres and they carried out crimes like kidnappings, bomb blasts and murder of migrant workers. In 2005, Bhutanese Army launched Operation All Clear to crack down on extremist outfits (including ULFA) operating from its territory. Though ULFA shifted to Bangladesh but it was weakened.

In 2009, the Chairman and Vice-chairman of ULFA were taken into custody by India. In 2011, Bangladesh also launched a major crackdown on ULFA leaders. All this helped the Indian government in bringing ULFA to talks on condition of dropping the demand for independent Assam and shun violence (suspension of operation) and a tripartite agreement was signed on 03 September 2011 between the Indian Government, State Government of Assam and ULFA. As of date, one faction of ULFA as ULFA (I) is functional under Paresh Baruah.

### Bodoland:

The second major point of contention in Assam is the Bodoland Territorial Region made of four upper Assam districts (Kokrajhar,

Chirang, Baksa and Udalguri) lying at the foothills of Bhutan. This region is inhabited by Boros/Bodos, also known as the Kacharis; forming the largest notified Scheduled Tribes group of Assam (5-6% of the state population).

This region is relatively backward and isolated in Assam. The British started tea plantations in the region and brought tribals from central India to work as tea labour. Under Gurudev Kalicharan Brahma, the first organization started among the indigenous Bodo people. But the first official demand for separate Bodoland state as 'Udayachal' was raised in 1967, after the formation of the Plains Tribal Council of Assam (PTCA) and All Bodo Students Union (ABSU).

But it remained dormant in operations. The signing of Assam Accord in 1985 served as an opportunity for ABSU (under its president Bodofa Upendra Nath) to once again revive the demand for a separate Bodoland State, as 'Bodoland'. The first Bodo militant group also emerged as the Bodo Security Force in 1986, later renamed as the **National Democratic Front of Bodoland** (NDFB). It started its operations with Bhutan as base and soon became the main militant face of demand for Bodoland. It targeted security forces as well as the non-Bodo people, particularly the tribals like Santhal, Munda or Oraon working in the region as labour in Tea Plantations.

In 1993, the first agreement was signed by the government with ABSU and Bodo Peoples' Action Committee (BPAC) in order to restore peace in the region. It led to the creation of Bodoland Autonomous Council with limited political powers in the region. But hardly any work was done towards the implementation of the agreement. In 1996, another group named Bodo Liberation Tiger Force (BLTF) came into the picture. 1996 was also the year of high violence during assembly elections from NDFB leading to the formation of Adivasi Cobra Force by other tribes in order to protect themselves from NDFB.

In 2003, the second Bodo Accord was signed with the militant group Bodo Liberation Tiger Force (BLTF) for creation of a Bodoland Territorial Council (BTC), to work as an autonomous body under the 6th Schedule of Constitution. The four districts of Bodoland were also classified as Bodoland Territorial Area District (BTAD) with BTC to look after 30 subjects in this area like education, forests, horticulture etc.

But the most active group which demanded Bodoland was still not on the table. In 2005, Bhutan launched Operation All Clear, a massive crackdown on all such militant organizations operating from its land. This weakened many while some moved to either Myanmar or Bangladesh. NDFB was also one among them and it signed a ceasefire agreement with the Indian Government.

This lead to factionalism in the group and by 2009 it got divided into two factions as-

I.    Pro-talks with no demand for secession under National Democratic Front of Bodoland- Progressive (NDFB-P), and

II.   Anti-talks with continued demand for secession under NDFB (ATF) with Ranjan Daimary as leader.

In 2010, Ranjan Daimary was arrested and more factions emerged in the group. One such faction was NDFB (R) under Ranjan Daimary which agreed to talks while the remaining anti-talk faction appointed I. K. Songbijit (from Karbi Society i.e. non-Bodo) as its leader. In 2013, another split happened and National Democratic Front of Bodoland- D.R. Nabia Faction emerged. Some other organizations are also present like National Democratic Front of Bodoland- Saoraigwra (NDFB-S) demanding Bodoland.

In 2014, a large scale massacre of tribals and other migrants was carried out by Songbijit group in order to reinforce his demand for a referendum and he tried to link other groups like Kamtapur Liberation Organisation (KLO) and ULFA but soon the NDFB removed him. With Indian Government growing a strong relationship with Myanmar, the Myanmar Army launched a massive crackdown to eliminate the operations of all Anti-India groups operating from its lands like ULFA-I, NDFB-S, NSCN-K, KLO and other Manipuri outfits in 2019.

This helped the government in gaining significant peace in the region and in January 2020, Saoraigwra group surrendered and on 27 January 2020 India signed the third accord with all the factions of NDFB along with other organizations like ABSU, United Bodo peoples' organisation for permanent peace in the region. Under the 3rd agreement, a series of steps are taken for the economic upliftment of the region and greater political empowerment of the Bodo people in a time-bound manner. The major points of this Bodo Accord include-

- To include all the Bodos dominated villages in the Bodoland Territorial Region which are outside BTAD while excluding the non-Bodo majority villages from it.
- A committee will be formed with members from ABSU and Bodoland Territorial Council (BTC) to decide the exclusion and inclusion of new areas and after such exercise, the Bodoland Territorial Council (BTC) will have 60 members in comparison to the existing 40.
- The non-Bodo majority of villages will have a Bodo-Kachari Welfare Council for focused development of Bodo villages outside BTAD.
- Bodos living in the hills would be conferred a Scheduled Hill Tribe status.

- Bodo language with Devanagari script would be the associate official language for the entire Assam.
- Overall, 1615 cadres from different factions of the NDFB surrendered and joined the mainstream. These people will be rehabilitated by the Assam Government and the Union Government.
- All non-heinous criminal cases are withdrawn against NDFB members while heinous crimes will be reviewed before an action
- A special development package of Rs 1500 crore will be given by the centre for specific developmental projects in the region and the families of all those people who were killed in the Bodo movement will get Rs 5 lakh each.

Many other organizations are also present in Assam with different demands like-

- Kamtapur Liberation Organisation (KLO, established in 1995) with demand for separate Kamtapur nation with districts from West Bengal and Assam), with demand for a separate nation;
- United People's Democratic Solidarity (UPDS, established in 1999 and disbanded in 2014) and Karbi Longri N.C. Hills Liberation Front (KLNLF, formed in 2004 as an armed wing) with demands for self-rule/self-determination by people of Karbi Anglong and Dima Hisao district.
- Muslim United Liberation Tigers of Assam (MULTA, established in 1996) is an Islamist extremist group with demand for the establishment of a Muslim state for Assam based on Sharia laws in districts of Dhubri, Nagaon, Morigaon and Darrang.

## NAGALAND

Before the arrival of British, Nagaland was among the most diverse parts of the North-East. It is dominated by different Naga tribes, who identify themselves to have origins from a common village, but over a time moved to different places taking separate identities with different customs and practices. Today, they live along the Himalayan Range in North East India with Nagaland as the mainland while some living in other States like Arunachal Pradesh and some living across Indian border in Myanmar.

The insurgency in Nagaland, also known as Naga Movement, started near the ending phase of colonial rule when Angami Phizo created the Naga National Council (NNC) in 1946. NNC demanded a separate nation for Naga people. Soon after independence, the movement started and the rising ideological contrast between the local leadership and the National leadership turned it into a violent movement. In 1975, a peace agreement was reached with NNC when it signed the Shillong Accord and gave up violence.

Some NNC members opposed it and in 1980 they formed NSCN (National Socialist Council of Nagaland). Within a few years, the leaders who played an important role in the formation of NSCN themselves got divided in two factions' as- NSCN-IM (lead by Isak Chishi Swu and Thuingaleng Muivah) and NSCN-K (lead by S.S. Khaplang) in 1988. The main demand of NSCN was to have a Nagalim, i.e. a Greater Nagaland State with full sovereignty. Later, they signed a ceasefire agreement for 14 years.

In August 2015, another peace accord was signed by the Government of India with NSCN-IM to further the dialogue process and ensure proper peace and stability for better growth of the region. Some other groups also joined the peace process. But NSCN-K isn't part of the accord as it is mainly composed of Naga people from Myanmar and it doesn't want peace in the region. E.g. in 2015, it played an important role in the creation of the United National Liberation Front of Western South East Asia (UNLFW) with other militant organizations to continue violence and carried out the 2015 ambush attack on Indian Army where 18 soldiers were killed.

This peace accord is significant as NSCN (IM) has given up its demand for 'Greater Nagaland' and vowed allegiance to the constitution of India. The Government of India has also made clear that existing boundaries of states will not be altered, giving much-needed assurance to neighbouring states. Recently, the Government of Nagaland has also initiated a Register of Indigenous Inhabitants of Nagaland (RIIN) to identify the indigenous people and restrict the enjoyment of local resources or government schemes for them, as guaranteed by Article 371 (A) of the Constitution. This will help in giving a greater sense of security and relief to the local people.

## MANIPUR

Manipur is unique in comparison to other states of North-East. Though we had kingdoms in other states also but Manipur has seen a continuity of such rule existing from the times of legendary kings from 50 BC to the last Kangleipak Kingdom, which ruled the region from $12^{th}$ century AD till the British rule. For a brief it acted as an independent state after independence, only to join India on 15 October 1949.

This unique situation of Manipur is made possible by the demographic features of Manipur, where nearly 70% of people identify to one community (Meitei Community) and rule of Meitei community over the valley, one-fourth area of Manipur. Tribals account for another thirty per cent of the State's population, with Naga, Kuki-Chin and Mizo groups as the main tribes.

Soon after its integration with India, problems started as Manipur was made part of Assam. The ongoing insurgency in the neighbouring regions like Nagaland and Mizoram enhanced division in Manipur as well. E.g. National Socialist Council of Nagaland (NSCN) started its operations in the Manipur region because of which other tribes like Kuki also formed guerrilla groups.

In the 1960s, the Meitei insurgency also started because of the resentment against its merger. In 1964, an insurgent group United National Liberation Front started its operation in Manipur with the aim of having a sovereign nation. Some Meitei people also started their own organizations like People's Revolutionary Party of Kangleipak (PREPAK, established in 1977), People's Liberation Army of Manipur (PLA, formed in 1978) and Kangleipak Communist Party (KCP, established in 1980). All of them are armed insurgent groups demanding a separate and independent homeland with affiliation to communist ideology of Mao Zedong, also known as Maoism. They used guerrilla warfare against Indian security agencies and Police forces. UNLF also established its own armed wing, the Manipur People's Army in 1987.

The prime source of finances for these groups includes extortion, arms trading etc. In 2011, another group came into the picture as Maoist Communist Party of Manipur while some of the previous groups started fading because of the arrest or neutralization of their commanders. On 05 October 2012, most of the active insurgent groups of Manipur joined one umbrella organisation CorCom (Coordination/Core Committee) to reverse the gains made by the security forces and to win people's support. Its members include PLA, PREPAK, KCP, UNLF, KYKL (Kanglei Yawoi Kanna Lup, formed in 1994) and UPPK (United People's Party of Kangleipak) joining it. But the unity was short-lived and all members of the UPPK surrendered in 2013 to join the peace process. Many other Meitei insurgent groups have also signed a Memorandum of Understanding (MoU) with the government of India and the state government in order to join the peace process.

Some are still active and in 2015 they joined another umbrella organisation, United National Liberation Front of Western South East Asia (UNLFW). UNLFW is led by the National Socialist Council of Nagaland- Khaplang (NSCN-K) and United Liberation Front of Assam faction ULFA (I) operating under Paresh Baruah. The UNLFW first meeting was organized at Taga, Myanmar. Seven major groups which operate in different parts of North-East and joined UNLFW include ULFS-Independent, KCP, KYKL, PREPAK, PLA, UNLF and NDFB-(Songbijit Faction).

Our intelligence agencies gathered information that Chinese agencies were behind the meeting and promised weapons and logistics to carry out the operations. In June 2015, UNLFW carried out its first major attack in Manipur leading to the death of 18 military personnel. Indian Army responded to the attack through the surgical strikes in Myanmar, targeting the NSCN-K and other probable available on the site.

The strong support shown by India to Myanmar in its ongoing crisis in the Rakhine region and other equipment to its armed forces has helped India to gain greater support from the Myanmar Army. Finally, in 2019 Myanmar Army carried out massive strikes against these groups, helping India in establishing considerable peace in the region. The political representatives also followed the steps to meet the demands of local people by giving approval to the long-pending demand for introduction of Inner Line Permits in Manipur.

**INNER LINE PERMITS (ILPs)**

Inner Line Permits is a mechanism, developed by the British regime, in order to remove the fears or concerns of the local tribes because of increased outsider's presence while protecting their own commercial interests (tea, oil and ivory trade) in the region. It was first introduced through **Bengal Eastern Frontier Regulation, 1873,** limiting the contact of British Subjects with local tribes in areas like Cachar, Darrang, Kamrup, Lakhimpur, Nagaon Sivasagar etc. and the Hill regions like Garo Hills, Khasi Hills, Jaintia Hills and Naga Hills spread across the Northeast region.

Post-independence, India continued with ILPs while altering its boundaries, by lifting ILP from some North-East states like Assam and Meghalaya along with the extension of special provisions to certain states. ILPs control the inflow of outsiders in the protected areas of Northeast by restricting entries without permission and putting a time limit on entries.

In 2015 and in 2018, the Manipur Government introduced 'The Manipur Peoples Bill, 2018' in order to protect the local people and ensure socio-economic and cultural balance. Finally, from the start of 2020, ILP was introduced in Manipur in order to allay the fears of the Citizenship Amendment Act and protect the local identity.

Apart from the valley people, we had considerable tension among the tribes themselves. It is estimated that because of the violence between Nagas and Kukis more than 2000 lives were lost since 1990. Under such circumstances, signing of Nagaland Peace Framework by the government with NSCN (IM) is a positive step. This framework gives assurance to safeguard the 'territorial integrity of Manipur', establishing comparative peace and calm among the tribes.

## TRIPURA

Though a tribal land for long, demography of Tripura quickly changed in 1947 when the partition of India happened and many Bengali speaking

Hindus migrated to Tripura moved from East-Pakistan. They took over the plains, which indigenous tribes considered as their agricultural land. By the end of the 1970s, the local tribes started their resistance as instead of reduction, more people started to settle in the region because of religious persecutions and other reasons from East-Pakistan (now Bangladesh).

Finally, by the end of 1980s militant outfits started to appear with Tripura National Volunteers (TNV) as the first group, formed in 1988 by indigenous people. In 1989, the National Liberation Front of Tripura (NLFT) and in 1990, All Tripura Tiger Force were established. The resultant tensions caused major violence and widespread terror with the tribal-dominated Tripura National Volunteers (TNV) emerging as one of the most violent extremist outfits.

The set up of Tripura Tribal Areas Autonomous District Council (TTAADC) under the TTAADC Act 1979 with its inclusion under the purview of the provisions of 'Sixth Schedule' (through 49th Amendment) has helped in effective decentralization in the 'non-scheduled areas'. TTAADC has 30 seats, with 25 being reserved for Scheduled Tribes and another 2 being nominated by the Governor. Around 68% of the State area, covering the hills and forests of the state, comes under TTAADC which enjoys the executive and legislative powers over it.

For reforms in plain cultivable areas, land reforms were introduced and agriculture was promoted among the tribes as well. Also, steps are taken to improve the connectivity of the region with the mainland and create infrastructure in order to increase participation from tribes. The signing of the Land Boundary Agreement with Bangladesh, resolving the dispute on land with better fencing of the border has further helped in easing tensions.

## MEGHALAYA

Meghalaya was carved out of Assam and the State of Meghalaya was formed in 1972, with Gharo, Khasi and Jaintia Hill areas as part of the State. Though a number of organizations like Hynniewtrep Achik Liberation Council (HALC, established in 1992) emerged but it soon divided into Hynniewtrep National Liberation Council (HNLC) and Achik Matgrik Liberation Army (AMLA). Some new organizations were also established like Garo National Liberation Army (GNLA, founded in 2009) for sovereign Garoland but they were largely limited to crimes like extortion, oil smuggling, coal mining or small scale violence against Bengali speaking migrants. The membership of these organizations is in two figures only and they lack people support because of the criminal element.

In the past, some bigger militant organizations with operations in other states like Assam (ULFA and NDFB) tried to make it their hub and established links with GNLA. Today, those outfits are part of the peace process or the operational factions lack the influence and capabilities to disturb the peace in Meghalaya. Because of this, Meghalaya is considerably peaceful in comparison to other areas.

## ARUNACHAL PRADESH

At the time of independence, Arunachal Pradesh was known as North-East Frontier Tract (NEFA, created by British in 1914). With Independence, it was merged into Assam and in 1954 it was established as North-East Frontier Agency, based on the Tribal Panchsheel model of Verrier Elwin and PM Jawaharlal Nehru with the Governor of Assam as administrative head. In 1972, it was converted into the union territory of Arunachal Pradesh and in 1987 full state status was given to Arunachal Pradesh.

The care shown by Indian Government since independence with tribal Panchsheel helping the local people to develop their own genius helped in keeping peace in the state and strong integration of its people with India despite the claims from China on a large part of it. Only some fringe elements like the National Liberation Council of Taniland (NCLT) demanding Taniland or the parts of Tirap District demanded by the National Socialist Council of Nagaland (NSCN) as part of Greater Nagaland were points of worry.

But the strong will with which the people of Arunachal Pradesh stand with India has kept the NCLT defunct and the dropping of the demand of Greater Nagaland by NSCN-IM has ensured peace in those parts of Tirap District as well. Today, Hindi is the lingua franca of the region and the only sour point is the question on the settlement of Chakma refugees from Bangladesh.

## MIZORAM

Mizoram represents the state which went to one of the most violent insurgency and subsequently returned to permanent peace with the signing of Mizo Accord of 1986 and the recent Bru accord. The insurgency in Mizoram started under Pu Laldenga because of the neglect of Mizo people in Assam with ghastly apathy shown by the central government during the dreadful famine of 1959.

In 1961, Pu Laldenga established the Mizo National Front (MNF). Many Chakma refugees also started to come and settle in the Mizo region from 1964, creating a further sense of anger among the Mizos. Finally, in 1966 a major revolt was organized by MNF to establish a sovereign state of Mizos. This included attacks on government offices and security agencies. Soon, security agencies reversed the gains made by the MNF and recaptured all the offices. This included the use of IAF, the only incidence of Indian history when India used IAF for airstrikes in its own territory.

In 1972, Mizoram was separated from Assam and established as a Union Territory. But the struggle continued till 1986 when the Mizoram Peace Accord was signed by MNF with the Government of India. On 20 February 1987, Mizoram was recognized as a state with Aizawl as its capital. This accord helped in the establishment of a decade of complete peace and harmony in Mizoram, only to be disturbed by the ethnic clashes of 1997 between Bru and Mizos, leading to the displacement of nearly 30,000 Bru tribes (also called Reang) from their home.

The Bru tribe is ethically different from the Mizos and traditionally settled in the region of Mizoram, Tripura and southern Assam. Most of them live in Tripura (around 2 lakh) and are recognized as a Reang Tribe. The prime reason for the 1997 clash was the demand from the Bru tribe to have an Autonomous District Council for western Mizoram Areas with a sizable population of Bru. This demand was partly influenced by the 1994 peace accord signed by the state government with Hmar People's Convention (HPC), which led to the formation of Sinlung Hills Development Council (SHDC, now renamed as Sinlung Hills Council in 2018). HPC represented the Hmar tribe spread in the North and North-West part of Mizoram.

But the demand for an Autonomous District Council took an ugly turn when it turned violent. A Bru militant group, named Bru National Liberation Front (BNLF) started the violence by kidnapping and murdering a Mizo forest official. Angry Mizos of nearby villages burnt the Bru huts, forcing nearly half of the Brus in Mizoram to take refuge in Tripura. Though some families returned to Mizoram because of support from the union government in 2010 and 2018 but many remained displaced.

The long period of other displaced people finally ended in January 2020, when a quadripartite agreement was signed by the Union Government with the State of Tripura, State of Mizoram and the Bru-Reang tribe. According to this agreement, the displaced Bru people who are living in the Tripura camps will have a permanent settlement in Tripura with a rehabilitation package of Rs 600 crore from the Union Government. Each Bru family will be given a plot of land and a fixed deposit of 4 lakh with Rs 5000 cash per month and free ration for two years. Additional help of 1.5 lakh will be given to them for the building of the home.

## Present Situation of North-East

In the last few years, a considerable sense of peace and calm has returned to the North-East region. The credit for it goes to the successive governments who understood the needs of some tribe and some region at different times and did their best to solve the issues. In the last 5-6years, a special focus is given to the problems of North-East and government has used all the resources at its disposal including the use of force, international cooperation, organizing bigger festivals and bringing economic prosperity to the region through improved connectivity and tourism development with a focus on preserving its ecology.

Part of the credit also goes to the state of Sikkim which has shown a developmental model for all the small yet ecological rich states through its tourism and organic farming. The Government of India is planning to extend the same model to the Union Territory of Ladakh. Today, the majority of the North-East tribes have overcome the hypothetical fears created for long about mainstream people diluting their socio-cultural identity.

The increasing tourism and removal of Armed Forces (Special Powers) Act or AFSPA from states like Tripura (2015) and Meghalaya (2018) is a welcome sign of returning peace. It shows that not just the local people but security agencies are also more confident of peace returning in the region. Arunachal Pradesh is at peace and with the signing of Bodo peace Accord, it is hoped that the struggle which claimed more than 4,000 lives will also come to an end. The final positive outcome on the Nagaland Peace Framework and the recent ILP in Manipur will help in bringing sustainable peace in the region with full integration through rail, road and air network by 2022, as promised by the ex-Home Minister Rajnath Singh. If the Ministry of Development of North Eastern Region carries its duty of planning, execution and monitoring of development schemes and projects in the North-Eastern Region with sincerity in next 5 years, the North-East region will become the biggest engine to India's dream of $ 5trillion economy by 2024.

## Language issues

India is a land of diversity. Like ethnic diversity, India displays a very high linguistic diversity in terms of the language and dialects spoken by people. This high linguistic diversity of language and dialects in India was first officially studied by the linguistic survey conducted by GA Grierson (1898-1927). In his Linguistic survey, GA Grierson identified 179 distinct languages with nearly 544 dialects across India.

These Indian languages are classified into four main language families, on the basis of origin, as:

a) **Indo-European language family:** These are the languages with origin in Aryan family, starting from the Vedic Sanskrit and having close contact with the European languages.

b) **Dravidian language family:** These are the languages which are spoken in the Deccan and South Indian regions, including the Munda language from central India.

c) **Tibeto-Chinese language family:** These are the languages which are believed to have origins from the Chinese mainland and spoken in the Indian States sharing a border or close to China like the Tibeto Himalayas, Sikkim, Assam and other North-Eastern states. These languages are also known as the KIRATA group of languages.

d) **Austro-Asiatic language family:** These are the languages which trace their roots to the Austric language family and spoken by the tribals of India living in central India. These languages are also known as the NISHAD group of languages.

During the British regime, the Indian National Congress (INC) started to demand the formation of states on linguistic bases. From 1920, INC started to establish its provincial committees on linguistic basis and in 1927 INC declared "the redistribution of provinces on a linguistic basis" as one of its major commitments.

At the time of independence, India had the big problem of not just the integration of the large number of princely states in India but to form a Union of states from them. Sardar Patel successfully carried out the integration of 552 princely states in the Indian Union and a number of states emerged as part of India. This organization of states created a challenge for the Indian Union, requiring careful reorganization of States.

Subsequently, a commission was set up under S. K. Dhar in June 1948 'to study the feasibility of State reorganization based on a linguistic basis.' The commission gave its report in 1948 and recommended state reorganization based on Geographical contiguity, Financial Self-reliance, Administrative viability and Potential for development rather than linguistic basis.

In 1948, Indian National Congress formed another committee under Jawaharlal Nehru, Sardar Patel and Pattabhi Sitaramayya (JVP Committee) to consider the recommendations of the Dhar Commission. It also rejected the reorganization of states on linguistic factors. It recommended that the reorganization of states should be on the basis of security, unity and economic prosperity of the nation.

In addition to the above challenge of linguistic based state reorganization we had another challenge in the form of national language of India. Many leaders from various regions were worried that the Hindi language will subjugate their language and culture. The constituent assembly also discussed it and based on the Munshi-Ayyangar formula, Part XVII of the Indian Constitution was added. This part was introduced to not just resolve the issue of national language but to protect and promote the linguistic diversity as well. Based on the Munshi-Ayyangar formula:

- India will have no National Language but Hindi in Devanagari script shall be the official language of the Union. The international form of Indian Numerals shall be the official form of numerals of the Union.
- States were given the freedom to choose own official languages,
- A number of languages will be recognized as scheduled Languages (presently 22 under 8th Schedule). The scheduled language status makes it a binding on the government to take measures for the development of a scheduled language in order to let it grow and become an effective means of communication in due course of time, and
- English will continue as an official language for the next 15 years after the enactment of the Constitution.

But both measures failed to calm the nerves and we faced two forms of linguistic agitations in India. The first form of agitation was the demand for reorganization of states on the basis of language. The second form of agitation was against the use of another language, seen as an imposition by other people. The 1950s started with linguistic bitterness in the newly created Union of India. The protests in Andhra Pradesh (a part of the State of Madras) for creation of a separate state for Telugu speaking people and death of Poti Sriramulu in the hunger strike, led to 1st state creation on the basis of linguistic identity, Andhra Pradesh under the State of Andhra Pradesh Act 1953. It gave rise to many other linguistic aspirations, forcing the Government to set up a new committee for Reorganization of State based on a linguistic basis.

This led to the formation of the 3rd Committee under Justice F. Fazl Ali (Chairman) with H. N. Kunzru and K. M. Panikkar as members. The committee submitted its report in 1955 and gave four major factors for the reorganization of states as:

a) Linguistic and Cultural Homogeneity,
b) Preservation and strengthening of the unity and security of the nation,
c) Financial, economic and administrative considerations, and
d) Planning and promotion of the welfare of the people in each state as well as of the nation as a whole.

Based on its report, the States Reorganization Act was passed by parliament, under Seventh Constitution Amendment in 1956; reorganizing the states of India on linguistic basis. The restructuring of Indian states under Constitutional (Seventh Amendment) Act, 1956 led to the division of Indian Territory into 14 States and 6 Union territories. Also, to remove the bitterness and to create a healthy inter-State and Centre-State relation, Zonal Councils were created under the State Reorganisation Act, 1956.

But the fears of language dominance have remained a cause of concern for many states especially in South India even before the independence. This has resulted in solely language-based agitations as well as agitations where the imposition of one language added to other grievances. E.g. The first Anti-Hindi agitations of Tamil Nadu happened in 1937 when Rajaji introduced Hindi as a compulsory part of secondary schools. The idea was to help the locals in moving beyond the Tamil region and utilize the jobs and business opportunities across India.

The agitations were led by E.V. Ramasamy (Periyar) with fasts, marches, picketing and protests as the ways of agitation. Though the Constituent Assembly settled the debate for 15 years but nearing the end of that period, fears started to reappear in South India. In order to allay those fears, Official language Act 1963 was enacted with Hindi as the official language with English to continue even after 1965. Due to some reservations on the language used in the Official Language Act and attempts to end English in a few states, Anti-Hindi agitations started again on 25 January 1965.

So, the Act was amended in 1967 to provide for the use of English until a resolution was passed to that effect by the legislature of every state that had not adopted Hindi as its official language, and by each house of the Indian Parliament. Similar fears were also present within states. E.g. The denial of entry to Mizo language in the Official Languages of Assam was one of the reasons for the Mizo uprising. Similarly, Gorkha people also showed unhappiness on the introduction of Bengali in the Hill area.

Similar agitations have happened many times because of various reasons/fears like the National Education Policy in 1985 or the recent draft Education Policy released by the government. Recently, in Karnataka, we had agitations because of three languages used on Bengaluru Metro (2017) and on the celebration of Hindi Divas (2019).

At the same time, we have seen a number of languages being vanished from India because of various reasons. In 2010, UNESCO released an Atlas of World Languages in Danger which identified nearly 2500 languages across the world as the languages under Danger. With India being the land of high linguistic diversity, maximum languages in danger were found to be from India (197 languages) with USA (191) and Brazil (190) as the other main countries with very high language threat.

Dr, B.R. Ambedkar also said, *"One language can unite people. Two languages are sure to divide people. This is an inexorable law. Culture is conserved by language. Since Indians wish to unite and develop a common culture, it is the bounden duty of all Indians to own up Hindi as their official language."* So, we need to take steps which not only remove the threats on the imposition of another language but also help in protecting the languages from going extinct.

The Bodo accord presents a model to protect smaller languages or languages/dialects with no script. Similarly, to remove the fears of imposition we need to present a lingua franca which goes beyond the present. One such language in older times was Sanskrit. Sanskrit is not just the language which is considered to be the oldest language with written texts but a language with rich vocabulary. E.g. Sanskrit contains 280 synonyms for water based on the not just the different forms or functions of water but also the diverse names by which it is called in different parts of the time.

But we need to see every issue and linguistic movement in detail. It is not just the question of language but we have seen that geography, ethnicity, religious identities and demographic features play an important role in these movements. We have seen situations where attempts are made to use language as a tool for political mobilization or to cut people from their history. An apt example of it was Macaulay, who wrote in a letter to his father, "No Hindoo who has received an English education ever remains sincerely attached to his religion."

## Left-Wing Extremism (LWE)/Naxalism

When in 2006, Prime Minister Dr. Manmohan Singh called Naxalism as the biggest threat to the internal security of India, many were taken aback. As we learnt earlier, Kashmir insurgency claimed far more life in comparison to any other insurgency, including the ones in North-East and the Naxalism. So, it becomes important to know the origins, expansion, present situation and philosophy behind the LWE which makes it the biggest threat to internal security. At the same time we need to find ways to address the challenges posed by it to the internal security.

**The Naxal movement** traces its history to May 1967 Naxalbari uprising, in Naxalbari village of Darjeeling district against the jotedars (local Zamindars or landlords). It started with the peasants taking over the land of jotedars by force and the subsequent violence which led to the killing of a few villagers and police personnel. One of the reasons for this situation was the poor implementation of the land reforms and the constitutional safeguards under the 5th schedule. E.g. Land reforms were introduced to put a ceiling on individual land holdings and to redistribute the land.

The major leaders of the movement included Charu Majumdar, Kanu Sanyal and Jangal Santhal, who were part of the Communist Party of India (CPI), founded before independence. In 1964, the CPI suffered a division and the Communist Party of India (Marxist) or CPI (M) came in the picture. Both of these parties believed in the politics of India and winning through elections. So, the far-left radical elements who believed in the idea of armed revolution separated from the party. This group was lead by the same three leaders of naxalbari movement. In 1969, they moved out of the CPI (M) and formed Communist Party of India (Marxist-Leninist) or CPI (ML).

The '*Historic Eight Documents*', a set of eight monographs written by Charu Majumdar during 1965-67 became the foundations of LWE. These documents focused on fighting the modern revisionism or the political democracy set up in India. Many other such organizations were established and focused on gaining power through armed rebellion. It largely attracted the tribals from the regions of high poverty and backwardness. At its peak, Maoists claimed to have influence from Pashupati to Tirupati, i.e. from Pashupatinath Temple of Nepal to Tirupati temple of Andhra Pradesh.

This was also known as the 'Red Corridor" or the Left-Wing Extremist influenced regions with presence in more than 200 districts of India. With Law and Order being a state subject, the state used police force supported by the Central Reserve Police Force (CRPF) to contain Naxalism. In 2004, most of the Left-Wing radical organizations like Maoist Communist Centre of India (MCCI), People's War Group and its People's Liberation Guerilla Army etc. joined and established Communist Party of India (Maoist). The main objective of the organization was to overthrow the government of India through the Maoist strategy of people's war[41].

Because of this basic idea behind the Naxal movement of using armed rebellion to overthrow government and the influence, it garnered over the Indian Territory, Dr Manmohan Singh said "Naxalism remains the biggest internal security challenge and it is imperative to control Left Wing Extremism (LWE) for the country's growth." In 2006, MHA also took note of the deteriorating law and order situation and created a Left Wing Extremism Division on October 19, 2006. This Division was created in order to have better coordination between all the Left-Wing affected states with the centralization of response against the increasing unification of extremist groups.

This lead to a series of steps from CRPF like the COBRA Battalion (**CO***mmando* **B***attalion for* **R***esolute* **A***ction*) established by it in 2008 with specialization in guerilla tactics and jungle warfare operations or the State Governments launching all-out offensives in coordination with the CRPF like Operation Green Hunt by Chhattisgarh Government. Some tribal groups also joined the efforts of the Government, as the

---

[41] *People's war is a strategy developed by Chinese leader Mao Zedong, focusing on gaining people's support by presenting it as people's war and using guerilla warfare tactics by drawing the enemy deep in its own bastion.*

Salwa Judum established under Mahendra Karma by the local tribals of Chhattisgarh to counter Naxalite violence.

The State Government also supported Salwa Judum initially but later withdrew its support, after the Supreme Court decision on declaring it illegal in 2011. Among all this, many tribes were mute spectators with slightly greater sympathy for the Naxals because of the absence of administrative structure with poor facilities and delayed grievance redressal. Naxals fill that vacuum and garner support for their activities by filling that space through various measures like quick justice through its Kangaroo courts.

Therefore, in 2009 the Government of India launched its Integrated Action Plan, focusing not just on dealing with Naxalism as a security issue but also a developmental issue requiring coordinated efforts from the centre and all concerned states. Idea behind IAP was to not just hit the Naxals in Combat but also to end the local support enjoyed by Naxals. The Integrated Action Plan works on achieving this through grass-root development projects, starting from the 78 highly affected districts of that time.

It gave importance to local administration and focused on the education and health infrastructure in the tribal areas. An increased focus is given to skill training of the tribal people as well. E.g. Roshini scheme is started for skill training of local youth with 50% women strength. Prayas initiative is taken by the Chhattisgarh government for the higher education and competition exam preparation of tribal students.

In 2015, a significant step was taken towards the welfare and development of Particularly Vulnerable Tribal Groups (PVTGs) through **Vanbandhu Kalyan Yojana**. This scheme tries to create high quality social and physical infrastructure in an accelerated manner through strategic interventions. It tries to have an integrated, holistic and inclusive development of tribal communities by focusing on quality education, health, livelihood development, housing, drinking water, cultural heritage protection etc.

Some of the objectives of the scheme include- the creation of Special Health Centres for PVTGs area beyond the National Health Mission with improved infrastructure, medicine availability and types of equipment with qualified manpower. Special focus is given on genetic diseases and to extend 100% health facility coverage of pregnant mothers and immunization of children.

It targets to achieve 100% physical enrolment in schools by setting up large residential co-educational schools in PVTG areas with training and engagement of local educated people along with special incentives to attract other good teachers. Other features include flexible schooling (for adjusting to local needs or festivals), special coaching before the start of the new session, special focus on dropped-out students, regular health check-up at schools etc. It will also promote Eco-tourism and revival of traditional nutritious crops with proper crop rotation and develop multi-cropping patterns.

After the physical and social infrastructure, the next important step is to improve livelihood. Therefore, under Special Central Assistance to Tribal Sub Plan, it works toward the convergence of resources between different agencies, like Integrated Dairy Development program, promotion of dairy cooperatives, set up of chilling plants in tribal regions with assured power supply and finance. Focus is also on bringing greater integration of the region with mainstream through MUDRA bank, rural connectivity (through PMGSY), electricity to all households (through Saubhagya Scheme) and other initiatives.

Similarly, different departments of the Ministry of Agriculture like Department of Agriculture, Cooperation and Farmers Welfare (DAC) and Department of Agriculture, Research and Education (DARE) work with KVIC, TRIFED etc. in order to promote scientific farming and bee-keeping. These initiatives not only provide scientific inputs but also the market linkages as well.

Also, in past few years, many new laws are framed to address the long-pending demands from the tribal groups like

- The Scheduled Tribes and Other Traditional Forest Dwellers (Recognition of Forest Rights) Act, 2006 to provide a framework recognizing and vesting **Land Rights** (up to 4 hectares), **Use rights** (to collect Minor forest produce, use of grazing grounds and water bodies) and **Right to protect and conserve the forests.**
- Panchayats (Extension to Scheduled Areas) Act 1996 **to promote self-governance in tribal areas in Scheduled Areas** under the 5th Schedule.
- Right to Fair Compensation and Transparency in Land Acquisition, Rehabilitation and Resettlement Act (2013) to limit land acquisition with fair compensation, proper rehabilitation and resettlement measures.

Because of the joint efforts from Security agencies with the State and Central Government, the sphere of LWE influence has rapidly reduced. Today, it is active mainly in Chhattisgarh, Jharkhand and Odisha region along with a few districts of neighbouring states. From 76 districts of 2013 with violence attributed to the Left-Wing Extremism the number of districts has reduced to 60 districts in 2018, with 89% of violence being concentrated in 30 districts only.

**Future of Naxal Movement:**

After a struggle of more than 50 years, a significant calm has reached in the region. More than 12,000 people have lost their lives in the process with 9,300 being civilians killed on the apprehension of the informer or caught in the crossfire. The Naxalite movement reached its peak in 2009-10 but the National Policy and Action Plan to address the LWE problem in a comprehensive manner through a multi-pronged strategy helped us in addressing security concerns with the promotion of rights and sense of entitlement among the local community.

Still we need to be careful in order to avoid the reemergence of the movement, as it can be a tactical pause or strategic rethinking from them. Our efforts to redress to the old problems of deprivation and displacement in the tribal regions are still in the early stage and government needs to make more efforts toward

a. Greater physical connectivity of tribal people with the mainstream through better physical infrastructure,
b. Greater financial connectivity through opening of bank accounts, loans, distribution of LPG-Stoves, LEDs etc., and
c. Greater knowledge connectivity through social infrastructure development like educational and health institutes.

These are the basic minimums expected by everyone from the government. The powers extended to local panchayats through PESA Act and other acts like FRA has helped in increasing the confidence of local tribes in governance. In comparison, the Naxal movement is shrinking to few tribes left as foot soldiers and largely the non-tribal leadership of the movement. We need to further consolidate our gains against the naxals and take further steps to:

- Block the supply of weapons to the Naxals,
- Restrict the supply of money for such operations and focus on removing the illegal trade measures used by them to generate funds,
- Keep a look at the movement of top leadership and counter any international help which might be coming to them,
- Ensure faithful implementation of all the constitutional safeguards, and
- Anticipate the future moves of the ideological backup behind the present Naxalite movement and counter it. E.g. Experts believe that so-called 'Urban Naxalism' is actively joined by the radical-left ideologues. The shrinking space of the Naxalite movement is more problematic for them rather than the foot soldiers. It is an onus on the security agencies and government to properly identify the risks involved. As Dr Manmohan Singh said, "Development is the biggest weapon against Naxalism", we should focus on overall development across India.

## Future of India: Capitalism with Socialism

We had long debates and ideological clashes in the past including the Cold War between the ideologies of Socialism and Capitalism. Even today, many people in India feel proud to be socialist while even the nations who succeeded with Socialism or its other branches like Communism, all adopted features from Capitalism to achieve economic success and have more sustainable prosperity. E.g. Whether it was the New Economic Policy of Vladimir Lenin or the Chinese economic reforms of 1978 all included the features of Capitalism.

In India, the State worked as a Socialist State. But the growth was too slow in those years and few economic failures were also faced by India. Because of one such failure, India moved more towards the capitalist model. The introduction of Liberalization, Privatization and Globalization (LPG) as economic reforms in the 1990s was part of it. With nearly 30 years of such reforms, we can fairly access the benefits of the rising MNC culture. Let's look at the economic comparison between an Indian MNC and its equivalence to the different states of India.

| Economic parameter | Performance of TCS | Equivalent To |
| --- | --- | --- |
| Total Revenue | 1 Lakh 30 Thousand crore | The budget of states like Haryana or Kerala |
| Corporate tax Paid | 10,000 crore | More than Budget of State like Sikkim and Mizoram |
| Employee Strength | 4 Lakh plus jobs with an entry-level income of 3.5 Lakh | Employees by a State like Haryana 2.5 Lakh with nearly 70% as Group C and D |
| Other Features | TCS earns a significant amount of foreign revenue with more than half of its revenue being earned from a global operation | |

If we don't get into the unwanted details of the type of operation or services offered by both and just stick to pure economic comparison (as the comparison isn't to show problems with state government but to show the importance of an entrepreneur or MNC), can someone claim that we don't need private corporations in India?

Today, the number of jobs created by such companies and the overall economic benefits created by an efficiently run MNC are vital to aid the efforts of the state government. Similarly, the Revenue of Reliance Industries (3,80,438 crores) is next only to the Budget of Uttar Pradesh and Maharashtra in India. It paid more than 12,000 crore of taxes in a year and created a significant number of jobs in India.

So, what is also needed is responsible capitalism having high standards of corporate governance which can add to the government efforts of creating more jobs and economic prosperity in India. It is also one of the reasons because of which parties with a basis in socialist or communist ideas are becoming less insignificant or moving to other issues. Today, a labourer working in a decent company wants his son or daughter to become engineer, doctor and join a reputed MNC rather than to live in ideas which are becoming less relevant today.

This comparison is done with the prime purpose of letting you know that the corporate organizations are as important as a private citizen and we need as much effort and care from the government to look after business needs as the private citizens. It will help us in generating not just the significant economic synergies but to fund the necessary basic services from the government like the security, law and order etc. through taxes.

## Communal Violence

Communal Violence starts from the idea of communalism. Communalism is defined as a positive integrating force among local communities, integrating people with each other with a sense of being one. When two or more communities belonging to different communalism have fallout against each other and violence happens, it is termed as communal violence. With such a high diversity, it becomes difficult to preserve the 'unity in diversity'.

Incidents of communal violence are common in India for long with recorded incidents in history since the 18th century. In India, it is mainly linked to the fallouts of ethnic or religious consolidation, i.e. when it is used to incite violence or to create a divide among people. The communal violence starts with the basic philosophy where we have a community with three beliefs as:

1) Belief in **common interests** among a group (these common interests can be the social, economic, political or cultural reason),

2) A belief that another groups interest is **different** from them, and

3) A belief that their interests are at a **crossroad** with another group's interest.

In Ancient India, because of its high diversity in terms of caste, ethnic and cultural differences marked with absence of modern communication means, such incidents were restricted to limited space with limited scale. In medieval times such incidents became more intense and frequent because of foreign invasions. Some of those invasions had the primary aim of loot with visible presence of religious calls for violence, recorded by people like Amir Khusrow or the subsequent texts with Timur's massacre in Delhi being the biggest one. Even during the

British rule, similar incidents of communal violence were recorded with basis in identities like religion, caste or any other ethnic differences.

With independence, it was hoped that the miseries of people will end and they will live in harmony. But the declaration of Indian independence also came with the ingredients for the biggest communal violence in the form of partition on religious lines, leading to the formation of East and West Pakistan. More than a million people lost their lives with many more being displaced because of the partition.

Such incidents of communal violence or riots also happened in certain parts within India during the integration of princely states like Hyderabad. According to Paul R. Brass, professor (Emeritus) of Political Science and International Studies in University of Washington with many books and articles on politics, ethnic and collective violence in South Asia post-independence, these incidents of communal violence or riots/pogroms/genocide occur in the wake of a psychological atmosphere produced by organized groups rather than a spontaneous outbreak of passion.

Paul R. brass further stressed that the riots, especially the Hindu-Muslim riots, for many years follow a dramatic production with three phases as:

1) Preparation/Rehearsal: As a continuous activity at the endemic site;

2) Activation/Enactment: Large scale riots under particular circumstances, most notably the intense political mobilization or electoral competition; and

3) Explanation/Interpretation: Broader struggle to control the explanation or interpretation of the causes of the violence. This involves the numerous elements of the society like politicians, journalists, social scientists and public opinion.

At times, the government and its agents do not act to control violence, but often engage in or permit gratuitous acts of violence against particular groups under the cover of the imperative of restoring order, peace, and tranquillity. Therefore, he stressed that '*secularism constitutes a countervailing practice, and a set of values that are essential to maintain balance in a plural society where the organization of intergroup violence is endemic, persistent, and deadly.*'

Since independence, we have had numerous incidents of riots/communal violence, with major one including the incidents like:

- Jabalpur Riots, 1961
- Gujarat Riots, 1969 and 2002
- Nellie Massacre of Assam 1983 and the 2012 Assam violence,
- Anti-Sikh Riots, 1984
- Bhagalpur Riots, 1989

- Anti-Kashmiri Pandit Riots, 1989-90
- Bombay (Mumbai) Riots, 1992-93 etc.

In India, we have many other reasons also which lead to communal violence like the uneven growth between various regions of a state or feelings of being deprived among certain ethnic groups. Such feelings lead to different political movements and subsequent violence during such movements by the protesting community or the other community. E.g. the Bru (Reang) incident discussed earlier or during 2017 Gorkhaland agitation.

The increasing penetration of modern-day communication systems like social media and ideological differences further influence the present-day communal violence as they are often used as the means to keep the preparation stage alive or to spread the stage of the enactment phase. E.g. because of the 2012 Assam Violence, we had many incidents of small scale violence and events of the exodus of Assamese people living in South India. The increasing incidents of mob-lynching with cases of vigilantism from citizens are also becoming more frequent.

At times, because of certain issues between two states regarding resource sharing (like River Water in Kerala-Tamil Nadu or Karnataka-Tamil Nadu), protests against the people from other states (like in Maharashtra against North Indian) etc. also leads to targeted violence against particular communities/identities. In 2017 alone, we had 822 incidents of communal violence leading to the killing of 111 people. In recent times, the incidents of Mob Violence i.e. a group of two or more individuals causing violence are increasing. Their sporadic nature with limited target and cause make it difficult to identify or issue a warning in advance. It can be in the form of mob lynching or displacing specific group of people from a place with actions like propagation of offensive materials, creating a hostile environment or creating obstructions in legal processes as common strategies.

Therefore, in order to secure India from the challenge of communal violence, the MHA needs to work on a larger scale as it worked against the Naxalite movement by following certain steps like:

- Establishing the new-age patterns and constantly track the means which can be used in communal violence in order to develop early-warning indicators.
- Initiate steps to use communalism in a positive way by creating the nation as the biggest and first identity group for the people and work on removing the inter-personal and inter-regional disparities.
- Keep a watch on the sectarian divides among people and create mechanisms which can stop its exploitation for political mobilization by political parties like the creation of interest groups.

- Making Zonal Councils more functional with focus on reducing the pending issues between states and promotion of steps to establish peace and harmony in diversity.

- Keeping a constant vigil on the religious fundamentalism and all organizations involved in such ideas should be constantly engaged in inter-religious harmony events.

- Better implementation of Law and order from sates in order to address mob lynching and vigilantism with building confidence among people. It may require changes in our criminal justice system as well, which itself is considered by people as obsolete and slow to the needs of the present.

- Better codification of the guidelines on government administration response to communal violence situations with the inclusion of members from all interest groups.

- Set up special investigation and prosecution agencies for swift handling of the incidents with better investigation and a quicker remedy in order to remove the deep anger and hatred among people.

## Socio-political and Economic isolation

One of the major issues with our democracy is that it is not inclusive and significant minority people or regions are often left behind in socio-political and economic development. This leads to unequal distribution of resources with the creation of pockets of poverty among people and regions, leading to greater distrust and feeling of being left out among people. E.g. Before the separation of Telangana from Andhra Pradesh, the Telangana region was facing high isolation in terms of unfavourable river water distribution to its districts. 9 out of the 10 districts falling in Telangana region (except Hyderabad) were among the most backward districts.

Similar feelings were prevalent in the territorial regions of present-day Jharkhand, Uttarakhand and Chhattisgarh. At community level also such socio-political and economic isolation exists. E.g. Muslims, with 14.2% of our population (2011 census) form the biggest minority group of India. But in terms of the social, political and economic status, Muslims are highly underrepresented.

The literacy rate, as per 2011 census, was only 57.28% among Muslims (aged 7 years and above). It is lowest among all major religions of India. Among the Hindu population, it was 63.60%. The number of graduates was also low at 2.76%. At political level, in 2014 Lok Sabha we had only 23 Member of Parliament (MP) from the Muslim community and in 2019 it has just inched to 27 (approx 5%). Similarly, in Uttar Pradesh with a 19.2% Muslim population, the number of Muslim MLAs in 2017 Legislative Assembly is only 24 or 5.9%.

Similarly, if we closely look at the Socio-economic Caste Census-2011 (SECC) we will observe widespread disparities among people of India. Overall, the SECC identified the presence of 24.39 crore households in India with 10.69 crore households among them fit to be considered as deprived because of various reasons. Based on its seven indicators of deprivation i.e. living in Kutcha house, no adult working-age member, headed by women with no working-age adult, having a disabled member, belonging to SC/ST, without literate adults over 25 years and landless engaged in manual labour, the picture of India identified by SECC in 2011 looked like following:

- 49% of the households can be considered poor in terms of facing some deprivation.
- In rural India, over 90% of rural India households (HH) lacked the presence of a salaried job member. Fewer than 10% HH had a member with higher secondary education and mere 3.41% HH had a family member who is at least a graduate.
- Only 30% of rural households had cultivation as their main source of income. And, 51.14% HH were living as manual casual labour (MCL).
- In nearly 75% of the rural households, the main earning family member makes less than Rs 5,000 per month (or Rs 60,000 annually). Only 8 per cent of households had a main earning member making more than Rs 10,000 per month.
- 56.25% of rural households hold no agricultural land.

According to the recent Oxfam report on inequalities "**Reward Work, Not Wealth**", the economic inequalities in India are at worse with ranking as the second most unequal region after the Middle East. The inequalities in India exceed the global average and the richest 1% of the Indian population holds over 58% of national wealth. Add to that, the richest 1% of Indians cornered 73% of the wealth generated in a year while the wealth rise for the poorest 67 crore people was just 1%. Overall, the top 10 percentile of India holds nearly 80.7% of wealth with the bottom 90% of Indians holding the rest.

If we look at the recent revolution of the Middle East and North Africa (MENA region), the main reason for the start of revolution was poverty and unemployment. The poverty or inequality discussed above and the present unemployment of India among youth at its highest of last 45 years, India faces a big risk by not working on the ways to remove them. It is vital for our internal security that we find alternatives to our present development model or add new dimensions to it which can help in removal of the different forms of socio-political and economic isolation faced by the people. Some of the steps in this direction can be:

- Formulate a comprehensive social security structure for the most deprived people in order to ensure good health, education and basic necessities to all.
- Identify the different forms of poverty present among others and tackle them through targeted interventions towards socio-economic needs like sanitation, basic income, affordable housing, disability etc.
- Provide structural solutions to the farming sector like consolidation of land holdings, farm mechanization and other inputs which help in increasing agricultural productivity.
- High focus on the creation of gainful non-farm labour-intensive employment by the policymakers. This includes the food processing industry, construction industry, textile sector etc. with a high focus on long-term sustainability.
- Skilling of educated people with advanced needs like Artificial Intelligence and Data Science (part of 4th industrial Revolution) needs to be promoted through a better structured and output-oriented approach in Startup India.
- Engaging the youth in constructive works which help in increasing their emotional attachment with the nation. It helps in stopping people from going against the state.

## Political Sub-state movements

Secessionism, i.e. withdrawal by a group from a larger entity, comes in different forms especially when it is related to a political entity. Based on its ethnic identity within or outside the greater identity of the home nation, the secessionism comes with the demand to bifurcate and, at times, trifurcate, into two or three basic nationalist orientations such as:

- Independentist nationalism,
- Autonomist nationalism (and its sub-variants),
- Federalist nationalism (and its sub-variants).

In India also we have different forms of such secessionism. E.g. The insurgency of Jammu and Kashmir and some parts of the North-East region was based on independence from India. Some demand greater autonomy within the state while some demand recognition as an independent political entity. The political sub-state movements are basically of the last two forms, i.e. decentralized arrangements featuring autonomous regions within the state or recognition as a separate political entity (state) under the union of India.

If the initial phase of India after independence was dominated by the demands for political reorganization based on linguistic identities, the second phase is dominated by the political sub-state movements caused because of following reasons:

- Linguistic identity,
- Historical reasons,
- Geographical reasons,
- Cultural anxiety,
- A feeling of the lack of fair treatment under present state or
- Deprivation of one region at the expense of others despite being rich in natural resources or other reasons.

These political sub-state movements are largely driven by the regional parties, formed to express the larger feeling of the local people and take its cause to higher forums i.e. Lok Sabha and Rajya Sabha. Being within the premise of the institutional and constitutional means prevalent in India these movements can also be supported by state and national parties.

This includes the successful movements for Uttrakhand, Jharkhand, Chhattisgarh and Telangana with a continuing movement for Gorkhaland in West Bengal, Vidarbha in Maharashtra, Purvanchal, Bundelkhand and Harit Pradesh in Uttar Pradesh with parts of Madhya Pradesh in Bundelkhand, Saurashtra in Gujarat etc.

Though political in nature at times it can take the form of violent agitation because of the increased fears of cultural hegemony or increased regionalism. E.g. in 2017, the Gorkhaland movement for separate state turned violent because of the fears of making Bengali mandatory in the hill region and upper hand shown by the state police while dealing with the agitation. Similar, violent agitations were also witnessed before the establishment of Gorkhaland Territorial Administration.

The moment they turn violent, it becomes a challenge to our internal security. Also, at the ideological level, they are against the concept of pluralism and unity in diversity of India as it represents the feeling of alienation present in our society. This can be because of the problems of unequal opportunities, imbalanced development and distrust against the present government.

Therefore, the solution to such political sub-state movements lies in the reversal of these insecurities/inequalities present within different regions of a state through good governance and adequate political representation; helping in the preservation of the concept of pluralism and unity in diversity.

## Espionage

Every nation has its own secrets and when it comes to information which can be useful to the enemy nations in wartime or terrorist/militant groups in carrying out their operation, means of espionage are used by them to extract this information. In India, such information isn't just sought by the foreign intelligence services of nations like Pakistan but also by the insurgents to gather intelligence on a broad range of subjects, including foreign policy, defence, financial, technological, industrial and commercial interests.

This is done by Espionage, defined as the process of obtaining information that is not normally publicly available, using human sources (agents) or technical means (like hacking into computer systems). This includes the military secrets (like technical information on weapons and their location) and operational details (troop's location and their movement). It may also involve seeking to influence decision-makers and opinion-makers to benefit the interests of a foreign power.

E.g. The attacks like the Pulwama Attack of 2019, Uri attack of 2016 or ambush of Manipur in 2015 involved pre-information on troop movement and location. Similar attacks are part of guerilla warfare tactics used by the Naxals. In wartime, such information can help an enemy to find weak points or launch surprise attacks against us. Apart from the information on armed forces, we have important industry secrets or technological details of research and production activities carried out by DRDO and other units, the signature of ships and submarines, nuclear plants and the scientific manpower which is as close on the radar of enemy nations/groups as the military secrets.

E.g. Under the guise of protests for safety from Kudankulam nuclear power plant we have incidents where the actual Blueprints with all technical details were demanded by some selective activists. Leakage of such information can be disadvantageous not just to the interests of India but to the partnering nation (Russia for Kudankulam) as well. Similarly, the cyber network of our armed forces, DRDO labs, nuclear plants etc. are always under attack from spies to extract technical details for commercial purposes or to shut the network.

Sometimes, it may include confidential information of politically sensitive nature or significant information related to security affairs, international negotiations, economic details or policy developments. As we can't restrict the existence of such information, we have only two ways to protect this information. This first is the denial of such information to spies or agents by ensuring passage of such information through secure networks. The second is to catch the spies or agents, their intelligence officers including the employees of the target organization.

The techniques used to gain access to the cyber network and collect information are discussed as part of the cyber threats. Under this heading, we are focusing on the intelligence officers and other spying agents used by them. The intelligence officers are the professionally trained members of foreign intelligence services or militant organizations active in the region. They are highly trained in espionage techniques and handling of agents. They can be operating in any part of India either as a covert or overt operator in an official or non-official capacity.

The other agents are the "covert human intelligence sources", providing secret information to an intelligence officer. They are usually the unprofessional spies lured/hired by the intelligence officer through money, honey-trap (i.e. using an attractive person to try to get information from someone) or other means (like ideological factors). They may be trained in some basic instruction on espionage methods. With the increased use of social networking websites, the methods of old physical honey-traps are replaced by online allurement (through images and videos), providing a swift and clean way to lure many past and present staff at one time with no risk of physical harm. E.g. in 2019, Indian agencies identified a Pakistani Spy named Sejal Kapoor on Facebook who hacked the computer systems of more than 98 defence personnel of various defence agencies.

## Solutions:

The basic solution to stop intelligence officers operating within India is to catch them and deny the fresh entry for those who try to enter India through unofficial ways. Those who come in the guise of a diplomat, staff or function in the guise of another job profile should undergo a thorough investigation from our intelligence agencies about their background and their movements within India. Also, the security at vital installations should be high and all suspicious movements or buildings should be kept under watch.

Though the steps toward protection of network and information are given under the cyber threat in order to protect the information at vital installations we need to have dos and don'ts to guide the functioning of officials and staff. Selective checks on phones, laptops and desktops of officers and others posted in sensitive areas can be handy in capturing or keeping the fear of being caught among agents. Establishment of an information warfare team by the armed forces to look after the online social presence of its people and to track suspected Twitter handles or Facebook accounts with frequent suspicious activities can be handy in catching allurement.

The official networks/websites should be secured through latest technologies for early and better detection of viruses with lighter solutions for the protection of staff devices. The people handling sensitive information should be regularly updated towards cyber risks with information on how to review and audit their own devices against spyware/malware.

### Security of the national infrastructure/assets related to the weapons of mass destruction

If we look around us, we will observe that we have different kinds of infrastructure or facilities built for different roles/purposes. Among them, National Infrastructure refers to those facilities, systems, sites, information, people, networks and processes which are necessary for a country to function and upon which daily life of its people depends.

When it comes to India, we have a large number of such facilities or infrastructure in the form of roads, railway network, airports, power plants (conventional and non-conventional), oil and gas (production, refining and distribution), educational institutions, digital infrastructure etc. which is essential part of the life of our citizens. With the 6th largest chemical industry of the world and presently the 13th biggest civil atomic power sector, a great potential danger can be created for the people and state by attacking it.

A gas leak like Bhopal Gas tragedy or nuclear radiation leakage can be far more dangerous and fatal even in comparison to Kargil war. It also includes agriculture, mining and other infrastructure or individuals in India and abroad which are vital for our core strategic interests. This includes our foreign missions, diplomats, industrialists and large Diaspora which helps our nation to reap economic, political, socio-cultural, and other benefits in India or abroad.

In the past, we had many incidents where railway stations, schools, our foreign missions, nuclear scientists etc. came under attack from terrorists. The insurgent groups of North-East and Naxals in Central India have often blocked roads or rail networks around them. With nearly US$1.1 trillion invested by India on building national infrastructure from 2008-17 and plans to further spend US$1.4 trillion (102 lakh crore rupee) in next five years (2020-25) through the National Infrastructure Pipeline, it is important that adequate security measures are taken to protect them.

The security of nuclear installation is carried out by RAW and till date, we have no untoward incident caused by external agents. With militants' preference for attacking soft targets, higher levels of effective and visible protective security cover at national infrastructure sites is an effective deterrent. Though the proposed federal anti-terror agency i.e. National Counter Terrorism Center (NCTC) is yet to take shape but efforts toward the synchronization of information and investigation under NIA has helped a lot in improving the internal security environment.

But we can't discount the ambition and evolution of terrorist organizations. Therefore, we need to find ways for setting up NCTC and need to build a greater internal intelligence network with greater insights on the continual diversification of the threats to internal security, in order to protect not just the national infrastructure but any other target also.

# Modern/Emerging Threats to the Security of India and their Solutions

We ended our previous discussion on the need for having greater insights on the continual diversification of the threats to internal security. Our policymakers and security establishments have also recognized a number of such challenges. Some of them are emerging with the latest technology while some are seeking revival from the past with a more organized form. Some are caused because of internal reasons while some are caused because of external reasons or mix of two. These challenges are also caused as the modern/emerging challenges and includes

### 1. CYBER THREATS

In the last few decades, Information Technology (IT) played a transformational role in the whole world. It not just connected the people but the nations and their future as well. It was part of the 3rd Industrial Revolution and provide foundations to the more exponential and disruptive Fourth Industrial Revolution[42]. Therefore, the integration of IT with economical, political, socio-cultural, legal and other processes/systems present in a nation is gaining the centre stage.

Integration of IT is carried through a global technology environment built over the electronic medium of digital networks for communication, also known as the **Cyberspace**. Cyberspace can store, modify and communicate information. With the increased importance of cyberspace, the new forms of challenges or vulnerabilities are also created not just at the user level but also at the national and global level. These challenges or vulnerabilities are recognized as Cyber threats. These Cyber threats are divided into four categories, based on the perpetrators and their motives, as:

***Cyber Crime (E-Crime):*** Any unlawful act where a computer or communication device or computer network is used to commit or facilitate the commission of a crime. Presently, our criminal justice system recognizes 24 types of crimes like cybercrime, such as cyber bullying, cyber stalking, child pornography/child sexually abusive material, cyber grooming, sexting, vishing, online sextortion, ransomware, data breach, etc. As per the data collected and published by National Crime Records Bureau (NCRB), cyber crimes in India have

---

[42] *Klaus Schwab, founder and executive chairman of World Economic Forum, defined Fourth Industrial Revolution (in his book "The Fourth Industrial Revolution) as a technological revolution which will blur the lines between the physical, digital, and biological spheres. These technological revolutions include the mobile devices (with unprecedented processing power, storage capacity, and access to knowledge) and the emerging technologies such as artificial intelligence, robotics, the Internet of Things, autonomous vehicles, 3-D printing, nanotechnology, biotechnology, materials science, energy storage, and quantum computing.*

nearly doubled within a span of just two years, i.e. 2015 to 2017, with 21,796 cases in 2017 as compared to 11,592 in 2015 and 12,317 in 2016. The common forms of cybercrimes include cyber frauds and online sexual exploitation/harassment.

***Cyber Espionage:*** It is a form of cybercrime, defined as the act or practice of obtaining data and information without the permission and knowledge of the owner. It is often done to gain illicit access to confidential information held by the government or related organizations. Some of the benefits offered by cyber espionage include its cost-effectiveness over the traditional means, remote nature of espionage adding an extra layer of deniability and a high volume of data that can be stolen by it.

***Cyber Terrorism:*** In simple words, cyber terrorism means the acts of terrorism committed through the use of cyberspace or computer resources. Cyber terrorism includes unlawful attacks and threats of attacks against computers, networks, and information stored therein with a purpose to intimidate or coerce a government or its people in furtherance of political or social objectives. It can also include simple propaganda pieces on the internet related to the threat of bomb attacks to cause fear or the serious attacks to cause violence against persons or property by organized groups within networks. It can also be done to demonstrate power or collecting information relevant for ruining peoples' lives, robberies, blackmailing, etc.

***Cyber Warfare:*** It is considered as the fifth domain of warfare (after land, sea, air and space) where the cyberspace (computers and networks) of the nation is attacked by another nation or its proxies with intentions of espionage or to cause harm comparable to actual warfare or disrupt life including economic activities. Under espionage, the activities include intelligence gathering and data theft. Some of the examples of such cyber-espionage include the Titan Rain (by China on US military contractors, government agencies etc.) and Moonlight Maze (by Russia on US military contractors, government agencies etc.).

The attempts to harm include defacement of web pages, Denial-of-Service (DoS) by taking them down, destruction of data, and insertion of malware or use of logic bombs (secret instruction in a program which cause harmful effects when certain conditions are satisfied) to set off a malicious function. It often includes the Stuxnet used by US and Israel against Iran or old attacks of Russia on Estonia and Georgia.

As the motives behind these cyber threats are different the sources through which cyber threats can be inflicted also varies a lot. It can be an individual hacker, organized cybercriminals, terrorist groups or nations. The targets also vary from an individual to more organized activities like businesses, governance systems, security agencies or the whole cyberspace. It has remained a challenge for governments and individuals around the world to avoid cyber threats.

The problem is further complicated by the ever-progressing technologies, making it difficult to frame one standard solution or law against it. The cyberspace suffers from inherent vulnerabilities like- Innumerable entry points for the attackers and ease with which the identity can be hidden or attributed to other parties, making it easy to carry out cyber attacks. Security software firm, Symantec Corp ranked India 3rd based on the number of cyber threats detected and 2nd in terms of targeted attacks in 2017.

In 2017 alone we had significant incidents like 17 million users data theft at Zomato and ransomware like Wannacry and Petya making their presence felt in India. This is caused by the high number of internet users with most of them naïve to emerging cyber threats. By 2020, we will have 730 million internet users with ever-increasing online money transactions. This cyberspace also monitors & controls the critical Infrastructure of a nation whose integrity & availability is critical for the economy, public safety, & national security. This includes sectors such as- Defence, Energy, Finance, Space, Telecommunications, Transport, Essential Services and Utilities for public, Law Enforcement and Security. Therefore, we need to protect both the critical infrastructure and users' information as well.

**Solutions**

The basic minimum required from the government to address these cyber threats includes:

- Having a legal framework to ensure the rights of all and provisions to punish the guilty;
- Agencies to identify and handle such cyber threats at national and international level based on national cyber security policy;
- Creation of a large talent pool with capabilities and capacities to man these agencies and perform the functions of R&D and security;
- Spreading awareness among the users on their rights and possible cyber threats;
- Implementation of standard protocols for safe use of cyberspace with an early warning and response mechanism; and
- Joining global responsible nations to promote the idea of safe use of cyberspace based on an international convention.

In the past few decades, a series of initiatives have been taken towards Cyber Security, covering different areas like security of information and the communicating channels, computing devices like computers and Smartphone's, computer networks including private and public networks, and the Internet as a whole. These steps include,

1) The first step in the direction of setting up a legal framework started with the Information Technology (IT) Act, 2000. But it lacked clauses related to data protection, cyber terrorism and cyber security. So, in the aftermath of the terrorist attack in Mumbai in November 2008, through the Information Technology (Amendment) Act, 2008, greater emphasis was given to data protection, cyber terrorism and cyber-crime. Today, it covers various aspects of cyberspace like the electronic transactions, digital signatures, cyber-crimes, cyber security and data protection, directly or through the Information Technology (Guidelines for Cyber Cafe) Rules, 2011.

2) In recent past, India has set up a number of agencies to deal with different aspects of cyber threats like- **National Technical Research Organisation** (NTRO, established in 2004) to develop technological capabilities of India in number of fields including cyber security, cryptology systems, strategic hardware and software development; **Indian Computer Emergency Response Team** (CERT-In, established in 2004) as the national nodal agency for coordinated efforts on cyber security issues and number of sectoral CERTs to look after specific sector; **National Informatics Centre-Computer Emergency Response Team** (NIC-CERT, established in 2017) with objective of creating a comprehensive framework that integrates world-class security components and inbuilt threat intelligence for detection, prevention and incident response. NIC-CERT will protect government networks from cyber attacks; **National Critical Information Infrastructure Protection Centre** (NCIIPC, established in 2014 under section 70A of IT Act, 2000) as national nodal agency to protect critical information infrastructure (CII) defined under the IT Act, 2000 as *those computer resource, the incapacitation or destruction of which, shall have debilitating impact on national security, economy, public health or safety.* This includes the information infrastructure of Defense, Space, Banking and finance, Power, Transport, Communications, water supply, Public Health, Law enforcement agency, Sensitive Government organizations, Critical manufacturing, E-Governance etc.

3) In 2018, **Indian Cyber Crime Coordination Centre** (I4C) was set up to combat cybercrime in India by acting as a nodal point in the fight against cybercrime and handle issues related to cybercrime in the country in a comprehensive and coordinated manner. I4C has seven components to handle various aspects of cybercrime as *National Cybercrime Threat Analytics Unit, National*

*Cybercrime Reporting Portal, Platform for Joint Cybercrime Investigation Team, National Cybercrime Forensic Laboratory Ecosystem, National Cybercrime Training Centre, Cybercrime Ecosystem Management Unit* and *National Cyber Research and Innovation Centre.* It will work towards the prevention of misuse of cyberspace by extremist and terrorist groups from furthering their cause. It will also identify the research problems/needs of Law Enforcement Agencies and take up R&D activities in developing new technologies and forensic tools in collaboration with academia/research institutes within India and abroad.

4) As we earlier discussed, the Defence Cyber Agency is established under the integrated defence staff to secure the armed forces.

5) Steps are also taken by the Central Government to spread awareness on cybercrime, to issue cyber-related alerts/ advisories, capacity building/ training of law enforcement officers/ judges/ prosecutors, improving cyber forensics facilities etc. to prevent cybercrime and expedite investigations.

6) In 2017, the first phase of the **National Cyber Coordination Centre (NCCC)** became operational. NCCC is a multi-stakeholder cyber-security and e-surveillance agency with powers based on section 69B of the IT Act, 2000 and it functions under the CERT-In. In simple words, NCCC will be responsible for scanning the web traffic in India in order to detect cyber security threats.

7) Some states have also taken initiatives in this direction like the Cyberdome project from Kerala Government, a high tech R&D centre of Kerala Police Department based on public-private partnership, to gain greater excellence in cyber security and get technological help in better policing. It plans to prevent cyber crimes through increased resilience in cyberspace through a collective coordination among the Government departments and agencies, academia, research groups, non-profitable organizations, individual experts from the community, ethical hackers, private organizations, and other law enforcement agencies in the country.

---

### National Cyber Security Policy, 2013

With a vision to build secure and resilient cyberspace for citizens, businesses and Government of India, **National Cyber Security Policy** was released in 2013. It outlined a road-map for the nation towards the creation of a framework for comprehensive, collaborative and collective responses to deal with the issue of cyber security at all levels within the country. The major **objectives** of the policy are:

- To secure cyber-ecosystem and enable adequate trust and confidence in electronic transactions and also guide stakeholders actions for the protection of cyberspace.
- To create an assurance framework for the design of security policies and enable actions for compliance of global standards.
- To strengthen the regulatory framework for ensuring a secure cyber ecosystem.
- To develop suitable indigenous technologies in the Information and Communication Technology (ICT) sector.
- To increase the visibility of the integrity of ICT products by establishing infrastructure for testing and validation of the security of such a product.
- To create a workforce of 500,000 professionals skilled in cyber security in the next five years.
- To provide fiscal benefits for corporations for the adoption of cyber security.
- To safeguard the privacy of citizen's data.
- To enable effective prevention, detection and investigation of cybercrimes.
- To create the culture of cyber security.
- To enhance global cooperation in cyber security.
- To enhance the protection and resilience of National Critical Information Infrastructure.
- To enhance national and sectoral 24*7 mechanisms for monitoring cyber threats.

The agencies/initiatives listed above are in line to achieve the objectives set by this policy. Once we will have the National Encryption[43] Policy (currently in draft mode), the cyber security environment on communication and transactions will further improve. It will also help in encouraging the use of digital technology by promising better public safety and helping in national security.

At the same time, we need to expand the ambit of our policy. Our cyber security strategy should focus not only on defence of our cyber

---

[43] *Encryption is defined as the process of encoding messages or information in such a way that only authorized parties can read it. Common ways of encryption include the use of an encryption algorithm, generating cipher text that can only be read if decrypted.*

infrastructure but on offence as well. When we focus just on defence we give the enemy an opportunity to dictate the targets, means and time to target our cyberspace. Our security agencies are forced to take the first hit and deploy countermeasures rather than to make the whole affair more unfavorable for the enemy. The New India, i.e. India with greater clarity on its national security priorities and ready to defend its core interests by going offensive (e.g. Balakot Strike), it is a must that we build a strategy which can itself act as a deterrent to the enemy.

## 2. ORGANIZED CRIMES LIKE HUMAN TRAFFICKING, MONEY-LAUNDERING AND NARCO-TERRORISM

Organized Crimes include the illegal activities carried by a group of individuals at local, national or transnational/international level under highly centralized criminal enterprises. *MCOCA defines Organized Crimes as any continuing unlawful activity by an individual, singly or jointly either as a member of Organized criminal group or on behalf of such group by use of violence or threat of violence or intimidation or coercion or other unlawful means with objective of gaining monetary benefits or gaining undue economic or other advantage for himself or any other person.*

These criminal enterprises are primarily engaged in the delivery of goods and services which are of illegal nature like drug trafficking, migrant smuggling, human trafficking, money laundering, firearms trafficking, illegal gambling, extortion, counterfeit goods/currency, wildlife and cultural property smuggling, and cybercrime etc. As we can see from the list, the organized crimes are crimes which are not just against an individual but also against the society, economy, and national security of a nation. We have a large presence of such organized crimes in India. E.g.

a) *Human Trafficking:* Trafficking in Human Beings or Persons is prohibited under the Constitution of India under **Article 23 (1)**. Being a signatory to the United Nations Convention on Transnational Organised Crime (UNCTOC, 2000) with Protocol to Prevent, Suppress and Punish Trafficking in Persons, we implemented it through amendments in the **Criminal Law (Amendment) Act** 2013. Under this, the Section 370 of the Indian Penal Code was substituted by new Section 370 and 370A of IPC. These sections provide for comprehensive measures to counter the menace of human trafficking including trafficking of children for exploitation in any form like physical exploitation or any form of sexual exploitation, slavery, servitude, or the forced removal of organs. In addition to it, we have many specific laws to protect the child and women like *The Immoral Traffic (Prevention) Act, 1956 (ITPA), Protection of Children from Sexual*

*Offences (POCSO) Act, 2012, Bonded Labour System (Abolition) Act, 1976 Transplantation of Human Organs Act, 1994 Prohibition of Child Marriage Act, 2006 etc. including* some laws from states like *The Punjab Prevention of Human Smuggling Act, 2012.* Apart from the State Police which is supposed to ensure implementation of these laws in its territory we have specialized anti-human trafficking units across the country along with NSA and Anti Trafficking Cell (under MHA, set up in 2006) to stop it.

Still, the problem of human trafficking exists in India on a large scale. Though we lack official data, NGOs estimate it to be anywhere between 20 million to 65 million individuals with women and children being the main victims. E.g. Every 8 minute a child disappears in India. While the women from neighbouring countries like Nepal are smuggled into India, from India many are smuggled to the Middle East for sexual exploitation.

According to the National Human Rights Commission (NHRC), India is the source, transit point and destination of women and child trafficking. While the women are forced to work at brothels or sold for marriages, the children are forced to work as bonded labour, beggar or to do petty crimes. Estimates suggest that nearly 70,000 children are working as bonded labour in private mines. Many NGOs or charity organizations like Missionaries of Charity Branch in Ranchi or Muzaffarpur Shelter home run by an NGO are some of the many incidents.

b) *Drugs Smuggling: Narcotic Drugs and Psychotropic Substances Act* (DPS Act, 1985) and the *Prevention of Illicit Trafficking in Narcotic Drugs and Psychotropic Substances Act* (1988) makes it illegal for a person to produce/manufacture/cultivate, possess, sell, purchase, transport, store, and/or consume any narcotic drug or psychotropic substance in India. India is still among the biggest consumers of such drugs. The main reason for this is the organized form of drugs smuggling with the lax implementation of laws by the Narcotics Control Bureau. E.g. section 31A of the NDPS Act, 1985 allows capital punishment for repeat offenders but same is not practised in India. Geographically, India is surrounded by the two biggest areas of illicit opium production in the world known as the Golden Crescent[44] and Golden Triangle[45].

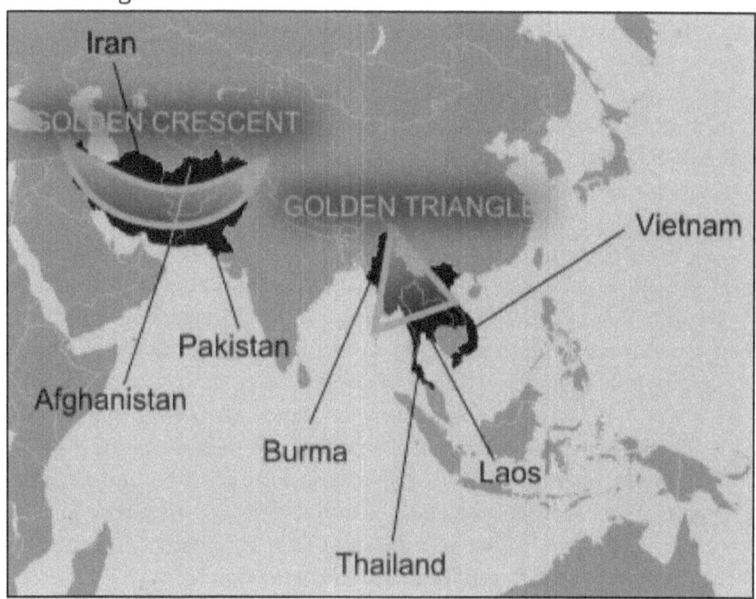

Figure 18 Major Drug Production Regions around India

Even within India, we have many states where illegal production activities are carried out. *The International Narcotics Control Board* (INCB) in its 2018 report found that in 2016 and in 2017 India seized 300 tonnes and 353 tonnes of cannabis herb (ganja) alone. Also, 3,400 hectares of land was cleared from the illicit cannabis plant. Still, the use of drugs is on the rise in India, as the seized drugs suggest that the consumption of synthetic drugs, particularly methamphetamine is on the rise.

The increasing presence of darknet to sell and purchase drugs and crypto-currencies to make a payment further helps the drug cartels to carry out illicit drug trade. The trend of drug-cartels being engaged in terrorist activities or close to terrorist organizations is concerning. E.g. The D-Company of Dawood is working with the Pakistan based terrorist organization with help from state establishments like ISI. In North-East,

---

[44] *Golden Crescent is the area along the mountains of Afghanistan, Pakistan and Iran which has been in the practice of growing illicit drugs for long. Today, it is the biggest illicit drug production region of the world with Afghanistan as the dominant.*

[45] *Golden Triangle is the area where the borders of Thailand, Laos and Myanmar meet. Though the production of drugs was prevalent in the region for a long time, it gained international prominence in the 1980s. In last few years it is on decrease because of changes in Myanmar, the second biggest producer of world after Afghanistan.*

we had many militant organizations involved in transportation and selling of drugs.

This is called as **Narco-Terrorism**, where people engaged in narcotics trade are also linked to terrorist activities or indulge in activities which lead to violence and intimidation. The major consumption centres of such drugs include the North-East Region, Punjab and the tourist spots or Educational hubs of India like Goa, Mumbai, New Delhi, Manali etc. with even involvement from local police officers.

    c) *Arms Trafficking:* Arms trafficking, also known as gunrunning, is the illicit trade of small arms, light weapons, ammunition and other parts/components of such arms and ammunition. In India, the illegal weapons largely enter from Pakistan, Myanmar and Bangladesh, suggesting close links with the insurgency. Within India, we have regions known for illegal arms manufacturing like Munger District of Bihar. This domestic manufacturing utilizes a network of international suppliers along with ordnance factories and arms depots present in India. Similar, illegal facilities are also available in West Bengal, Uttar Pradesh, Jharkhand and Madhya Pradesh with Maoists/Naxalites as the main buyers.

    d) *Money-Laundering:* The word Money-laundering is made of two words, money which is generated by the criminal activities and Laundering from word Launders meaning wash or clean. So, Money Laundering is a process used for the concealment of the origins of illegally obtained money, typically by means of transfers involving foreign banks or legitimate businesses in order to show it as legitimate.

Prevention of Money-Laundering Act, 2002 defines it as, "*Whosoever directly or indirectly attempts to indulge or knowingly assists or knowingly is a party or is actually involved in any process or activity connected with the proceeds of crime and projecting it as untainted property shall be guilty of the offence of money-laundering.*"

The process of Money-Laundering starts with its 1st step of **Placement**, i.e. to put the illegally obtained money into the legitimate money channels/financial system. This is considered as the riskiest and often carried in a manner to avoid suspicion.

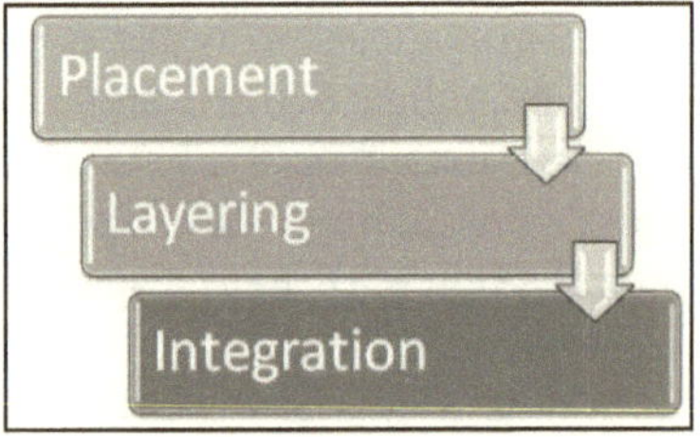



Figure 19 Steps in Money-Laundering (Starting from Top)

Most commonly, it is done through a cash-intensive business like a restaurant or hotel with inflated cash receipts. It can also be done through structuring or smurfing i.e. executing financial transactions through banking channels in under-the-radar patterns in order to avoid financial institutions' trigger or suspicion from law enforcement agencies.

The 2nd step is **Layering**, i.e. carrying out a series of complex transactions or bookkeeping tricks which helps to conceal the source of money. This can be done through existing financial channels or using own captured financial institutions. Hawala[46] and Round tripping[47] are other methods through which layering can be done. The increasing presence of crypto-currencies and other online systems like gaming, auctions, Peer-to-peer transfers etc. has made the process of placement and layering easier than the traditional means.

The last step is **Integration**, i.e. the withdrawal of the illegitimate money from the legitimate channels and use it for any purpose. But it is not compulsory to always follow all the steps and one may just place and integrate, a common practice followed by many during demonetization to turn unaccounted cash into new currencies by giving the money to a servant and taking it back.

Money-laundering is primarily linked to the organized criminal activities like drug trafficking, arms trafficking or terrorist funding because of the large amount of money generated in these activities and the illegal nature of such money. So, money may be left at layering level by ending it with own businesses engaged in real estate, movies etc. or the shell companies/trusts.

Internationally, the Financial Action Task Force or FATF is working to control Money-Laundering. It was created in 1989 by G-7 with HQ in Paris, as an intergovernmental organization to design and promote policies and standards to combat financial crime or money-laundering. In October 2001, the FATF mandate was expanded to incorporate efforts to combat terrorist financing, in addition to money laundering. In April 2012, it added efforts to counter the financing of proliferation of weapons of mass destruction.

The objectives of the FATF is to set standards and promote effective implementation of legal, regulatory and operational measures for combating money laundering, terrorist financing and other related threats to the integrity of the international financial system. The FATF has 39 members including 37 nations of the world (including India) and

---

[46] *Hawala meaning trust is a parallel money transfer system which transfers money without actual movement of the money, i.e. transferring money from one place to another place without any real money movement. It is an informal method of money transfer (considered illegal in India) where money is given at one hawala dealer point and taken from another hawala dealer point.*

[47] *Round Tripping is a process, commonly used for money-laundering and tax-evasion, where the money is first transferred to another nation (mostly a tax-haven nation) and then invested back into the home country as FDI.*

2 regional organisations (European Commission and Gulf Cooperation Council) and Indonesia as a FATF observer.

**Other organized crimes**

Apart from the above main crimes, crimes like counterfeit currency wildlife and cultural property smuggling, gambling, extortion, migrant smuggling etc. are present in India. Some of them like wildlife and cultural property smuggling are prevalent for being one of the oldest centres of civilizations and rich flora and fauna of India. Similarly, gambling and extortion are prevalent because of the poor law and order situation in India.

The criminal enterprises engaged in such crimes don't have a single structure. Some enterprises operate through hierarchies, some through clans/networks/cells. These enterprises are self-perpetuating and continue to function even without direct leadership engagement or their elimination. These groups are typically insular and protect their activities through corruption, violence, international commerce, complex communication mechanisms, and an organizational structure exploiting national boundaries.

Therefore, the solutions also need to address the problem through a 360-degree approach, i.e. not just targeting the criminal enterprises but also their supporters, their countries of operation and their processes. Following steps can help in addressing the problem of organized crimes.

- Improve the law and order situation in India.
- Remove the corruption from politics and government organizations.
- Spread education and remove poverty from India in order to protect the victims of crimes like human trafficking.
- Work closely with other nations and organizations like FATF, Interpol and our neighbouring nations in order to attack the transnational network and routes used by them.
- Keep a close watch on the activities of the NGOs and charity missions which often indulge in such crimes in the garb of service to mankind.
- Filter the money transactions and catch the attempts of money-laundering by limiting cash dealing and promoting digital transactions.

**Differences between the Organized Crime Group v Terrorist Group**

| Parameters | Organized Crime Groups | Terrorist Groups |
| --- | --- | --- |
| **Main Objective** | To gain Financial Benefits | To gain Political Benefits |

| **Means to Achieve** | Non-confrontational (at times use state institutions through bribe) with violence directed mainly towards private individuals | Confrontational with use of extreme violence against state and private individuals. Use individuals working in state institutions because of ideological similarities |
|---|---|---|
| **Responsibilit y for Actions** | Concealed actions with no or little desire to take responsibility for own action | Keen to take responsibility for actions in order to gain media coverage |
| **Territorial hold an ambition** | No desire to take control over territory | Have control over some territory and desire to further extend it |

Despite these differences it is not the usual case that both, i.e. the organized crime groups and terrorist groups, will have a **coexistence** with little or no interaction. Based on interests and prevailing environment, they can have a symbiotic relationship of **cooperation** with each other or a deeper **confluence** where both are difficult to segregate. In India, different organized crime groups have some confluence with the militancy in Kashmir, insurgency of North-East and the Left Wing Extremism.

### 3. DEMOGRAPHIC CHANGES

Demography is formed by a combination of Greek words '*Demos*' meaning people and '*graphy*' meaning description or measurement. So, demography is the statistical representation of the people in terms of their age, gender, religion, caste, ethnicity, education or any **criteria which can** be used to identify different groups of people. Demographic changes are the changes or transitions gone by these demographic criteria.

When a society is perfectly integrated and demographic changes are because of natural or biological processes, these demographic transitions are considered normal and each society goes through such demographic transitions without much challenge. But when such transitions are induced by man made processes or socio-cultural attempts, it becomes an existential risk for one community and a challenge to internal security.

Such challenges were faced by India for the past many centuries, leading to a decrease in the area belonging to India. The partition of India was one such incident which was accepted to avoid the likely internal security challenge in the form of a Civil War. Even before that, they introduced the Inner Line Permits to allay the fears of North-East people from any demographic change. The Constitution of India carried those provisions but threats still persist.

E.g. The Assam movement is primarily based on the fears of demographic changes among indigenous people because of large scale migrations from Bangladesh and other parts of West Bengal. Similar incidents are seen in other states and cities, where local people demand restrictions on the outsiders to protect their culture or economic resources. Similarly, the large youth population of India is also becoming a challenge and if the problems like unemployment are not solved our demographic dividend will soon become a demographic burden.

The gravity of such demographic changes becomes far more severe when such changes are introduced to harm the strategic or core interests of India. In fact, one of the reasons for removing all provisions of Article 370 except 370 (1) and the Reorganization of the Jammu and Kashmir State is the ongoing attempts to change the religious demography of the region for past few decades. At the time of its integration with India, the State of Jammu and Kashmir was unique in terms of three regions with each region being dominated by one religion.

The Kashmir region was dominated by Muslims, the Jammu region by Hindu and Ladakh by Buddhists with the presence of other religions. But the militancy of Kashmir became the first nail towards changing demography when more than 5lakh Hindu (Kashmiri Pandits) left the Kashmir valley because of targeted killings. The low level of voting in the region can also be attributed to the fact that the winner is pre-decided from one community.

Before the restructuring of 2006, Jammu and Kashmir had 14 districts. This included 6 districts of Jammu region with 3 being dominated by Muslims and other 3 by Hindus. In 2006 restructuring, the number of districts was raised to 22. It also increased the number of districts in the Jammu region to 10 with 6 being dominated by Muslims and 4 by Hindus. As the people from any other part of India can't purchase land in the region, so the demographic changes were made through internal mechanisms like the Jammu and Kashmir State Lands (Vesting of Ownership to the Occupants) Act, 2001, popularly known as the Roshni Act.

Similarly, in the Ladakh region, we have a very thin majority of Buddhist over the Muslims. In 2017, we had protests in Ladakh from Buddhists because of increased Love Jihad or conversion to Islam through marriages with ignorance from state machinery. Such conversions are very effective in bringing demographic changes in a few generations, as it is not just the conversion of 1 woman. In biological terms it means that one reproductive person is taken out from one community and merged into another, increasing the population growth of the merged community while other communities will have reduced growth.

Earlier, in 1989 also we had similar incidents in Ladakh leading to violent riots and calls for the social and economic boycott between communities. The wafer thin population differences makes it a cultural issue and a threat to internal security. Similar concerns are also raised by others like the recent Kerala's Syro-Malabar Church with concerns of joining the agenda of Islamic State (ISIS) and movement to Syria is reported. Even NIA is involved in the investigation of some incidents which not only involve the question of love and conversion but also of other illegal activities like blackmailing through obscene videos, violence and threats.

Whether love is genuine or a tool for conversion is a different question but such incidents create a dent in the society. This has been observed in Ladakh. The investigation agencies like NIA should investigate whether it is organized or not rather than to look at the specific case referred to it. Also, efforts are required to build confidence among people or communities which are somewhere lost. The fears of the North-East region are addressed through ILPs and we need to make them more functional. The signing of Bodo-peace accord after the CAA act suggests that the people of Bodo region had overcome the fears and we need to generate such confidence among the other districts also.

### 4. STRESS IN FINANCIAL INSTITUTIONS

In the last few years larger stress is visible on the overall economic system, especially the financial institutions, of India. The high NPA of banks, crisis of IL&FS, DHFL and the recent Yes Bank are all the visible signs of that greater stress. Among the various reasons for present stress in financial institutions, the culture of non-compliance created in India by Black Money is a major one.

Black money refers to the money which is not fully legitimate in the hands of the owner either because of illegitimate earning means or because of non-disclosure to authorities in order to avoid tax. Black Money has been a persistent problem in India for a long time. It created a parallel or unaccounted economy in India with varied estimates on its extent. With Black money as the base, many sectors of India outshined the others and became the biggest cash cows of India like real estate, bullion and jewellery market, informal sectors, Trusts/Non-profit organizations etc.

The presence of tax havens and exemptions on capital gain tax on investment from countries like Mauritius helped in increasing the quantum of black money in Indian economy. E.g. 39.6% of FDI in India from 2001 to 2011 came through Mauritius only. It is believed that it helped in re-routing the Black Money back to India by using other financial instruments like Participatory Notes. It kept the whole system running and the lack of capital gain taxes on it furthered the culture of non-compliance.

High corruption at various levels of government further weakened the political, legal and administrative institutions of India. The low or nil capital gain tax on investments through offshore financial centres promoted corrupt businesses headed by dishonest persons. It created a barrier even for genuine and honest businesses.

In the last one decade, India tried to solve the problems created by the vicious cycle of Black Money by setting up a Special Investigation Team (SIT) on Black Money under Chairmanship and Vice-Chairmanship of two former Judges of Hon'ble Supreme Court. Under the guidance of SIT and the political leadership, India has taken a large number of initiatives at various levels like:

**Legal:** Introduction of new laws or making the old laws stronger such as:

- Amendments to Prevention of Money Laundering Act 2002 in 2015 which added provisions to enable the attachment and confiscation of property equivalent in value held within the country where the property/proceeds of crime are taken or held outside the country;
- Amendments to Prevention of Corruption Act, 1988 with a direct liability of the commercial organizations involved in bribery in India with reduced immunity to bribe giver even if it turns witness;
- Amendments to Benami Transactions Prohibition Act, 1988 in 2016 to enable confiscation of Benami property and prosecution of benamidar and the beneficial owner;
- Black Money (Undisclosed Foreign Income and Assets) and Imposition of Tax Act-2015;
- General Anti-Avoidance Rules (GAAR) in 2017 as an anti-tax avoidance law under the Income-tax Act, 1961; or
- Fugitive Economic Offenders Act, 2018 to declare a person a Fugitive Economic Offenders by special courts under the Prevention of Money Laundering Act, 2002 and to confiscate the properties of the person if the amount involved is over Rs. 100 crore.

**International Cooperation:** Joining the International fight against Black money by:

- The signing of Double Taxation Avoidance Agreement (DTAA) with a number of nations especially the tax havens like Mauritius in 2016 (which is also extended to Singapore under our treaty with Singapore);

- Tax Information Exchange Agreements (TIEAs) with nations like the Foreign Account Tax Compliance Act (FATCA) with the USA;
- The signing of Information Exchange pact with the Swiss National Bank to get information about Indian residents having accounts in Switzerland banks, etc.

<u>**Administrative measures:**</u>
- Launch of **Operation Clean Money** on 31 January 2017 for collection, collation and analysis of information on cash transactions, extensive use of IT and data analytics tools for identification of high-risk cases, expeditious e-verification of suspect cases, and enforcement actions in appropriate cases, which include searches, surveys, enquiries, assessment of income, levy of taxes, penalties, etc. and filing of prosecution complaints in criminal courts, wherever applicable
- Launch of an Information Technology based **Project Insight** for strengthening the non-intrusive, information-driven approach for improving tax compliance,
- Voluntary disclosures scheme with alternatives like Pradhan Mantri Garib Kalyan Yojana, 2016, or
- Various tax reforms like Goods and Services Tax and digital reforms with an increased focus on online tax filing, online transactions through BHIM etc.

While the real impact of these measures was yet to come, in terms reduced corruption, punishments for corrupt and financial recoveries, but it has already shaken and stressed the whole financial system of India. E.g. a large portion of money got stuck in real estate, creating the first major cycle of NPA for banks. It was followed by closure of some companies operating in various sectors.

Today, the situation has reached to a distressing situation where not just the banks are suffering from high Non-Performing Assets (NPA) but the Shadow lenders, i.e. the Non-Banking Financial Companies (NBFCs) are also facing high NPAs with the problems of reduced liquidity in the system.

From the below 3lakh crore of Gross NPA level in 2014 or 4.4% of advances the Gross NPAs of Indian Banking Sector has reached to nearly 10.35 lakh crore or above 9% of total advances by March 2018. Nearly 85% of those NPAs include loans and advances from public sector banks. The actual picture can be even worse as the present NPAs levels is because of a moratorium on declaring stressed assets of small and mid-size businesses as non-performing assets till March 31 2020.

Once moratorium is lifted it will lead to recognition of more such NPAs. The risks of NPA are also spreading to other loans and advances like farm-loans, educational loans, MUDRA loans etc. E.g. The RBI data reveals that nearly 11% or 1.04lakh crore rupees from the total credit of

9.42 lakh crore rupees given by the PSU banks to the farm sector and allied activities have turned NPA. The stresses are also visible in the telecom sector with over 92,000 crore advances due to the burden of Adjusted Gross Revenue (AGR) and the intense competition.

This can further stress the financial system by reducing the government revenues through the telecom license sale in coming months. Though some silver linings are visible in terms of the resolutions completed on some big-ticket NPAs like Essar Steel, Bhushan Steel and Ruchi Soya, a lot is yet to be done. The increasing failures like IL&FS and slow speed of resolution at National Company Law Tribunal (NCLT) and other levels is another cause of concern.

Questions are also raised on abrupt policy decisions and problems associated with steps like demonetization by various economists including our ex-Prime Minister Manmohan Singh. One of the reasons behind these concerns is the liquidity concerns in our economy. The major impact of the liquidity crisis is felt by NBFCs which have reached the levels of 6-7% NPA's, as a whole, probably the first time since their inception.

It is true that National security is threatened because of the presence of black money but the security is also threatened when we have no credit growth and wealth creation in the nation. In the last few years, the credit growth in India has remained abysmal, leading to reduced greenfield projects and even closure of many existing units.

The dream of reaching the US $5 trillion economy by 2024-25 requires a credit growth of nearly 15%, i.e. more than double of the present 7%. It also requires aggressive participation from the private sector which will be a far-fetched dream in the present atmosphere of large business uncertainty and frequent policy changes. Recent initiatives like reduced corporate taxes and schemes like Vivad se Vishwas for dispute resolution on pending income tax litigations may help in addressing the worsening business confidence in India and improve the credit culture with creation of jobs in our economy.

### 5. PROBLEMS OF CRIMINAL JUSTICE SYSTEM

Criminal Justice refers to the agencies of government, charged with the function of enforcing the law, adjudicating crime, and correcting criminal conduct. It is used as an instrument for social control by promoting some social behaviours and punishing other social behaviours which are considered to be dangerous for continuity of the society and dignity of an individual.

The Justice Malimath Committee on 'Reforming Criminal Justice System' said that "The entire existence of the orderly society depends upon sound and efficient functioning of the Criminal Justice System."

Therefore, a good criminal justice system is supposed to prevent the occurrence of crime and maintain law and order in society by creating deterrence through punishment. A good criminal justice system also looks at the rehabilitation of the criminals along with compensation to the victim in order to build the lost trust and discourage the repeat of such crimes at least by the same offenders.

These objectives are achieved by the criminal justice system through its three components, as-

1) **Law Enforcement:** Agencies to report and investigate the crimes which happen against the laws. It includes the police and other investigative agencies like CBI, NIA etc.

2) **Adjudication:** This is the next step in the criminal justice system. Based on the report and evidence, the guilty is punished through a judicial process involving judges and lawyers with existing courts or special courts established to handle specific cases.

3) **Prisons and Correction Centre:** This is the last step. If the accused is found guilty, then he is sent to prison or correctional centre based on the magnitude of the crime, age of the criminal and the other factors.

But it isn't as simple as it looks in the steps. Many crimes are committed, especially the organized crimes by hardened and sharp criminals making it difficult to trace and investigate. The situation is further worsened by the situation of our law enforcement agencies which suffer from problems like lack of manpower, lack of technology and resources, limited talent, high political involvement, the prevalence of corruption etc. The poorly designed procedures and lack of empathy towards the victim further aggravate the situation.

E.g. The number of policemen per 100,000 people in India is 137.8 as compared to the United Nations recommended Standard of 222. Even among them, 86% are at constable level. The budgetary allocations toward Police are a mere 3% in India with a lack of proper training and dedicated units to look at different crimes. The first contact police officer is often not the expert of matter and the lack of forensic knowledge can be against the cause of justice. The increased workload and lack of support system can further impact the mental health of police personnel leading to high incidents of drinking, suicides, fratricides etc. among them.

In Prakash Singh vs Union of India case, Supreme Court gave 7 steps for structural and functional reforms in the police but as on date, these steps are implemented by some states with modifications. These steps and some other steps mentioned by the Second Administrative Reforms Commission (ARC) and initiatives toward modernization of the police are important to have a highly motivated, professionally-skilled and sophisticatedly trained police force.

Like Police, the **adjudication** system of India also suffers from the infrastructure and manpower bottlenecks. According to National Judicial Data Grid, the backlog/pending number of cases in Indian Courts are as high as nearly 3.3 crores (2018). Out of it, nearly 2.84 crores are pending at the subordinate courts level, 43 lakh at High Courts and 57,987 at Supreme Court. The present ratio of about 13 judges per million people is one of the lowest in the world. The low number of public prosecutors further increases the trial duration.

Though most of them are very old and related to small issues they eat up most of the time and effort of judges and advocates. The multiplicity of laws and procedures in India further helps in prolonging the case. This delay in justice delivery not just promotes the interests of criminal elements but it also reduces the faith of people in the judicial system.

Therefore, India needs to set up more alternative and innovative solutions like Lok Adalat, Fast Track Courts, Gram Nyayalayas etc. to reduce the backlog and give time for judges to focus on criminal cases. The Judges are also required to be sensitized on prioritizing the cases. The recruitment of new judges to either look at civil cases or to look at criminal cases after necessary training can help in reducing the backlog. This can also help in moving towards the Inquisitorial System of Justice over the present Adversarial System of the common law.

The difference between the two is of intention. In an adversarial system two advocates, representing their parties', present argument before an impartial judge. In the inquisitorial system, a judge or group of judges investigates the case. This helps in increasing the contact of judges with the investigating agencies rather than advocates, helping in not just getting direct insights but also improving the investigation system.

A large number of problems also exist in the Prisons and Correction Centre because of the old Prison manuals to control the overcrowded inmates in jails. E.g. India's under-trial population remains among the highest in the world. Estimates suggest that 2/3rd of the people languishing in Indian jails are under-trials. The poor infrastructure and facilities at the prison centre further makes it difficult to reform the prisoners. In fact, they are more counter-productive rather than productive as it helps even the small criminals to become more hardened with jails as places of recruitment.

Therefore, we need to properly identify the reason for having the jails and correction centres and develop them to bring positive changes in the attitude of criminals. Some of such initiatives are introduced by aspirational police officers like Kiran Bedi towards increasing computer literacy among inmates in order to have better rehabilitation through employment after release.

The promotion of open prison system and legal business engagements like Swiggy tie-up with Jails in Kerala is a good initiative and we need to check the impact of such tie-ups. The old prison manuals from states should be replaced by a central manual with the inculcation of all the good initiatives from across the Indian State and world, based on the feasibility in India.

The recent encounter in Hyderabad of four rape accused in December 2019 with large-scale support from people was an alarm against the slow pace of our judicial system. It signifies the loss of faith of people in the judiciary. If we don't address the problem of our slow and inefficient criminal justice system we are surely inviting troubles in the form of increased criminal minds in our society. It will further uproot the faith citizens have in the government agencies and without adding speed, accuracy and transparency we can't keep that faith intact.

## 6. Revival of Khalistan

With decreasing penetration abilities of Pakistan in Jammu and Kashmir region, the revival of Khalistan movement is a natural element of Pakistan's strategic policy of bleeding India with thousand cuts.

The origins of earlier Khalistan movement are traced to 1973 demand for higher autonomy through Anandpur Sahib Resolution from Akalis. In the 1980s, Pakistan's ISI started to actively support the Khalistan movement by providing training and supply of arms and ammunition. Under the leadership of Jarnail Singh Bhindranwale, the movement was declared as Dharam Yudh Morcha in 1982. This was followed by violent attacks and counter-attacks ending only in 1995 with the death of Punjab CM Beant Singh.

The strong political leadership of Indian National Congress in Punjab and the strong love of the people of Punjab towards India (as displayed by their high presence in Indian Armed Forces) helped in keeping the Khalistan movement as a fringe movement with little support. Even today, it is mainly an aspiration shared by some of the old Khalistan movement participants living in Pakistan or outside India.

The only worrying factor for India in Punjab is the lack of effective steps taken by the government against the menace of drugs in Punjab. Though Law and order is a state subject, the Central Government is also required to take effective steps as securing the border lies in its domain. Also, rehabilitation and awareness is something which can be done by anyone rather than just restricting it to the State Government.

Lack of effective measures against the menace of drugs can be projected by people as an action against the community. The involvement of non-state actors from Pakistan in drugs trade further intensifies the damages as the money generated from it might be used for financing terrorism and other organized crimes.

## 7. SOCIAL MEDIA AND THE SELF-RADICALIZATION

In the recent past, the majority of the terrorist attacks in the USA and European countries were planned by local residents. The common traits shared by them include support for violent extremism, previously engaged in Islamist extremist activities overseas or getting self-radicalized through the videos and images seen on social media. In India also, many people have returned who fought for extremist groups overseas.

So, one of the major risks felt by Indian intelligence agencies to internal security is the lone-wolf attacks carried out by people who are self-radicalized through social media posts or videos. The members returning from overseas can further aid in it by radicalizing others or by using acquired skills to organize attacks under direction from outside India, or on their own initiative.

ISIS or DAESH always made effective use of social media and modern communication methods towards publicizing or glamorizing their acts with calls for others to join them. More often, few people get inspired, take training and come back because of other emotional attachments such as family. With family, more often they appear normal but the influence of training remains and any spark to the individual, either through social media or incident, the individual might decide to conduct a terrorist attack.

Such self-organized attacks are difficult to detect and more damaging to the social fabric of a nation. E.g. the November 2015 attack in Paris which killed 130 people and injured 368 more has sent the French society to a point where they have closed a large number of mosques, schools etc. linked to political Islam.

## 8. WATER SCARCITY

After air, water is the next important intake of our survival. It is the basic building block of our cells and required for carrying out many processes inside our body. Therefore, it is important to have adequate clean water availability to all. It is also required for growing the food we eat and many other mundane activities like cooking, washing, bathing etc. The other life forms also depend on it in some form or another.

But despite being covered by seawater from three sides and having a large number of perennial and seasonal rivers flowing across our nation, water is a scarce resource in India. India supports nearly 17% of the world population on meager 2.4% of global land and, just 4%

of the world's renewable water resources. In 1950, India had more than 5,000 cubic metres of water per person per year. Today, the average water availability has gone down to less than 1,200 cubic metres per person per year. Reasons include increase in our population, poor planning and management of water resources.

India extracts around 24 billion cubic meters (bcm) of groundwater in order to fulfil 85 per cent of the country's drinking water needs. Because of this excessive groundwater extraction around 256 districts of India is suffering from an acute water crisis. Niti Aayog, in its Composite Water Management Index, stressed that India is on the brink of water scarcity. 21 cities of India including Delhi, Chennai, Bengaluru etc. will run out of groundwater by 2020. By 2030, the annual water demand of India will outstrip the supply and 40% of Indian population won't have access to drinking water.

The poor water quality further worsens the situation. Nearly 70% of our freshwater resources are contaminated. The quality of groundwater is also not good. Because of it, the disease burden due to unsafe water and sanitation in India is 40 times higher than China. Natural as well as manmade pollutants are present in Indian water like arsenic, Fluoride or faecal contamination.

Therefore, we need to properly use our water and create an infrastructure to store and manage the highly concentrated Monsoon water (70% of rainfall in India takes place in the 4-month monsoon season). This water management can be done through the building of storage and check dams with a focus on groundwater recharge as well. The inefficient irrigation practices should be replaced by new technology with the promotion of rain-water harvesting.

Extension of access to clean drinking water and basic sanitation services to all (as desired by the SDGs), will help in solving the high water-borne disease burden. As of July 2018, out of the 17.87 crore rural households of India only 3.27 crore were getting water through piped connections. The recent merging of all water-related ministries, i.e. the Ministry of Water Resources, River Development and Ganga Rejuvenation with the Ministry of Drinking Water and Sanitation, under the newly created **Jal Shakti Ministry** is supposed to bring better synchronization of the government's efforts towards water management.

Primary aim of the ministry is to provide clean drinking water to all by 2024 under the Jal Jeevan Mission in a sustainable manner. It is expected that with increasing pace of ground work in this direction will provide more insights to fight India's water woes. Some of the present solutions include the formation of an integrated water data management system and addressing the long pending issues of inter-state water disputes, international waters, cleaning of rivers through projects like the Namami Gange project and interlinking of rivers.

The community-driven projects at local level with capacity building and training of local populace to increase their participation in In-situ conservation of rainwater will certainly help in making the mission more sustainable. Water conservation methods may include rainwater harvesting structures at the field, village and watershed levels, recharging the primary sources of water (either ground or surface) in order to make them sustainable before taking water out from them, increasing the number of check dams or digging new ponds etc.

Strong relations of India with Israel can help a lot in this, as Israel is known for the most efficient water supply (minimum pipe losses) and use of innovative techniques in order to ensure safe and sufficient supply of water to each household.

## 9. CLIMATE CHANGE

Climate Change is an emerging problem for the world with some nations already feeling the heat of climate change while others are still in an early stage of it. In the coming times, the impact of climate change is likely to increase further. Certainly, the climate change will become a game-changer at a global level but any change in the global power equations will be driven by the challenges it will create towards the internal security of a nation.

The common changes in our atmosphere under climate change include the rise in temperature with subsequent changes in the climate or seasons. The visible impacts of it include the changes in rain patterns, increased forest fires, rapid melting of glaciers and higher evaporation rates with a rise in sea level. Because of this many small island nations are already at the risk of getting completely submerged in a few decades.

With a large coastal area on the mainland and number of islands, India also faces the risk of considerable land getting submerged under the sea. This will cause **greater migrations** from the coastal regions to the mainland and even from some of our neighbouring nations like Bangladesh. This will also increase the organized crimes like migrant smuggling, human trafficking etc. because of high poverty.

The next major impact of climate change is visible on our monsoon pattern where the rainfall is becoming more erratic and concentrated with increased incidences of weather outbursts. With Indian agriculture being highly dependent on Monsoon, the production of crops will reduce and chances of crop failure will increase. This will further stress the rural areas which already suffer from the problems of the poor physical and social infrastructure and poor economic opportunities.

This will further increase the rural-urban gap and more people will be forced to migrate towards the urban centres, i.e. push-migration (repulsion) and look for better opportunities in already stressed urban infrastructure. The increasing suicides among farmers because of crop failure and cattle dying because of lack of water are somewhere linked to climate change also. At the same time, any reduction in agricultural production will further increase the problem of poor public health status with large scale problems of malnutrition, stunting or higher disease burden.

The increased melting of glaciers will lead to more natural disasters like floods and cloudbursts in the Himalayan region with higher flows in the perennial rivers while the time of seasonal river flow and quantity of water in Peninsular India is getting reduced because of higher water evaporation. The decreased forest cover is further reducing the rainwater and small contributing channels/streams are getting extinct.

These changes will further intensify the struggle for river water between the South Indian States. Even river water politics between nations will also intensify. Biggest threat it will lead to is tension and pressure in the mind of people, especially youth. Therefore, we need to work harder towards the set objectives like:

- Doubling of farmer income by making agriculture more remunerative and diversified with better resistant crops and alternative sources of income through Kisan Urja Suraksha evam Utthaan Mahaabhiyan (KUSUM) and other schemes;
- Providing all-weather roads for better connectivity of rural centres with urban areas with enhanced electrical and educational connectivity;
- Setting up MSME units in rural areas to provide more work opportunities to the landless laborers in the rural region;
- Getting some more visible outcomes from the Smart cities and AMRUT Yojana to have more sustainable infrastructure in urban areas;
- Alternative economic development on coastal areas which is least affected by the rising seawater and helping our neighbours also to avoid any wider migration;
- Reducing environmental stress on natural resources like Rivers through increased green cover and revival of natural contributing streams with small dams to ensure greater water availability throughout the year;
- Promotion of better cattle rearing practices; etc.

## 10.  **UNEMPLOYMENT**

Though India is young its youth lack participation in its growth. The unemployment rate in India is at its highest of the last 45 years. According to the Periodic Labour Force Survey for 2017-18 by NSSO, the unemployment rate in India has jumped to 6.1%, with 5.3% in rural

India and 7.8% in the urban area. The unemployment among youth, i.e. unemployment among those in the 15-29 years age category has reached a high of 17.8%, with the percentage being highest among educated urban women at 27.2% (more than double from 2012 figure). The comparative figure for urban men is equally high at 18.7%.

The recent figures on unemployment in India (February 2020) from Centre for Monitoring Indian Economy (CMIE) suggest that the unemployment has reached a record 7.78%. The problem of unemployment in India is further aggravated by the high dominance of unorganized sector or the informal jobs in our economy. E.g. The Economic Survey of 2018-19 says that nearly 93% jobs are informal in India (though Niti Aayog reports it around 85%) with the largest number of jobs created in the informal sector only.

For a young nation like India, high unemployment and lack of decent work opportunities (i.e. jobs with decent work, income, social security, better career prospects etc.) is a cause of concern. It diminishes not just the potential of the present generation but of future generations as well. It shows the failure of India as a nation to best utilize its human resources. It also shows lack of vision towards the problems created by unemployment in terms of increased crime, low productivity, more caste-class struggles and higher affinity to getting attracted towards anti-India forces.

So, it should be the utmost priority to properly utilize our demographic dividend before it turns into a demographic burden. As per the Labour Bureau Report, 2014, the current size of India's formally skilled workforce is only 2 per cent in India. It means that though the Indian education system has been churning out brilliant minds they lack in the skill set required for a specific job. So, we need to increase the skill level of our youth and improve the linkage of Skill India with industry in order to generate jobs for skilled people.

The available NSSO data shows that the 15-24-year-old cohorts face the greatest risk of working poverty if they enter the labour market as a low paid worker. The chances of their withdrawal from the market are highest if they fail to get suitable employment. So, along with the right skill, we need to increase the formalization of jobs in order to add dignity to the work with increased social protection to the workers.

Integrating the youth of India with programmes like Make in India, Digital India, and Smart Cities etc. can be a good initiative to make them part of new India makers. Skilling our youth in advanced technological innovations like Artificial Intelligence and Data Science with better structured and output-oriented programs can help a lot in keeping the nationalistic feeling more vibrant and wise among them.

We can also take a number of other steps to avoid any untoward act towards our internal security like:

- The revival of labour-intensive sectors with increased participation from the youth in agriculture and related sectors like food-processing;
- Lowering the cost of credit by improving the health of the financial sector through the resolution of liquidity issues like NPAs for easy credit availability in the market.
- Take advantage of the problems of China like economic slowdown, trade-war with USA or coronavirus by replacing it as the world factory and promote Indian MSMEs to create greater international supplies with higher credit.
- In the last few years, India has made great progress in the mobile manufacturing sector. We need to identify more such sectoral clusters and work on creating the enabling infrastructure and talent pool to serve.
- Helping the old world through our youth, i.e. as the western economies are growing old, Indian youth can get a huge opportunity by getting work from them. It will also help these nations in overcoming the fatigue set in their economies since 2008.

# CHAPTER 5 - Challenges to External Security of India & Solutions

The United Nations has lost its sheen which it enjoyed once, especially after the end of the Cold War. The Global West is getting replaced by the USA with the rise of Asian countries like China and India, especially after the 2008 financial crisis. This has made global power more diffused with new alignments and more bilateral/trilateral/quadrilateral relationships, helping in building up greater informal networks based on interests rather than traditional multilateral power blocs like the North Atlantic Treaty Organization (NATO).

This has helped national governments to not just influence the economic, social, and political affairs of a nation but also in giving rise to a greater nationalistic role by resolving the complex security challenges which were once dealt as a block. Higher nationalistic aspirations have also changed the regional equations.

Because of these changes, the challenges to our external security are joined by new challenges including the risks of resource constraints, global infectious disease outbreaks and international institutions trying to question the state on its governance. As a nation, India also faces many external challenges and has many new opportunities to overcome those challenges. But this requires the government to be more futuristic and more innovative in approach.

## What is External Security?

Traditionally, External Security was considered as the security of a nation from any attack on its territory. With changing time and changing nature of threats, external security means the security of the nation and its assets from any threat from any foreign country or any other actor. This threat can emerge from not just the physical attacks but also from any aggression toward its economy, its people or any other interest outside the borders of India, including foreign partners across the world.

So, in order to feel externally secure, a nation needs to think beyond its own boundaries. Today, an orbiting INSAT satellite or the oil production from Bombay High (an offshore oilfield in our Exclusive Economic Zone of Arabian Sea) is as vital to us as our territory. Therefore, the challenges to our external security don't end at our land borders, coastline or airspace above it but it includes everything on earth which is strategically important for us.

Kautilya also identified two ways in which the threats to the external security of a nation can emerge, as- external threats caused by reasons outside the nation and external threats caused by Internally-aided reasons. If we look around us, we will observe that India faces multiple challenges to its external security from a range of external actors. And, the steps to externally secure India not just depend on the strength of our armed forces but also on our leadership, our diplomacy and the partnerships we build with other nations or regions.

The Ministry of Defence and Ministry of External Affairs are the main administrative bodies which look at these two aspects. But in recent past, many other ministries have also taken initiatives to make India more secure from any incident outside India. It has helped India to overcome all the existential threat to our security. Today, India is far more forthcoming and far more capable in the expression of its core interests and working towards its security.

This is made conducive by the changing global world and strong support our leadership has gained from valuable nations. But this also means that the global environment is still in the phase of churning and we need to be far more concerned and far more practical in our approach to looking at the global events. This chapter is divided into two broad parts with the first part dealing with the traditional challenges or the physically visible threats to our external security. The second part deals with the subtle future challenges which may not look like a threat to the naked eyes but a threat for an analytical mind.

## Visible Threats to our External Security

Securing the available territory and everything within that territory from any external attack is the basic minimum on which no State can falter. This is also known as national security for a nation and the armed forces of a nation are raised to fulfil this duty. It helps the nation in remaining sovereign and to handle any challenge to its interests through hard power, diplomacy or any other means at its disposal. So, the first goal is to save the very existence of a nation, before any other facets.

And, it has remained the goal of every kingdom from time immemorial. Chanakya in his book Arthashastra emphasized on the need for a well-organized army for state security and advised the king to have a special focus on the art of war. Today's war is fought in different theatres with different actors and strategies focusing on different dimensions and advancing technologies.

India's national security concerns can also be looked at from those theatres of threat along with our troubled neighbourhood. This is visible from the fact that most of the wars India fought after its independence or the major violent internal security threats it faces, all can be linked to ideological basis or material and operational support in our neighbourhood.

This includes the terror-infested and terror-nurturing State of Pakistan in our north-west and rising belligerent China above the Himalayas. The situation is made furthermore challenging for us by the close relationship enjoyed by China and Pakistan. Even bigger challenge is the unsettled borders with some parts of Indian territory being occupied by both of them. Some of the major problems of India with direct/indirect support from them include terrorism, secessionism, drug peddling, Counterfeit Currency circulation, cyber threats, the proliferation of weapons of mass destruction, and the upcoming challenges in the Indian Ocean.

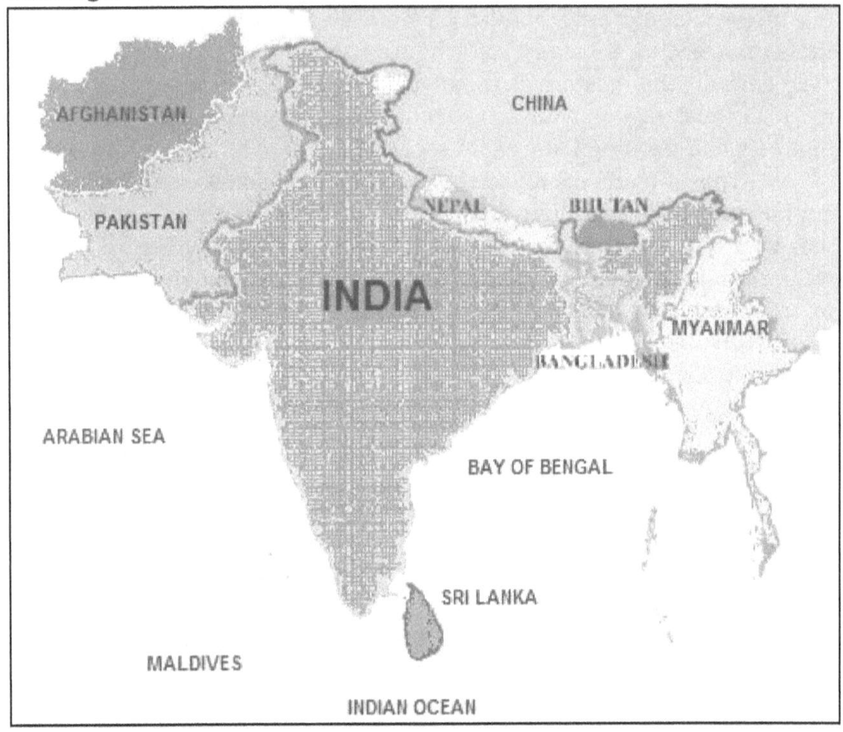


Figure 20 Map of India and its Neighborhood

The traditional external security challenges from an armed forces strategy point of view are based on the battlespace, which under present conditions include- Land, Air, Sea, Cyberspace, Information and Outer Space. India faces all these forms of threat. Out of them, the threats faced by Indian cyberspace in terms of cyber warfare are already discussed in the previous chapter. So, in this chapter, we will give information on the threats which can emerge from the rest.

## Land

The first and oldest field of human warfare is **Land.** From animals to humans, all fight for land in one form or another and even among modern nations we often see the struggle for land. India has a land boundary of nearly 15,200 km, originally shared with seven countries in descending order as- Bangladesh (4,096 km), China (3,488 km), Pakistan (3,323 km), Nepal (1,751 km), Myanmar (1,643 km), Bhutan (699 km) and Afghanistan (106 km).

With unsettled borders and expansionist neighbourhoods, India is pushed since its independence by few of its neighbours to retaliate against the wars started by them. Even in case of no war, the infiltrations from the Army of these nations led to border skirmishes. E.g. in 2013 at Daulat Beg Oldi of Ladakh and in 2017 at Doklam (Bhutan), the entry of Chinese Army in Indian Territory or in the territory of our friendly nation Bhutan led to a face-off between the army of two nations.

From Pakistan side border skirmishes mainly take place in the form of ceasefire violations, cross-border firing and attack on patrolling parties. These are also used by Terrorist Groups. The reason for most of the present border issues of India goes to the British regime but after independence, most of the issues are still present with some being further intensified. Therefore, it is worthwhile to look at the brief history of India with these two nations and the reasons for the present struggle.

## India-China:

India and China share some of the oldest civilizational ties going beyond the trade between the two nations. Among this, Buddhism is the greatest export from India which not only spread the value system of Gautama Buddha but also the Shaolin (a form of martial art spread by BodhiDharma) and the medicinal system of Sowa Rigpa. In 1914, under the British administrator Henry McMohan, British India signed a convention (known as Simla Convention) to demarcate the borders between China, Tibet and India.

The borderline demarcated by McMohan and Tibetian representative Lonchen Satra, also known as McMohan Line, is regarded as the official borders of India by India in the North-East region with Tibet. Initially, China also accepted it and moved forward with the idea of Panchsheel (signed in 1954 by Nehru and Zhou Enlai) for peaceful coexistence with India. With the establishment of complete occupation over the Tibetan region in 1959, the intentions of China changed.

Since then, China has rejected the border agreement from Tibet and claims nearly 65,000 sq km area of Arunachal Pradesh as part of South Tibet. The Cuban missile crisis of 1962 between the USSR-USA provided an opportunity for China to attack India. The crisis started on 16 October 1962 and on 20 October Chinese forces attacked India, leading to a brief war between the two nations. China briefly occupied a significant part of India on both sides of McMohan Line but left the Arunachal side and kept the Aksai Chin (an area of 37,244 sq km) region on Ladakh side under their occupation.

Today, the border shared by the two nations in the Ladakh region is called the Line of Actual Control or LAC (separation between India-controlled territory and China-controlled territory). With the shift of Chinese focus to its economy and greater aspirations towards the South China Sea and competition against the USA, no war has taken

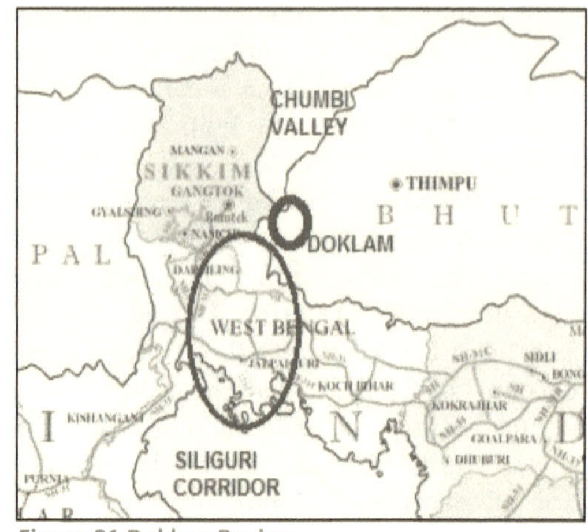


Figure 21 Doklam Region

place between India and China after the 1962 war. But we often see the intrusions from the Chinese side on Indian Borders in Uttrakhand, Ladakh etc. and even in friendly nation's territory of strategic importance. One such major intrusion was the Doklam intrusion, present in Chumbi valley.

Doklam (in Bhutan) lies at a strategic location with the Chumbi Valley of China lying above it while Indian "chicken's neck" corridor or the Siliguri Corridor lie below it. This is useful for India in checking the military movement of China in Chumbi Valley, keeping a check on any untoward incident towards Sikkim. Therefore, occupation of Doklam by China will not only endanger Indian security of Sikkim but also bring China closer to the Siliguri Corridor, blocking of which will block the land connection of India with its North-East region.

## India-Pakistan:

Before the partition of India, the territory of Pakistan and Bangladesh was part of India. Because of the demand for two-nations on religious lines and the communal violence which started from the Direct Action Day, British divided India into two dominions through the Indian Independence Act, 1947. The division was based on the Mountbatten Plan and the borders were divided by the boundary commission under Cyril Radcliffe.

Because of this, the border between the two nations is called to be separated by the Radcliffe line. After killing of many people on both sides, the borders seemed to settle but Pakistan's desire for Kashmir led to many complete and brief wars between the two nations. E.g. Just after a month of independence, the first war between the two nations started with Pakistan's attempts to forcefully occupy Kashmir (around 22 October 1947) before the local King decided on merging its territory with any nation.

Though it became counter-productive and the king merged its territory with India but it helped Pakistan to gain 13,297 sq km area of Kashmir to govern, also known as Pakistan occupied Kashmir (PoK). With the separation of East Pakistan, as Bangladesh, the border issues on one end are completely settled (after the Land Boundary Agreement of 2015) but the Pakistan side remains unsettled.

The Simla Agreement of 1972 tried to settle borders by making the Cease-fire Line as the Line of Control (LoC) between two nations but the aspirations of Pakistan still remained unsettled. Many security experts believe that the very existence of Pakistan as a nation and dominance of Pakistan Army over its polity is dependent on the continued confrontation with India. Because of it, our north-western neighbour never wished for any settlement and half-heartedly reciprocated towards all peace gestures from India.

**China-Pakistan Nexus:**

China is considered as the all-weather friend of Pakistan. Whether it is the supply of weapons to Pakistan or restricting any global action against the terrorism in Pakistan, China has remained at the forefront to support Pakistan. Recently, both nations came together to built the China-Pakistan Economic Corridor (CPEC) under the One Belt One Road[48] (OBOR) initiative of China. It is a US$ 46 billion project with the declared purpose of connecting the less developed South-West China with the Arabian Sea via the road and rail network from Kashgar (China) to Gwadar Port (Pakistan).

But most experts see it as a tool of neocolonialism or the Chinese debt-trap policy, with additional concerns for India because of its passage through the PoK region (disputed region between India and Pakistan). It undermines the sovereignty and territorial integrity of India. This corridor can also serve the interests of both nations' military

---

[48] *One Belt One Road, also known as Belt and Road initiative was first announced by Chinese President Xi Jinping in 2013 to revive the old silk routes between China and Europe. This is called the Silk Road Economic Belt, connecting China and Europe through Central Asia. Add to that, China has launched 21st Century Maritime Silk Road, a sea-based link to get greater maritime access and develop sea routes. As of date, OBOR has spread to 78 different countries from Asia, Africa and Europe. At face value, it is projected as an ambitious economic development measure to construct a unified large market by increasing trade connectivity and cooperation through building of roads, railways, maritime ports, energy grids, oil and gas pipelines etc.*

towards squeezing India in Jammu and Kashmir, i.e. attack from East, West and North on Jammu and Kashmir. CPEC calls for a relook on the strategy of both nations and our armed forces are already working out strategies to respond against any such situation imposed on India by both nations. E.g. Work is on to restructure our armed forces under the newly appointed Chief of Defence Staff with a focus on restructuring our armed forces to meet the demands of future needs. One such proposal is the establishment of a separate Jammu and Kashmir theatre command in Indian Army.

**<u>Other Borders and Land-based threats:</u>**

India's relationship with other South Asian neighbours is governed by the Neighborhood First Policy (launched in 2014) and the Gujral Doctrine, a set of five principles to guide India relationship with its immediate neighbours as:

    i.    With neighbours such as Bhutan, Bangladesh, Nepal, Maldives and Sri Lanka, India does not ask for reciprocity but gives and accommodates what it can in good faith and trust.

    ii.    No South Asian country should allow its territory to be used against the interest of another country of the region.

    iii.    No country should interfere in the internal affairs of another.

    iv.    All South Asian countries must respect each other's territorial integrity and sovereignty.

    v.    They should settle all their disputes through peaceful bilateral negotiations.

Also, we have had strong friendship agreements with Nepal and Bhutan since the 1950s. Because of such policy measures, India doesn't face any state-sponsored land-based risk from these nations. The only source of future worry can be the unsettled Nepal border, where Nepal claims some territory in Kalapani region (part of Pithoragarh district, Uttrakhand) and Susta with some part of it being under the administration of West Champaran district of Bihar).

The worries for India from some of the nations have remained. This includes the use of their territory for operations and infiltration into India by terrorist groups and insurgents. These terrorists and insurgents often cross the borders of Myanmar, Nepal, Bhutan and Bangladesh to avoid actions by Indian forces and use foreign territory for illegal activities against India. Another worry relates to organized crime enterprises which use neighboring countries as a base it for various crimes like human trafficking, migrant smuggling, wildlife trade, antiquities, fake currencies etc. If not handled carefully, these threats can endanger the external and internal security of the nation in future.

**Sea**

After Land, the second field of human warfare is Sea. The importance of protecting water bodies and having a strong Navy to thwart any attempt of attack from water can be traced to the writings of Kautilya. During Colonial times, sea worked not just as a means of exploration and travel but also as a means to attack, occupy and consolidate various nations. E.g. the Portuguese, Dutch, British and French, all came to India through the sea-routes. So, for India, the risk of external threats from the Sea side is very high. It has faced such risks earlier and even today it faces greater risk through those water bodies.

The external risks from water bodies can also come from Rivers, Lakes etc. The shared Himalayas with China, Nepal and Bhutan puts India as the lower riparian state and the risks of blocking water supply to India, causing floods in India or increasing the chances of the earthquake in the region by building large dams is also present for India.

But the good thing is that the Hydro-power projects of Nepal and Bhutan are in collaboration with India. The risks mainly appear to emerge from China, which doesn't want to share its resources with other nations and shows higher tendencies to go to any extent for self-interests.

If we look at the Map of India shared earlier, we will find that the mainland of India is surrounded by the Arabian Sea on the western side and Bay of Bengal on Eastern side with the vast Indian Ocean lying South to it. Apart from the mainland, we have two major island groups-
  i.   Andaman and Nicobar Island Groups (in the Bay of Bengal region), and
  ii.  Lakshadweep Island Groups (in the Arabian Sea).
This gives India a coastal boundary of 7516.6 km with nearly 6100 km as part of the mainland. These coastal areas play an important role in our economy through different purposes served by them like fishing, transportation, tourism, coastal economic zones etc. Presently, 95% of India's trade by volume and 70% by value happens through maritime transport. We have 13 major ports and 205 small and intermediate ports along the coastal boundaries with a plan to establish 14 Coastal Economic Zones.

In addition to that, India has an Exclusive Economic Zone[49] of 2.172 million sq km with a large amount of explored and unexplored natural resources to fulfil the needs of India and its people. So, the challenges to our external security from the Sea side are not just the territorial sabotage but also of economic sabotage. This is further

---

[49] *Exclusive Economic Zone is a sea zone prescribed by the 1982 United Nations Convention on the Law of the Sea (UNCLOS) over which a state has special rights regarding the exploration and use of marine resources, including energy production from water and wind. The present limit of it is 200 nautical miles from the baseline.*

intensified by the threats faced by them from natural and manmade reasons.

The natural reasons include events like Tsunami, Climate Change etc. We discussed climate change earlier. In that, it is worthwhile to explain that the increased risk of climate change and Tsunami are also caused by our activities which damage the natural barriers like Mangroves. Some potential risks are also identified in terms of increasing dead zones, risk of the release of greenhouse gases like methane from methane gas hydrates stored in the sea etc. These risks are discussed in the Sustainable Development Goals book or the natural disaster. Here, our focus is on manmade risks or the risks from state and non-state actors.

## External Security Risks from State and Non-state Actors

Post-independence, the first sea-based challenge was faced by India in the 1965 war when Pakistan was able to restrict Indian Navy involvement in the war, partly because of our unpreparedness with a majority of ships under refit. India learnt its lessons and in 1971 war, our Navy reversed the situation by denying West Pakistan access to East Pakistan through sea-route.

Though the risks from the Pakistan Navy still exist Indian Navy has developed greater capabilities over Pakistan in Sea. Pakistan also realizes it and it has restricted itself from any sort of war from the sea during the Kargil War or any retaliation from the sea after the recent Balakot strike. But it is only a matter of time and technology. As and when its economy improves or some other nation helps it by leasing submarines/ships with better technology than India, they may try to seek adventurism through the sea.

India is also aware of it and the modernization of Indian Navy is one of the topmost priorities for India. Apart from the list of the submarine, aircraft carriers and other technological advancements we discussed earlier, Indian Cabinet Committee on Security has cleared the purchase of 24 MH-60R Seahawk multi-role aircraft from USA (built by Lockheed Martin). These helicopters will help Indian warships and aircraft carriers in performing anti-surface and anti-submarine missions in open oceans and littoral zones through the precision kill weapon system installed on it along with Hellfire missiles and MK 54 Torpedoes.

If we look at the external threats emerging for India in the Indian Ocean region, we will observe that modernization of Indian Navy will be of great help to India in the coming years. These emerging risks to the external security of India are primarily created by the rising sea activities from China in the Indian Ocean Region and its aggressive violations of International Laws in the South China Sea.

Geographically, India shares its maritime border with seven nations form west to east as- Pakistan (at Sir Creek), Maldives (at eight-degree channel, locally known as Maliku Kandu), Sri Lanka (at Katchatheevu Island), Indonesia (at six-degree channel between Indira point of India at Rondo island of Indonesia), Thailand (Andaman Sea separating Indian Islands from Similan Islands of Thailand), Myanmar (the Andaman Sea separating Indian Islands from Coco Islands of Myanmar) and Bangladesh (at New Moore Island). Among them, except the Pakistan and Bangladesh maritime borders, all are settled. In 2014, the Permanent Court of Arbitration gave its award on maritime border dispute between India and Bangladesh and both nations accepted it.

So, the only unsettled maritime border remains the Sir Creek (between Sindh of Pakistan and Gujarat of India) between India and Pakistan. On Sir Creek, the international tribunal gave its verdict in 1968. Based on the area claimed by India, India received 90% of its claim while the rest 10% of it was given to Pakistan. But Pakistan doesn't accept it as the area demanded by it is more. At the same time, it doesn't agree to resolve the issue bilaterally (as both nations agreed under the Simla Agreement, 1972) nor does it accept the Indian suggestion of having demarcation of the boundaries as per the Technical Aspects of Law of Sea (TALOS), an international law which is often called as the constitution of the oceans.

Though all other international laws or doctrines like UNCLOS and Thalweg Doctrine[50] support Indian position or give it advantage, Pakistan claims of complete control over Sir Creek are based on old Sindh Government Resolution of 1914 forgetting that the whole region was under Bombay Presidency of British India at that time.

## The South China Sea and the Chinese String of Pearls

If we look at the coastline of China, we will observe that its sea access is limited to the South China Sea and the East China Sea. Even in it, the East China Sea is shared by North Korea, South Korea and Japan. Similarly, the South China Sea is traditionally the territory of Vietnam with some other smaller nations also having presence and interests in it. This gives China a very narrow sea sphere to influence and an EEZ of only 0.877 million sq km (if the disputed islands claimed by China aren't included).

---

[50] *Thalweg Doctrine, also known as the Thalweg principles, are the legal principles to demarcate boundaries between two political entities in the waterways separating the two. According to it, the centre of the principal navigable channel (presumably the deepest part) should serve as the boundary. In case of multiple channels, the one which is principally used for downstream travel (likely with the strongest current) is used to set boundaries.*

In comparison, the USA, Russia, India etc. enjoys access to a large unclaimed sea to explore and extract resources. E.g. The USA enjoys unhindered access to the Pacific and the Atlantic Ocean with the presence of naval bases in the Indian Ocean. It shares access to the Arctic along with other powers like Russia. India enjoys free access to the Indian Ocean.

If we look at it in terms of Exclusive Economic Zone of different nations, France enjoys world's biggest EEZ with area of over 11.6 million sq km, USA enjoys an EEZ of over 11.3 million sq km, Australia over 10 million sq km, Russia Enjoys an EEZ of over 8 million sq km, Indian EEZ is above 2 million sq km. In comparison, even if we include all the disputed islands EEZs to Chinese EEZ, it goes up from 0.877 to 3.877 million sq km only; Significant addition of 3 million sq km but too little in comparison to the aspirations of China.

It restricts the development of the Blue Economy in China and limits the future growth opportunities by putting limitations on its access to a large amount of natural resources available in the seabed. If we look at the economy of China, it is largely based on large scale exports (because of which it is known as a world factory) requiring high oil and gas imports from other nations to run it. Under such a situation, any strong naval power like the USA can easily contain China in its two seas and destroy the economic superpower of China.

E.g. nearly 70 % of Chinese oil imports come from the Middle East and African nations. Therefore, it started to protect its strategic interests by:
   a) Taking control of the oil and the gas-rich South China Sea by expanding its control over the region, and
   b) Securing safe access to energy and exports by taking control of the critical sea lines of communication,
The start of oil exploration activities by other nations in the Spratly islands served as immediate interest and the exit of the USA from the South China Sea in 1991 served as a golden opportunity for China to expand its occupation without forceful opposition.

Traditionally, the Spratly and Paracel islands are considered to be part of Vietnam territory. The Geneva Accord of 1954 gave South Vietnam access to the whole Vietnam lying below the 17th parallel, including the Spratly and Paracel Islands. In 1994, China started its occupations by taking control of Mischief Reef, part of Spratly Island with proximity to the Philippines Coast.

With increased economic strength and aspirations of making the 21st century as the century of China, it started to call the South China Sea as its core interests with Chinese indisputable sovereignty over the region based on the nine-dash line. The nine-dash line represents the nine dotted lines marked by Zhou Enlai on the South China Sea.

Though in 2011 it signed a Declaration of Conduct of Parties in the South China Sea with Taiwan and four ASEAN nations (Malaysia, Vietnam, Brunei and Philippines), as guidelines to resolve disputes, China neither follows it nor does it allow the application of international laws to solve problems. E.g. in 2011, it opposed the agreement signed by ONGC Videsh Ltd with PetroVietnam for oil and gas exploration in the blocks under Vietnam.

Chinese expansionist attitude has increased a lot in the last few years. In 2014, it occupied Subi Reef and stationed its troops on the island to block the entry of warships of any other nation. It is also claimed by Taiwan, Vietnam and the Philippines. A similar military base is also developed at Mischief Reef with the installation of anti-aircraft and missile defence systems.

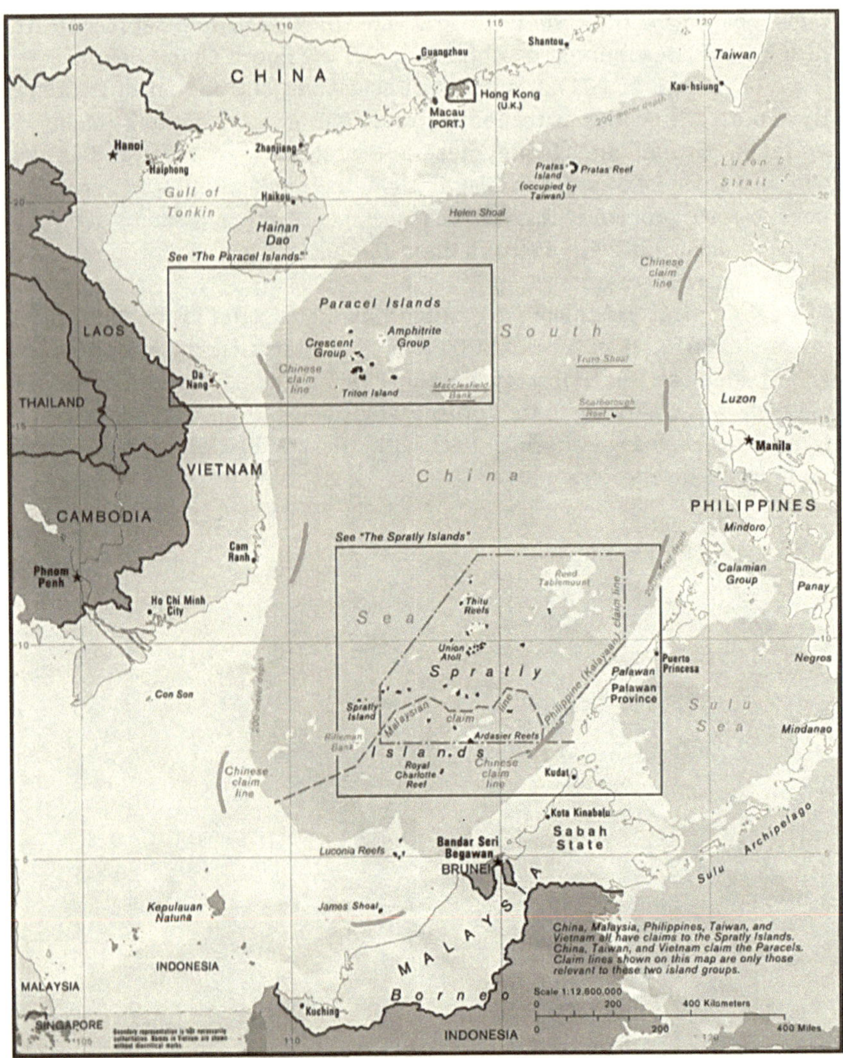


**Figure 22 Nine-Dash Line**

With no concern for the ecology of the region, China has started even building artificial islands at strategic locations to further restrict navigation in the region, coined by US Admiral Harry Harris in 2015 as "Great Wall of Sand", involving large scale reclamations at seven different locations in order to strengthen the territorial claims of China as per the Nine-Dash Line.

India opposes such occupation from China and through various platforms it has stressed on the need of upholding international laws in the South China Sea region and resolution of all disputes in the region

234

based on international laws. In the last few years, the USA has also started to increase its presence in the region to save freedom of navigation and contain China.

Similar concerns are also shared by other nations like Japan and Australia. In 2007, Japanese PM Shinzo Abe called a Quadrilateral Security Dialogue (QSD), also known as Asian Arc of Democracy, with Japan, India, USA and Australia as its four participants. But it went to latent mode soon. The idea of QSD, was again revived during the 2017 ASEAN summit by making it an inter-governmental security forum.

Today, QSD works toward a free and open Indo-Pacific by putting a curb on the territorial ambitions of China. At the same time, to allay the Chinese concerns on QSD as a military block to restrict its movement, India has remained away from the formation of any exclusive group. E.g. India and the USA have been holding joint naval exercise 'Malabar' since 1992. In 2015, Japan was made a permanent member of the exercise. Though others want to induct Australia as a permanent member to the exercise, India refuses such participation. It helps in keeping the QSD focused on the maritime concerns of Indo-Pacific region rather than the development of a military association against China.

But China doesn't share such concerns when it comes to the Indian Ocean. The Indian Ocean is among the busiest oceans of the world with half the world's container traffic, one-third of bulk cargo transport, and around two-thirds of the world's maritime oil shipments passing through it. The sea lines of communication in Indian Ocean also contains a number of straits, also known as chokepoints by maritime experts, like **Bab-el-Mandeb** (connecting Red Sea and Gulf of Aden between Yemen on Arabian Peninsula and Djibouti and Eritrea on Horn of Africa), **Strait of Hormuz** (connecting Persian Gulf with the Gulf of Oman between Iran and the Oman and UAE), **Strait of Malacca** (connecting Indian Ocean with Pacific Ocean between Malaysia and Indonesia), **Sunda Strait** and **Lombok Strait** (connecting Indian Ocean with Pacific Ocean between Bali and Lombok Islands of Indonesia).

The first two straits, i.e. Bab-el-Mandeb and Strait of Hormuz, are important passages of world oil and gas. E.g. The Strait of Hormuz is the only Sea link for Iraq, Kuwait, Bahrain and Qatar. Many oil shipments from UAE and Saudi Arabia also pass through it. Similarly, Bab-el-Mandeb is a vital link between Asia and Europe, with the Suez Canal in North of the Red Sea and the Indian Ocean down South.

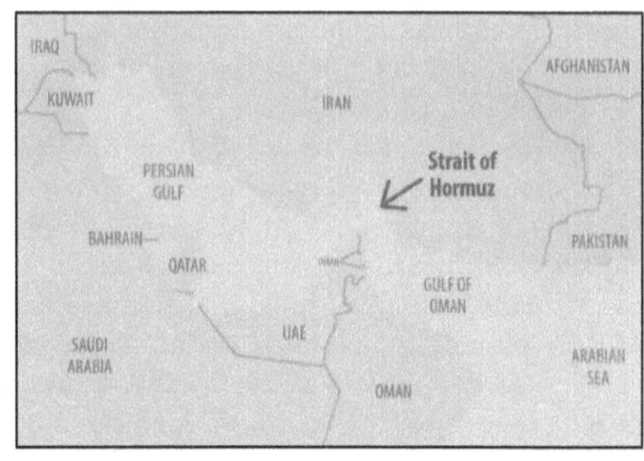


Figure 23 Strait of Hormuz

The other Straits, i.e. The Strait of Malacca, Sunda Strait and Lombok Strait are important points through which sea lines of communication connecting the Indian Ocean with the Pacific Ocean pass through. Under normal circumstances, all straits function normally and merchant ships move from one region to another region without any obstruction through the International Shipping Lanes (ISL). ISL represents the most suitable routes of trade with the shortest and safest sea routes with staging ports en route.

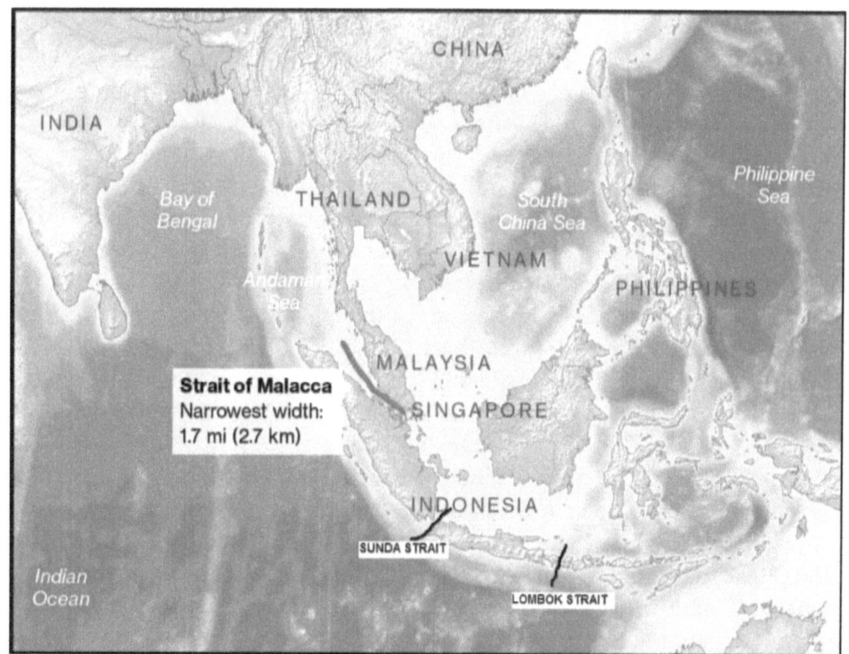



Figure 24 The three Straits of the Indian Ocean and the Pacific Ocean

Though China claims to have a peaceful rise for long but somewhere it feels that it will have a confrontation with nations because of its core interests. Therefore, to overcome any challenge to its core interests, energy security and exports; China started gaining access to ports near the straits. In 2004, a USA consulting firm published a study *"Energy Futures in Asia"*, with **String of Pearls** as the name for Chinese strategy to overcome any challenge to its energy security and protect its supply lines.

Therefore, China wants to take control of the Sea Lines of Communication (SLOC) which are used by a nation during tension or conflict. The first fear of China is the USA with a high presence in all these regions. E,g, USA has Camp Lemonier as a naval base in Djibouti. It has similar naval, air or military bases in Bahrain, Kuwait, Qatar, Iraq, Diego Garcia etc. The next fear is India, as the primary focus area of Indian Navy, expands from the Strait of Hormuz and the Strait of Malacca.

E.g. as early as in 2003, India showed its first interest in the development of Chabahar Port in Iran. The Malacca Strait is close to Andaman and Nicobar with ships passing through the Andaman Sea region of India before going through the Malacca Strait. Since 2001, India has had a tri-force base at Great Nicobar. Looking at the vast expanse of Indian EEZ around Andaman and Nicobar Island, such security measures are natural for India.

China also denies such fear but the work on a policy similar to the **String of Pearls,** first described by the Chinese strategic policy document of the 1990s is visible. The document favoured the attempts to win the military of small nations by paying a small friendship price in terms of military equipment with some economic assistance in order to gain access to the Indian Ocean Region. Today, China has gained control over 15 civilian and naval ports of the small nations, which starts from the South China Sea but most of them are in Indian Ocean Region with nearly half of them encircling India.

E.g. China has encircled India through its development of ports at Gwadar (Pakistan), Marao Port (Maldives), Hambantota port (Sri Lanka), Chittagong (Bangladesh), a naval base in Coco Island of Myanmar and Kyaukpyu Sittwe in Myanmar and Port near Kra Canal of Thailand. A naval base is also established by China in Cambodia. In 2015, only a change of guard in Sri Lanka was able to stop its plan of developing a naval base in Sri Lanka.

China has increased its presence in the Seychelles and Mauritius with more infrastructure projects and flow of investment, especially after the end of favourable tax treatment to Mauritius route by India. But India shares a strong relationship with both nations and it has offered to build a naval base at Assumption Island in Seychelles and Agalega Island in Mauritius, to help both the nations in their fight against piracy while protecting the Indian Ocean from excessive militarization.

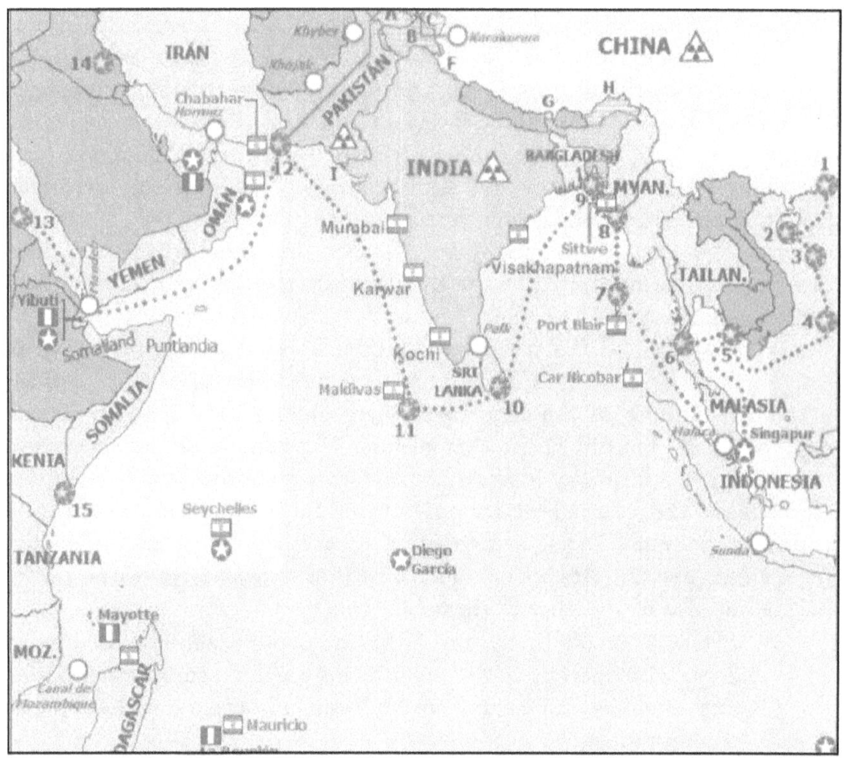


Figure 25 Chinese ports under String of Pearls and the presence of others in the Indian Ocean

These excessive militarization risks of the Indian Ocean are not just from China (which added another base at Djibouti and working on some others in Africa). The Indian Ocean is already frequented by many powers of the world. E.g. The USA is operating from Diego Garcia, part of Chagos Island and counted by Britain as its Indian Ocean Territory. The USA is also trying to expand its operation in the region by developing Cocos Keeling Island, an external Australian territory in the Indian Ocean as its naval base. It will help the USA in keeping watch over the Malacca Strait and the South China Sea. In 2011, the Japan Maritime Self-Defense Force established its base at Djibouti. France is already present in the region with Reunion Islands as part of its territory.

Reasons for the same can be attributed partly to history, geostrategic significance of Indian Ocean Region and high frequency of Piracy in the region (especially from Somalia) and other parts of Indian Ocean Region. E.g. As part of the Combined Maritime Forces of USA (started in 2002 with 33 partnering nations) and Operation Atlanta of Europe (started in 2008 with 18 participating nations) to fight piracy, the whole region remains heavily militarized. It multiplied the woes of India in the region as the pirates started to shift towards the Arabian Sea.

In 2012, the longitudinal marking of the high-risk areas for piracy was moved from 65° East to 78° East in the Arabian Sea by the International Maritime organisation. It essentially meant that the pirates are more active in the region around Indian EEZ. Because of perceived danger, the merchant ships shifted their routes towards Indian coastline for safety. It increased the fuel and insurance costs for all, especially Indian Ships. The risk of ships carrying weapons, toxic materials etc. coming near Indian coastline also increased and Indian fishermen also faced threat, as happened in the Enrica Lexie incident (2012) when two Indian fishermen were killed.

Indian Navy and Coast Guard identified the risks and in a period of 4-5 years, they were able to regulate the activities of pirates. It also helped in shifting of the high-risk longitudinal in 2015, when it was shifted back to 65° East Longitude. But the risk of excessive militarization and piracy in the Indian Ocean remains, posing a serious challenge to the external security of not just India but of all other littoral countries as well. The activities of state and non-state actors in the region increase the risk of not only piracy and blockades of the choke points but also many other challenges, like:

- *External Risks*, in terms of threat to our Exclusive Economic Zone with increased risk of attacks on our sea-based facilities like Bombay High and to our coastal areas or the fishing communities;
- *Internal Risks*, in terms of increased incidences of not just piracy but also of maritime terrorism, smuggling of narcotics, oil, arms, gold and other weapons with the threat of establishing contacts with the organized crime enterprises of India and around;
- Environmental Risks, in terms of threat to the ecosystem of the region which is already stressed due to global warming and climate change.

In the coming years, this struggle for domination in the Indian Ocean Region is more likely to increase and the external threats to India will also multiply with it. E.g. China has already refined its strategy from the string of pearls, in order to gain support for the increased Chinese involvement across the world and in Indian Ocean Region (IOR) through One Belt One Road (OBOR) in 2013. As OBOR talks in terms of economic partnership, the reactions from other nations are becoming mild and they are easily disguised by China through OBOR.

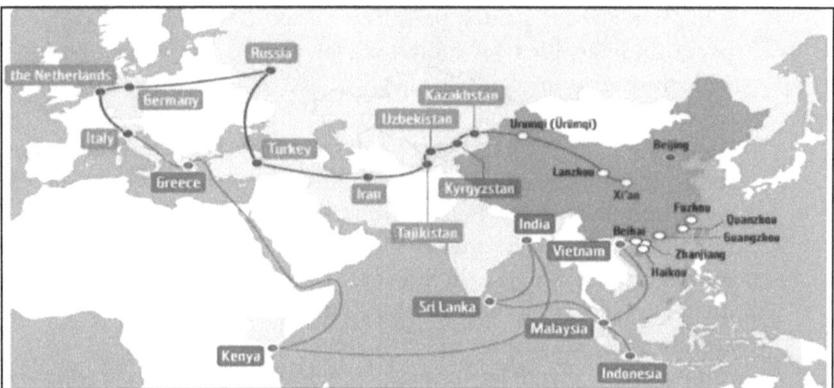


Figure 26 One Belt One Road connecting Asia, Africa and Europe through Sea and Land

India also knows the risks involved and the importance of the greater need of better maritime cooperation and surveillance with urgent need of suppressing the incidents of gunrunning, narcotics smuggling, piracy, and poaching in India's EEZ. With the high risk of natural disasters like cyclones and tsunamis in the region, India also needs to build a greater technology network for early risk warning and provide humanitarian assistance to small island nations in any disaster relief. A number of steps are already taken in this direction like:

- In 2007 India established the Indian Tsunami Early Warning Centre as part of the Global Tsunami Warning and Mitigation System under the Intergovernmental Oceanographic Commission (IOC) of UNESCO;
- In 2012, India consolidated the Tri-Service command in Andaman and Nicobar with commissioning of INS Baaz, the southernmost air station of Indian armed forces to consolidate our presence in the Bay of Bengal and increase safety in East and South-East Asia;
- In 2016, India signed Logistics Exchange Memorandum of Agreement (LEMOA), a reciprocal logistics support agreement with the USA. It will help India in gaining access to US bases in not just Indian Ocean like Diego Garcia, but also in other regions like Guam, on the edge of the Pacific Ocean. It will help India to work along with the USA or alone in humanitarian assistance and defence needs through Logistic Support, Supplies, and Port Services;
- In 2018, India signed a similar reciprocal logistics support agreement with France, allowing India access to the strategically important French base in the Reunion Islands near Madagascar and Djibouti, helping India to overcome the recent protests against the Indian naval projects in Seychelles and Mauritius.

- India has already gained permission from Singapore on use of its ports and facilities by Indian naval vessels for longer periods, with authority to conduct maritime surveillance missions in the South China Sea.
- Since 1995, India has been holding MILAN naval exercises and today it has become one of the biggest naval exercises of the world like Rim of the Pacific Exercise (RIMPAC) from the USA. If all the 41 nations invited by India for the 2020 exercise participate, it will be greater than RIMPAC and will help in bringing synergies across the Indian Ocean and the Pacific Ocean.

This importance given by India to the Indian Ocean is necessary. Like China, India also depends a lot on the oil imports to run its economy and the modern-day information and communication technologies which are based on the large under-sea data cables in the region.

## Airspace

After Land and Sea, the third traditional battlespace is **Airspace**. For a long time, our legends talked about wars fought in the air and it emerged as one of the biggest battlefields of the modern world during the Second World War. Since then the threat levels have multiplied and a wide range of technologies like aircraft, missiles, UAVs etc. are built to use the air.

In recent past, the risk of its use by terrorists as a tool to create fear among people has multiplied through different forms of attacks like hijacking of planes (Indian Airlines Flight 814 in 1999 by Harkat-ul-Mujahideen with support from ISI, Pakistan), blasts in planes (Air India Flight 182 in 1985 by Khalistani terrorists killing 329 people) or the attacks like 9/11 in USA by hitting important commercial and defence installations through plane.

The Airspace of a nation is identified as the 3-dimensional atmosphere above its territory, including the atmosphere above its territorial waters. While the length and breadth of airspace can be defined easily based on the borders and territorial waters, the height or altitude isn't standardized through the international convention. Some call for 30 km or the maximum height at which aircraft go while others call to extend it till 160 km. The most followed convention is to consider the atmosphere below the outer space, i.e. atmosphere below the Karman Line or the edge of earth's atmosphere with a height of 100 km above Earth's mean sea level as airspace.

The nations are also free to take control of the airspace above oceans for civilian purposes i.e. to have executive control over the airspace in order to help the air traffic. If we look at the airspace of India, it is estimated to be 40 million cu km. Most of it is opened for civil use while some of it, around 35% has been earmarked for defence use. Such large airspace is also among the busiest airspace of the world with India as the 3rd largest civil aviation market of the world and presence of vital inter-continental routes over India.

To guard this airspace from the hostile neighbourhood of India with continued risk, the need for greater surveillance and air defence capabilities over the region are of prime importance. In the past, we have seen serious incidents of unauthorized arm drops (Purulia 1995), a mid-air collision between civil aircraft (in 1996), or Indian Air Force and Coast Guard planes/helicopters going off the radar or crashing.

In the last few years, the incidents of Malaysian MH 370 going missing or another MH 17 being shot by non-state actors has opened new challenges and closer look over the neighbouring airspace as well. If we look at the air network of India, the flights from Delhi towards Russia, Europe, Middle East etc. passes from the airspace of our troubling neighbour Pakistan and some over Afghanistan. The incidents like MH 17 over Ukraine can be repeated if the non-state actors get hold of such surface-to-air firing equipment. The increased use of UAVs or drones for surveillance by external enemies or even internally for espionage purposes is another challenge from airspace.

The last and most damaging challenge to our security is the missiles fired by our enemy nations. With both Pakistan and China being nuclear powered, the warhead of missiles can cause severe damage to India. Therefore, the need for securing airspace is as important as any other battlespace. The first step to mitigate any external threat from the air include tracking of all civil aircraft flying in the security layer of Indian Air Defence Identification Zone[51] (ADIZ). Being responsible for the security of Indian airspace, Indian Air Force keeps a close watch over it through military and civil radar with different capabilities of surveillance in terms of altitude (low, medium and high) or range/distance. We can add UAV and Satellite tracking also to it.

IAF is helped by the Air Traffic Service (ATS) in control over the civil aircraft with Indian Navy and Indian Army adding to its firepower. The second step in this direction is the presence of a sound Air Defence

---

[51] *Air Defence Identification Zone (ADIZ) is the airspace beyond the land and territorial waters of a nation which is identified by a nation as vital for its security. First ADIZ of the world was identified by the USA in 1950 and soon many other nations followed. India also identifies its ADIZ at a distance of 15NM (Nautical Miles) from its border or territorial waters in Indian Ocean. Though it is part of International airspace, every civil flight is required to share its identity and follow the routes established by India or specially permitted to it over the Indian airspace. Any aircraft without air defence clearance or not following the permitted route is liable to interception from India as long as it remains in the ADIZ.*

system against alien fighter planes and UAVs. In the last few decades, greater importance is given to it and a range of air-defence systems are made available to our forces as following:

- AWECS system to identify enemy aircraft.
- Defence aircraft with quick response teams of IAF.
- Surface-to-air missiles and air defence systems. The deal to purchase S-400 from Russia is already done and talks on purchase of USA air defence system NASAM-II (National Advanced Surface-to-Air Missiles System-II) are in an advanced stage.

Once purchased, it will add to the mix of air defence systems of India including our own air defence systems (AAD and PAD), Akash missile, Israeli Barak-8 Missile and the Russian security. The post-Balakot attempts from Pakistan to enter into Indian airspace and the quick reply given by IAF shows that India is well prepared to handle the aircraft based intrusion. Once all the air defence systems are installed, India will develop capabilities to not just protect its airspace from missiles, aircraft or UAVs but also give us the abilities to track and destroy missiles in the exosphere, i.e. beyond our atmosphere.

To protect India from the events of espionage or other security threats from Unmanned Aerial Vehicles, also known as UAVs/Drones or Remotely Piloted Aircraft System (RPAS), flying within the Indian airspace, the Ministry of Civil Aviation has launched use guidelines in 2018 with following mandatory requirements as:

- All RPAS except nano and those owned by NTRO, ARC and Central Intelligence Agencies are to be registered and issued with a Unique Identification Number (UIN).
- Unmanned Aircraft Operator Permit (UAOP) shall be required for RPA operators except for nano RPAS operating below 50 ft., micro RPAS operating below 200 ft., and those owned by NTRO, ARC and Central Intelligence Agencies.
- The mandatory equipment required for operation of RPAS except nano category are
  a. Global Navigation Satellite System (GPS),
  b. Return-To-Home (RTH),
  c. Anti-collision light,
  d. ID-Plate,
  e. Flight controller with flight data logging capability, and
  f. RF-ID and Subscriber Identity Module (SIM)/ No-Permission No Takeoff (NPNT).
- These RPAS will operate within visual line of sight (VLoS), during day time only, and a maximum of 400 ft. altitude.

- The airspace has been partitioned into Red Zone (flying not permitted), Yellow Zone (controlled airspace), and Green Zone (automatic permission).
- The Red Zones or no drone zones are identified at various locations like airports, international borders, Vijay Chowk in Delhi; State Secretariat Complex in State Capitals, strategic locations/vital and military installations; etc.
- For flying in the Yellow Zone, i.e. controlled Airspace, filing of the flight plan and obtaining Air Defence Clearance (ADC) /Flight Information Centre (FIC) number shall be necessary.
- The ADC/FIC will be given through the 'Digital Sky Platform', a national level unmanned traffic management system to implement the policy of NPNT (No Permission, No Takeoff). The users will be required to ask for permission to fly through a mobile app and an automated process permits or denies the request instantly.
- In case of any violation, the enforcement actions are, (a) suspension/ cancellation of UIN/ UAOP in case of violation of regulatory provisions, (b) actions as per relevant sections of the Aircraft Act 1934, or Aircraft Rules, or any statutory provisions, and (c) penalties as per applicable IPCs (such as 287, 336, 337, 338, or any relevant section of IPC).

## Space

Space or the outer space i.e. space above the Karman line is an emerging battlespace where nations are likely to fight future wars. The race for the establishment of dominance in space started between the USA and USSR in the early years of the Cold War even before the launch of the first satellite. In the 1960s, both nations started to test systems which can check the satellites from other nations and damage them, if required. This is also known as space-to-space warfare and the **outer space treaty** of 1967 tried to restrict such activities in space by making space free for exploration and use by all nations with no nation to claim sovereignty of outer space or any celestial body.

Under the present time, the outer space treaty is considered to be outdated and insufficient towards stopping future battles of space as it suffers from certain limitations. E.g. The outer space treaty prohibits the placing of nuclear weapons in space but it doesn't put a limit on placing any other weapon system in outer space. Similarly, it limits the use of the Moon and all other celestial bodies for peaceful purposes only but it doesn't specify whether mining on celestial bodies is peaceful or not.

Similarly, the treaty prohibits the use of space for testing weapons of any kind, conducting military maneuvers, or establishing military bases, installations, and fortifications but the USA and USSR in the 1980s and China in 2007 conducted Anti-Satellite Missile Test. The test from China has changed the geopolitics of outer space, especially the regional security balance in outer space.

In the last 2-3 decades, Satellites have become an important part of national security and society. The satellites orbiting in different orbits help in carrying out a range of services like remote sensing of the earth, weather information, communication, Internet, banking and navigation etc. It also helps our armed forces and intelligence agencies in their day-to-day functioning and in carrying out special missions. Under such situation, the Anti-Satellite Missile Test (ASAT) from China with capabilities to even attack Medium and Geo-Earth Orbit, removing one navigation and communication satellite from the large constellation of satellites launched by ISRO can have a crippling effect on the functioning of not just our economy but on capabilities of our armed forces to carry out any large-scale military operations as well.

In order to secure our regional interests and ensure the safety of our space infrastructure, India test-fired its Anti-Satellite (ASAT) missile to shoot down its Low Earth Orbit Satellite in 2019 under Mission Shakti. This test will help in securing the regional balance and keep the Outer space protected for the modern society which is dependent on outer space for a lot of needs. It will also help India in the following ways:

- With voices being raised to replace the outer space treaty with the new treaty because of the merging challenges of mining, space debris and narrowing down of space available for satellite launch, especially in fixed orbits; ASAT will protect India from any discriminatory policy. E.g. the Non-Proliferation Treaty on Nuclear Weapons or NPT allows the vertical proliferation of nuclear weapons by allowing the nuclear-weapon states to modernize or advance their existing weapons technologies while states not possessing nuclear weapons on 01 January 1967 are restricted from acquiring nuclear weapons;
- It helped India in demonstrating its capabilities to protect its satellites and restrict other nations to launch any satellite with capabilities to spy on India;
- It will give voice to India in framing the text of any future treaty on outer space; and
- Most importantly, it helped India to gain insight on the intricacies of the whole subject. After the successful test, we carried a successful space warfare simulation exercise IndSpaceEx about the threats and inputs for joint space warfare doctrine.

The work has already started in the direction of joint space warfare doctrine by setting up of a Defence Space Agency (a Tri-Service command) to protect Indian space assets and operate the space warfare assets of India. Defence Space Agency can help India in identifying the existing gaps in state-of-the-art technologies of outer space and the solutions which will not only enhance the future capabilities of our defence forces towards the security of India, but also help DRDO and ISRO in exploring the technologies to better serve the present and future needs of a vibrant space industry in India.

## The proliferation of weapons of mass destruction

Even before becoming a member of international treaties like the Chemical and Biological Weapons Conventions and the Missile Technology Control Regime, India followed the principles similar to the international obligations against the proliferation of the weapons of mass destruction (WMD). It helped India in gaining entry to most of the treaties which work towards the non-proliferation of WMD.

But a handful of nations with poor track records against the protection of WMDs and its technology still continue to hold WMD and also harbor terrorist groups. This creates a potential threat to the security of India in the form of proliferation of weapons of mass destruction (WMD) with the terrorist organizations gaining access to the WMDs. These WMDs include nuclear, biological and chemical weapons. E.g. in 1998, Al-Qaeda chief Osama Bin Laden called it an Islamic duty to acquire weapons of mass destruction in order to kill masses. As part of it, anthrax was used for attacks in the USA. Globally, the Weapons of Mass Destruction includes-

- Destructive devices such as an explosive or incendiary bomb, rocket, or grenade;
- A weapon that is designed to cause death or serious injury through toxic or poisonous chemicals;
- A weapon that contains a biological agent or toxin;
- A weapon that is designed to release dangerous levels of radiation or radioactivity.

Among them, nuclear weapons are something which we discussed earlier. The Chemical Weapons are based on toxic chemicals and their precursors. The Biological Weapons includes the microbial or other biological agents, or toxins whatever their origin or method of production, of types and in quantities that have no justification for prophylactic, protective or other peaceful purposes.

As we know that India houses one of the biggest chemical industries in the world with a pharmaceutical industry which serves the world, India identified the risks of proliferation. Accordingly, many laws were enacted over the years to provide legal and administrative control over the WMDs, their means of delivery and related dual-use materials. Few of those laws include- *The Atomic Energy Act, 1962; The Customs Act, 1962; The Environment Protection Act, 1986; The Foreign Trade*

*(Development and Regulations) Act, 1992; The Chemical Weapons Convention Act, 2000; The Unlawful Activities (Prevention) Amendment Act, 2004* etc.

Still, some points were missing towards the fulfilment of India's obligations towards UN Security Council Resolution 1540 on non-proliferation of WMDs. Accordingly, in 2005 THE WEAPONS OF MASS DESTRUCTION AND THEIR DELIVERY SYSTEMS (PROHIBITION OF UNLAWFUL ACTIVITIES) ACT was enacted to prohibit unlawful activities, in relation to weapons of mass destruction and their delivery systems by prohibiting the possession, manufacture, transportation, acquisition, development of nuclear weapons, chemical weapons or biological weapons by non-State actors.

It prohibits the export of any good or technology from India if the exporter knows that it is intended to be used in a WMD programme and introduces transit and trans-shipment controls, re-transfer provisions, technology transfer controls, brokering controls and end-use based controls, which were missing in earlier acts. The 2005 Act was an important step to reaffirm India's commitment to safeguard its security as a nuclear weapon state and to avoid the transfer of WMDs, their acquisition by non-state actors and its commitment towards global nuclear disarmament.

Still, the risks remain because of India being surrounded by two nations with nuclear weapons and active nuclear power installations. Even a nuclear accident of any kind in Pakistan can cause significant damages in Indian Territory as well. The use of chemical weapons in the Syrian conflict despite a ban suggests that many nations still hold chemical weapons which can be accessed by terrorist organizations.

Our neighbours may also possess them. Another emerging worry under the WMDs for India is the rapid developments in biotechnology leading to the birth of increasingly complex and dangerous microorganisms. While Pakistan lags far behind India in biotechnology but China is actively engaged in this field with many advanced laboratories and facilities. It is not confirmed but some conspiracy theories published by newspapers claim that the recent coronavirus outbreak In China is caused by an accidental release of virus from a state laboratory in Wuhan rather than exotic seafood market.

While the conspiracy theories need a lot more evidence, major learning's can be taken from the outbreak in terms of the problems faced by China. As we know, China is better equipped in terms of hospitals, healthcare professionals, masks etc. in comparison to India. Despite this, China is facing a lot of supply and infrastructure constraints. With a death toll of 3,802 and 109,648 active cases of coronavirus by 03 March

2020, the damage which can be caused by any such outbreak in India can be enormous.

India also faced one such catastrophic event when tons of methyl isocyanate gas was released in the 1984 Bhopal Chemical disaster. As per National Disaster Management Authority, we are still underprepared to face the problems of WMDs as we lack vulnerability assessments, have limited ability to track the sale and purchase of hazardous chemicals, inadequate security at "large institutions and isolated storage sites," and inadequate surveillance of the movement of hazardous chemicals.

This is partly because of India's knee jerk reaction to such incidents by making laws more strong rather than to work on all aspects like mitigation, prevention, preparedness, response and recovery to a disaster. At the global level, the world also seems to be more conservative towards nuclear disarmament with the main focus on non-proliferation. In 1954, India called the world at UN Disarmament Commission to end the nuclear testing and a freeze on fissile material production.

From time to time, India has reiterated its stand of a global, non-discriminatory, verifiable nuclear disarmament in a time-bound manner. But the global response was shallow, first in the form of the Partial Test ban Treaty followed by a biased NPT and Comprehensive Test Ban Treaty. As long as the international community remains divided and doesn't work towards a universal commitment of disarmament, the threats of the proliferation of WMDs will continue to remain in the world and India.

## Subtle Future Challenges

If we look at the world around us carefully we will observe that despite no immediate threat of war the world looks far more disturbed and nations are far more assertive to protect themselves. The rising right with increasing nationalistic pitches among different nations including India is a sign of changing world with the security of a nation being perceived beyond the power of armed forces.

The precise need of a National Security Strategy with DIME (Diplomacy, Information, Military and Economy) and organizations working in cohesion becomes more prominent in wake of rising threats to national security which isn't confined to its borders or disturbances within. From the Chinese perspective, One Belt One Road is vital to safeguard itself from upcoming challenges of energy security.

But OBOR Association poses a subtle challenge of Debt-trap diplomacy for smaller countries. Other such subtle future challenges likely to be faced by nations (including India) are the challenges caused by trade imbalances, lack of access to natural resources, misuse of technology, world without sustainable development etc.

Being the trendsetter on national security, the USA was the first to realize a number of them. Whether it is the ongoing renegotiations on trade pacts to correct trade imbalances or the US objections to Huawei 5G installations in US or advice to its allies or friendly nations, all suggests toward the rising risks of technological and information warfare.

## 5G Technology:

5G or fifth-generation wireless technology is the next generation of technology to drive digital cellular networks. The infrastructure used by the telecom companies for 5G is provided by 4-5 major players like Samsung, Nokia, Ericsson, Huawei and ZTE.

For India, all of them are foreign-based companies. If we focus on economic considerations and sideline security concerns then 5G products from Chinese companies are the cheapest, saving 15-20% price. If we go by security concerns, then the next-generation applications which will drive businesses across India and the world with people getting connected with the government and others will use this 5G technology. Therefore, we need companies which can cooperate with India and don't misuse the sensitive and personal information which will be assessed by the carrier equipment like base stations, antennas and switching gears.

This is called as backdoor access to information and if not controlled, it will not just violate the privacy of individuals (by selling the information to others) but it can also jeopardize the security of nation as in few years our agriculture, manufacturing, public transport, healthcare, tourism, weather forecasting, environment monitoring, early warning systems against natural disasters etc. all will be based on 5G technology.

If we look at the previous history of Chinese equipment, then questions were raised about mobiles. Even our armed forces asked its personnel not to use Chinese mobiles. So, it is important that we carefully analyze the risks involved in allowing the Chinese company to gather information which will drive the next generation industries (including the trade secrets). The Chinese companies are always known for opaqueness in their connection with the Government and use of information.

Presently, India is in the trial stage and the government has allowed the telecom companies to conduct trials with participation from Chinese companies. The USA is asking India to not allow Chinese companies. China has advised that any such measure will hurt India-China relations. The trials may help us in finding those potential vulnerabilities and searching for better solutions but some solutions which India can try based on the other examples to overcome its 5G dilemma can be:

- Categorization of parts into core and non-core like the United Kingdom, which is planning to allow the participation from Huawei in non-core parts of the UK's 5G network, the masts and towers, with a 35% cap on the use of the firm's equipment;
- Another solution is to have multiple players with a cap on all participants in market irrespective of core and non-core;
- The USA is looking to establish its control on Nokia and Ericsson through purchase or other means. India can also look for such measures; or
- Introduction of limitations on taking such information out of India and technological initiatives to monitor the activities of backdoor access to information.

On one hand, advancing technologies are bringing benefits to people through dramatic changes in our ecosystem. On another hand, they are posing new challenges which can jeopardize the security of the nation by introducing new systemic fragilities in our socio-economic life which can be exploited by state and non-state actors for their interests. It can also impact the interests of domestic companies and India's relationship with other nations. 5G technology is one such technology and we have many other such technologies or services like Social Media, Artificial Intelligence, Cryptocurrency, nanotechnology etc. which offer such dual-use opportunities which can threaten national security.

## Natural Resources

In 2014, China and Russia signed a US$400 billion deal to supply gas from Russia to China for 30-year. From Indian perspective, we can look at this deal from number of perspectives, such as:

A. The first and the more natural perspective is that such a deal helps China in overcoming the threats it perceives to its economy in case of no energy security or tensions at the choke points of the trade.

B. The second perspective is that both nations are facing sanctions from the USA in one form or another for long. So, as long as the USA domination over the world doesn't end, both nations should behave as realpolitik. Thus, China and Russia signed the deal which can help both nations in overcoming past differences and create trust through long-term economic cooperation.

C. The third and most strategic reason can be the increasing competition for scarce natural resources, including energy resources. In future, we are likely to have increased tensions within a nation and between nations for scarce natural resources. The factors like climate change and excessive exploitation of resources have multiplied these threats. So, China has tapped a prospective resource opportunity in its neighbourhood to negate any negative development in the global energy market and gain spin-off benefits from it in the form of getting latest military help from Russia (which was largely denied by Russia to China because of its past experience of reverse engineering), more synergies in solving its dispute with Russia and getting Russia on its side against USA in next few years.

We may have many other perspectives to look at the deal but this deal becomes vital for India to think about future scenarios and our national security interests. E.g. the total trade between India and Russia in 2018-19 was US$8.3 billion only. Under such a situation, it will be naïve to believe that Russia will support India in case of any future challenge from China. The geopolitical situations are favouring Russia and China to become natural allies rather than to act against each other.

Also, it makes little sense for India to counter its impact on its relationship through similar purchase from Russia. In 2014, India asked for the extension of the Russia-China pipeline till India but Russia declined, probably because of Chinese reservations. As an alternative, India and Russia are working on the feasibility of a pipeline from Serbia to India through Central Asia or other routes.

But India knows that this plan won't be completed in the near future. Our long-term interests lie in reducing oil and gas imports, which meets 80% of our oil and gas needs but cost heavily on the exchequer. When we purchase crude oil/gas from Middle East nations, it helps these nations to host large Indian Diaspora and in return, India gets high remittances. So, India has developed many other solutions to secure its energy security. E.g. in collaboration with some Middle East nations, India is working on building Strategic Petroleum Reserves in India which can help in facing any supply shock by extending the buffer stock of India. We have already completed work on 5.33 MMT (Million Metric Tonnes) of strategic crude oil storages at **Mangalore (Karnataka), Visakhapatnam (Andhra Pradesh) and Padur (Karnataka)** under Indian Strategic Petroleum Reserves Limited. The plan is to build another 6.5 MMT strategic reserve caverns at Chandikhol (Odisha) and Udupi (Karnataka).

Once completed India will have 22 more days buffer in addition to the 65 days industrial stock kept by Indian refineries. It will help India in achieving the International Energy Agency suggested 90-day reserve stock. Analyzing in terms of long-term energy security, 90 days buffer appears to be too small. For long-term energy security, India is working on a number of solutions as:

- Increased use of solar and other renewable energy resources. India has set a target of 175 GW of renewable energy (by 100 GW Solar, 60 GW wind, 10 GW bio-power and 5 GW by small hydro-power) by 2022 and in last few years renewable energy sector has seen a significant increase;

- One alternative is increased use of our coal reserves but they can't be used in automobiles and cause more environmental pollution. Because of it, India is not working aggressively on coal and we are spending more on the expansion of renewable energy rather than coal, which dominated our expenditures before;

- The third step is the increased use of Electric vehicles rather than Petrol and Diesel vehicles. For this India has introduced 'The National Electric Mobility Mission Plan (NEMMP) 2020' for faster adoption of electric vehicles and their manufacturing in the country. NEMMP is supposed to enhance our energy security along with addressing the issues of climate change, promote our advances in renewable energy with solutions to the increasing problem of pollution in Indian cities and development of Indian automotive industry as a global manufacturing hub. The major change in this policy over the earlier FAME policy is the incentive from the government in terms of reduced GST (12%) on an electric vehicle with no cess and active promotion from the government through the purchase of electric vehicles by government ministries and state transport departments.

- The fourth step which the government is exploring is the sale of BPCL to any gulf company especially from Saudi Arabia, with the largest oil reserves. It will help in creating shared interests for India and other nations towards energy security.

- The fifth step is to set up a buyer's bloc with China. Plans are on to bring South Korea and Japan also onboard. It mayn't help in energy security but it will help in short-term bargaining on price.

We have many more solutions and we are already working on them in order to ensure long-term energy security for India. But the same situation is likely to be faced in other fields as well. E.g. the present technology of electronic equipment and devices used in satellites, mobile devices, healthcare (MRI) and even nuclear reactors, is based on various rare earth metals. Presently, China produces nearly 90% of such metals as it has mastered the technology to produce it which for others is very difficult and expensive under the current scenario.

Similarly, if we look at the Lithium, used in various electronic appliances, especially batteries, the global race for Lithium is intensifying and its reserves are mainly restricted to few nations like Chile, Australia, Argentina, China, Zimbabwe, Portugal, Brazil etc. The Lithium reserves of India are around 14,100 tonnes only.

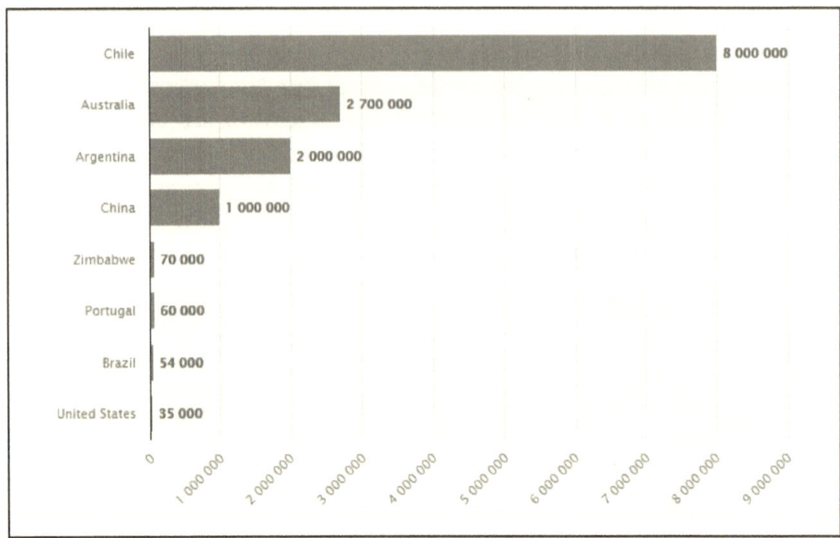


Figure 27 Major Lithium Reserve Countries of the world and their reserves

Therefore, our dream of becoming an electric vehicle manufacturing hub will remain a dream as long as we don't work in the direction of removing the dependence of our automobile industry on supplies from other nations. One solution on which India is working is the Joint Venture between different mining PSUs of India with NALCO as the main lead and Niti Aayog as a guide. We can also promote private players to acquire rights in foreign mines and set up production facilities as they did in Africa.

## Partnership of 21$^{st}$ Century: Indo-US and Trade Deals Concerns

Under the changing geopolitical conditions and the reducing relevance of UN India needs a strong economic and security partner which can propel its growth and help in building international order and peace. The natural fit nation in this scheme for India is the USA. For last few years, many initiatives are taken from both nations including the highest office of US i.e. President.

E.g. from Indian Independence to the end of last century only three out of its nine Presidents visited India. But since 2000, all Presidents of the USA have visited India at least once including the recent visit from President Donald Trump on 24-25 February 2020. The grandeur of the whole visit suggests the investments India is making to build a strong partnership with the USA.

This increased cooperation is developed over a series of confidence-building measures and partnership initiatives taken in the past like US-India High Technology Cooperation Group (2002), Indo-US Nuclear Deal (2008), Defence Technology and Trade Initiative (2012) and so on. All this helped the two nations in understanding each other better and it helped India in becoming part of MTCR, Australia Group etc. This has also helped both nations through increased defence cooperation with greater synchronization of efforts in the Indo-Pacific region.

Under such blooming partnership between the two nations, one major concern which can have a negative influence on our relationship is the India-USA. In recent times, we have witnessed the ugly tariff war between USA and China which started in July 2018. In less than a year both nations imposed more than $470 billion tariffs on each other (more than $360bn from the US on Chinese goods, and more than $110bn from China on US products).

It shows the intensity of negotiations between the two nations and the uncertainty faced by the industry of both nations and beyond. Even today, only the 1st phase of the deal or a preliminary deal is signed. If we compare India's trade with US ($142.6bn) with the US-China trade ($737.1bn in 2018), we can realize that we have far less leeway to bargain. An already precarious situation of our economy increases the stakes involved for India.

At the same time, the US-China trade negotiations are uglier because of the high stakes from the US as trade deficit between US and China was nearly $378.6 billion dollar in 2018 ($179.3 billion of exports and $557.9 billion of import). In comparison, the trade deficit between India and the USA was only $25.2 billion in 2018 in favour of India. Further, the high-end defence purchases and LNG agreement from India has relaxed the situation by decreasing the trade deficit.

The concerns from India are primarily because of the suspension of India's tariff-free access for approx $5.6 billion in exports under the 1970s-era Generalized System of Preferences. While the US wants removal of price caps on medical equipment with greater market access for its farm goods, dairy products, mobile phones, motorbikes and high-end IT products.

This makes it tough for India as we have very limited scope of negotiation on such items. E.g. because of the systemic neglect of our agriculture and allied activities, India is not in a situation to face any foreign competition. The outcome of the deal will also be crucial for our Information Technology and Pharmaceutical Industry, for which the USA is the biggest market. Any negative development can worsen the internal security situation of India which is already going through the phase of unemployment and reduced wealth creation.

Only a favourable trade deal with the USA can help India in long-term wealth creation while an unfavourable trade deal may cause greater challenges to our own trade deficit economy. The Indo-US trade deal also gains importance because of other opportunities both nations hold in the coming decades. Whether it is the defence cooperation or exchange of information, India has obliged the USA through favourable response.

In this process, some of our old partners (Russia) are distanced or at times we were forced to overlook our interests (as happened in case of oil imports from Iran). The USA also understands the importance of India for selling its defence equipment and most importantly, the role played by Indian market in US wealth creation through the soared market capital of US companies like Google, Facebook, Twitter, Netflix etc.

India and the USA need to close the deal quickly, in a manner which favours the economy of both nations. This will lead to a stronger and stable relationship between two nations. The success of our innovative public diplomacy in last few years has helped in bringing the two nations together and we need such innovative steps in the economy which can bring the economy of two nations together, helping us in building a far more secure and safer India and world.

# Epilogue

National Security is discussed for a long time by political representatives as the ultimate dream they want to achieve but the state always remains divided on ways to achieve it. Armed forces tried to achieve it by becoming more lethal and brute. Diplomacy tried to achieve it through continuous diplomatic engagements irrespective of the security environment. The economists gave priority to the economy over other factors and our information collection agencies remained scattered with no synchronization of information.

The escalation of the Kashmir problem is a manifestation of such divided state thinking. The Army felt that greater power (under AFSPA) with greater retaliation will solve the problem. The Planning Commission and others felt that greater monetary help from the central government will solve the problem. Our diplomacy felt that it can solve the issue through talks. And among all of them, our information agencies were left with little motivation when nothing favourable happened on the given information and our own agencies negated the advances made by others.

After the 9/11 attacks, the US displayed that it has overcome the failures of Vietnam through its National Security Strategy. National Security Strategy helps in bringing all executive organizations, especially DIME, in close working coordination. The success of the US in Afghanistan (2001) and again in Iraq (2003) proved the benefits of the National Security Strategy. Since then, many nations are working on their unwritten National Security Strategy and India is also one among them. But as long as we are not aware of the challenges to our national security we can't decide on the solutions, solutions which not only protect our borders but also protect our present and future interests.

National Security Strategy is a process to synchronize all those interests and create solutions which try to achieve maximum interests of our nation in a coordinated manner. It helps in identifying our enemies and allies from not just present or past perspective but also from a future perspective, helping in giving a pragmatic approach to our decision-making. Such pragmatic thinking from Kautilya laid the foundations of a strong pan-Indian empire for Chandragupta with boundaries expanding till modern-day Afghanistan. As Kautilya said,

*Before you start some work, always ask yourself three questions - Why am I doing it, what the results might be and will I be successful. Only when you think deeply and find satisfactory answers to these questions, go ahead.*

Through National Security Strategy, India will also incorporate such a pragmatic approach to its decision making. But it also requires leadership which owns the risks and work on including key principles and interests of DIME in order to know why we are doing it and what results it will achieve before each strategic decision. It helps them in identifying the chances of success and work on achieving success through effective oversight through all the obstructions which may emerge from other state and non-state actors. But as a process National Security Strategy requires strong leadership and wise institutions to implement it.

The results also depend on the wisdom of incumbents who act through the process. The leadership of a nation is the first incumbent. It helps in shaping the work culture of our organizations and the values they carry while working towards National Security. Without work culture and values, our organizations can't work effectively towards the goal of National Security Strategy and advise the leadership in a manner which helps the leaders to better understand our world and work on building protective security measures at the strategic level. As a team, our leadership and organizations help in building a holistic security culture, supported by effective governance structures. As our poet Thiruvalluvar said,

*The enemies cannot destroy the king who has at his service the respect and friendship of the wise men who can find fault, disagree, and correct him.*

The first visible signs of some form of National Security Strategy with DIME working in cohesion were displayed in the response from India after the Pulwama attack of 2019. It started with the suspension of trade relations (Economic) with Pakistan and Diplomacy took it forward by creating a global opinion against Pakistan. Our information (intelligence and Satellite network) followed it by giving detailed inputs on terrorist hide-outs and Indian Air Force (IAF) hit that terrorist centre in Balakot, deep inside Pakistan. At the ground, Military and Central Reserve Police Force (CRPF) helped in controlling the separatist's with active engagement/encounters of terrorists to remove the internal support to Pakistan.

Europe is a land of diversity but it is divided into different nations based on that diversity. Africa is a land of diversity but it is also divided into different nations based on that diversity. India is among the league of very rare nations like Brazil and the United States of America (a newly created nation of diversity) which hold such a significant diversity in its fold. National Security is one major factor which will further integrate the people of India in order to strengthen our union. The coordinated efforts on Pakistan suggest that Indian executive agencies has evolved a consensus on national security and working on following:

1) The priorities of our Defence establishments through better identification of their future needs, better coordination among them and restructure them for future security risks;

2) Assessing the strategic environment around us, including the most critical and enduring threats to the national security of India and its allies from state or non-state actors with possible solutions;

3) Assessing the national environment and work on providing solutions to all internal threats with a priority on threats which undermine Indian sovereignty and integrity;

4) Fixing the size and role of various Government agencies with their governance mechanism including the informational role of them; and

5) Most importantly, developing a plan for the holistic development of our national security ecosystem including our defence capabilities, physical infrastructure, the readiness of our forces, development of human resources, technological capabilities, environmental protection and any other element which is necessary to support it.

It will also help India in overcoming the problems of regionalism as people start supporting the actions of the government towards national Security. The peaceful resolution of some long-pending problems is a step in this direction. At the same time, it is vital to understand that fundamentals of the world and human wisdom don't change with geopolitical changes. As long as India carries its old ethos and values of *'Vasudhaiva Kutumbakam'* and works towards bringing the world towards one common goal of peace, India will always find ways to solve any problem. As our poet Thiruvalluvar said,

*To embrace the whole world in friendship is wisdom. This wisdom is not changeable like the flowers that bloom and fade*

# Miscellaneous Information

- **Sam Manekshaw was the first Field Marshal of India, and he was awarded this title in January 1973.** The second person to receive the title of Field Marshal was 'Konderera M. Cariappa', who was given the rank on 14 January 1986.
- Limited or Partial Test Ban Treaty (LTBT/PTBT) is an arms control agreement of 1963 intended to prohibit the testing of nuclear weapons in outer space, atmosphere and underwater.
- The Comprehensive Test Ban Treaty (CTBT) is an arms control agreement of 1996 intended to prohibit any testing of nuclear weapons anywhere in the world.

## Major Operations from Indian Forces

| S. No. | Operation | Year and Region |
|---|---|---|
| International | Operation Lal Dora | In 1983 to help Mauritius government for avoiding a coup |
| | Operation Meghdoot | In 1984 against Pakistan to gain control over Siachen Glacier |
| | Operation Flowers are Blooming | In 1986 to help Seychelles government for avoiding a coup |
| | Operation Pawan | In 1987 to take control of Jaffna from LTTE |
| | Operation Cactus | In 1988 to help Maldives government for avoiding a coup |
| | Operation Vijay | In 1999 by Indian Army to clear Kargil Sector |
| | Operation Talwar | In 1999 by Indian Navy to block Pakistan use of Arabian Sea |
| | Operation Safed Sagar | In 1999 by Indian Air Force to Indian Army in Kargil War |
| National | Operation Blue Star | In 1984 against Khalistani militant inside Golden Temple, Punjab |
| | Operation Black Thunder | In 1988 against Khalistani militant inside Golden Temple, Punjab |
| | Operation Vajra Shakti | In 2002 against the terrorists who attacked Akshardham Temple, Gujarat |

| | Operation Black Tornado | In 2008 against the terrorists who attacked Mumbai |
|---|---|---|
| | Operation Green Hunt | In 2009 against Maoists inside Red-corridor present in five-states |
| | Operation Dhangu Suraksha | In 2016 against the terrorists who attacked Pathankot Air Force Station |

## Major International Exercises Held or Participated by Indian Forces

| S. No. | Exercise Name | Participant/s |
|---|---|---|
| **INDIAN ARMY** | | |
| 1. | AUSTRA HIND | Australia |
| 2. | SAMPRITI | Bangladesh |
| 3. | HAND IN HAND | China |
| 4. | SHAKTI | France |
| 5. | GARUDA SHAKTI | Indonesia |
| 6. | DHARMA GUARDIAN | Japan |
| 7. | PRABAL DOSTYK | Kazakhstan |
| 8. | KHANJAR | Kyrgyzstan |
| 9. | EKUVERIN | Maldives |
| 10. | HARIMAU SHAKTI | Malaysia |
| 11. | NOMADIC ELEPHANT | Mongolia |
| 12. | IMBEX | Myanmar |
| 13. | SURYA KIRAN | Nepal |
| 14. | AL NAGAH | Oman |
| 15. | INDRA | Russia |
| 16. | LAMITIYE | Seychelles |
| 17. | BOLD KURUKSHETRA | Singapore |
| 18. | MITRA SHAKTI | Sri Lanka |
| 19. | MAITREE | Thailand |
| 20. | AJEYA WARRIOR | United Kingdom |
| 21. | YUDHABHAYAS & VAJRA PRAHAR | United States of America |
| 22. | VINBAX | Vietnam |
| 23. | FORCE 18 | Multinational |
| 24. | MILEX-18 | Multinational by BIMSTEC (except Thailand and Nepal) |
| 25. | PEACE MISSION | Counter Terror EX by SCO (only exercise with the |

|  |  | participation of India and Pakistan) |
|---|---|---|
| **INDIAN NAVY** | | |
| 1. | AUSINDEX | Australia |
| 2. | IN-BN CORPAT | Bangladesh |
| 3. | IBSAMAR | Brazil & South Africa |
| 4. | VARUNA | France |
| 5. | IND-INDO CORPAT, IND-INDO BILAT | Indonesia |
| 6. | IN-MN TABLE TOP | Malaysia |
| 7. | IMCOR, IN-MN BILAT | Myanmar |
| 8. | NASEEM-AL-BAHR | Oman |
| 9. | INDRA | Russia |
| 10. | SLINEX | Sri Lanka |
| 11. | SIMBEX | Singapore |
| 12. | INDO-THAI CORPAT | Thailand |
| 13. | IN-UAE BILAT | United Arab Emirates |
| 14. | KONKAN | United Kingdom |
| 15. | MALABAR, RIMPAC | United States of America |
| 16. | SAHYOG HOP TAC | Vietnam |
| 17. | ADMM+ | Multilateral Exercise by Brunei |
| 18. | KOMODO | Multilateral Exercise by Indonesia |
| 19. | MILAN | Multilateral Exercise by India |
| **INDIAN AIR FORCE** | | |
| 1. | TABLE TOP | Bangladesh |
|  | GARUDA | France |
| 2. | BLUE FLAG-17 | Israel |
| 3. | EASTERN BRIDGE | Oman |
| 4. | AVIAINDRA | Russia |
| 5. | JOINT MILITARY TRAINING | Singapore |
| 6. | SIAM BHARAT | Thailand |
| 7. | DESERT EAGLE-II | United Arab Emirates |
| 8. | INDRADHANUSH-IV | United Kingdom |
| 9. | RED FLAG 16-1 | United States of America |
| 10. | SAMVEDNA | Multilateral Humanitarian |

| | | Assistance & Disaster Relief Exercise by India |
|---|---|---|

*In addition to the above Exercises, Indian forces carry out different domestic exercises individually or in collaboration like Vayu Shakti, Vijay Prahar, Paschim Lehar etc.*

## Important Laws related to Security

With detention of a number of Jammu and Kashmir politicians under Jammu & Kashmir Public Safety Act, 1978 and LG of Delhi authorizing Delhi Police to put Delhi under National Security Act amid the Citizenship Amendment Act protests, it is important to know about the various laws related to preventive detention.

Article 22 of our constitution provides for protection against arrest and detention in certain cases with its clause (1) and (2) dealing with the punitive detention/arrest and clause (4) to (7) dealing with preventive detention.

**Punitive Detention** is defined as a penalizing or disciplinary arrest of a person for commission or suspicion of engagement in crime. For punitive arrests, Article 22 provides certain inalienable rights like-

a. **Right to Know:** Every person has the right to know about the reasons of his/her detention,

b. **Right to Consult:** They have the right to consult and get themselves defended by a legal practitioner of their choice, and

c. **Proper Hearing:** Within 24 hours of the detention they should be presented before the nearest magistrate, and

d. **Fixed time of Detention:** No person can be detained for a time beyond the time allotted by Magistrate unless the magistrate extends such duration.

Under clause (3) of Article 22, enemy aliens and detentions under preventive detention laws are excluded from the provisions of the first two clauses or these inalienable rights, and Clause (4) to (7) deals with preventive detention.

**Preventive Detention** is defined as the precautionary or protective custody/arrest of a person by the state on grounds of reasonable suspicion or scepticism that the person is likely to cause harm or threat to the peace of society. Under Article 22, parliament holds the power to make such laws (including state legislative assemblies, as law and order comes under the state list) on preventive detention with an advisory board (with persons qualified to be appointed as High Court judges) to identify the sufficient cause for such detention.

In India, we have seen many preventive detention laws enacted to control terrorism (with some still working while others have lapsed). E.g. we had *Terrorist and Disruptive Activities (Prevention) Act (TADA)* (from 1985-95); *Prevention of Terrorist Activities Act (POTA)* (from 2002-04); *Unlawful Activities (Prevention) Act (UAPA)*, in force since 1967 etc. with many state laws like *Maharashtra Prevention of Dangerous Activities Act (MPDA)*. Two important laws which are in news include:

1) **National Security Act, 1980:** It is a national level law which allows the preventive detention of a person for 10 days without being informed about the charges against them and for 12 months if authorities are satisfied that a person is a threat to national security or law and order. The person can be kept in preventive detention without being charged during this period of detention on state government approval within 12 days of reporting to the state government about the grounds. The primary goal of law is to prevent individuals from- a) acting in any manner prejudicial to the defence of India, the relations of India with foreign powers, or the security of India, b) regulating the continued presence of any foreigner in India or with a view to make arrangements for his expulsion from India, c) preventing them from acting in any manner prejudicial to the security of the State/ maintenance of public order/maintenance of supplies and services essential to the community.

2) **Jammu & Kashmir Public Safety Act, 1978:** Jammu and Kashmir State law which allows the preventive detention of any person above 16 years without trial for a period of two years in order to prevent him or her from acting in any manner that is prejudicial to the security of the state or the maintenance of public order. The detention order is required to be referred to an advisory board within four weeks of passing the detention order and the advisory board is expected to give recommendation within eight weeks to continue the detention.

## Other Laws related to Security

### Armed Forces (Special Powers) Act (AFSPA):

A central government law based on the lines of 1942 Ordinance, which allows the Indian Armed Forces to use special powers under the law to maintain public order in "disturbed areas". Post-independence, it was 1st enacted for Assam and Manipur in 1958. In 1983 it was enacted for Punjab and Chandigarh (withdrawn in 1997) and in 1990 it was enacted for Jammu and Kashmir. According to The Disturbed Areas (Special Courts) Act, 1976 once an area has been declared 'disturbed', it has to maintain the status quo for a minimum of 3 months.

### Anti-Hijacking Act, 2016: A central government law to replace the earlier Anti-Hijacking Act (1982) and introduce a new law to give effect to the Hague Hijacking Convention of 1971 and the Beijing Protocol of

2010. The new act broadens the term hijacking over the earlier by including the making of threat to commit an offence of hijacking as part of hijacking with universal jurisdiction with extradition provisions and capital punishment even to conspirators and abductors of the hijacking act with power to confiscate the moveable and immoveable property of the convict with designated courts for speedy trial.

**The Anti-Maritime Piracy Bill, 2019:** The new bill from External Affairs Ministry, presently with Standing Committee, is meant to give effect to the United Nations Convention on the Law of the Sea (UNCLOS) of 1982 and promote the safety and security of India's maritime trade and the crew in all parts of the sea adjacent to and beyond the limits of Exclusive Economic Zone of India. The bill has provisions of stringent punishment provisions for those involved in acts of piracy at sea including the death penalty. It will help in the formation of a specific law with effective prosecution on issues of piracy rather than the present provisions of the Indian Penal Code. The punishments for "whoever commits any act of piracy, include imprisonment for life and capital punishment if a death is caused or an attempt is made by such person while committing the act of piracy. Like the Anti-Hijacking Act, it also provides for punishment for attempting to commit an offence of piracy or being an accessory to the commission of an offence and making the offence extraditable with designated courts for speedy trials.

**Five Principles of Panchsheel** (Sanskrit word 'Panch' meaning five and 'Sheel' meaning Virtues)

1) Mutual Respect for each other's territorial integrity and sovereignty;
2) Mutual non-aggression;
3) Mutual non-interference in each other's internal affairs;
4) Equality and mutual benefit; and
5) Peaceful co-existence.

## Special Protection Group (SPG)

It was raised in 1985 with the intention to provide proximate security cover to the Prime Minister, former Prime Ministers and their immediate family members.

## Railway Protection Force (RPF)

The Railway Protection Force established by the Railway Protection Force Act, 1957 for "the better protection and security of Railway property. It has nearly 75,000 personnel and can be helpful in national security efforts if required.

# Previous Year Civil Services (Main) Examination Questions and Answers (2015-2019)

**2019**

**1. The banning of 'Jamaat-e–Islami' in Jammu and Kashmir brought into focus the role of over-ground workers (OGWs) in assisting terrorist organizations. Examine the role played by OGWs in assisting terrorist organizations in insurgency affected areas. Discuss measures to neutralize the influence of OGWs. (150 words, 10 Marks)**

Terrorism, i.e. use of violence and threats to intimidate or coerce citizens is largely done for political purposes. These political purposes are often achieved by diluting the perceived control of the State over law and order, i.e. creating lawlessness and presenting their own alternatives to it. These alternatives are often served by the over-ground workers (OGWs), who act as a medium to help the terrorist organizations in carrying out terrorist activities and alienate people from the state by spreading terrorist's alternatives.

In Jammu and Kashmir, Jamaat-e-Islami was found to be one such socio-political organization, serving the terrorist organizations and their efforts of promoting insurgency in Jammu and Kashmir region through an **active role** in activities like-

- Mobilization of masses to **support Terror and Secession** activities through **radicalization** among local populace. This includes **proselytization** and **propaganda** activities in order to provide ideological background to the terror outfits,

- Create political support for the terrorist organizations through **persuasion, threat, violence** and **intimidation**,

- Identify and neutralize the support for **armed forces** by keeping a watch over informers and people at large who support the State,

- Provide necessary **Food** and **Logistics support** to terrorist organizations for meeting basic needs. This includes the help given to Foreign terrorists by arranging **weapons** and **shelter** for them,

- Helps the terrorist organizations in **finding new recruits** (for direct or indirect help) by finding youth or the administrative/political actors who can extend help. E.g.

Jamaat-i-Islami set up its student wing named Islamic Jamiyat-ul-Talba for early catching of youth. Similarly, the coordination with secessionist leaders or other political actors was function of OGWs,

- To act as the **channel for carrying out the organised crime activities** like illegal trade, flow of counterfeit currency, Hawala transactions or promote tax-evasion under guise of different businesses. It helps the terrorist organizations in gaining access to resources and work independently. This can be used to meet their own expenses or to instigate anti-state protests like the one in 2008.
- Act as a local **intelligence network** for terrorist organizations, providing assistance in **planning and execution of terror activities** by providing information about security agencies' preparations/activities and help terrorist organizations in operational planning, providing safe exits or any other input needed by terror operations.

Therefore, it is important for the State to check the activities and minimize their influence by:

- Addressing the **root causes of alienation** through development of proper infrastructure, providing educational and job opportunities with solution to the problems suffered by the region,
- Enhancing the socio-political integration with mainstream through **awareness campaigns**, countering false propaganda and use of **confidence-building measures** by security agencies to dispel fear and alienation,
- Strengthening own **intelligence network** (human and/or electronic surveillance) to keep a check over the radicalization, fundamentalist or exclusivist activities along with the financial transactions,
- Strengthening of the **grass-root democracy** with greater transparency and engagement of masses via. education, media voices, local recruitment drives by security agencies etc.,
- Implement proper **rehabilitation** measures of youth who surrenders or the **orphans and women** who suffer because of violence,
- Improving the **Law and Order** situation by keeping the **unlawful activities** in check. and setting up **Fast track courts** for swift action against terrorists and OGWs on matters related to public safety acts, i.e. speedy ban on Unlawful Associations working as OGWs under sub-Sections (1) & (3) of Section 3 of the [Unlawful Activities (Prevention)] Act,

- Work for **International cooperation** in order to reduce safe havens for terrorist organizations and stopping their access to international monetary channels.

Controlling subversive activities against the territorial integrity and sovereignty of Indian state are vital for our existence. However, the state and its security agencies should be careful and wise enough to allow dissent which helps in making our democracy stronger and more vibrant. The tendency of misusing legal provisions in order to create a strong deterrent among its own citizens or excessive use of force should be avoided. The Constitution of India gives enough power to the State for protecting our nation. Ensuring greater political participation with equitable social and economic development for all can be the first step in removing people's support for insurgency, as done in Northeast.

**2.   What is the Cyberdome Project? Explain how it can be useful in controlling internet crimes in India. (150 words, 10 Marks)**

Cyberspace, is a global technology environment built over the electronic medium of digital networks for communication. It is the modern day highway for functioning of a nation and day-to-day activities/interests of its people. It links people with institutions and stores vital public and private information, which is the most sought information by the criminals for internet-based crimes. This is corroborated by the increasing internet crimes in India with increasing penetration of cyberspace in the life of people. According to a recent Assocham-NEC study titled Digital Policing – Smart Policing for Public Safety, from 2011 to 2016, India has witnessed a 457% rise in cybercrime incidents under the Information Technology (IT) Act, 2000.

For tackling such crimes, our security agencies have taken various initiatives and one such unique initiative is the Cyberdome Project by the Kerala Police. Cyberdome Project is a Centre of Excellence for Kerala Police, established to meet the long term security challenges in the digital arena of the modern world. As a high end technological research and development centre, cyberdome will help in bridging the gap between the latest changes and innovations in the cyber space and the skill set development of Kerala Police, in combating the emerging cyber threats. It is envisaged as a public-private collaboration Centre where both can converge and share information, as well as resources, that will escalate the safety of our cyberspace. These cyber centres will help the police in its efforts towards smart and effective policing. Other features of the Cyberdome Project through which it will help the police in tackling cyber crimes in a proactive manner are:

- Creation of an **online portal or digital repository** of all the police records (data of stolen vehicles, lost vehicles, criminals record etc.) to provide quick and easy access to this data across the state police department.

- Improving the **in-house technological capabilities** of the state police department and help in manpower training and development through utilization of the expertise of participating technical experts, ethical hackers and cyber professionals at the centre as cyberdome volunteers.

- Adapt to the **rapidly changing technological and crime capabilities** through a resilient and dynamic network system. E.g. The Anti-Cyber Terror Cell under the Cyberdome project will keep **real time watch over cyberspace**. The online activities of the criminals, including the social networking sites and financial transactions of illegal nature (check over money laundering and other dubious transactions) will become easy.

- Engaging people with efforts of the police and to **increase awareness** among the users, especially the children using the internet. It will help in protecting children from the online games like Blue Whale or keep a vigil over the crimes like cyber bullying with online complaints and its redressal over different communication channels like social media by its centres.

- It will help the police officials in ensuring cyber security with aid to the **investigation of cyber crimes** by providing vital leads in cyber offences through use of Artificial Intelligence and other technological advancements in the field of information technology.

- It will help in keeping a **close watch over serious internet-based crimes** like child porn, sale of illegal products or services through the covert cyber-surveillance and infiltration measures under the project.

- It will help in keeping a **watch over the local and global extremist outfits** like ISIS engaged in online radicalization and extremist activities.

- The Cyberdome project involves the establishment of a ransomware school, helping in understanding the nature and pattern of ransomware infections.

Cyberdome project is an important and much needed technological help to aid the police efforts in mitigation of emerging future challenges through establishment of better standard operating procedures and reach against cyber crimes. It will also help in making people aware about the precautionary and cure measures.

3.    **The Indian government has recently strengthened the anti-terrorism laws by amending the Unlawful Activities (Prevention) Act (UAPA), 1967 and the NIA Act. Analyze the changes in the context of the prevailing security environment while discussing the scope and reasons for opposing the UAPA by human rights organizations. (250 words, 15 Marks)**

In the aftermath of 2008 terrorist attack on Mumbai, National Investigation Agency (NIA) was established as the first truly federal investigation agency of India (on lines of FBI) as per National Investigation Agency Act, 2008. It was called truly federal as NIA enjoys power to investigate terrorism cases across India without need of state government approval. In the last one decade, the nature of security threats to India and the linkages of terrorist organizations have changed a lot. To keep pace with the changing nature of terrorism and to make India more secure, the Union Government amended the NIA Act and UAPA Act in 2019.

### The Unlawful Activities (Prevention) Act (UAPA), 1967:

The **Unlawful Activities (Prevention) Act (UAPA), 1967** is meant to outlaw unlawful activities of the individuals and organizations. In 2004, after the repeal of TADA and POTA, the law was amended to penalize the terrorists and prevent other unlawful activities, which pose a threat to the integrity and sovereignty of India. Under the 2004 amendment, Central Government was empowered to designate an organisations as **'terrorist organisations'**, if it commits or participates in acts of terrorism; promotes terrorism; or is otherwise involved in terrorism under the Fourth Schedule of the act.

In 2019, various provisions of the UAPA act are further amended, especially the Chapter VI, section 35 and 36 of the UAPA, to empower the Central Government for designating an individual also as terrorist if suspected to have terror links under the Fourth Schedule of the act.

### The National Investigation Agency Act (NIA), 2008:

The NIA Act, 2008 was enacted to constitute an investigation agency at the national level for investigation and prosecution for offences which affect the sovereignty, security and integrity of India, security of states, friendly relations with foreign States and offences under Acts enacted to implement international treaties, agreements, conventions and resolutions of the United Nations, its agencies and other international organisations and for matters connected therewith or incidental thereto. This act allowed the NIA officers to investigate and prosecute offences within India or to conduct raids, and seize properties that are suspected to be linked to terrorist activities without taking prior permission of the

Director General of Police of a state (the designated sanctioning authority for NIA is the Director General of NIA).

The 2019 amendments made to **NIA Act** enhances the powers of NIA by **widening the scope** of its investigation and allowing NIA to investigate and prosecute for the crimes related to human trafficking, counterfeit currency or banknotes, manufacture or sale of prohibited arms, cyber-terrorism and offences under the Explosive Substances Act, 1908, which were traditionally done by the State police.

Provisions are also made to increase the speed of investigation and carry out prosecution for certain offences, including those committed outside India. The amended act allows the central government to designate Sessions Courts as Special Courts for the trial of scheduled offences under the Act after consultation with the Chief Justice of the respective High Court. It empowers the NIA to register and investigate offences committed outside India, if directed by the Central Government to do so, subject to international treaties and domestic laws of other countries. Over such cases, the NIA special court in New Delhi will have jurisdiction.

Allowing individuals to be designated as terrorists by the Central Government is important to stop the old tactic of terrorists to form new terrorist organizations, as and when the functioning organizations are banned. This issue came to fore during India's push to designate Masood Azhar as international terrorist as India's domestic laws were silent on an individual's designation as terrorist. The changes in the NIA act gives more power to NIA, by **expanding the scope of its investigation**, considered as necessary by the security experts because of the increasing confluence or linkages between the terrorist organizations and the organized crime activities like human trafficking, counterfeit currency, sale of prohibited arms etc. The above amendments will also help the agency in quicker persecution, helping in improving the national security environment and implement the **zero-tolerance policy against terrorism**.

## Reasons for Opposition to UAPA:

The biggest reason for opposition to the amendments by human rights organizations is the arbitrary and unfettered power given to the executive while declaring individuals as terrorists. Designating an individual as terrorist without specifying the grounds of it is against the due process of law and violates the individual's right to dissent and the right to reputation. This violates the fundamental rights enjoyed by an individual under Article 14 (Right to Equality), Article 19 (Right to Free Speech) and Article 21 (Right to Life) of the Constitution.

The Supreme Court of India, in Sri Indra Das v the State Of Assam (dealing with Section 10 of UAPA and TADA of that time), opined that mere membership of a banned organization is not criminal, as it violates the Article 19 and 21 of the Constitution. In Arup Bhuyan's case, the court held that 'unless a person resorts to violence or incites people to violence or creates public disorder by violence or incitement to violence, he is not criminal'. Designating an individual as terrorist without proving the guilt violates the doctrine of presumption of innocence, i.e. innocent until proven guilty. It can curb the freedom of speech and expression by introducing undefined exemptions to it and creates an authoritarian regime rather than strengthening the Indian Democracy.

On one hand we need to strengthen the rights of our citizens and on another we need to act hard against the terrorists and terrorist activities. Clarity on the reasons for designation of an individual as a terrorist and allowing the judiciary to decide the merits of such a decision before any official word can help in balancing both ends while meeting the changing needs of the security environment.

**4.   Cross-border movement of insurgents is only one of the several security challenges facing the policing of the border in North-East India. Examine the various challenges currently emanating across the India-Myanmar border. Also, discuss the steps to counter the challenges. (250 words, 15 Marks)**

Despite our good territorial relationship with most of the nations surrounding North-East India (except China) the cross-border insurgency has remained a big security challenge. Almost all nations at different times are used by the insurgent groups. The efforts made by Indian Government and our security forces with neighboring nations on resolving pending border disputes, strengthening military co-operation and carrying out joint operations against insurgent groups has helped in bringing greater peace in the region. Exceptions still remain and one such exception is the Indo-Myanmar border. The Manipur ambush of 2015 showed that the cross-border movement of insurgent groups is unabated despite our standing boundary agreement since 1967 and the work started on border fencing in 2003-04.

The India-Myanmar border is a 1,643 km long geographical border (along the Indian State of Arunachal Pradesh, Nagaland, Mizoram and Manipur) with mountain ranges of the Patkai Bum, Naga Hills and Mizo Hills as the physical separation between the two nations. These mountains are not as high as Himalayas and contain various passes and valleys which makes the Indo-Myanmar border highly porous. The generational socio-cultural relationship of the tribal communities and presence of same tribes on both sides of the border, makes it further difficult to properly fence and guard the borders. Because of all this, number of challenges emanates from the India-Myanmar Border like:

- **Illegal drug trade** from Myanmar with Myanmar being part of Golden Triangle (cultivating opium),
- The **remote location** of the region and its **underdeveloped economy** with free movement of people across the border (16 km as limit for without Visa movement) is used by various insurgent groups and others for organized crimes like wildlife trade, migrant smuggling, arms trade etc.
- The confrontation between the Myanmar Army and the Rohingya community also led to a greater influx of **migrants** from the Rohingya community and other bordering nations as well. With local tribes being against outside influence for long, the new entry has further raised the fear among the local populace with increased demands for removal of the illegal migrants and use of local resources by locals through Inner LIne Permits.
- The **difficult terrain** of the region with high forest cover and wildlife makes it difficult to fence the border or to carry out surveillance activities.
- Presently Assam Rifles is playing the role of peace-keeping force (countering insurgency) in the North-East region as well as doing the duty of guarding the Indo-Myanmar border.
- Development of infrastructural facilities in the region and have functional Integrated Check Posts (ICPs) in the region is another challenge.

Peace and development in North-East is essential not just for internal reasons but also for the success of our international policies like Act-East Policy (erstwhile Look-East Policy). It is the gateway to Southeast Asian countries with Myanmar as the first stop. India is engaged with Myanmar at various fronts through multilateral forums like BIMSTEC, BCIM as well as bilaterally. Under such situation, it is important that some immediate steps are taken to counter these challenges by:

- Hastening the work on Indo-Myanmar border fencing through Comprehensive Integrated Border management System (CIBMS) to overcome the problems of difficult terrain with porous borders.
- Complete the long pending establishment of a dedicated Indo-Myanmar Border Force on the lines of BSF, a relief to Assam Rifles as well.
- The next step is to complete the connectivity projects from Indian side related to the railways, roads etc. and help Myanmar in early completion of the pending projects like the Kaladan Multi-modal Transit Transport Project. This will help in strengthening

our relationship with Myanmar and improve the cross-border trade.

- Increased infrastructure and trade in the region will help in proper immigration and custom crossing or functional Integrated Check Posts. These check posts will help in keeping a check over the free movement of people or to have registration based travel without locals' resistance.
- Implementation of confidence building measures from the security forces for reciprocal community interaction and awareness campaigns against drugs and other illegal activities.
- Successful completion of the Nagaland Peace Accord and maintenance of law and order in other bordering states will further help in bringing the cross border challenges under control.

In the last few months, significant progress has been achieved in blunting the cross border insurgent groups because of the massive crackdown from Myanmar Army against all Anti-India groups working from its soil. It is hoped that the growing defence relationship between India and Myanmar will bring both nations further closer to achieve greater economic integration with sustained people to people contact.

## 2018

**1.    The China-Pakistan Economic Corridor (CPEC) is viewed as a cardinal subset of China's larger "One Belt One Road" initiative. Give a brief description of CPEC and enumerate the reasons why India has distanced itself from the same. (150 words)10**

The China-Pakistan Economic Corridor (CPEC) is a flagship project under the One Belt One Road (OBOR) initiative of China, costing nearly US\$ 62 billion (earlier projected to cost 46 billion US dollar) to connect Kashgar (part of South-West China) with Gwadar Port of Pakistan in Arabian Ocean. Though part of "One Belt One Road" initiative it differs from other trade and transport initiatives under OBOR by expanding CPEC scope of work from road and rail network development to a complete economic corridor involving the development of Gwadar Port, energy projects, Special Economic Zones and other infrastructure along the CPEC like airport, gas pipelines, fibre optic network etc.

**Reasons for India's distance from the project:**

S. Jaishankar, during his tenure as foreign secretary, clearly articulated the Indian viewpoint on the CPEC, as- "China should respect India's territorial sovereignty as Beijing is 'very sensitive' to matters relating to its own sovereignty". The reasons for India distancing itself from the project and even objecting to it are as follows:

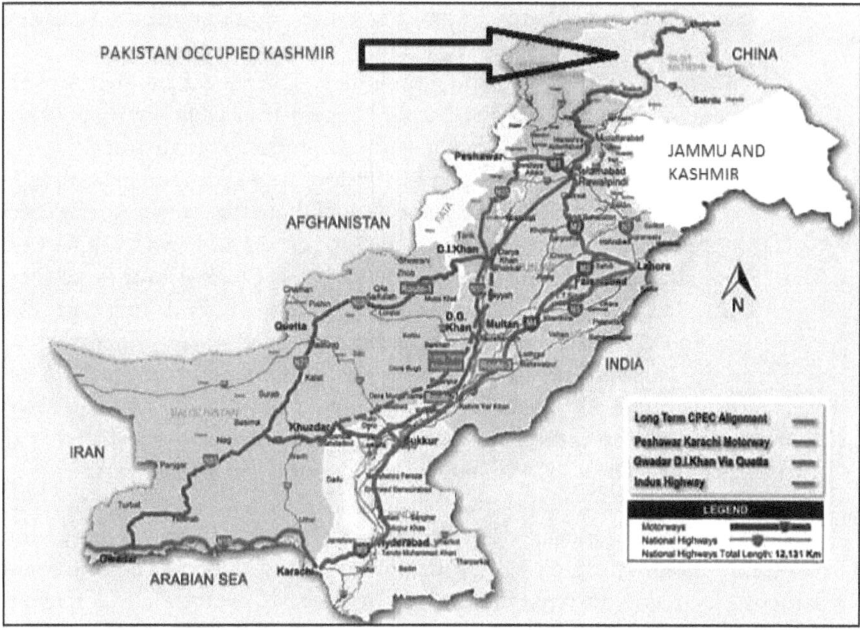


Figure 28 China-Pakistan Economic Corridor

- The CPEC project was started in 2013 without any consultation with India despite its passage through the Gilgit-Baltistan region of the Pakistan Occupied Kashmir (PoK). This region is part of Jammu and Kashmir region (now under the Union Territories of Ladakh and of Jammu and Kashmir). So, CPEC undermines the sovereignty and territorial integrity of India and shows the insensitivity from China towards India despite being the follower of One China Policy on territorial integrity.
- Like other projects from China in our neighboring countries CPEC violates the international norms of mutual growth, peace and prosperity. The project is built by the Chinese Companies using Chinese labor. Maintenance and operation of CPEC and various manufacturing activities along the CPEC is largely under the control of Chinese Companies.
- OBOR in general and CPEC in particular violate the principles of openness, transparency and financial responsibility as it largely serves the strategic and political endeavours of China. The project will help China in gaining footholds in key regions.
- The industrial activities along the CPEC corridor focus mainly on the extractive sectors like energy and related infrastructure. These extractive sectors are of little help to the host nation and look only at the viability of the CPEC.

- Like most of the OBOR, the CPEC passes through weak and politically unstable regions of the poor nations. Such big projects by a foreign company in another nation don't stand the financial wisdom and principles of economics unless state security from China is extended to the companies. The recent incidents of 99 year port lease from Sri Lanka suggest that CPEC will also be a part of debt-trap diplomacy or the Chinese colonialism.
- Growing Chinese presence in the Indian-ocean region is already a concern for the peace and stability in the region. The new access point to the Arabian Sea through Gwadar port will further jeopardize the security of the region. It will be harmful to not just the Indian interests in the region but it will increase the weaponization of the Indian Ocean.

We need to look at the June 2017 joint statement by India-USA on 'Prosperity through Partnership' or the September 2017 joint statement by India-Japan. The underlying call of all connectivity partnerships is to help all nations through the bolstering regional economic connectivity based on transparent development of infrastructure using responsible debt financing practices, while ensuring respect for sovereignty and territorial integrity. It cares for the rule of law and the environment through an open, transparent and non-exclusive use of such corridors. The Chinese OBOR and its flagship project CPEC fails to ensure these basics.

**2.　　Left Wing Extremism (LWE) is showing a downward trend, but still effects many parts of the country. Briefly explain the government of India's approach to counter the challengers post by LWE. (150 words) 10**

Extremism in its broadest sense refers to an individual or a group of individuals holding extreme political or religious views. These extreme views are the basis of fanaticism or radicalism which wants to suppress all other opposite views through violence. Left Wing Extremism is one such thought based on the Maoist ideology which considers the modern revisionism or the political democracy of India in opposition to Maoist ideas. It wants to gain power over India through armed rebellion, i.e. through violent actions.

In India, Left Wing Extremism traces its origin to the 1967 Naxal movement. At its peak LWE had influence over 200 or more districts of India. In the last one decade, the influence of LWE has reduced significantly. According to MHA, by 2018 only 60 districts had incidents related to violence from the Left Wing Extremism with 89% of this violence being limited to 30 districts only. Though reasonably below from its peak but it is significant as 60 districts mean nearly 10% of Indian

Districts with mineral rich states like Chhatissgarh, Jharkhand and Odisha as main focus and some neighboring states like Maharashtra, Andhra Pradesh, Telangana etc. also suffering in some pockets.

The credit for this downtrend in the LWE goes to the two-pronged approach adopted by the Government of India in 2009. It was called an Integrated Action Plan and focused on dealing with the LWE not just through force but changes in the region through an inclusive development model. Inclusive development helps in removing the problem of maldevelopment or the feelings of marginalization in the less developed regions of India, one of the prime reasons of Left Wing Extremism. Apart from solving the developmental issues, the holistic approach of Integrated Action Plan focuses on-

- ***Governance Reforms:*** The governance reforms in the Left Wing Extremism influenced areas focus on building capabilities of local administration and develop local leadership to provide governance to the region. Need to further strengthen the local Panchayts (set up under the PESA Act) and proper implementation of laws like Forest Rights Act-2006 with focus on tribal rights in order to serve as the medium to implement the constitutional safeguards meant for such regions.

- ***Infrastructure Development:*** The presence of physical (road, railway, airport, telecommunication network etc.) and social (health and education) infrastructure is a must to bring all people in the mainstream and make them feel part of one nation. Schemes like PMGSY have helped in improving the connectivity in the region. Similarly, Union Government as well as State governments have taken initiatives towards education through schemes like Roshini (for skill training of local youth) or Prayas Residential School by the Chhattisgarh Government for education and preparation for competitive examinations for admission in the IITs and other higher educational institutions.

- ***Schemes and financial help:*** Though the exclusive schemes for these areas are introduced since the 1960's, in the last few years schemes with targeted interventions like Van Bandhu Kalyan Yojana, Ujjwala, MSP for Minor Forest Produce and the institutional loans through MUDRA Loans has helped in linking local tribes interest with government and work for greater prosperity in the life of local people.

- ***Strengthening Security Agencies:*** Improved coordination among the different security agencies i.e. State Police and the CRPF with modernization of the forces are given higher importance. Standard operating procedures are developed for them and the latest technology has aided the security forces efforts by acting as a force multiplier through better training, weapons and use of technological aids like UAVs.

- ***Strong Action against LWE outfits with generous Surrender-cum-Rehabilitation policy:*** The improved capabilities have helped the security forces in effective neutralization of the LWE outfits. Recent Union Government initiatives helped in reducing Left Wing outfits access to financial resources and the weapons. The state governments have also played their role by implementing a generous Surrender-cum-Rehabilitation Scheme to ensure easier integration with the mainstream.
- ***Public Perception Management:*** Education is the biggest resistance against extremist ideologies and the improving educational scenario in the LWE affected region has helped in it. The interaction of security forces with local people and celebration of tribal festivals is of great significance. It helps in reducing apprehensions among local people and bridge the gap between Security Forces and local people.

Meeting the basic needs of the people with increasing development has helped in gaining faith of the citizens living in LWE affected areas. It has helped in synchronization of the people's aspirations with the state vision. Peace and harmony are the automatic dividends of that development and synchronization of interests. Today, local people want reduction in violence and conflicts in the region through establishment of law and order, so that they can use the special safeguards provided for them by the Constitution of India.

But winning the ideological battle is not enough. We need to win the physical battle as well. In 2017, Ministry of Home Affairs (MHA) introduced the new strategy 'SAMADHAN', to completely wipe out the Left Wing Extremism from India. SAMADHAN stands for **S-smart leadership**, **A-aggressive strategy**, **M-motivation and training**, **A-actionable intelligence**, **D-dashboard-based KPIs** (key performance indicators) and **KRAs** (key result areas), **H-harnessing technology**, **A-action plan for each theatre** and **N-no access to financing**.

**3.    Data security has assumed significant importance in the digitized world due to rising cyber crimes. The Justice B.N Sreekrishna Committee Report addresses issues related to data security. What, in your view, are the strengths and weaknesses of the Report relating to the protection of personal data in cyberspace? (250 words)15**

With increasing digitalization of India the cyber crimes are also increasing in India at an alarming pace. One of the common targets of these cyber crimes is the common citizens and their personal data.

Though Right to Privacy is declared the fundamental right of every citizen (Justice K. S. Puttaswamy v Union of India), we lack a Data Protection Framework to address the privacy concerns of every citizen.

The Justice BN Srikrishna committee has submitted its report on data security, titled as "A Free and Fair Digital Economy – Protecting Privacy, Empowering Indians". This Committee proposed a draft Personal Data Protection Bill to provide a framework for the government towards bringing of new data protection legislation for the country. The draft bill tries to balance the interests of the citizens and the responsibilities of the state by extending protection to both without any tradeoff between them. Some of the strengths of the draft are:

1. The **Individual Consent** is kept as the centerpiece for data sharing. The individual holds the veto to give consent on use of personal data.

2. At the same time, bill imposes **obligations on the data fiduciaries** (i.e. trustees like state and private entities which will process the data) to determine the purpose (**Limiting the Purpose**) which is clear, specified and lawful with collection limitation i.e. to collect only data necessary for the purpose and store as long as reasonably necessary for the purpose.

3. These entities will specify the means of data processing and are responsible for ensuring **data privacy by design** of data processors with proper definition on the frequently used terms like consent, sensitive data, data breach etc.

4. The individuals will hold the **Right to be forgotten** with easy access to options related to delete, delink or limit the personal information to be disclosed on the internet, protecting him from misleading, irrelevant or anachronistic use of such data.

5. Set up the Data **Protection Authority (DPA)** as an independent regulatory body with responsibility towards effective enforcement of the law. The DPA will be responsible for- monitoring and enforcement of law; carry out research activities and create awareness among people; to set policy standards and its implementation; and to conduct inquiry, handle grievance and adjudication.

6. Same law will be applied on **all data processing entities** (public and private) if such data has been used, shared, disclosed, collected or otherwise processed in India.

7. It **protects the critical personal data** of Indian Citizens through mandatory data localization. All entities will have an obligation to keep a copy of all other data within India. Cross border data transfers, other than critical personal data, will be done through model contract clauses containing key obligations with liability of

the transferor for any harm caused to the data principal for violations of the provisions.

8. A **long list of sensitive information/personal data** is given in the draft like passwords, sexual orientation, caste, religion, tribe, political beliefs/affiliations, biometric data, genetic information, health data, financial information, official identifier etc. The DPA will have the residuary power to add further categories to it as per the criteria set by law.

9. The draft act covers the personal data collected, used, shared, disclosed or otherwise processed by companies incorporated under Indian law, irrespective of where it is actually processed in India. However, the data protection law may empower the Central Government to exempt such companies which only process the personal data of foreign nationals not present in India.

10. It empowers the Central Government to establish an **Appellate Tribunal or grant power to an existing tribunal** to hear and dispose of appeals against the order of DPA.

11. The draft covers the provisions of **penalties for violations** of the data protection law. The committee has suggested the criteria as well as the suitable amount with Rs. 15 crore or 4% of the total worldwide turnover of the preceding financial year for data collection/processing entities, whichever is higher. The failure to take prompt action on a data security breach will attract further penalties of Rs. 5 crore or 2% of turnover, whichever is higher.

12. It provides for the set up of a **Data Protection Fund** to which the penalty amount will be deposited and the same funds will be used to finance the functioning of the Data Protection Authority.

13. Entities using the data will ensure **no harm to the user** through necessary security safeguards. They will ensure transparency and whenever new technologies will be introduced, a data protection impact assessment will be the necessary requirement. These entities will appoint a data protection officer and its data policies will be audited regularly by the data auditors.

14. It lists the **impact of new data protection framework on the allied laws**, like Aadhaar Act and the RTI Act, with the necessary amendments in those laws to add provisions on data protection with remedial measures and power of the implementing agencies like UIDAI for Aadhaar.

15. It provides for **certain exceptions for state**, i.e. to process data without user consent on the grounds of public welfare, law and order or any other emergency situation where the individual is incapable of providing consent, for employment or other

reasonable purpose. The processing of data for security purposes, legal proceedings or the research and journalistic purposes can be exempted from certain obligations as per the draft.

16. Special and stringent provisions are provided for the protection of children data. It will **strengthen the child data protection measures** by moving away from the present system of parental consent. The Data Protection Authority will have the power to designate large child data processing websites or online services as guardian data fiduciaries. It also puts limitations on certain types of data processing such as behavioral monitoring, tracking, targeted advertising or any other type of processing which is not in the best interest of the child. This is vital for child data protection because of the complex and opaque data collection and processing technologies with the inability of a child to fully understand the consequences of these actions.

As we can observe, the committee has given a comprehensive draft to ensure data security. Still, certain limitations or weaknesses can be observed in the draft bill, requiring greater public and parliamentary debate on issues like-

- No retrospective application of law gives a leeway for misuse of data collected earlier,
- The state is allowed to process the data for its various welfare and other such functions. It is against the informed consent principle given in the Aadhaar Judgement. Also, it is silent on safeguards against the misuse of data by the State or its agencies,
- The draft bill lacks any specific guidelines on the surveillance activities, related agencies and legal framework. The surveillance system of India is not much regulated by the legislature and judiciary. It gives free hand to the executive and the storage of all data within India will further increase the power of the executive.
- TRAI recommended that the ownership of data should lie with the individual. But the draft bill is not specific on the ownership of data.
- The data breach is to be first reported to the Data Protection Authority rather than the individual. The empowerment of citizens is incomplete without specifying the reasons for them being treated second on their own data.
- The right to be forgotten usually means the right to erase data. But the Srikrishna committee has given an ambiguous understanding to the right to be forgotten by adding too many technicalities.

With a large number of internet users being below 18, having a law on data security is vital to build a digitally secure India. Data security is essential for protecting an individual's right to privacy and giving more power to people over their own data. It will make data processing entities more responsible and reduce the commercial exploitation of individual data with a safety net for our growing digital economy.

**4.    India's proximity to two of the world's biggest illicit opium-growing states has enhanced her internal security concerns. Explain the linkages between drug trafficking and other illicit activities such as gunrunning, money laundering and human trafficking. What countermeasures should be taken to prevent the same? (250 words)15**

Almost all of South Asia suffers from the problem of illicit opium. The problem becomes more intense for India because of being sandwiched between the two biggest illicit opium-growing regions of the world. The first is the Golden Crescent (situated in Pakistan, Afghanistan and Iran) and another is the Golden Triangle (situated at the tri-junction of Myanmar, Laos and Thailand borders). Together these two regions produce most of the illicit opium in the world. A large number of methamphetamine manufacturing facilities are also prevalent along the Golden Triangle.

India is among the major markets for them because of its porous land and sea borders, poor law and order and its large population. The presence of multiple terrorist organizations, insurgent groups and organized crime cartels being active in India makes it far more vulnerable than other nations with drug trafficking as the enabler for establishing linkages with other illicit activities such as gunrunning, money laundering and human trafficking. This can be understood as follows:

- What oil was for ISIS, Opium is for Taliban. Around 85% of the opium growing area of Golden Crescent falls under the Taliban's control. It helps Taliban in financing its operations and to buy necessary weapons for itself. The contacts established by Taliban are used by drug cartels and gunrunners.

- Similar situation existed in Myanmar and nearby regions where Opium became the main source of income because of the non-suitable environment of the region towards other crops. The weak establishments (even patronage at times) helped in easy growth with insurgent groups becoming part of it to meet their own expenses.

- The poor law and order situation helped in development of established routes for drugs. These routes are based on land as well as through sea. E.g. methamphetamine is commonly transported to all BIMSTEC nations through sea because of its use for recreation activities at bars, casinos etc. along coastal areas.

- With India being the destination, source and transit point for human trafficking groups, through the routes which overlapped with the established drug trafficking and gunrunning activities, mutual help and shared logistics became advantageous for both. The presence of some organizations in 2-3 activities further helped in it. E.g. the Russian and Ukrainian groups are active in gunrunning, drug trafficking and human trafficking. Similarly, the Dawood Group is engaged in drug trafficking and human trafficking activities.

- The huge amounts of money flow require money laundering activities to gain access to global financial systems. The casinos, bars, hotels etc. at tourist spots like Goa for Russian groups, Bollywood and real estate for D-Group are the major fronts for money laundering and at times some of them serve as direct points for sale of drug or human trafficking.

*The countermeasures which can help India in overcoming such crimes include:*

- With major opium growing regions being outside India, the first basic step is to engage these nations through multilateral forums like SAARC (for Golden Crescent) and BIMSTEC (for Golden Triangle). E.g. in the last few years, the change of regime in Myanmar has helped in significantly reducing the opium production and operations from insurgent groups.

- After international cooperation, the next important step is to make our borders impermeable or difficult to penetrate for the drug smuggling and human trafficking groups. These drugs are often transported inside human bodies; stopping one will help in reducing other activities as well. The recommendations given by Madhukar Gupta Committee on strengthening our border protection and addressing vulnerabilities in fencing Indo-Pakistan border can be replicated at other land borders and similar exercise can be taken to address coastal borders.

- The next vital countermeasure is to improve the law and order within Indian boundaries through modernization of our police force and make them accountable towards reducing such crimes. E.g. in the last few years, use of darknet with courier/postal deliveries have made the drug trafficking more anonymous in nature. The police need to be ahead on all these latest modus operandi.

- The next countermeasure is to sensitize our people to be vigilant about the ills or negative fallouts of drugs, human trafficking, money laundering etc. Forming local groups of elders or other responsible persons at schools, colleges etc. can help in proper awareness and to coordinate with the police.

- The health and education departments need to work on rehabilitation programmes, psychological training and awareness among children which can help in creating strong deterrence and enable a more responsible generation in future. E.g. one of the main reasons for HIV spread in India; especially in North-east is injectable drug usage.

Keeping problems pending for too long is not in the interest of the nation. In the last few years, different crime groups are coming closer. Increasing technical and multi-lateral challenges require a comprehensive solution with all responsible nations coming together to protect its people.

**2017**

**1. Discuss the potential threats of Cyber attack and the security framework to prevent it. (150 words, 10 marks)**

With increasing use of cyberspace by the citizens, government and businesses in day-to-day life the risk of its exploitation is increasing beyond proportion. This exploitation is done through manipulation of technology and users' awareness being limited to the use of cyberspace only. One such manipulation method is cyber attack.

A cyber attack is defined as a random or targeted assault launched by cybercriminals using one or more computers against a single or multiple computers or networks. A cyber attack is mainly targeted towards computers or mobile devices with the motive of maliciously disabling computers, stealing users data, or to use a breached computer as a launch point for other attacks. These cyber attacks can be launched through installation of a malware or inclusion of malicious codes in existing softwares, evasive email phishing or attack on cloud-computing devices to gain access to stored information or sensitive data.

**Three major potential threat of cyber attack in recent past:**

1. ***Ransomware:*** In 2017, WannaCry and NotPetya ransomwares became the biggest cyber attacks of the world. These ransomwares are the form of malicious softwares used to encrypt the computer or device data in order to remove access of the user and demand ransom in order to restore access to the device.

2. ***Denial of service:*** These attacks are mainly targeted at the websites or apps of the organizations which serve citizens or use them for internal purposes in order to deny the services availed by users. If from foreign enemies, these targets can be comprehensive in terms of bringing down the whole or part of the Critical Information Infrastructure of a nation or takeover the whole system to prove a point.

3. ***Phishing:*** These are the email based cyber attacks targeted to get the sensitive details (passwords, banking details etc.) of an individual by posing as an email from a genuine institution. Phishing can also be used by ransomware attackers to send the initial file containing malicious macros in the guise of word file or other crimes like hacking, cyber bullying, cyber financial frauds etc.

Digitalization is increasing across the changing networks (from traditional networks to cloud computing) of the world, adding new devices to access it (increasing use of mobile, watch, TV etc. along with the computers). Because of these expanding vectors the need of having a preventive security framework is also increasing.

The Government of India has been working on a preventive security framework since the start of this century and in 2013 the first holistic preventive security framework was presented in the form of National Cyber Security Policy, 2013. This policy looks towards the creation and maintenance of a secure cyber ecosystem in line with global security systems. It focuses on prevention rather than detection by setting a regulatory framework to cover all vectors and institutions along with necessary manpower to develop advanced technologies which can withstand such attacks. Recently, the Government of India sought details on data security protocols followed by the smartphone manufacturers in India.

The participation from the private sector is increasing and the Data Security Council of India (established by NASSCOM in 2008) is working along with other private organizations to improve their trustworthiness. DSCI work is not just limited to the private sector cyber security enhancement through best practices and standards but to engage with government and its agencies (like CERT), regulators etc. for capacity building, policy advocacy etc. Recently, Data Security Council of India (DSCI) and the Technology Development Board came up with a joint strategy to promote cyber security startups in India.

**2.    The north-eastern region of India has been infested with insurgency for a very long time. Analyze the major reasons for the survival of armed insurgency in this region. (150 words, 10 marks)**

Insurgency, i.e. a violent rebellion or uprising against the legitimately recognized authority, is a form of irregular warfare against the State. The North-east India is more vulnerable to such insurgencies because of its remote location and the presence of distinct ethnic identities. These insurgencies started during the British Regime and even after independence many of them continued or new rebellions emerged in the region. E.g. The Nagaland movement started soon after the independence and as of date we are yet to reach a conclusive Nagaland Peace Accord. Based on the motive, the insurgencies of North-Eastern region can be divided into categories as:

I.    Insurgency with demand of Secession from India, and
II.   Insurgency with demand for new state or sub-region with greater autonomy within the state.

Apart from its remote location and distinct ethnic identities, the main reasons for the survival of armed insurgencies in this region are:

- Lack of development in the region and poor connectivity. Development and connectivity is the bridge between people from different groups. The absence or limited development and connectivity creates a feeling of being neglected or sidelined leading to resentment among people. Either people on their own or the insurgent groups take advantage of these feelings to get popular support for its demands.
- Difficult topography of the region with presence of dense forests and absence of proper security structure makes it easy for the insurgent groups to challenge the might of security agencies through indirect or guerilla warfare. The porous boundaries with the neighbouring nations make it easy for them to hide during anti-insurgency operations.
- The increasing migration of outsiders is another reason for the continued fear among the local people. It creates fear of cultural subjugation among local people and the outsiders are always looked at with suspicion.
- The little presence of national political parties is another reason. Usually, the aspirations of the local people in troublesome regions are often linked to the local political parties. The insurgent groups further ignite people's passion through calls for boycott of the electoral process as well as the dialogue process.
- The poor implementation of the constitutional safeguards in some parts of the region which are ensured under Schedule VI and other special safeguards is another reason for insurgency as it increases suspicion on state motives.
- The traditional insecurities or unsettled issues between different local tribes are another reason for insurgency. The presence of

strong laws like AFSPA in parts of North-East which gave greater power to the Armed Forces was another tool used by the insurgents group to create fear among locals to gain support.

- The political, monetary, operational and logistics support from other nations to the insurgent groups is another reason for continued insurgency. It makes it difficult for the state and security agencies from all-out attacks against the insurgent groups.

In the last few years, the development of the North-Eastern region has been given special focus while continuing the strong actions from our security agencies including cross-border surgical strike. Most of the neighboring nations and the insurgent groups are also taken on board to resolve all the pending issues and reach a political solution to establish peace for prosperity of the region.

**3.     Mob violence is emerging as a serious law and order problem in India. By giving suitable examples, analyze the causes and consequences of such violence.  (250 words, 15 marks)**

Mob Violence is a form of informal execution carried out by a mob or large crowd of people in public to punish an alleged transgressor, convicted transgressor or to intimidate other groups. Though mob violence is part of almost all societies, in India such incidents are more prevalent because of large ethnic identities and poor law and order situation. Mere suspicion of being a child abductor or robber causes people to take law in their own hands. Because of this, the incidents of mob violence are emerging as a serious law and order problem.

E.g. in 2015 a mob broke into a jail in Dimapur (Nagaland) and lynched an accused rapist. In the same year a Muslim was lynched in Dadri (UP) on suspicion of slaughtering a cow. Similar mob lynching incidents have happened in regions like Alwar (Rajasthan), Latehar (Jharkkhand). In 2020, a similar incident happened in Palghar (Maharashtra) when two Sadhus were lynched along with the driver. The **main causes** for increasing mob violence are:

- The decreasing mutual trust between people of different ethnic or religious identities because of increased spread of rumors through social media or whatsapp groups with targeted and motivated messages.
- The hostile climate is further mystified by the poor law and order maintenance on both fronts, i.e. in controlling crimes of abduction, killing of cows etc. and to stop the vigilante from committing mob lynching.
- The support from political parties or local functionaries of different groups further reduces the chances of people getting

punished for mob violence. Sometimes, police fail to act even if they reach the spot because of political pressure. This further erodes the people's trust in institutions and encourages the mob to take law in their own hand.

- The indifferent attitude from bystanders or little/no effort towards stopping people from violence shows the decreasing humanity in the society. It is seen as tacit approval by the violators and encourages them to commit further violence.

The major consequences of increasing Mob Violence are:

- Reduced faith of society in the judiciary and police because of the justice deficit in society. Violators roam freely without any fear or fervor.
- Goes against our long cherished idea of Unity in Diversity because of increased tensions within different ethnic or religious groups.
- Take away the fundamental rights of individuals like Right to have dignified life because of constant fear of mob violence in unknown terrain.
- It diminishes India's image of a peaceful and democratic nation globally, impacting tourism and other opportunities from outside.

Mob Violence is a serious crime against the whole nation and people at responsible places need to bridge the increasing divide among people through improving awareness against rumors, instant justice and reforming the legal system through comprehensive police and criminal justice system reforms.

4. **The scourge of terrorism is a grave challenge to national security. What solutions do you suggest to curb this growing menace? What are the major sources of terrorist funding? (250 words, 15 marks)**

Since the early 1990's, the lackluster approach from India against terrorism has only lead to develop terrorism as a grave challenge to national security. E.g. in the last 30 years or more we have had terrorist attacks from small to large nature like 1993 Bombay blasts, 2001 Parliament attack, 26/11 Mumbai attacks etc. The India's approach to tackle terrorism changed only after the Uri attack (or the surgical strikes), sending a message across borders that the terrorists aren't safe even on Pakistan soil. It has increased the cost of terrorism for our neighboring nation and shows the resolute behavior from security agencies against the terrorist organizations.

So, based on the positive leadership scenario of present, the solution to curb the growing menace lies with the National Security Strategy and the four vital tools of national security strategy, i.e. Diplomacy, Information, Military and Economy.

- *Diplomacy* is the first need as it can help in having a peaceful solution by bringing responsible nations on one platform and put international pressure on rogue nations like Pakistan.
- The second need or step is to strengthen our *information access* i.e. intelligence network to gain beforehand information on the location of terrorists and their motives so that the security agencies can plan in advance the ways to tackle the situation. Strong information also helps in exposing the nations who support terrorism at international forums like United Nations and FATF to impose sanctions against the supporting nations.
- The next step is to *strengthen our armed forces* through the latest equipment and training with enhanced coordination among them. It helps in avoiding any mishap by spoiling infiltration attempts through enhanced border security or in giving a befitting reply to every action from the terrorist groups. It also helps in boosting the morale of our security forces.
- The next step is to strengthen our own *economy* with effective curb on the terror financing activities like illicit drugs, human trafficking, money laundering, etc. Strengthening Indian economy will help in increasing our capabilities to meet the expectations of each section of our society.
- The ongoing efforts on engaging with civil society, local communities or educational establishments can be of great help in countering radicalization. They can help in taking care of the vulnerable sections of our society and enhance their integration with India through celebration of various festivals and the Rashtriya Ekta Diwas (31st October) to establish unity in India. Education can be of great help against radicalization and even deradicalize the vulnerable sections with help of religious teachers to counter internet based propaganda.

The major sources of terrorist funding are:

- Help from sponsoring nations like Pakistan or through the network of international NGOs, charities and donations which are politically or religiously inclined towards terrorism.
- Self-financing through increased linkages with the organized crime organizations or engagement in activities like Counterfeiting of Indian currency, drugs smuggling, human trafficking, extortion etc.
- With increasing use of technology cyber frauds, ransomware, crypto-currency and other money generating things through Darknet are also likely to be used by some terrorist organizations.

**2016**

**1.    The terms 'Hot Pursuit' and 'Surgical Strikes' are often used in connection with armed action against terrorist attacks. Discuss the strategic impact of such actions.**

Hot Pursuit, i.e. a close continuous pursuit of a fleeing hostile military, terrorist groups or belligerents across territorial lines or sea and Surgical Strikes, i.e. a swift military attack against a legitimate military targets like terrorist launch pads with no or minimal collateral damage to surrounding structures, people etc., are becoming a new normal for our forces in our transformation from a weak state to a strong state.

E.g. in 2015, India carried out surgical strikes across Myanmar. In 2016, our military forces carried out surgical strikes across the Line of Control or the regions of Pakistan Occupied territory of India, The Indian Coast Guard also apprehended a Pakistani fishing vessel off the Gujarat coast in hot pursuit for carrying narcotic drugs worth Rs. 600 crore.

If we talk about international norms, Article 2(4) of the UN Charter requires Member States to *"refrain in their international relations from the threat or use of force against the territorial integrity or political independence of any state"*, Article 51 recognizes the *inherent right of self-defence*, upon the incidence of an *armed attack*, thereby allowing states to use force in such circumstances. Further, UN Security Council resolutions 1368 and 1373 recognise acts of international terrorism as an actionable threat to international peace and security.

Similarly, the doctrine of Hot Pursuit is recognized by international laws (Article 111 of the 1982 UNCLOS), giving the State authorities right to continue its pursue and seize a vessel belonging to a foreign state even outside the territorial waters which has violated any law within its territorial boundaries and jurisdiction, an exception made to the principles of freedom on the high seas.

**Strategic Impact of such actions:**

- The first and most important strategic impact is the change of stance from India by moving away from its past as a soft state against terrorism by shedding the self-proclaimed policy of "strategic restraint".
- Though such incidents mayn't be new but sharing its details publicly shows the strategic shift among our policy think tank and desire to pursue the strategy of a strong State with greater confidence in the improving operational and technical capabilities **(Command, Control, Communications, Computers, Intelligence, Surveillance and Reconnaissance — C4ISR)** of our armed forces.

- Though surgical strikes and hot pursuit are allowed under international laws and chances of full blown war are rare still it indicates a silent shift from the fears of "preemptive strikes" from India becoming the reason for a full blown nuclear war between the two nations.
- The surgical strikes signify the attempt to cause maximum damage to enemy capabilities, making them and the host nation realize that the costs of supporting or allowing terrorists to operate from its soil will be high. E.g. India has ended the trade with Pakistan and the strike inside territory controlled by it sends the message of no immunity for terrorists even on foreign soil.
- It may also help in Pakistan taking effective steps to stop activities of terrorist groups in its territory because of increased international pressure and avoid isolation from other nations for being the safe haven for terrorists.

Indian Government and security agencies have shown the courage to make a strategic shift within the limits of international law. At the same time, we are cautious on chances of escalating the situation to the stage of war as well. The immediate release of the operation and the reasons or operation helps us in making the world realize our motives behind such action and to put the necessary evidence in public domain based on which such action was carried out.

**2.    'Terrorism is emerging as a competitive industry over the last few decades." Analyze the above statement.**

The desire for power and money among people is present from time unknown. The terrorist organizations are also not untouched and the emerging competitiveness in terrorism is a natural outcome of the desire for power and money. The ideological differences and the operational differences add to it and create factionalism or rise of new organizations.

The competitiveness among the terrorist groups can be seen from two perspectives. The first is the traditional competition where multiple terrorist organizations operate from the same or adjacent territory and gain new recruits based on the ideology and relationship with the sponsoring state. The terrorist organizations had particular areas and ways of attack with the sponsoring state often having the last say.

The second and more intense competition in the terrorism has started after the desire of ISIS to have influence across the world. The global operations of ISIS with higher monetary resources helped it in establishing itself as a global force. The extremists from all across the world, including India, started to join it. It forced other organizations to either owe allegiance to ISIS or try to become more competitive in order to keep their flock together. Such desires of one central authority are very much visible among terrorist organizations operating in India as well.

E.g. The 2016 Pathankot attack by the Pakistan based United (Muttahida) Jihad Council was an attempt to prove one-upmanship over Indian terrorists under increasing challenges from Al-Qaeda and ISIS. It was supposed to limit the increased extremists and global charity aligning with ISIS after Charlie Hebdo and other attacks across the globe, drying local groups' funding and popularity among possible recruits, i.e. fear of losing out financial resources and influence over people.

This competition for having large money to buy weapons and more people to fire is visible through the increasing appetite for big-risk attacks for greater publicity. Also, the drying of charity from NGOs and people has forced many of them to take control over organized crimes or establishing linkages with them or even with legal businesses. Today, many terrorist organizations are in competition with each other to get control over the natural resources such as oil reserves in Middle East countries, cultivation of Opium, arms trafficking etc. This provides money which is important for them to carry out operations, spread their own ideology among the large number of groups and use the publicity to attract new recruits.

The path taken by ISIS of having targets where it can gain more publicity with new forms of intense attacks (like lone-wolf attacks) has not just enhanced the violence and bloodshed but the terrorist groups are also forced to either out-do each other or to accept guardianship from other groups. The limitations put by the international financial institutions or bodies like FATF further makes it difficult for new organizations or splinter groups to operate unless someone else is taken out of the competition.

**3.    Border management is a complex task due to difficult terrain and hostile relations with some countries. Elucidate the challenges and strategies for effective border management.**

Securing a nation territory from any external attack through effective border management is the most basic necessity of every nation. India is no exception to it and our task of border management is made complex by a number of factors including the difficult terrain and hostile relations with some neighboring countries. E.g. The land boundary of India is nearly 15,200 km with 7 nations sharing it with us. The major challenges in our effective border management are:

- *Unsettled boundaries* with some of our neighboring nations leading to the problem of having proper border fencing. E.g. The China and India border is mainly based on the Line of Actual

Control (LAC) while the Pakistan and India border is based on Line of Control at various parts.

- *Varied and difficult Terrain* along the borders of India because of our borders being defined by nature through its harsh and extreme climatic conditions. This includes the high mountains of the Himalayas and other ranges with rivers, valleys and passes along them; the deserts of Thar and the marshy land of Kutch; and a large number of rivers or water streams across the expanding Delta of the Himalayan Rivers. Therefore, from extreme conditions of above 50 degree Celsius temperature to the -50 degree or more of the Siachen Glaciers is part of the border to be managed by India.
- Old relationships with cross border regions and the presence of terrorists as well as organized crime groups across border regions is another challenge as complete stoppage of the cross border movement from people and animals is quite challenging. Because of this, we see a number of international drug smuggling, human trafficking, illegal arms etc. routes passing through India.

**Strategies for effective border management:**
After the Pathankot Air Base of IAF, MHA constituted the Madhukar Gupta Committee with a mandate to look at all types of gaps in our border fencing and all other vulnerabilities in the International Border and to suggest a comprehensive approach to fix these gaps in fencing and other vulnerabilities on interim and permanent basis.

Though the committee recommendations are based on the Indo-Pakistan border conditions, the same grid border protection can be used at other borders as well instead of linear security. The grid based border protection is designed with an integrated surveillance and monitoring system using physical and non-physical barriers with coordination among all security and intelligence agencies (IB) responsible for border management. This includes smart border management techniques using latest drones, laser fencing, night vision cameras, sensors etc. to detect the movement with effective communication and coordination among the forces to neutralize any illegal movement.

The states which are part of our international borders are also made part of it through a state-level standing committee set up under the chief secretary. It helps the state feel more responsible and the active participation helps in building mutual trust along with better coordination from state police. This makes the border security more resilient against the cross border infiltration. The settlement of our long-pending border disputes with Bangladesh and the subsequent establishment of grid border protection has provided a way for border management with peaceful neighbors. For others, we can carry with the setup of grid border protection till a solution is reached to the border problem.

**4. Use of the internet and social media by non-state actors for subversive activities is a major security concern. How have these been misused in the recent past? Suggest effective guidelines to curb the above threat.**

The increasing penetration of internet and social media in the routine life of the people has attracted the interest of everyone. Whether it is the State or non-State actors (i.e. an individual or organization that has significant political influence but is not allied to any particular country or state) both are trying to influence the people through the internet and social media. Among them, certain non-State actors like ISIS and the unethical hackers, also known as black hat, misuse it for subversive activities. E.g. Terrorist organizations like **ISIS** use the internet and social media platforms to exploit religious divisions for personal gains (brainwashing of youth), recruiting youth from all around the world and to plan lone-wolf attacks or other attacks in different parts of the world.

Similarly, unethical hackers or state-sponsored hackers use it for Cyber warfare and Cyber attacks. E.g. **Stuxnet**, a computer worm aimed to target Iran's nuclear facilities, attacked not just Iran's Nuclear facilities but it spread to other industrial and energy-producing facilities as well. Similarly, we had many cyber attacks in the form of malware threats or ransomware attacks like cryptolocker, mydoom etc. at different times. Cyber espionage is another growing challenge, exposing different nations, organizations and even individuals (especially females) to gain access to sensitive information. E.g. Zomato, Unacademy and many other organizations had to suffer because of such attacks.

Such espionage activities are also carried out through social media. The women and children are main targets and often other crimes like cyber-bullying, sexual exploitation and blackmailing are part of such espionage. In the recent past, the use of social media is increasing among like-minded people or interest-based groups. They use it for radicalization or gather public for violence during riots etc. Because of such subversive uses of the internet, cyber security has largely remained in use for wrong reasons. The exponential growth of internet and social media has made it necessary that the guidelines which are made to curb this threat are not just holistic but more practical. It will help them to be easily disseminated and implemented in our nation despite the present information gap among people. Some of the guidelines which are recommended by different study groups or used by India and other nations to control these subversive activities and build a secure cyberspace are:

- The earliest implementation of National Cyber Security Policy or the basic minimum measures on ensuring network security and cyber security must be taken on priority.
- The digital literacy component of digital India should focus not just on functional information on the internet and social media, it should also attempt toward comprehension based digital literacy.
- The appointment of Chief Information Security Officer (CISO) in all ministries/departments, PSU's etc. based on the Ministry of Electronics and Information Technology guidelines is a welcome step. CISO will help in the implementation of cyber security programs and coordinate in the security policy compliance efforts across the organisation and interact regularly with agencies like CERT-In.
- Similar steps can be implemented by private organizations or use various Information Security Management Systems which can help against any cyber espionage or cyber attack.
- To check the subversive activities which try to incite hatred among people for personal benefits by terrorist groups or interest based groups on social media platforms we need to have a holistic policy with participation not just from state intelligence and security agencies but from religious and political leaders in order to counter attacks as well as the propaganda.
- Agencies like CERT-In which are responsible for coordination of crisis management efforts can be aided by our intelligence agencies such as RAW and IB to check the radicalization as well as the state police through initiatives like Cyberdome of Kerala.
- The data protection law for individuals will act as another firewall for citizens and the private users are required to be made aware of the security threats and vulnerabilities as part of the digital literacy campaign.

*Social Media: It is defined as the computer-based technology that facilitates the sharing of ideas, thoughts, and information through the building of virtual **networks** and communities. The common examples of social media platforms or websites are Facebook, Instagram, WhatsApp, Twitter, TikTok, Pinterest etc. By design, they are internet-based and give users quick electronic communication of content from across the globe. In 2019, India had nearly 351 million Social media users. With a large youth population of India, it is expected to reach 450 million by 2023.*

*On one hand, such a large population of social media users can have a positive impact on India by increasing people's participation in the governance activities or gain support for important national projects/policies. It can also be used in disasters or calamities to communicate with people or remove distress in situations like the recent Coronavirus. If used properly, it can help in early detection of crimes/criminals through use of Artificial Intelligence, Big data analytics etc. E.g. Mumbai Police has established a dedicated cyber cell to check for signs of radicalization, false trends or for tracking the criminals. During recent Delhi Riots (February 2020) a number of twitter handles were identified with spreading false rumors or using fake news/videos to incite religious hatred.*

*At the same time, if social media helped in identifying people spreading false rumors or fake news/videos it was also the initial source of such fake news/videos spread by the Indian users or from outside India. Similar misuse can be identified during incidents of mob violence or the 2012 exodus of North-East people from South India, especially Bangalore. The terrorist organizations also find them lucrative because of their reach and anonymity offered in setting and operation of social accounts. Often, the crimes are also streamed live on social media in order to create greater terror as it happened during the Christchurch mosque shootings. The organized crime groups are also increasing their presence on social media and often it is used for match-fixing, human trafficking, wildlife trade, drug trafficking etc. Even some militaries of the world like Pakistan use it for honeytrap in order to extract sensitive information about our armed forces without coming to India for espionage. The political parties also misuse it for influencing users to vote through various means including agencies with technical expertise and celebrities who can influence others through posts, doctored videos etc.*

*Therefore, it is important to have better regulation over the social media platforms (either by themselves or from the Government). But the concerns on users' privacy and foreign-based parent companies with data being stored on foreign servers make it a challenge to address the regulation concerns. The large number of users of these platforms with large amounts of live and past data along with the changing features further increases the challenges for security agencies to handle them alone. While the USA came out with a recent executive order to make the social media platforms responsible for users' posts, in India it is difficult to establish their accountability as these companies are considered as Intermediaries under Section 79 of the IT Act, 2000. As an intermediary, they are not liable for the user's post. The Government can only give direction to them for removing an objectionable content under Section 79(3)(B). Because of this, the social media platforms are emerging among themselves as the censor authorities with power to restrict, edit, promote or hide users' thoughts based on preferences or hidden motives. They are also criticized for reading the personal information of its users for commercial exploitation i.e. targeted ads of present time.*

## 2015

**1.    Human rights activists constantly highlight the view that the Armed Forces (Special Powers) Act, 1958 (AFSPA) is a draconian act leading to cases of human rights abuses by the security forces. What sections of AFSPA are opposed by the activists? Critically evaluate the requirement with reference to the view held by the Apex Court.**

Armed Forces (Special Powers) Act (AFSPA) is an act from the Indian parliament, first passed in 1958 to deal with the Naga insurgency. This Act granted special powers to the Indian Armed Forces and the state and paramilitary forces in areas classified as "disturbed areas", including the power to kill.

Post 1958, the AFSPA Act was enacted at two other moments. The 1st was in 1983 for Punjab & Chandigarh and the 2nd time in 1990 for the Jammu and Kashmir region. The main objective behind the implementation of AFSPA Act is to restore law and order in the **disturbed areas**, as identified under Section 3 of the AFSPA. Under the present AFSPA provisions, the Governors of the States, the Administrators of the Union Territories and the Central Government are empowered to declare any part or full of any state as a disturbed area if according to their opinion it has become necessary to disrupt terrorist activity or any such activity that might impinge on the sovereignty of India or cause insult to the national flag, anthem or India's Constitution. The state governments can suggest whether the act is required to be enforced or not but their opinion can be overruled by the governor or the Centre. The major sections/provisions of the AFSPA act which are opposed by the human rights activists are the provisions under section 4 and 5.

- These provisions empowers the commissioned, non-commissioned, warrant officer or any other army officers to fire upon or use force if he is of the opinion that *in order to maintain public order* it is necessary to do so, even to the extent of *causing death*, against any individual who is deemed to be acting in contravention of any law that is in force in a disturbed area, after giving such due warning that is necessary.

- The army officers can *destroy any arms* dump, prepared or fortified position or shelter from which armed attacks are made or are likely to be made or are attempted to be made, including the structure/s used as a training camp for armed volunteers or utilized as a hide-out by armed gangs or absconders wanted for any offence.

- He can prohibit,
  - the assembly of five or more persons,
  - carrying of weapons or of things capable of being used as weapons,
  - fire-arms, ammunition or explosive substances.
- The security forces can arrest any individual without a warrant for committing a cognizable offence or on reasonable suspicion of committing or likely to commit such offence.
- They can enter and carry out searches without warrant at any location for such arrests or to apprehend any individual believed to be wrongfully restrained or confined or any property reasonably suspected to be a stolen property or any arms, ammunition or explosives believed to be kept unlawfully in such premises and for this purpose reasonable amount of force can be used if necessary.
- Once a person is taken into custody, he/she has to be handed over to the nearest police station as soon as possible.
- Prosecution of the officer on duty for alleged violation of human rights requires the prior permission of the Central Government.

Because of these provisions, AFSPA is considered to violate various human rights or the rights conferred by the Constitution of India and other laws, International Conventions etc., like the Right to Life (Article 21), Protection against arrest and detention (Article 22), Universal Declaration of Human Rights, International Covenant on Civil and Political Rights, Convention against Torture, Criminal Procedure Code (CrPC) for the immunities granted to the security forces. E.g. The members of the armed forces can't be arrested for anything done within the line of official duty. They are granted immunity for all the atrocities committed under the AFSPA and the citizens need to first seek the permission of the central government in order to file a suit against a member of the armed forces for any violation.

Therefore, the act is challenged in the Supreme Court by the human rights activists and in 1997, while upholding the constitutional validity of AFSPA, Supreme Court said that "Section 3 of AFSPA does not confer an arbitrary power to declare an area as a 'disturbed area' and that 'a declaration under section 3 of AFSPA has to be for a limited time period and there must be a periodic review of the declaration every six months prior to its expiry'. Again, in July 2016, the Supreme Court questioned the validity of AFSPA which has been in force in the state of Manipur since 1958. As per its judgement, the state or the central government can impose AFSPA in a disturbed region to enforce normalcy within a stipulated time period and the armed forces should not be used to control its own citizens. For all killings, whether insurgent or civilian, a thorough enquiry by the CID shall be done on the instance of the NHRC.

In July 2017, on PIL filed by the Extra Judicial Execution Victim Families Association Manipur, which has recorded 1,528 deaths between 1979 and 2012, the Supreme Court overruled the centre and army submissions, directing the CBI to setup a Special Investigative Team (SIT) to investigate the allegations of fake encounters and human rights violations under the AFSPA in Manipur. While recognizing the presence of state violence in conflict areas, the Supreme Court noted that the victims of such violence have no access to justice, a basic human right recognized by the Constitution. It is vital to remove the absolute immunity given even to the acts which can be of criminal nature.

Along with them, the Supreme Court Guidelines during the ***Naga People's Movement of Human Rights vs. Union of India,*** 1998 are important. The five judge bench concluded that the act cannot be considered as violative of the Constitution (as challenged for law and order being a state subject) and the powers conferred under the section 4 and 5 of the Act are not arbitrary and unreasonable and therefore not in violation of the provisions of the Constitution. The Supreme Court said that the army personnel are required to strictly follow minimum force under Section 4 against suspected of violating prohibitive orders. Any person arrested and taken to custody under section 4 has to be handed over to the nearest police station within 24 hours of such arrest and the act has to be reviewed every six months by the state for its continuity.

Apart from the Supreme Court, two committees are also appointed at different times. The first was Justice B P Jeevan Reddy Committee because of the protests after the killing of Thangjam Manorama by the Assam Rifles in Manipur. This committee was of the firm opinion that the Armed Forces (Special Powers) Act, 1958, should **be repealed** with amendments to be made in the UAPA to allow its use for disturbed areas. Also, the security forces must be brought under the purview of ordinary criminal law rather than under army law. The second Administrative Reform Commission also suggested repealing the AFSPA Act.

In 2013, a second committee headed by Justice Santosh Hegde was appointed to review the encounter killing of 1528 people in Manipur from 1979 to 2012. In its report, the committee observed that five of the six encounters were **not genuine** and **disproportionate force was used** against persons with no known criminal antecedents. AFSPA gives sweeping powers to men in uniform, even greater than the state of emergency as Right to Life and personal liberty (Article 21) and certain rights under article 20 cannot be suspended, without granting citizens protection against its misuse. Greater power requires greater restraint with strict mechanisms to prevent its misuse or abuse. The National Human Rights Commission and the Supreme Court in 2014 laid down the guidelines to be followed by the state in case of encounter deaths through filing of the FIR and an investigation conducted by an independent agency and not by officers of the same police station and a magisterial enquiry needs to be held.

**2.    Religious indoctrination via digital media has resulted in Indian youth joining the ISIS. What is ISIS and its mission? How can ISIS be dangerous for the internal security of our country?**

ISIS (Islamic State of Iraq and Syria), also known as ISIL (Islamic State of Iraq and the Levant) or Daesh, is a Salafi Sunni jihadist group with a particularly violent ideology with its leader Abu Bakr al-Baghdadi calling itself a caliphate, claiming religious, political and military authority over all Muslims. ISIS originated from *Jama'at al-Tawhid wal-Jihad,* a militant group established by *Abu Musab al-Zarqawi* in 1999. Following the 2003 invasion of Iraq by Western forces, he pledged allegiance to Al-Qaeda and participated in the Iraqi insurgency. In 2013, *Abu Bakr al-Baghdadi* became its leader and in June 2014, the group proclaimed itself a worldwide caliphate along with a change of name to ISIS.

ISIS is dangerous for the internal security of our nation because of its extreme violent methods like beheadings and executions of soldiers and civilians on religious or sectarian lines with videos. Along with these war crimes, genocide and crimes against humanity, ISIS is a major threat for its appeal of caliphate and the people who joined the group since this call from its leader Abu Bakr al-Baghdadi. E.g. Our security agencies reported that nearly 180-200 people from India went to join ISIS and fight the war. In 2014, a Bengaluru techie Mehdi Masroor Biswas was found to be a propagandist of ISIS ideology. This is a cause of concern as it cannot just influence people in India but it influences them against some of the nations with which India has friendly relations.

The influence of ISIS is visible in some of our neighboring countries, like Sri Lanka and Bangladesh. In these nations, ISIS has played a role in the revival of Islamic militancy. With the death of Baghdadi, it is hoped that the Islamic State's command and control network will weaken. But it can turn into another concern for India as some of its affiliates or people who joined ISIS will either assert for more independence or retreat back into the localized conflicts or home nations while continuing to believe in the philosophy of ISIS. As a precautionary measure, we need to not just profile the Indian people who were influenced by ISIS and worked for it before returning to India but to engage the faith-based organizations, religious and political leaders to disengage the minds which were influenced by ISIS.

3.     **The persisting drives of the government for development of large industries in backward areas have resulted in isolating the tribal population and the farmers who face multiple displacements. With Malkangiri and Naxalbari foci, discuss the corrective strategies needed to win the left wing extremism (LWE) doctrine that affected citizens back into the mainstream of social and economic growth.**

The Naxalbari region of Siliguri (West Bengal) and Malkangiri region of undivided Koraput (now Malkangiri is turned into a district of Odisha) represent two stories of state apathy being utilized by the Left Wing Extremism doctrine and the need from state to have a corrective strategy. The Naxalbari region is the original epicenter of LWE. The rebellion started in 1967 at Naxalbari because of the extreme land inequality and the exploitation of the tribes (mainly Santhals) by the big landlords through insecure tenancy and use of goons.

Soon the landlords were replaced by the large industries and the enabling infrastructure which caused a large number of people, especially tribals, to be displaced. It is estimated that from 1947 to 2000, around 60 million people have been displaced in India for development projects. Among them, some of the large projects like building of dams or irrigation projects, setting up mining and other industrial complexes have caused displacement of over 21 million people with tribal people constituting nearly 40% of this displacement.

Often, this displacement is forced and the poor rehabilitation has caused them to relocate to unfamiliar and hostile environments. With habitat playing a major role in their life materially and spiritually (Nature-Man-Spirit Complex), such relocations create further stress in their life and often make them more vulnerable to exploitation, poverty and poor health apart from the psychological trauma of losing home. This happened in the Malkangiri region, because of its hilly and forested region considered to be suitable for building dams or multipurpose projects. The seven multipurpose projects of Odisha displaced a total of 52,584 families out of which 10,498 families were scheduled tribes. In the undivided Koraput district alone, tribal displacement was 58 percent of the total. Under major irrigation projects, the displacement of tribals was about 42.73 percent. But the lack of adequate compensation paid to the displaced tribes with little or no efforts toward rehabilitation, the tribal dissatisfaction grew further.

This feeling of neglect was used by the naxals fleeing from Andhra Pradesh because of tough police action and in 1990's, Malkangiri became the hotbed of Naxalism. E.g. In 2001, the Collector and Superintendent of Police of the Malkangiri ran away from the district. On the Chief Minister's request, the Central Government sent four battalions of Central forces as well as a helicopter to let the administration function. The grip of naxals over the Malkangiri grew so much that they started to oppose the development projects which could integrate the tribes with the mainstream, reducing the power of extortion and terrorism. At times, despite the issuance of a work order, the contractor either doesn't start work or start by paying money.

In 2013, 65 representatives of the Panchayati Raj Institutions (PRIs) in Malkangiri resigned en masse protesting against the apathy of the State government. All belonged to different tribes and the principal demand was the extension of an irrigation canal, road repair, and the supply of drinking water to villages. This shows that even the benefits of the development are not even and the tribals get them at the end and the state is least concerned to make it happen. Therefore, some of the corrective strategies which can help in winning over the LWE doctrine and bringing the tribals and others strongly into our mainstream of social and economic growth can be:

- Inclusive growth,
- Strengthening of our democracy with greater power to the PRIs,
- Making people realize that the projects like dams, irrigation canals etc. are as helpful to them as to other people. E.g. In the western part of Odisha, particularly the districts of Kalahandi, Bolangir, Sambalpur severe drought occurs frequently which leads to problems of poverty, hunger, outbreak of serious diseases etc. Though these projects the government gets help in controlling the floods, withstand impact of droughts, cyclones or other natural calamities.
- Using institutions like the Ministry of Tribal Affairs, National Commission for Scheduled Tribes for solving the problems of the displaced and vulnerable tribes of rehabilitation, compensation etc. along with the Judiciary. This helps in reducing the influence of Jan Adalats or the Kangaroo Courts run by naxals for hearing local people's problems.

**4.	Considering the threats cyberspace poses for the country, India needs a "Digital Armed Force" to prevent crimes. Critically evaluate the National Cyber Security Policy, 2013 outlining the challenges perceived in its effective implementation.**

The rising cyber attacks on the networks and softwares used by government agencies, private organizations and individuals show that along with the creation of Digital India we also need to protect our digital infrastructure for a secure India. For creating a secure India, a strong digital defence mechanism becomes important with a Digital Armed Force to protect it. The National Cyber Security Policy of 2013 also outlined it and aspired to build a workforce of 5 lakh professionals skilled in cyber security in the next 5 years.

The purpose of such attacks varies from espionage to Denial-of-service, Phishing and spear-phishing attacks, defacing of websites etc. The threats multiply further as digital technologies become an integral part of our lives. E.g. Under the Digital Army Programme, the armed forces are moving to cloud data centres on lines of Meghraj used by the government. With increased digitalization, the people to be affected by the attacks on servers and electronic devices will be huge.

So, a critical appraisal of our National Cyber Security Policy (NCSP) becomes important in order to find its positives and what needs to be changed or added in order to create a digitally secure India. Some of the important points under such appraisal and challenges which are perceived in its effective implementation are:

- Use of indigenous designed or developed products: Countries like China restricted the use of American company's products like Microsoft, Cisco, Apple etc. in government offices after the PRISM incident. Recently, the US also advised against the use of Huawei or ZTE products in its 5G network or by its strong partners. But India still seems indifferent and uses nearly 60% Chinese products based on its freely available products approach while some are from US based companies. While our NCSP aspires to develop suitable indigenous technologies in the Information and Communication Technology (ICT) sector it is silent on specifying anything further. Therefore, we need to consider it as an important component of 'Atma Nirbhar Bharat' and work on not just the hardware and network but the software's as well.
- While the policy talks about the protective or defence measures including the Digital Armed Forces, testing and validation of the security, involving the corporate sector etc. it is silent on building the offensive capabilities.
- The NCSP is piecemeal in nature and only talks about safeguarding the privacy of citizens and building trust and confidence in digital transactions. It lacks further details on the data security, encryption policy etc. which are must to do so.
- The policy talks about enhancing protection and resilience of National Critical Information Infrastructure with monitoring of cyber threats 24X7. But it is silent on how to make people more aware about these vulnerabilities and how to deal in cases of such attacks. Providing for another way is also part of addressing a crisis, reducing panic among people while our Digital Armed Force looks for solutions.

With increased focus on digital India we strongly need a cyber agency to safeguard India from Digital enemies. This cyber agency can steer our planning on cyber attacks and play an important role in cyber warfare. But it needs help from the domestic manufacturing capabilities (on hardware and software) to use an indigenous component for building technological components for our high-level intelligence and digital security infrastructure.

*We hope that the above detailed answers were enough to give greater information on the topic. You are supposed to write only 150 or 250 word answers in the examination. Therefore, the 2014 and 2013 questions are left for your practice. To some questions, references are given to the specific pages of the book where you can find answers while for some you need to understand the whole crux of the book.*

## 2014

1. **The diverse nature of India as a multi-religious and multi-ethnic society is not immune to the impact of radicalism which has been in her neighborhood. Discuss along with the strategies to be adopted to counter this environment.**

*Refer Page No. 161 and 162 along with some previous answers on radicalization.*

2. **International civil aviation laws provide all countries complete and exclusive sovereignty over the airspace above the territory. What do you understand by airspace? What are the implications of these laws on the space above this airspace? Discuss the challenges which this poses and suggests ways to contain the threat.**

*Refer Chapter 5 "Challenges to the External Security of India" from page number 239*

3. **How illegal trans-border migration does pose a threat to India's security? Discuss the strategies to curb this, bring out the factors which give impetus to such migration.**

*Refer Chapter 4 "Challenges to the Internal Security of India". The answer will be based on the analysis of the problems in Northeast India, overall crime in India, Drug Smuggling, Human Trafficking etc.*

4. **In 2012, the longitudinal marking of the high-risk areas for piracy was moved from 65° East to 78° east in the Arabian Sea by International Maritime organisation. What impact does this have on India's maritime security concerns?**

*Refer Chapter 5 "Challenges to the External Security of India" from page number 237*

5. China and Pakistan have entered into an agreement for development of an economic corridor. What thread does it dispose for India's security? Critically examine.

*Refer the answer to Q.1 of 2018 regarding China-Pakistan Economic Corridor (CPEC)*

## 2013

1. Money laundering poses a serious threat to country's economic sovereignty. What is its significance for India and what steps are required to be taken to control this menace?

*Refer Chapter 4 "Challenges to the Internal Security of India", from page number 204*

2. What are social networking site and what security implications do these sites present?

*Refer the information (in italic) at the end of Q.4 of 2016*

3. Cyber warfare is considered by some defense analysts to be a larger threat than even Al Qaeda or terrorism. What do you understand by Cyber warfare? Outline the cyber threats which India is vulnerable to and bring out the state of the country's preparedness to deal with the same.

*Refer Q.4 of 2015 and Cyber Warfare covered under Chapter 4 "Challenges to the Internal Security of India" from page number 196*

4. Article 244 of Indian Constitution relates to Administration of Scheduled areas and tribal areas. Analyze the impact of non implementation of the provisions of fifth schedule on the growth of Left Wing Extremism.

*Refer Chapter 4 "Challenges to the Internal Security of India" from page number 180 and some previous answers*

5. How far are India's internal security challenges linked with border management, particularly in view of the long porous borders with most countries of South Asia and Myanmar?

*Refer Chapter 5 "Challenges to the External Security of India" regarding Border Management and answer to Q.4 of 2019*